ISLAMIC IMPERIALISM

ISLAMIC IMPERIALISM

A HISTORY

EFRAIM KARSH

YALE UNIVERSITY PRESS
NEW HAVEN AND LONDON

For information about this and other Yale University Press publications, please contact:
U.S. Office: sales.press@yale.edu   yalebooks.com
Europe Office: sales@yaleup.co.uk   www.yalebooks.co.uk

Set in Minion by J&L Composition, Filey, North Yorkshire
Printed in the USA

Library of Congress Cataloging-in-Publication Data

Karsh, Efraim.
    Islamic imperialism: a history/Efraim Karsh.—1st ed.
        p. cm.
    Includes index.
    ISBN 978-0-300-12263-3 (cl.: alk. paper)
1. Islam—History. 2. Islamic Empire—History. 3. Imperialism—History. 4. Jihad.
I. Title.
    BP52.K37 2006
    325′.32091767—dc22
                                                                        2005034836

A catalogue record for this book is available from the British Library

10 9 8 7 6 5 4 3 2 1

For Matan, Roy, and Rachel

Contents

List of Maps   ix

Introduction   1

1   The Warrior Prophet   10

2   The Rise and Fall of Islam's First Empire   23

3   The Best of Times, the Worst of Times   43

4   The House of Islam and the House of War   66

5   The Last Great Islamic Empire   88

6   The Price of Empire   109

7   Mishandling the Great Game   119

8   The Rise of the Arab Imperial Dream   132

9   An Arab Caesar   149

10 A Reckoning of Sorts   170

11 The Tail That Wags the Dog   191

12 Renewing the Quest for Allah's Empire   212

13 Bin Laden's Holy War   225

Epilogue   234

Notes   242

Index   273

Maps

		page
1	The Middle East on the Eve of Islam	3
2	Islam's First Empire	34
3	The Abbasid Empire at its Height	56
4	The Crusading Kingdoms	75
5	The Ottoman Empire in the Late Eighteenth Century	98
6	Sharif Hussein's Imperial Dream	136
7	The Sykes–Picot Agreement	194
8	The Contemporary Middle East	209

Figures

1	The Family of the Prophet	10
2	The Rightly Guided Caliphs	29
3	The Umayyad Dynasty	39

Tables

1	The Abbasid Dynasty	58
2	The Ottoman Dynasty	105

Introduction

"I was ordered to fight all men until they say 'There is no god but Allah.'"
Prophet Muhammad's farewell address, March 632
"I shall cross this sea to their islands to pursue them until there remains no one on the face of the earth who does not acknowledge Allah."
Saladin, January 1189
"We will export our revolution throughout the world . . . until the calls 'there is no god but Allah and Muhammad is the messenger of Allah' are echoed all over the world."
Ayatollah Ruhollah Khomeini, 1979
"I was ordered to fight the people until they say there is no god but Allah, and his prophet Muhammad."
Osama bin Laden, November 2001

The 9/11 attacks have inspired two diametrically opposed interpretations regarding their "root causes." According to the first school of thought, the attacks were the latest salvo in the millenarian "clash of civilizations" between the worlds of Islam and Christendom, a violent backlash by a deeply frustrated civilization reluctant to come to terms with its long-standing decline. "For many centuries Islam was the greatest civilization on earth—the richest, the most powerful, the most creative in every significant field of human endeavor," wrote a prominent exponent of this view. "And then everything changed, and Muslims, instead of invading and dominating Christendom, were invaded and dominated by Christian powers. The resulting frustration and anger at what seemed to them a reversal of both natural and divine law have been growing for centuries, and have reached a climax in our own times."[1]

Not so, argues a vast cohort of academics, journalists, writers, and retired diplomats. The attacks were a misguided, if not wholly inexplicable, response to America's arrogant and self-serving foreign policy by a fringe extremist group, whose violent interpretation of Islam has little to do with the actual spirit and teachings of this religion.[2] Not only does Islam specifically forbid the massacre of innocent civilians but the evocation of a *jihad* in the context of 9/11 makes a travesty of this concept, which means first and foremost an inner quest for personal self-improvement and not a holy war as is widely believed. "Muslims have never nurtured dreams of world conquest," runs a typical argument in this vein. "They had no designs on Europe, for example, even though Europeans imagined that they did. Once Muslim rule had been established in Spain, it was recognized that the empire could not expand indefinitely."[3]

Neither of these interpretations is particularly novel. Both echo the received wisdom in the field of Middle Eastern studies since the early twentieth century, which views the region's history as an offshoot of global power politics. To many educated Westerners, "empire" and "imperialism" are categories that apply exclusively to the European powers and, more recently, to the United States. In this view of things, Muslims, whether in the Middle East or elsewhere, are merely objects—the long-suffering victims of the aggressive encroachments of others. Lacking an internal, autonomous dynamic of its own, their history is rather a function of their unhappy interaction with the West, whose obligation is to make amends. Some date this interaction back to the crusades. Others consider it a corollary of the steep rise in Western imperial power and expansionism during the long nineteenth century (1789–1923). All agree that Western imperialism bears the main responsibility for the endemic malaise plaguing the Middle East to date, as implied by the title of a recent book by a veteran observer of the region: *What Went Wrong? Western Impact and Muslim Responses.*[4]

But there is another argument, one that holds that the Middle East's experience is the culmination of long-existing *indigenous* trends, passions, and patterns of behavior, first and foremost the region's millenarian imperial tradition.[5] External influences, however potent, have played only a secondary role, constituting neither the primary force behind the Middle East's political development nor the main cause of its notorious volatility.

Contrary to the conventional wisdom, it is the Middle East where the institution of empire not only originated (for example, Egypt, Assyria, Babylon, Iran, and so on) but where its spirit has also outlived its European counterpart.[6] At the time of the rise of Islam in the early seventh century of the Common Era (C.E.), the Middle East was divided between the two great rival empires of Byzantium, successor to the Roman Empire with its capital in Constantinople, and Iran, ruled since the third century by the Sasanid dynasty, with its capital at Ctesiphon, where Baghdad stands today.[7] Though the Arabian Peninsula, birthplace of Islam, was on the fringes of this bipolar system, it was deeply implicated in its activities. The Iranians had colonies throughout eastern and southern Arabia, in Najd and in Yemen, and their

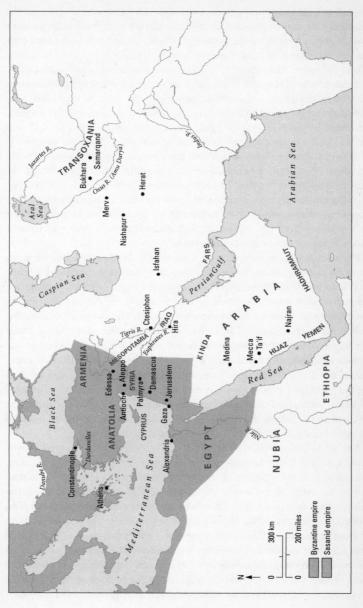

Map 1 The Middle East on the Eve of Islam

influence extended all the way to the Hijaz, the northwestern part of the peninsula. Byzantium's power was felt throughout western Arabia from the Syrian Desert, where it had client kingdoms, to Yemen, where its Ethiopian allies had ruled until they were expelled by the Iranians.[8]

This pervasive penetration led a prominent scholar of Islam to insist that any examination of the rise of this religion and the sources of its spectacular success must depart from the impact of Byzantium and Iran on Arabia. One possible way to do so would be to view nascent Islam "as a nativist movement, or in other words as a primitive reaction to alien domination of the same types as those which the Arab conquerors were themselves to provoke in North Africa and Iran, and which European colonists were later to provoke throughout the Third World ... the object of the movement being the expulsion of the foreigners in question." As a seventh-century Muslim leader explained regarding the contemporary Islamic conquests: "Other men trampled us beneath their feet while we trampled no one. Then God sent a prophet from among us ... and one of his promises was that we should conquer and overcome these lands."[9]

This thesis is true as far as it goes, yet it overlooks the imperialist impetus behind those early Islamic conquests. Expelling occupiers from one's patrimony is an act of self-liberation. Conquering foreign lands and subjugating their populations is pure imperialism. Neither North African Berbers fighting their Islamic conquerors nor twentieth-century Third World movements resisting European colonialism aspired to conquer the homeland of their imperial masters. Yet as the above quotation makes clear, this is precisely what Muhammad asked of his followers once he had fled from his hometown of Mecca (in 622) to the town of Medina to become a political and military leader rather than a private preacher: not to rid themselves of foreign occupation but to strive for a new universal order in which the whole of humanity would embrace Islam or live under its domination. As he told his followers in his farewell address: "I was ordered to fight all men until they say 'There is no god but Allah.'"[10]

This appealed to the warlike spirit of the Arabian nomads. Though vastly outnumbered by their settled counterparts, these tribes exploited the vicissitudes in imperial control in the decades preceding Muhammad's advent to break longstanding political and economic constraints and to encroach on the peninsula's sedentary populations. As pastoral practices progressively superseded agricultural and commercial interests, with trade routes increasingly harrassed by marauders, violence became endemic to Arabian society. This was vividly illustrated by the numerous fratricidal clashes known as *Ayyam al-Arab* ("the days of the Arabians"), arising from disputes over such material issues as cattle, pasture-lands or springs and glorified by contemporary poetry as an ideal of heroism and manhood. "We slew in requital for our slain an equal number [of them] and [carried away] an unaccountable number of fettered prisoners," one pre-Islamic poet boasted, "the days have thus raised us to be foremost with our battles in warfare after warfare; men find in us nothing to point their finger of scorn." While a convert to Islam was equally proud of his military exploits: "When I thrust in my sword it bends almost double, I kill my opponent with a sharp Mashrafi sword, and I yearn for death like a camel overful with milk."[11]

No single activity of pre-Islamic society epitomized this warlike ethos more succinctly than the raid (ghazw, or razzia as it is commonly known), a marauding expedition aimed at seizing camels, horses, livestock, or, less frequently, women from a hostile tribe. For most bedouins the razzia was not merely a means of subsistence but rather an exciting social endeavor that helped reaffirm tribal solidarity and win invaluable military experience. So much so that some scholars described it as "the national sport" of the nomadic Arabians.[12]

Indeed, Muhammad initially devised the concept of jihad, "exertion in the path of Allah," as he called his god, as a means to entice his local followers to raid Meccan caravans, instantaneously transforming a common tribal practice into a supreme religious duty and the primary vehicle for the spread of Islam throughout the ages. He developed and amplified this concept with the expansion of his political ambitions until it became a rallying call for world domination, and he established the community of believers, or the umma, as the political framework for the practice of this religion in all territories it conquered.

In doing so Muhammad at once tapped into the Middle East's millenarian legacy and ensured its perpetuation for many centuries to come. From the first Arab-Islamic empire of the mid-seventh century to the Ottomans, the last great Muslim empire, the story of Islam has been the story of the rise and fall of universal empires and, no less important, of never quiescent imperialist dreams. Politics during this lengthy period was characterized by a constant struggle for regional, if not world, mastery in which the dominant power sought to subdue, and preferably to eliminate, all potential challengers. Such imperialist ambitions often remained largely unsatisfied, for the determined pursuit of absolutism was matched both by the equally formidable forces of fragmentation and degeneration.

Tension between the center and the periphery was thus to become the hallmark of Islam's imperial experience. Even in its early days, under the Umayyads, the empire was hopelessly overextended, largely because of inadequate means of communication and control. Under the Abbasids, a growing number of provinces fell under the sway of local dynasties. With no effective metropolis, the empire was reduced to an agglomeration of entities united only by the over-arching factors of language and religion. Though the Ottomans temporarily reversed the trend, their own imperial ambitions were likewise thwarted by internal fragmentation.

In the long history of Islamic empire, the wide gap between delusions of grandeur and the centrifugal forces of localism would be bridged time and again by force of arms, making violence a key element of Islamic political culture to date. No sooner had Muhammad died than his successor, Abu Bakr, had to suppress a widespread revolt among the Arabian tribes. Twenty-three years later, the head of the *umma*, the caliph Uthman ibn Affan, was murdered by disgruntled rebels; his successor, Ali ibn Abi Talib, was confronted for most of his reign with armed insurrections, most notably by the governor of Syria, Mu'awiya ibn Abi Sufian, who went on to establish the Umayyad dynasty after Ali's assassination. Mu'awiya's successors managed to hang on to power mainly by relying on physical force, and were consumed for most of their reign with preventing or quelling revolts in the diverse corners of their empire. The same was true for the Abbasids during the long centuries of their sovereignty, and this process gained rapid momentum during the last phases of the Ottoman Empire, culminating in its disastrous decision to enter World War I on the losing side, as well as in the creation of an imperialist dream that would survive the Ottoman era to haunt Islamic and Middle Eastern politics to the present day.

It is true that this pattern of historical development is not uniquely Middle Eastern or Islamic. Other parts of the world, Europe in particular, have had their share of imperial powers and imperialist expansion, while Christianity's universal vision is no less sweeping than that of Islam. The worlds of Christianity and Islam, however, have developed differently in one fundamental respect. The Christian faith won over an existing empire in an extremely slow and painful process and its universalism was originally conceived in purely spiritual terms that made a clear distinction between God and Caesar. By the time it was embraced by the Byzantine emperors as a tool for buttressing their imperial claims, three centuries after its foundation, Christianity had in place a countervailing ecclesiastical institution with an abiding authority over the wills and actions of all believers. The birth of Islam, by contrast, was inextricably linked with the creation of a world empire and its universalism was inherently imperialist. It did not distinguish between temporal and religious powers, which were combined in the person of Muhammad, who derived his authority directly from Allah and acted at one and the same time as head of the state and head of the church. This allowed the prophet to cloak his political ambitions with a religious aura and to channel Islam's energies into "its instrument of aggressive expansion, there [being] no internal organism of equal force to counterbalance it."[13]

Whereas Jesus spoke of the Kingdom of God, Muhammad used God's name to build an earthly kingdom. He spent the last ten years of his life fighting to unify Arabia under his reign. Had it not been for his sudden death on June 8, 632, he would have most probably expanded his rule well beyond the peninsula. Even so, within a decade of Muhammad's death a vast empire, stretching from Iran to Egypt and from Yemen to northern Syria, had come into being under the banner of Islam in one of the most remarkable examples of empire-building in world history. Long after the fall of the Ottoman Empire and the abolition of the caliphate in the wake of World War I, the link between religion, politics, and society remains very much alive in the Muslim and Arab worlds.

If Christendom was slower than Islam in marrying religious universalism with political imperialism, it was faster in shedding both notions. By the eighteenth century the West had lost its religious messianism. Apart from in the Third Reich, it had lost its imperial ambitions by the mid-twentieth century.[14] Islam has retained its imperialist ambition to this day.

The eminent Dutch historian Johannes Kramers (d. 1951) once commented that in medieval Islam there were never real states but only empires more or less extensive, and that the only political unity was the ideological but powerful concept of the House of Islam (*Dar al-Islam*), the common "homeland" of all Muslims.[15] This observation can also be applied to the post-World War I era, where the two contending doctrines of pan-Islamism and pan-Arabism have sought to fill the vacuum left by the collapse of the Ottoman Empire by advocating the substitution of a unified regional order for the contemporary Middle Eastern system based on territorial states. Yet while pan-Islamism views this development as a prelude to the creation of a Muslim-dominated world order, pan-Arabists content themselves with a more "modest" empire comprising the entire Middle East or most of it. (The associated ideology of Greater Syria, or *Surya al-Kubra*, for example, stresses the territorial and historical indivisibility of most of the Fertile Crescent.)

The empires of the European powers of old were by and large overseas entities that drew a clear dividing line between master and subject.[16] The Islamic empires, by contrast, were land-based systems in which the distinction between the ruling and the ruled classes became increasingly blurred through extensive colonization and assimilation. With the demise of the European empires, there was a clear break with the past. Formerly subject peoples developed their distinct brands of state nationalism, whether Indian, Pakistani, Nigerian, Argentinean, and so on. Conversely, the Arabic-speaking populations of the Middle East were indoctrinated for most of the twentieth century to consider themselves members of "One Arab Nation" or a universal "Islamic umma" rather than patriots of their specific nation-states.

If a nation is a group of people sharing such attributes as common descent, language, culture, tradition, and history, then nationalism is the desire of such a group for self-determination in a specific territory that it considers to be its patrimony. The only common denominators among the widely diverse Arabic-speaking populations of the Middle East—the broad sharing of language and religion—are consequences of the early Islamic imperial epoch. But these common factors have generated no general sense of Arab solidarity, not to speak of deeply rooted sentiments of shared history, destiny, or attachment to an ancestral homeland. Even under universal Islamic empires from the Umayyad to the Ottoman, the Middle East's Arabic-speaking populations did not unify or come to regard themselves as a single nation: the various kingdoms and empires competed for regional mastery or developed in parallel with other cultures formally under the same imperial aegis. In the words of the American Arab scholar Hisham Sharabi, "The Arab world has not constituted a single political entity since the brief period of Islam's expansion and consolidation into a Muslim empire during the seventh and eighth centuries."[17] Rather, the perennial tension between center and periphery manifested itself in a constant flux in which vigorous, numerically small but militant groups quickly rose to the pinnacle of imperial power, only to disintegrate just as quickly into a number of smaller principalities, which in turn succumbed to new empires.[18]

Arabic, like other imperial languages such as English, Spanish, and French, has been widely assimilated by former subject populations who have had little else in common. As T. E. Lawrence ("Lawrence of Arabia"), perhaps the most influential Western champion of the pan-Arab cause during the twentieth century, admitted in his later years: "Arab unity is a madman's notion—for this century or next, probably. English-speaking unity is a fair parallel."[19]

Neither did the Arabic-speaking provinces of the Ottoman Empire undergo a process of secularization similar to that which triggered the development of modern Western nationalism in the late eighteenth century. When the old European empires collapsed a century and a half later, after World War I, individual nation-states were able to step into the breach. By contrast, when the Ottoman Empire fell, its components still thought only in the old binary terms—on the one hand, the intricate webs of local loyalties to clan, tribe, village, town, religious sect, or ethnic minority; and on the other, submission to the distant Ottoman sultan-caliph in his capacity as the temporal and religious head of the world Muslim community, a post that now stood empty.

Into this welter of parochial allegiances stepped ambitious leaders hoping to create new regional empires out of the diverse, fragmented tribes of the Arabic-speaking world, and wielding new Western rhetoric about "Arab nationalism." The problem with this state of affairs was that the extreme diversity and fragmentation of the Arabic-speaking world had made its disparate societies more disposed to local patriotism than to a unified regional order. But rather than allow this disposition to run its natural course and develop into modern-day state nationalism, Arab rulers and Islamist ideologues systematically convinced their peoples to think that the independent existence of their respective states was a temporary aberration that would be rectified in the short term.

The result has been a violent dissonance that has haunted the Middle East into the twenty-first century, between the reality of state nationalism and the dream of an empire packaged as a unified "Arab nation" or the worldwide "Islamic umma."

1

The Warrior Prophet

According to Muslim tradition, it all began one night during the latter part of Ramadan, the ninth month of the lunar year, around the year 610 C.E. Muhammad ibn Abdallah, a forty-year-old merchant from the town of Mecca in the Hijaz, the northwestern part of the Arabian Peninsula, was sleeping soundly in a cave on nearby Mount Hira, where he used to spend several nights at a time in prayer and meditation, when he was suddenly awoken by a heavenly voice telling him that he was the Messenger of God. Muhammad was terrified. "I was standing, but I fell on my knees and crawled away, my shoulders trembling," he was reported to have recalled. "I went in to [my wife] Khadija and said, 'Cover me! Cover me!' until the terror had left me. He then came to me and said, 'O Muhammad, you are the Messenger of God.'"

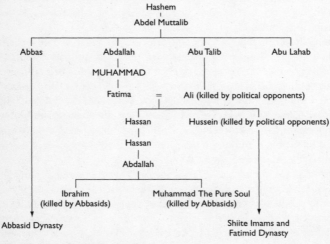

Figure 1 The Family of the Prophet

Unable to rationalize the ordeal he had just experienced, Muhammad concluded that he was possessed with an evil spirit and was thinking of committing suicide, when the mysterious figure reappeared. Presenting himself as the angel Gabriel, he told Muhammad again that he was the Messenger of God and ordered him to recite. "What shall I recite?" asked Muhammad. The angel did not reply. Instead he caught the terrified Meccan in a vice-like embrace until Muhammad heard God's words squeezed out of his mouth: "Recite: in the Name of thy Lord who created, created Man of a blood-clot. Recite: And thy Lord is the Most Generous who taught by the Pen, taught Man that he knew not." Thus came the first in a long string of revelations, which would eventually be grouped into chapters (or *suras*) of the holy book that would come to be known as the Qur'an: "The Recitation."[1]

The traumatized Muhammad returned to his wife and told her what had transpired. "I never hated anything more than idols and soothsayers," he said, "and I am afraid that I am becoming a soothsayer myself." Khadija was duly impressed. A strong-willed woman of independent financial means, she had exerted a profound influence on Muhammad, her third husband, fifteen years her junior. Once told of Muhammad's extraordinary ordeal, she quickly expressed her belief in the revelation's authenticity and took him to see a monotheistic cousin of hers who was well versed in the Jewish and Christian Holy Scriptures. "He asked me, and I told him what had happened," Muhammad recalled. "He said, 'This is the Namus which was sent down to Moses, son of Imran. I wish I were young now. I wish I could be alive when your people drive you out!' I said: 'Will they drive me out?' He said, 'Yes. No man has ever brought something akin to what you have brought without arousing antagonism.'"[2]

Emboldened by these prophetic words, yet reluctant to risk a premature public backlash, Muhammad went on to receive additional revelations but kept them secret from his townsmen for three full years. The first converts to the new faith were his most intimate circle: his wife Khadija, his freedman and adopted son Zaid ibn Haritha, his ten-year-old cousin Ali ibn Abi Talib, and his close friend Abu Bakr, later to become his direct successor. Ordered by Allah to make the nascent religion public, Muhammad then quickly acquired a local following, mainly from the town's marginal elements but also from a number of leading families and clans.

The Meccans initially viewed Muhammad's burst of prophetic energy with bemused indifference. As pagans worshiping a variety of gods, they were not averse to people choosing religions as they saw fit. As members of a merchant community, with trade relations with Syria, Egypt, and Yemen, they had been well aware of the existence of the monotheistic faiths.[3] Nor was there anything special in Muhammad's claim to divine guidance: the peninsula was rife with poets and ecstatic soothsayers claiming divine inspiration for their preaching. It was only after he launched a frontal assault on their most cherished beliefs and values, deriding their gods, emphasizing the perdition of their ancestors who had died in disbelief, and demanding an unequivocal profession of belief in Allah and total submission (the meaning of "Islam" in Arabic) to His will, that Muhammad incurred the intense enmity of the city's leadership.[4] Even then, however, the authorities seem to have been motivated as much by practical considerations as by religious outrage. Not only was the deity known as Allah, "the god," already being widely worshiped in southern Syria and northern Arabia, but by the time of Muhammad's early activity it had become *primus inter pares* in the Meccan pantheon of gods. Allah's elevation to a position of exclusivity was certainly a revolutionary move, yet it might not have been wholly traumatic for the Meccans. He already had attributes not shared by any other gods and was perceived, owing to Jewish and Christian influences, in more abstract terms, being the only god that was not represented by an idol.[5] At the same time, certain aspects of Muhammad's preaching, especially his emphasis on the equality of all believers, challenged long-standing social and genealogical structures of Mecca's tribal society. Besides, Arabian tradition tended to equate leadership with superior wisdom and judgment. Acceptance of Muhammad's claim to religious authority, let alone endorsement of his incipient faith, would have amounted to acknowledgment of his political leadership, something that Mecca's elite was loath to do.[6]

For a while Muhammad managed to hold his ground, largely due to the protection of his influential uncle Abu Talib. Though an unreconstructed pagan, Abu Talib had raised the young Muhammad following the early death of his parents and rallied his clan, the Banu Hashem, or Hashemites as they are commonly known, behind his protégé. Yet with Abu Talib's death in 619, the headship of the Hashemite clan passed to his brother, Abu Lahab, whose enmity to Muhammad was so virulent as to buy him a special Qur'anic sura (No. 111), detailing the torment he and his wife would endure in hell. Having initially promised to protect Muhammad, Abu Lahab quickly reneged on his word on the pretext that the Prophet had besmirched his own pagan grandfather by alleging him to be in hell. In these circumstances, Muhammad concluded that his position in Mecca had become untenable and that he had better look for an alternative venue from which to spread his divine message.

As early as 615 Muhammad sent a group of his followers to Ethiopia to escape persecution and to explore the possibility of cooperation with its Christian king. But Ethiopia was too remote and isolated to serve as a permanent base of operations, so Muhammad began to look closer to home. After a humiliating rebuff by the notables of Taif, a hilly town some sixty miles southeast of Mecca, and a string of abortive overtures to neighboring Bedouin tribes, Muhammad eventually reached an agreement with a group of Muslim converts from the town of Yathrib, some 275 miles north of Mecca, whereby they gave him their oath of allegiance and undertook to fight with him against his enemies.

A well-watered desert oasis on the merchant route to Syria, Yathrib had originally been settled by Jewish refugees fleeing Roman persecution and their local Arab proselytes.[7] They were organized in three tribes—Nadir, Quraiza, and Qainuqa—and their thriving farming and commercial enterprises attracted a substantial number of pagan Arabs to the site, notably the Aws and Khazraj tribes, who dominated the Jews yet remained torn by internal strife. The invitation to come to Yathrib as a peacemaker, made by representatives of the feuding tribes, thus provided Muhammad with a golden opportunity for spiritual and political pre-eminence, which he did not fail to seize. In the early summer of 622 about seventy of his followers quietly left Mecca in small groups for Yathrib. A few months later, on September 24, Muhammad himself arrived in the town, accompanied by his close associate Abu Bakr.

The *Hijra*, as the migration of Muhammad and his followers from Mecca to Yathrib has come to be known, was a watershed in Islamic history, aptly designated after the Prophet's death as the official starting point of the Muslim era. At one fell swoop Muhammad was transformed from a private preacher into a political and military leader and head of a rapidly expanding community, and Islam from a persecuted cult into a major religious and political force in the Arabian Peninsula. "Hitherto it had been a religion within a state," wrote the historian Philip Hitti, "in Medina ['the city,' as Yathrib came to be called after the Hijra] it passed into something more than a state religion—it became the state. Then and there Islam came to be what the world has ever since recognized it to be—a militant policy."[8]

Muhammad created this inextricable link between religious authority and political power shortly after the Hijra in the form of the "Constitution of Medina," which organized his local followers (*Ansar*) and those who had migrated with him from Mecca (*Muhajirun*) into "one community (umma) to the exclusion of all man," designed to act as a unified whole against external enemies and internal dissenters. The document wisely refrained from specifically abolishing existing tribal structures and practices, yet it broke with tradition by substituting religion for blood as the source of social and political organization and by making Allah, through the aegis of His chosen apostle, the supreme and exclusive sovereign: "If any dispute or controversy likely to cause trouble should arise it must be referred to God and to Muhammad, the apostle of God. God accepts what is nearest to piety and goodness in this document."[9]

Having established himself as the absolute religious and political leader of his community of believers, Muhammad spent most of his Medina years fighting external enemies and domestic opponents. During the first eighteen months after the Hijra he carried out seven raids on merchant caravans as they were making their way to Mecca. This was an attempt to build up the wealth and prestige of his followers, who had lost their livelihood as a result of their move to Medina, and to weaken Mecca's economic lifeline. It was also the logical thing to do. The caravans from Syria to Mecca passed between Medina and the Red Sea coast and were militarily unprotected, which made them easy prey for potential raiders who could intercept them at a substantial distance from their base and then disappear before the arrival of a rescue party. Yet as the Muslims lacked military experience, having themselves been merchants rather than fighters in their Meccan years, they normally returned home empty-handed. It was only in January 624 that Muhammad scored his first real success. A small raiding party of eight to ten Muslims, disguised as pilgrims, ambushed a convoy at Nakhla, southeast of Mecca, killed one of its attendants, captured another two (the fourth attendant managed to escape), and led the caravan to Medina. Yet as the raid occurred during the holy month of Rajab, when bloodshed was forbidden according to pagan convention, it was met with a wave of indignation in Medina. The embarrassed Muhammad claimed that his orders had been misunderstood and waited for a while before distributing the booty.[10] Eventually a new Qur'anic revelation appeared to justify the raid, and two months later the incident was all but forgotten as a Muslim contingent headed by Muhammad himself routed a numerically superior Meccan force near the oasis of Badr, southwest of Medina, carrying home substantial booty and a few dozen prisoners.

The battle of Badr boosted Muhammad's position in Medina, which seemed to have been deteriorating during the previous months, and allowed him to move against his local opponents. The first to find themselves in the line of fire were the Jews, who had refused to acknowledge the validity of Muhammad's revelations, and whose affluence made them a natural target for plunder. Using a trivial incident as a pretext, he expelled the weakest of the three tribes, the Qainuqa, from the city and divided their properties among the Muhajirun. (Muhammad had originally meant to kill the Qainuqa men but was dissuaded from doing so by the Khazraj sheikh.) One year later, in March 625, after a Muslim defeat in the battle of Mount Uhud, near Medina, had dented Muhammad's prestige in the eyes of the neighboring Bedouin tribes, it was the turn of the Nadir to pay the price of the Prophet's setback: after a few weeks' siege they were driven from the city and their lands were taken over by the Muslims. The last and most powerful Jewish tribe—the Quraiza—suffered more profusely following the abortive Meccan siege of

Medina in the spring of 627. Charged with collaboration with the enemy, the tribe's six to eight hundred men were brought in small groups to trenches dug the previous day, made to sit on the edge, then beheaded one by one and their bodies thrown in. The women and children were sold into slavery and the money they fetched, together with the proceeds from the tribe's possessions, was divided among the Muslims.[11]

The physical elimination of the Medina Jews was accompanied by Islam's growing break with its Jewish (and to a lesser extent Christian) origins. Upon moving to the town, Muhammad had sought to woo the local Jewish population by emphasizing the similarity between his incipient religion and Judaism, and by adopting a number of religious Jewish practices and rituals. These included the fast of Yom Kippur, the Day of Atonement, turning toward Jerusalem in prayer, raising the number of daily prayers from two to three, and accepting a number of dietary restrictions such as eating no pork or blood. These gestures failed to impress the Medina Jews. Rather than endorse Islam or unite with Muhammad against the local idolaters, they became his staunchest critics, highlighting the gaps and inconsistencies in the Qur'an and its misrepresentation of the Old Testament stories. The embittered Muhammad began to cast the Jews in his revelations as a devious and treacherous people, who had persecuted past prophets and falsified the Holy Scriptures. The direction of prayer was changed from Jerusalem to Mecca, Friday was substituted for Sabbath as the holy day of rest, the muezzin and minaret replaced the Jewish trumpets (and Christian bells) as the means of summoning to prayer, and Ramadan was designated as a month of fasting. This disengagement was completed on Muhammad's deathbed in the form of an injunction ordering the expulsion of Jews (and Christians) from the peninsula: "Two faiths will not live together in the land of the Arabs."[12]

The substitution of Mecca for Jerusalem as Islam's holiest site was also a shrewd piece of political expediency that allowed Muhammad to tie his nascent religion to pagan reverence of the city. He further reinforced this link by endorsing the annual pilgrimage to the Kaaba, Mecca's central shrine containing the images of the local gods, and by sanctifying the fetish of kissing the shrine's Black Stone, the source of Mecca's holiness. By way of giving this pragmatic move an ideological grounding, he claimed that the Kaaba had been built by the biblical figure of Abraham, together with his son Ishmael, to whom many Arabians traced their descent. In doing so, Muhammad tapped into prevailing Arabian practices and beliefs by conferring a monotheistic status on ancestral practices. He moreover dissociated Abraham, whom he presented as the first monotheist (or *hanif*), from Judaism and Christianity, and linked him to Islam and more specifically to himself by creating a direct line of succession in the development of monotheism.[13]

By now Muhammad had consolidated his power to a considerable extent. The Uhud defeat, where over seventy Muslims were killed, including some of Muhammad's oldest and most trusted followers and his formidable uncle Hamza, was a humbling experience for the Prophet. Yet the Meccans failed to achieve their strategic goal of destroying the umma and were increasingly forced to rely on a network of alliances with Bedouin tribes in their fight against the Muslims. Muhammad, however, was not to be easily upstaged. He managed to maintain the loyalty of the tribes around Medina, conducted a string of successful raids throughout the peninsula, and even resorted to the assassination of political rivals. These efforts did not prevent the Meccans from forming a grand alliance against Muhammad, nevertheless they did keep many potential participants out of this grouping, thus ensuring a more equal balance of forces in the final encounter.

This came at the end of March 627, when a ten-thousand-strong Meccan-Bedouin force advanced northward and laid siege to Medina, only to be confronted with a number of tactical surprises. To begin with, the Muslims had dug a trench around the city wherever it lay open to cavalry attack, a hitherto unknown defense method in Arabia. This caused considerable operational confusion among the Meccans, whose hopes of victory largely rested on their superior cavalry, which was further compounded by Muhammad's negotiations with the main Bedouin group in the coalition, the Ghatafan, aimed at bribing them out of the war. While the talks came to naught since the Medinese considered such a deal as being beneath their dignity, the Ghatafans had been sufficiently compromised in the eyes of their Meccan allies to preclude a cohesive military effort. After two weeks of abortive attempts to break the resistance of the far more committed and disciplined Muslims, the coalition disintegrated and its members went their separate ways.

With the failure of the siege of Medina, Mecca ceased to pose a threat to Muhammad, and in the spring of 628 he felt confident enough to attempt to make the "little pilgrimage" (umra) to his native city. As the Meccans vowed to prevent him from doing so, Muhammad stopped in the small nature spot of Hudaibiya, some ten miles northwest of the city, where the two sides negotiated a ten-year truce. The Muslims were given the right to carry out the pilgrimage the following year and the Meccans would vacate the city for three days to allow them to perform their religious duties unhindered. Muhammad agreed to send back anyone who came to him from Mecca without the explicit permission of his guardian, while the Meccans were not obliged to reciprocate this move.[14]

Many Muslims viewed these conditions as an unnecessary and humiliating surrender. They were particularly resentful of Muhammad waiving any reference to himself in the treaty as Allah's Messenger, and were indignant at the loss of booty attending the stoppage of raids on the caravans to Mecca that was implicit in the agreement. To deflect this simmering discontent, Muhammad found a handy scapegoat that had served him well in the past: the Arabian Jews. Having eliminated the Jewish presence in Medina, he now turned to the affluent Jewish community in the oasis of Khaibar, some ninety miles north of the city. After a month of siege the Jews surrendered and were stripped of their possessions and granted free passage with their women and children. Yet as Muhammad could not find the necessary manpower for tilling the site, he relented and allowed the Jews to stay on their land in return for an annual tribute of half of their produce.[15] A number of neighboring Jewish communities surrendered shortly afterward under the same terms, thus laying the ground for what would become the common arrangement between the umma and its non-Muslim subjects.

In the end, Muhammad proved more far-sighted than his critics. Not only did the Hudaibiya agreement not divert him from the ultimate goal of occupying his native city, it actually turned out to be a Trojan Horse facilitating the attainment of this objective. Aside from putting the umma on a par with Mecca, the treaty gave both signatories a free hand in their dealings with the nomadic tribes. On the face of it, this provision was of a reciprocal nature. In fact it worked in Muhammad's favor, as increasing numbers of tribes, including some that had previously been aligned with Mecca, sought to associate themselves with the umma.

When in 629 Muhammad performed the deferred "little pilgrimage," the event made a great impression. A fresh influx of converts flocked to the Prophet's camp, and Muhammad decided to strike while the iron was still hot. Using the killing of a Muslim by a Meccan in the course of a private dispute as a pretext for reneging on the Hudaibiya agreement, on January 1, 630, he set out from Medina at the head of a formidable force. Ten days later Mecca surrendered without offering any serious resistance.

The capture of Mecca was the jewel in Muhammad's crown. Less than eight years after his undignified departure, the ridiculed and despised preacher had returned as the city's undisputed master and Arabia's most powerful leader. In the course of the following year a steady stream of tribal dignitaries from all corners of the peninsula would flock to the warrior-prophet to profess their subservience. For many of them, this was a pragmatic response to the newly established balance of power rather than a true conversion to Islam. Yet being the astute politician and statesman that he was, Muhammad was prepared to content himself initially with a merely verbal profession of faith and a payment of tribute. He knew full well that paganism, as a social and political phenomenon, was virtually a spent force and that there was no need to bring about an instantaneous transformation of these independent-minded tribes. So long as they gave him their political obeisance and financial tribute, he could afford to wait and allow the socio-economic dynamics, which now favored Islam, to run their natural course.

Even in Mecca Muhammad refrained from following up his victory with mass conversions. He smashed the numerous idols kept in the Kaaba but left the population very much to its own devices, and incorporated many of the local leaders into his administration. Some of them, including his arch-enemy and the city's grand old man Abu Sufian ibn Harb and his two sons—Yazid and Mu'awiya, the future founder of the Umayyad dynasty—were given handsome rewards.[16] It was only a year later, during the annual pilgrimage festival, that Ali ibn Abi Talib, Muhammad's cousin and son-in-law, read a decree on the Prophet's behalf forbidding infidels from entering the Kaaba during the annual pilgrimage season.

In March 632 Muhammad performed for the first time the annual pilgrimage to Mecca, or the *hajj*. This turned out to be his last visit to his native city. Three months later the Prophet suddenly developed a high fever and excruciating headaches, succumbing to his brief illness on June 8, 632. He left behind a new universal religion and a community of believers organized on its basis—an unprecedented phenomenon in Arabian history that made Islam's imperial expansion inevitable.

To be sure, as evidenced by the common Qur'anic phrase "an Arabic Qur'an," Islam was initially conceived as a distinctly Arab endeavor, designed to set apart the "clear speakers" from other monotheistic groups such as the Christian Ethiopians and Byzantines, the Zoroastrian Iranians, and the Jews. This was particularly the case in the early Meccan period, when Muhammad viewed his mission along similar lines to those of numerous past prophets, namely to warn his Quraish tribe in its own language and to show it the road to salvation. He did not seem particularly interested in establishing an entirely new religion, let alone a universal one, and neither did his early supporters, whose preference for Islam over Christianity or Judaism was as much an act of rejection of foreign influence as religious devotion.[17]

With the growth of his political and military prowess, however, Muhammad increasingly fashioned himself, and by extension his religion, in universal terms. This is vividly illustrated by the concept of the "Seal of the Prophets," which casts Muhammad as the last, and the definitive, of the great prophets sent by Allah to pass His divine message to humanity: Abraham, the founding father of monotheism; Moses, to whom the Old Testament was revealed; and Jesus, who received the Gospel, confirming the Old Testament. Yet Muhammad is far more than a mere successor to them. According to the Qur'an, his future mission was foretold in the early scriptures and heralded by none other than Abraham and Jesus, which makes Muhammad nothing short of Allah's chosen Messenger to humanity, and Islam the one and only true religion: "Say: O mankind, I am Allah's Messenger to all of you . . . . There is no god but He . . . . Believe [then] in Allah and in his Messenger."[18]

This absolutist claim to universalism was amplified by a series of actions on the ground, beginning with the creation of the borderless and timeless umma. It is true that Muhammad's community was predominantly Arab in composition, but this was merely an historical accident attending Muhammad's Arabian descent and the environment in which he operated. Even before the establishment of the umma, some of the first converts to Islam had been of foreign extraction, notably Byzantine and Ethiopian,[19] and in creating his community the Prophet took great care to ensure its universal nature by substituting religion for tribal kinship as the basis of social and political affinity. At a stroke the past was wiped clean. One's ethnic origin and traditional ties and relationships counted for nothing, only one's faith and piety. The umma was not merely a novel form of socio-political communal organization. It was a divinely ordained brotherhood, bound together by something far stronger than blood and far wider than the Arabian Peninsula: the great equalizer between Arabs and non-Arabs, free men and freed men. As Muhammad put it in his farewell address during his pilgrimage to Mecca: "O people, your Lord is one and your ancestor is [also] one. You are all descended from Adam and Adam was [born] of the earth. *The noblest of you all in the sight of Allah is the most devout. Allah is knowing and all wise* [Qur'an xlix, 13]. An Arab is superior to a non-Arab in nothing but devotion."[20]

This unique fusion of religious and temporal authority, established by the Constitution of Medina, sowed the seeds of Islam's millenarian imperial experience. Muhammad was, of course, not the first political leader to have associated himself with divine guidance. Numerous rulers of all hues had done this before. Yet in pagan societies the authority of gods was limited to specific territories and/or functions, and it was generally accepted that there could be other deities in different places. The authority of Allah, as embodied in the person of His Messenger, was all-encompassing and left no room whatsoever for other gods. This made the worldwide expansion of the umma, as both the constituency in which Allah's authority had been established and the tool for its further dissemination, only a question of time. For if Allah is one and His Messenger is one and the two are fundamentally indivisible, then all humanity should believe in the one and only true religion—Islam—and be organized in one universal community living by its laws.[21]

Aside from its divinely ordained universalism, the socio-economic structure and political modus operandi of Muhammad's umma, endorsed by successive generations of Middle Eastern rulers to remain the basis of the Islamic perception of international relations to the present day, contained strong imperialist elements. To begin with, notwithstanding its tiny size and the theoretical

equality of all believers, this community was organized along classical imperial lines, with Medina acting as the metropolis of Muhammad's rapidly
expanding Islamic order and its other constituents serving as the periphery or
even colonies. The city was the seat of government, where the Prophet resided
and made his decisions and where taxes and other revenues were received and
distributed (Mecca took a back seat as a religious center).

Similarly, by substituting absolutist rule for the pluralistic system of traditional tribal organization, based as it was on a series of agreements among
equals, the umma created a powerful drive for expansion. Since it was answerable directly to Allah, through the aegis of His Messenger, it could tolerate no
dissent. Whoever acted contrary to the rules of the umma, let alone broke ties
with it, could not expect the protection of even his nearest relatives, for he
would be breaking with both God and man. So long as there were Arabs who
defied Muhammad's authority, the ideological foundation of his Islamic order
and its political standing were under challenge. This meant that "the umma
could not stand still, it had to expand or disintegrate."[22]

More importantly, the formation of the umma created a sharp dichotomy
between Muslims and "infidels" and presupposed a permanent state of war
between them. This vision was already expressed in the Constitution of
Medina, which declared the believers "friends one to the other to the exclusion
of outsiders" and forbade fighting and killing among them, let alone aiding
infidels against Muslims or making peace with them as long as "believers are
fighting in the way of God."[23] It was further underscored by Muhammad's
farewell address, which bequeathed to all Muslims a mission "to fight all men
until they say 'There is no god but Allah,'"[24] and by countless sayings and
traditions attributed to the Prophet (hadith). "The gates of Paradise are under
the shadow of the swords," runs one famous saying, while another hadith stip-
ulates that: "A morning or an evening expedition in God's path is better than
the world and what it contains, and for one of you to remain in the line of
battle is better than his prayers for sixty years."[25]

The Qur'anic revelations during the Medina years abound with verses
extolling the virtues of jihad against idolaters, infidels, and hypocrites
(munafiqun), who had ostensibly embraced Islam but effectively remained
entrenched in their non-belief. Those who participate in this holy pursuit
"with their property and lives" will be generously rewarded, both in this life
and in the afterworld, where they will reside in shaded and ever-green
gardens, indulged by pure women. The enemies of Islam will burn in hell,
having "no protecting helper nor friend in the earth." Those killed in the
course of the jihad should not be mourned as dead as they have made their
contract with Allah: "Allah has bought from the believers their soul and their
possessions against the gift of Paradise; they fight in the path of Allah; they kill

and are killed . . . and who fulfils his covenant truer than Allah? So rejoice in the bargain you have made with Him; that is the mighty triumph."[26]

There was an important material aspect to this militant doctrine. By forbidding fighting and raiding within the umma, Muhammad deprived the Arabian tribes of a traditional source of livelihood and drove them inexorably toward imperial expansion. A well-known Muslim tradition tells of a prominent tribe, which, on the verge of joining the victorious Prophet, had second thoughts owing to its reluctance to give up its previous way of life. "The religion of the grandchild of Abdel Muttalib [i.e., Muhammad] forbids its followers to go to war with each other," they are reported to have said. "It condemns to death a Muslim who kills another (even if he be of a different tribe). Thus we should have to refrain from attacking and robbing tribes who, like us, accept Islam." In the end they devised an ingenious solution: "We will undertake one more expedition . . . and then we will become Muslims."[27]

This story may or may not be true, but it certainly grew out of real conditions and underscored the dilemma confronting Muhammad. For a time he could rely on booty from non-Muslims as a substitute for the lost war spoils, which is why he did not go out of his way to convert all tribes seeking alignment with his Pax Islamica and preferred their attachment as tributaries. Yet given his belief in the supremacy of his religion and his relentless commitment to its widest possible dissemination, Muhammad could not deny conversion to those tribes wishing to undertake it. Were the whole of Arabia to become Muslim, a new source of wealth and an alternative outlet for the bubbling energies of the Arabian tribes would have to be found north of the peninsula, in the Fertile Crescent and the Levant.

The early Arab historian al-Waqidi (d. 823) narrated a tradition that Muhammad was destined to extend his domination over the lands of the Byzantine and Iranian empires, which had dominated the Middle East for centuries.[28] The Prophet certainly acted as if this objective were on his agenda. As early as the summer of 626 he sent a small force to fight some hostile tribes in the area of Dumat al-Jandal, some five hundred miles northeast of Medina. The ease and rapidity of the operation seemed to have whetted Muhammad's appetite, and in the following year he sent his freedman and adopted son Zaid to Syria on a trading mission. This failed to produce concrete results, but another mission in the same year resulted in a treaty of alliance with the Dumat prince.

At this stage, Muhammad was apparently not interested in occupying these territories on a permanent basis or converting their largely Christian populations to Islam. Yet during the last three years of his life he attempted to incorporate the tribes on the road to Syria into his Islamic order and even made overtures to the tribes in the direction of Iraq. Muhammad was also reported to have sent emissaries to a number of prominent Arab and non-Arab rulers, including the Byzantine, Iranian, and Ethiopian emperors, with the demand that they embrace Islam.[29] In October 630 he ventured toward the Byzantine frontier at the head of a thirty thousand-strong army. Advancing as far as the oasis of Tabuq, some five hundred miles north of Medina, Muhammad camped there for twenty days, during which time he negotiated a peace treaty with the Christian prince of Aylah (the biblical Eilat), at the northern tip of the Gulf of Aqaba. In return for an oath of allegiance and an annual tribute, the Christians were placed under the protection of the umma and granted freedom of worship. At this point Muhammad decided to return to Medina, having apparently realized the impracticability of his Byzantine ambitions. Yet this did not imply the disappearance of his interest in northern expansion. No sooner had he returned from his pilgrimage than he began preparations for a campaign in Transjordan and southern Palestine, which were only brought to an abrupt end by his sudden death.[30] And while it is unlikely that Muhammad had imagined the full scope of Islam's future expansion, let alone planned it in detail, "his was the far-seeing mind which directed the Arabs' attention to the strategic importance of Syria for the new Islamic state."[31]

The Rise and Fall of Islam's First Empire

Few events have transformed the course of human history more swiftly and profoundly than the expansion of early Islam and its conquest of much of the ancient world. Within twelve years of Muhammad's death in June 632, Iran's long-reigning Sasanid Empire had been reduced to a tributary, and Egypt and Syria had been wrested from Byzantine rule. By the early eighth century, the Muslims had extended their domination over Central Asia and much of the Indian subcontinent all the way to the Chinese frontier, had laid siege to Constantinople, the capital of the Byzantines, and had overrun North Africa and Spain. Had they not been contained in northwest France by the nobleman Charles Martel at the battle of Poitiers (732), they might well have swept deep into Europe. "A victorious line of march had been prolonged above a thousand miles from the rock of Gibraltar to the banks of the Loire; the repetition of an equal space would have carried the Saracens to the confines of Poland and the Highlands of Scotland," wrote the eighteenth-century British historian Edward Gibbon contemplating the possible consequences of a Christian defeat in Poitiers. "The Rhine is not more impassable than the Nile or the Euphrates, and the Arabian fleet might have sailed without a naval combat into the mouth of the Thames. Perhaps the interpretation of the Qur'an would now be taught in the schools of Oxford, and her pulpits might demonstrate to a circumcised people the sanctity and truth of the revelation of Mohammed."[1]

What were the causes of this extraordinary burst of energy and the sources of its success? To traditional Islamic historians the answer is clear and straightforward: religious zeal and selfless exertion "in the path of Allah." The problem with this view is that the Arab conquerors were far less interested in the mass conversion of the vanquished peoples than in securing their tribute. Not until the second and the third Islamic centuries did the bulk of these populations embrace the religion of their latest imperial masters, and even this process emanated from below in an attempt to escape paying tribute and to remove social barriers, with the conquering ruling classes doing their utmost to slow it down.

Nor were the early conquests the result of dire economic necessity, let alone "the final stage in the age-long process of gradual infiltration from the barren desert to the adjacent Fertile Crescent, the last great Semitic migration."[2] Far from a mass migration of barbarian hordes in desperate search of subsistence, the Arab invasions were centrally organized military expeditions on a strikingly small scale. The celebrated battle of Qadisiyya (637), which broke the backbone of the Iranian Empire, involved between six and twelve thousand fighters, while the number of Arab fighters active in southern Iraq was estimated at between two and four thousand men. There is no evidence of whole tribes migrating into the Fertile Crescent during this period, or of the poorer segments of Arabian society, the natural candidates for migration, accompanying the invading forces, or of warriors taking their own families and herds with them (apart from a few isolated cases). It was only after the consolidation of the initial conquests that substantial numbers of Arab colonists arrived in the newly acquired territories.[3]

This makes the conquests first and foremost a quintessential expansionist feat by a rising imperial power, in which Islam provided a moral sanction and a unifying battle cry rather than a driving force. In the words of the eminent German historian Theodor Noeldeke (d. 1930):

It was certainly good policy to turn the recently subdued tribes of the wilderness towards an external aim in which they might at once satisfy their lust for booty on a grand scale, maintain their warlike feeling, and strengthen themselves in their attachment to the new faith.... Mohammed himself had already sent expeditions across the Roman frontier, and thereby had pointed out the way to his successors. To follow in his footsteps was in accordance with the innermost being of the youthful Islam, already grown great amid the tumult of arms.[4]

Throughout history all imperial powers and aspirants have professed some kind of universal ideology as both a justification of expansion and a means of ensuring the subservience of the conquered peoples: in the case of the Greeks and the Romans it was that of "civilization" vs. "barbarity," in the case of the Mongols it was the conviction in their predestination to inherit the earth. For the seventh-century Arabs it was Islam's universal vision of conquest as epitomized in the Prophet's summons to fight the unbelievers wherever they might be found.

This vision, together with Islam's unwavering feeling of supremacy and buoyant conviction in its ultimate triumph, imbued the early believers with the necessary sense of purpose, self-confidence, and revolutionary zeal to take on the region's established empires. "We have seen a people who love death more than life, and to whom this world holds not the slightest attraction," a group of Byzantine officials in Egypt said of the invading Arabs.[5] The great Muslim historian and sociologist Abdel Rahman Ibn Khaldun (d. 1406) expressed the same idea in a somewhat more elaborate form: "When people possess the [right] insight into their affairs, nothing can withstand them, because their outlook is one and they share a unity of purpose for which they are willing to die."[6]

Whether the conquests were an opportunistic magnified offshoot of small raiding parties or a product of a preconceived expansionist plan is immaterial. Empires are born of chance as well as design. What counts is that the Arab conquerors acted in a typically imperialist fashion from the start, subjugating indigenous populations, colonizing their lands, and expropriating their wealth, resources, and labor.

Already Muhammad had skillfully couched his worldly objectives in divine terms, as illustrated by such sayings as "Stick to jihad and you will be in good health and get sufficient means of livelihood."[7] This fusion of the sacred and the profitable was endorsed by future generations of Islamic leaders. Abu Bakr, Muhammad's father-in-law and immediate successor (khalifa, or caliph), sought to lure the Arabs to his campaigns of conquest by linking the call for jihad with the promise of "the booty to be won from the Byzantines."[8] So did Umar ibn al-Khattab, who in 634 succeeded Abu Bakr in the caliphate, as well as Ali ibn Abi Talib, the Prophet's son-in-law and the fourth caliph (656–61). "Sacrifice yourselves!" he told his troops on the eve of a crucial battle against a contender to the caliphate. "You are under Allah's watchful eye and with the Prophet's cousin. Resume your charge and abhor flight, for it will disgrace your descendants and buy you the fire [of hell] in the Day of Reckoning." And as if this religious prodding was not enough, Ali added a substantial carrot: "Before you lie these great sawad [the fertile lands of Iraq] and those large tents!"[9]

Abu Bakr and Umar apparently made no personal profit by the conquests (both were said to have lived in modest households and on a humble subsistence).[10] Yet their immediate successor, Uthman ibn Affan, another son-in-law of the Prophet and the third caliph, exploited expansion for unabashed self-enrichment. By the time of his assassination in June 656, he had netted himself a fortune of 150,000 dinars and one million dirhams in cash, and the value of his estates amounted to 200,000 dinars, aside from a vast herd of camels and horses.[11] This fortune paled in comparison with the fabulous wealth amassed by some of Muhammad's closest companions. The invested capital of Zubair ibn Awam amounted to some fifty million dirhams and

400,000 dinars, and he owned countless properties in Medina, Iraq, and Egypt. Talha ibn Ubaidallah, one of the earliest converts to Islam to whom Muhammad had promised a place in Paradise, was similarly a proprietor of numerous estates in Iraq and Transjordan. He left, according to some authorities, 200,000 dinars and 2.2 million dirhams in cash, and his estates were valued at thirty million dirhams. His investments in Iraq alone yielded him one thousand dinars per day. "I will reserve comment on what is in the city I have captured," Amr ibn al-As, the conqueror of Egypt, reported to Umar upon the occupation of the port town of Alexandria, "aside from saying that I have seized therein four thousand villas with four thousand baths, forty thousand poll tax-paying Jews and four hundred places of entertainment for the royalty." He was peremptorily ordered to ship a year's supply of food to Medina for the upkeep of the Muslim community, which he dutifully did.[12]

It was during the caliphate of Umar (634–44) that the Arabs made their greatest conquests and institutionalized their absolute domination of the nascent Islamic empire. In a move that was to have a profound and lasting impact on the course of Middle Eastern history, Umar forbade the invading forces from settling on the conquered lands, placing the whole empire in trust for the Muslim community. "Allah has made those who will come after you partners in these spoils," the caliph is reported to have said when asked to divide the Iraqi and Syrian lands among the conquering Arabs. "Were I to divide these lands among you, nothing will be left for them. Even a shepherd boy in San'a [Yemen] is entitled to his share."[13]

Whether Umar actually justified his action in these particular words or whether they were a later attempt to legitimize an existing situation (it is common in Muslim tradition to represent rules established after Muhammad's death as ordinances of Umar), the decision effectively extended Muhammad's designation of Islam as the cornerstone of the political order to the entire Middle East. This principle would be maintained for over a millennium until the collapse of the Ottoman Empire in the wake of World War I and the subsequent abolition of the caliphate.

On a more immediate level, Umar's decision enabled the continuation of the conquests: had the vast majority of the Arabs settled on the conquered lands, fighting would have ground to a halt. According to numerous traditions about Muhammad's life, this fear had preoccupied the Prophet, who had reputedly warned that "the survival of my Community rests on the hoofs of its horses and the points of its lances; as long as they keep from tilling the fields; once they begin to do that they will become as other men."[14] Umar resolved this problem by devising a register (*Diwan*), which remunerated the fighters out of the proceeds from the conquered lands and thus allowed them to continue prosecuting war operations without worrying about their subsistence.[15]

Last but not least, since the umma at the time consisted almost exclusively of the conquering Arabs, by proclaiming the empire an Islamic trust Umar institutionalized their position as the new imperial ruling class. Viewing Arabs as superior to all other peoples and creeds, the caliph went to great lengths to make Islam synonymous with Arabism. He achieved this goal in the Arabian Peninsula by summarily expelling its Christian and Jewish communities, in flagrant violation of the treaties they had signed with the Prophet.[16] Yet this option was hardly available in the vast territories conquered by the Arabs, both because the populations involved were far too large to make their expulsion practicable and because their tribute was indispensable in enabling the Arabs to enjoy fully their privileges as conquerors.

In these circumstances, Umar contented himself with perpetuating complete Arab domination of the empire. For him, there was only one ethnic group destined to rule while all others were fated to serve and to toil as subject peoples. By way of preventing assimilation and ensuring Arab racial purity he forbade non-Arab converts to marry Arab women, sought to dissuade the Prophet's companions from marrying Jewish women, though this was not prohibited by the Qur'an, and pressured the many companions who did so to annul their marriages. He also settled the Arabs in garrison cities (*Amsar*), in total segregation from the indigenous population, from where they administered their newly conquered territories in a kind of inverted colonial rule similar to that of the coastal outposts of the British Empire. Two large Amsar were established in Iraq, by far the largest site of Arab colonization: Kufa, on the Euphrates River southwest of the site that was to become the city of Baghdad, and Basra, at the head of the Persian Gulf. In Syria the southern city of Djabiya, home to the Ghassanid dynasty that had ruled the area under Byzantine suzerainty, was chosen as the main camp of the Arab army, while in Egypt the garrison city of Fustat was established to become the province's capital until the foundation of Cairo in the late tenth century.[17]

To be an Arab in Umar's empire was to be at the pinnacle of society. It meant paying a modest religious tithe, which was more than compensated by the booty received in accordance with the Diwan. No Arab, Umar insisted, could be a slave, either by sale or capture; on his deathbed he ordered that all Arab slaves held by the state be freed. Even those Arabs outside the peninsula who did not embrace Islam were considered by Umar his primary subjects, as illustrated by his readiness to incorporate the north Iraqi Banu Taghlib tribe into the Arab army and to place it on a similar tax footing to that of the Muslims, despite its refusal to give up its Christian faith.[18] This stood in stark contrast to the heavy taxation levied on the rest of the non-Muslim populations, or *Dhimmis* as they were commonly known. These "protected communities" (the term was originally applied to Christians and Jews, but was subsequently expanded to other non-Muslim groups) were allowed to keep their properties and to practice their religions in return for a distinctly inferior status that was institutionalized over time. They had to pay special taxes (regularized at a later stage as land tax, *kharaj*, and the more humiliating poll tax, *jizya*) and suffered from social indignities and at times open persecution. Their religious activities outside the churches and synagogues were curtailed, the ringing of bells was forbidden, the construction of new church buildings prohibited, and the proselytizing of Muslims was made a capital offense punishable by death. Jews and Christians had to wear distinctive clothes to distinguish them from their Muslim lords, could ride only donkeys, not horses, could not marry Muslim women, had to vacate their seats whenever Muslims wanted to sit, were excluded from positions of power, and so on and so forth.[19]

Yet while this institutionalized discrimination secured the Arabs' short-term pre-eminence, it also contained the seeds of their eventual decline and assimilation into the wider regional environment. Unlike Muhammad's umma, where Dhimmis constituted a negligible minority, in Umar's empire the Arab colonizers were themselves a small island surrounded by a non-Muslim and non-Arab ocean, something that condemned their apartheid policy to assured failure.

The staggering magnitude of the conquests, together with Arab bureaucratic and administrative inexperience, forced the victors to rely on the existing Byzantine and Iranian systems for the running of their nascent empire, thus leading to greater mingling with the indigenous populations. In their capacity as the centers of government the Amsar quickly became hubs of vibrant economic and commercial activity, while the growing numbers of Arab colonists allotted plots of state lands (*qata'i*) during the caliphate of Uthman, and in its aftermath relied by and large on the indigenous population for their cultivation. With the intensification of interaction between conqueror and conquered, the Arabs adopted indigenous—especially Iranian—habits, manners, and ways of life. They embraced the refined Iranian cuisine and wore Iranian clothes. Meanwhile the early prohibition on Muslims from using foreign languages, as well as the prevention of Christians from learning the Arabic language and using the Arabic script, gave way to a growing sense of linguistic and cultural unity as the second generation of Amsar residents tended to be of mixed parentage and bilingual. On the other hand, Arabic penetrated the conquered peoples to such an extent that at the beginning of the eighth century it had evolved into the official imperial language.

The implications of this move cannot be overstated. For one thing, by adopting the Arabic language, the conquered peoples—Iranians, Syrians, Greeks, Copts, Berbers, Jews, and Christians—placed their abundant talents and learning at the service of their conquerors, thus leading to the development of a distinct Islamic civilization. For another, the Arabization of the imperial administration unleashed a process that blurred the distinctions between the Arab imperial elite and the indigenous non-Arab populations and culminated in the creation of a new Arabic-speaking imperial persona, a reincarnation of sorts of the old Roman subject. The term "Arab" itself in Arabic usage was subsequently restricted to the nomads.[20]

This development, however, was something that would take a century or two to materialize. In the meantime, the Arabs frowned upon the growing numbers of non-Muslims knocking at the gates of Islam in an attempt to improve their socio-economic conditions. As far as they were concerned the vanquished masses had only one role in life: to provide a lasting and lucrative source of revenue for their imperial masters, and, since religion constituted the sole criterion for social mobility, they were determined to perpetuate this state of affairs by keeping Islam a purely Arab religion. Non-Arabs were thus allowed to enter the faith only through the humiliating channel of becoming clients (*Mawali*, sing. *Mawla*) of the persons at whose hands they had converted. A vestige of the legacy of pagan Arabia, where clients were lesser members of an Arab clan (e.g., slaves and freed slaves promoted to a position of clientage),[21] this mode of conversion placed the new Muslims in a position

Figure 2 The Rightly Guided Caliphs

of institutional inferiority to their Arab co-religionists and subjected them to blatant social and economic discrimination.

In many cases the Mawali failed to escape their excessive tributes or even ended up paying higher taxes than before. They could not inherit equally, were denied the material benefits of Islam, and were treated with such contempt that in certain neighborhoods an Arab risked social ostracism merely by virtue of walking down the street in the company of a Mawla. Even the pious caliph Umar II (717–20), who attempted to equalize the Mawali's standing, was reputed to have taken a dim view of Muslims and Mawali intermarrying, and forbade Mawali from selling their lands to Muslims. Little wonder that this state of affairs turned the Mawali into an embittered and disgruntled group whose actions were to shake the empire to its core before too long.[22]

The Mawali were by no means the only disaffected group. From the start, the Islamic order had been beset by the perennial tension between center and periphery that has plagued imperial powers from antiquity to the present day. Muhammad's success in unifying most of the peninsula under a single authority may have been without parallel in Arabian history, but it was still far from complete. Many tribes regarded their inclusion in the umma as a personal bond with the Prophet that expired upon his death, not least since Muhammad had refrained from designating a successor and had emphasized time and again his irreplaceable historical role as the Seal of the Prophets. They therefore refused to acknowledge Abu Bakr's position as caliph and suspended their tribute payments and treaty relations with the umma in what came to be known in Muslim tradition as the *ridda*, "the apostasy."

This, however, is something of a misnomer. The urge for secession was predominantly political and economic rather than religious: some of the rebels failed to repudiate their Islamic faith while others had joined the umma as tributaries without embracing Islam. Some of the rebellious tribes were headed by self-styled prophets offering their own brand of religious belief, but for most the revolt represented an atavistic attempt to exploit the sudden weakening of the central government in order to free themselves from the less savory aspects of their subjugation (notably the payment of taxes), if not to end this status altogether.[23]

Abu Bakr's suppression of the revolt and his successful extension of Muslim control to the entire peninsula thus signified the first triumph of the imperial order over the centrifugal forces of tribal separatism. This was not achieved, though, without the massacre of the foremost rebellious faction—the central Arabian confederates of Banu Hanifa headed by the self-styled prophet Masalma ibn Habib—in a grim foretaste of countless such violent confrontations between the center and periphery throughout Islamic history.[24] Indeed, no sooner had the umma weathered the storm attending the demise of its creator than it experienced yet another peripheral backlash that culminated in the murder of its supreme ruler: the caliph Uthman, who in 644 had succeeded Umar.

Enforcing central authority over disparate provinces has been an intractable problem for most empires even in modern times, let alone for classical and medieval empires with their far less advanced means of communication and control. The stability of these early empires depended to a large extent on the existence of powerful governors capable of maintaining law and order within their domains while deferring to their imperial masters. This was especially pertinent for the nascent Arab-Muslim empire, where the age-old Arab traits of particularism and individualism had been suppressed but not totally extinguished and where clans and tribes not only remained the real units of social activity but paradoxically grew in weight and importance. Unlike pre-Islamic times, where tribes were relatively small units and their perennial squabbles were of a localized nature, the post-conquest migration and colonization in garrison cities brought many tribes into close contact with each other and created far larger leagues and alliances. The best known of these were the Qays and the Yemen, whose bitter enmity was to plague the region for centuries.[25]

Umar, who was keenly aware of this reality, sought to foster an overarching imperial unity that would transcend the traditional tribal system and ensure Medina's continued domination. He did this by cultivating a strong provincial leadership comprising the Prophet's companions and prominent commanders of the early conquests, and by encouraging the nomadic tribes that participated in the campaigns to settle in the Amsar where they could more easily be monitored by the central government. But this system, which worked reasonably well initially, began to falter after Umar's death as Uthman attempted to tighten his grip on the empire and to catapult his Umayyad clan, and the Quraish tribe more generally, into a position of imperial pre-eminence.

Unlike Umar, who had allowed the conquering commanders to govern the territories they had occupied, Uthman vested all key posts in the hands of his family members, many of whom abused their appointments for self-enrichment. This nepotism earned the new caliph hostility from all quarters. The Medinese elite resented its growing marginalization in the running of the empire, while the provincial leadership was incensed by Uthman's efforts to increase the central government's share in the distribution of local revenues, most of which had hitherto been retained in the provinces. These grievances were further exacerbated by the temporary halt of the conquests in the early 650s and the attendant reduction in the spoils of war on the one hand, and the continued influx of Arab colonists into the provinces on the other, which further strained their economic and financial resources.

Things came to a head in January 656 when disgruntled elements in Egypt seized Fustat, prevented the governor from returning from Medina, and issued a call for the removal of Uthman. A few months later, several hundred malcontents left Egypt for Medina, converging on the way with similarly disaffected groups from the Iraqi garrison cities of Kufa and Basra. The star- tled caliph accepted most of the demands put to him, including the dismissal of his Egyptian governor, and the group set out to return to Egypt, only to intercept a message sent in Uthman's name ordering the governor to deal harshly with the rebels. Viewing this as a blatant act of betrayal, the enraged Egyptians returned to Medina, where they laid siege to Uthman's residence. Ignoring the caliph's emphatic denials of having anything to do with the secret message, they murdered him on June 17, 656.[26]

Uthman's murder was much more than a tactical victory of provincial strongmen over their lawful ruler. It signified the periphery's ultimate triumph by heralding the permanent shift of the imperial center of gravity away from Medina, indeed from the Arabian Peninsula, to the Fertile Crescent. Within months of his election, Uthman's successor to the caliphate, Ali ibn Abi Talib, decided to make Kufa the center of his operations. This was apparently an ad hoc decision, deriving from the need to suppress an uprising in Basra by a group of distinguished Meccans who blamed the new caliph for his predecessor's murder. Yet what was conceived as a temporary move was to acquire permanence. Having defeated the renegades, Ali encountered a further and far greater challenge to his authority which forced him to stay in Kufa. Mu'awiya ibn Abi Sufian, the long-reigning governor of Syria and Uthman's cousin, refused to recognize the validity of Ali's appointment and demanded vengeance for the slain caliph. In late July or early August 657, after a few months of intermittent skirmishes, Ali confronted his challenger at the site of Siffin, on the right bank of the Euphrates near the Syrian border. As the battle went the caliph's way, the Syrians hoisted copies of the Qur'an on the points of their lances to demand that the dispute be decided through arbi- tration rather than war. Under tremendous pressure from his followers to give peace a chance, Ali, who suspected a trick, begrudgingly accepted the proposal, and the two armies departed for home.[27]

This proved to be a mistake. Not only were the arbitrators to rule against Ali, putting him on a par with his challenger and thus implicitly rejecting the validity of his claim to the caliphate, but he was also confronted with wide- spread desertions by his followers. Foremost among these was a group that came to be known as *Kharijites* (those who "went out" or "seceded"), who opposed the arbitration on the ground that "decision is with Allah alone" and claimed that in accepting this process the caliph had not only forfeited his right to the title but had effectively excluded himself from the community of believers. Ali managed to reduce them in a bloody engagement in July 658,[28] but was unable to arrest the steady disintegration of his authority and was forced to watch from the sidelines as Mu'awiya added Egypt to his possessions and made repeated incursions into Iraq. Shortly afterward the Syrian governor openly staked his claim to the caliphate, and there is little doubt that Ali would have suffered the ultimate ignominy of the loss of supreme office had he not first been murdered by a Kharijite on January 24, 661. His eldest son, Hassan, quickly renounced his right to the throne in favor of Mu'awiya, who was now hailed as caliph and the empire's new master.

From his newly proclaimed capital of Damascus Mu'awiya presided over the foundation of Islam's first imperial dynasty by having his son, Yazid, succeed him to the throne. This proved a shrewd move that allowed Mu'awiya's Umayyad family to retain power for the next ninety years and established the principle that was to dominate Middle Eastern political life up to the early twentieth century, and in some parts of the region to the present day.

In one fell swoop the umma was transformed from "Allah's Community" into an ordinary empire. Although Islam retained its position as the empire's pre-eminent organizing principle and its rallying point for further expansion, with the Umayyad monarchs styling themselves as "Allah's caliphs" and portraying their constant wars of expansion as a "jihad in the path of Allah,"[29] this was largely a façade that concealed what was effectively a secular and increasingly absolutist rule. The Umayyad caliphs adopted a lax attitude toward Islamic practices and mores. They were said to have set aside special days for drinking, specifically forbidden by the Prophet, and some of them had no inhibitions about appearing completely nude before their boon companions and female singers.[30] Little wonder that Islamic tradition tends to decry the Umayyads for having perverted the caliphate into a "kingdom" (*mulk*), with the implicit connotation of religious digression or even disbelief.

Moreover, the murder of Uthman had irrevocably changed the rules of the game. Three decades after the creation of the umma as a divinely ordained community answerable directly to Allah, the seemingly inextricable link between religious and temporal power was abruptly severed. So long as Muhammad was alive, this was inconceivable. He was Allah's Apostle, the true theocratic ruler. To defy him was to defy Allah Himself. Abu Bakr and Umar could claim no such religious prowess, yet by basking in the Prophet's reflected glow they managed to sustain the umma as a working theocracy, although Umar took care to emphasize the temporal aspects of his post by assuming the title "Commander of the Believers" (*Amir al-Mu'minin*).[31] Once the sanctity of the caliphate had been violated, its uninterrupted reten-tion and natural transition could no longer be taken for granted. During the

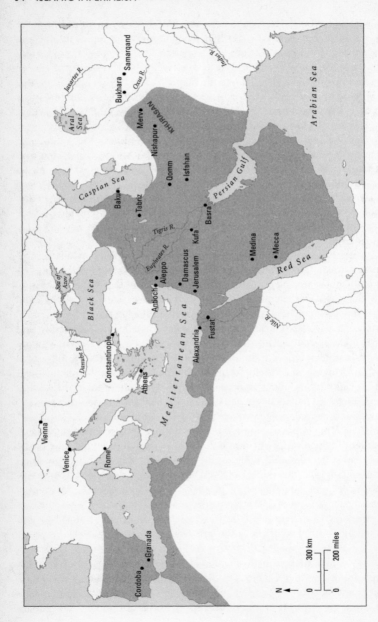

Map 2 Islam's First Empire

next millennium this coveted post would incessantly be contested by force of arms, making a mockery of the categorical prohibition of internecine fighting among Muslims underlying Muhammad's universal vision of the umma.

The Umayyads themselves succeeded in maintaining their position mainly through reliance on physical force, and were consumed for most of their reign with preventing or quelling revolts in the diverse corners of their empire. Mu'awiya had attempted to wrest the caliphate from Ali, and while his nineteen years on the throne (661–80) were characterized by relative calm and stability owing to his formidable political and administrative skills, his son and heir, Yazid I, faced widespread disobedience on several fronts. Particularly threatening was the revolt by Abdallah ibn Zubair, son of a prominent companion of Muhammad, who refused to acknowledge the validity of the Umayyad line of succession and sought to establish himself as caliph. Ibn Zubair was supported in his endeavor by the people of Medina, who withdrew their allegiance from the caliph and circulated damning stories about his alleged religious and personal indiscretions, including his propensity for wine and singing girls and his obsession with his pet monkey, which was constantly by his side and to which he gave the dignified title of Abu Qays. When Abu Qays was accidentally killed, the caliph was inconsolable. He gave the monkey a state funeral and had him buried in accordance with Muslim rites.[32]

These tales were but the tip of a huge iceberg of resentment within the traditional Islamic ruling elite over the shift of the imperial center to Damascus. This elite consisted initially of the small circle of Muhajirun who migrated with the Prophet to Medina and the local Ansar. These were the people who spread Muhammad's message and enforced his authority throughout the peninsula, whose opinion he sought on matters of import, and who enjoyed the material benefits of the umma's steady expansion. Following the conquest of Mecca in 630 this group was dramatically and swiftly expanded through the incorporation of Muhammad's Quraish tribe, as the Prophet sought to harness the organizational and administrative skills of his kinsmen to the service of his continued expansion. Much to the resentment of Muhammad's companions, this process gained considerable momentum during the wars of the ridda attending the Prophet's death, when Abu Bakr was forced to rely on the alignment between the Quraish and the Taif-based tribe of Thaqif as a springboard for reasserting Islamic domination over the rebellious tribes.

Umar restored the political pre-eminence of the early believers by appointing some of them to key positions in his nascent empire and, more importantly, by using precedence in Islam as the chief criterion for remuneration from the proceeds of the conquests. Yet during the caliphate of Uthman the Quraishis regained their predominant position to the detriment of the Ansar and the Muhajirun. These early believers (and their descendants) were particularly incensed by the meteoric rise of the Umayyads, who had long been at the forefront of the Meccan opposition to Muhammad and who joined Islam only after its ultimate triumph. They therefore sided with Ali in his confrontation with Mu'awiya, and quickly challenged the legitimacy of Umayyad dynastical claims upon the demise of its founding father.

The traditional Islamic aristocracy was fighting a rearguard action. Its commanding position in the imperial order of things had irrevocably been lost. An expeditionary force sent by Yazid routed the rebels and sacked Medina for three full days.[33] It then proceeded to lay siege to Mecca, where Abdallah ibn Zubair and his supporters had barricaded themselves in, but failed to take the city, and in November 683 was forced to return to Syria following the caliph's death. As Yazid's youthful and sickly successor Mu'awiya II proved to be a nonentity, Ibn Zubair quickly proclaimed himself caliph and asserted his authority throughout much of the empire. It was only after the accession of another branch of the Umayyads, headed by Marwan ibn Hakam, that the dynasty managed to reclaim its lost territories. In July 684 the Yemen tribe, associated with the new Umayyad caliph, defeated the rival Qays, aligned with Ibn Zubair, in a particularly bloody battle near Damascus. Shortly afterward Marwan recaptured Egypt, only to die a few months later in April 685. It thus fell to Marwan's able son and designated successor, Abdel Malik (685–705), to complete the suppression of the revolt. This was achieved in November 692, with the occupation of Mecca and the killing of Ibn Zubair.[34]

Iraq constituted the hard core of violent anti-Umayyad opposition. It was there that most Arab colonists had settled during the conquests, especially in the large garrison cities of Kufa and Basra, where they subsisted mostly on government stipends from the war spoils. Having enjoyed unprecedented pre-eminence as the imperial center during Ali's brief tenure, Iraqis resented the shift of the caliphate to Damascus and their attendant relegation to a position of subservience to Syria, which, they feared, would deprive them of their fair share of the spoils. This sentiment was further exacerbated by such factors as intertribal rivalries, personal and dynastical ambitions, and religious radicalism. The substantial numbers of Syrian forces permanently deployed in Iraq to enforce the regime's authority only served to sharpen anti-Syrian sentiments and to reinforce Iraqis' distinct sense of local patriotism. Especially powerful and astute governors were required to keep the Iraqi province in check and even then matters often necessitated mass physical repression. Hajjaj ibn Yusuf, who ruled the area for twenty years (694–714), was the epitome of such single-minded ruthlessness. "I see heads that are ripe for plucking, and I am the man to do it; and I see blood between the turbans and the beards," he famously told the people of Kufa upon his arrival in the city.[35] He made good on his threat. When many Iraqi Arabs, who had become accustomed to settled life, refused to participate in the campaigns of expansion, Hajjaj summarily beheaded the draft dodgers. When the number of Mawali and Dhimmis flocking to the towns in search of socio-economic advancement rose so high as to threaten a substantial drop in government revenues from agricultural produce, Hajjaj took draconian measures to discourage conversion and to drive the new converts back to their villages, including having the names of their villages branded on people's hands to prevent them from returning to the towns. One of his favorite modes of torture was to apply hot wax to his victims' naked bodies. This was then pulled off till the flesh was all lacerated, following which vinegar and salt were poured on the wounds until death ensued.[36]

Hajjaj's heavy-handed policy failed to prevent the Iraqi cauldron from repeatedly boiling over. The appalling conditions of the East African black slaves known as *Zanj* sparked a protracted revolt in Basra, while the weakening of the local Iraqi dignitaries (*Ashraf*) resulted in a number of uprisings, some of which were suppressed only with great difficulty.[37] Yet it was the activities of two radical religious movements—the Kharijite and the Shiite—that constituted the most dangerous and intractable source of turbulence. Both viewed the Umayyads as opportunistic latecomers to Islam who had unlawfully usurped and perverted its most cherished institution. But while the Shiites advocated the vesting of the caliphate in the Prophet's family, or more specifically in the house of the slain caliph Ali (their name originated in the designation *Shiat Ali*—the faction of Ali), the Kharijites acknowledged no authority but that of the Islamic community, which could elect or disown any caliph who went astray. Foreshadowing radical twentieth-century Islamic thinkers, they considered themselves the only true Muslims and had no scruples about shedding the blood of fellow co-religionists, for it was against these "heretics" alone that they waged the holy war. In the late 680s and early 690s one of their sects managed to occupy parts of Arabia (Bahrain, Yemen, Hadramawt) from where it harassed the caravan trade in the peninsula. Another sect controlled the former Iranian provinces of Khuzistan, Fars, and Kirman, using them as a springboard for repeated attacks on the city of Basra. They were eventually suppressed, but as late as the mid-740s Kharijite uprisings throughout Iraq were still causing the authorities a real headache. Their influence reached as far as the Maghreb, where in the 740s the indigenous Berber population temporarily drove the Arabs out of the area, raised the Kharijite banner, and even chose its own local Amir al-Mu'minin. "They strove most openly and decisively for the Kingdom of God, and also most fiercely for a pitiless Utopia," wrote a prominent student of Islam.

They renounced success; their only wish was to save their souls. They were content to meet death on the battlefield, and with it pardon in the sight of God; they sold their lives for the price of Paradise. In spite of this, perhaps because of it, they often overcame great armies, and for a time were the terror of the Muslim world, and although they always were only a small sect, still they could not be extirpated.[38]

The Shiites might not have been as fanatic as their Kharijite counterparts, but they had a far more profound and lasting impact, not least since they could stake a real claim to the caliphate based on descent from the prophet's family. As they saw it, the umma should be headed by a prodigious spiritual leader, or *imam*, possessing superhuman religious knowledge and interpretative powers, who would also act as the community's political leader, or Amir al-Mu'minin. The caliph Ali was the last person to have held both titles, while Mu'awiya and subsequent Umayyad rulers were (unlawful) secular practitioners of power rather than religious authorities, and it was for the restoration of this dual power to the Alid family that the Shiites pined.[39]

As early as 671 Mu'awiya was confronted with a pro-Alid revolt in Kufa. This was summarily suppressed, but nine years later Hussein, son of Ali and the Prophet's daughter Fatima, was lured by his Kufan supporters to stake a claim to the caliphate. The Umayyad governor uncovered the plot and intercepted Hussein's party. After a short battle, in which he received no support from the Kufans, Hussein fled to the small town of Karbala where he soon found himself under siege. The governor called upon him to surrender but Hussein, believing in his inviolability as the Prophet's favorite grandson, remained defiant. He was killed in the ensuing battle, on October 10, 680, and his head was sent on a platter to Damascus after being paraded in Kufa.[40]

Hussein's death was to prove a watershed in the history of Islam. It helped cement the small group of Ali's followers into a significant and cohesive religious movement; Hussein's grave in Karbala was to become the most revered site of pilgrimage for all Shiites. His day of martyrdom (*Ashura*, the tenth day of the Arabic month of Muharram) is commemorated every year in the most emotional way. More immediately, the Karbala massacre led to a revolt by Mukhtar ibn Abi Ubaid, scion of a distinguished Thaqifite family, under the slogan "Vengeance for Hussein."

Having driven Ibn Zubair's governor from Kufa and established himself as the city's master, Mukhtar proclaimed Muhammad ibn Hanafiyya, Hussein's half-brother, not merely a caliph but also a *Mahdi*, the "rightly guided one" or "redeemer," who would transform society and establish a reign of justice on earth. This was a powerful and novel idea that struck a deep chord among Kufa's disenfranchised masses and was to provide a lasting source of inspira-

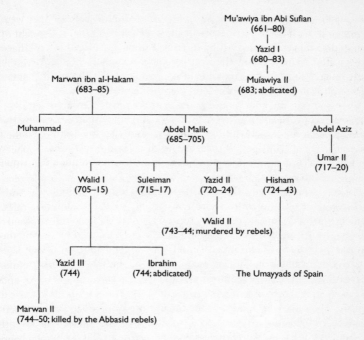

Figure 3 The Umayyad Dynasty

tion for numerous revolutionary groups and individuals throughout the ages. It nevertheless failed to save the day for Mukhtar. He was killed on April 3, 687, and thousands of his followers were slaughtered in cold blood after laying down their weapons. Initially the commander of the victorious forces wanted to execute only the non-Arab prisoners of war but was dissuaded by some of his aides who argued that this contradicted Islam's universalist spirit. "What kind of religion is this?" they reasoned. "How do you hope for victory when you kill the Iranians and spare the Arabs though both profess the same religion?" Impressed by the force of this argument, the commander ordered that the Arab prisoners be beheaded as well.[41]

Notwithstanding its short duration and limited geographical scope, Mukhtar's revolt had far-reaching historical consequences. By demanding the restoration of the caliphate to the Prophet's family and equating such a move with a return to "the Book of Allah and the *Sunna* [practice] of his Prophet," Mukhtar introduced a powerful political and religious concept that was to become the main rallying cry of the anti-Umayyad revolution. By endorsing

Ibn Hanafiyya as head of the Muslim community Mukhtar extended the range of potential Hashemite contenders to the caliphate who had hitherto been confined to descendants of Ali by his wife Fatima (or Fatimids as they are often called). This opened the door to other members of the House of Muhammad, such as the Abbasids, descendants of the Prophet's paternal uncle Abbas, to style themselves as the rightful caliphs.[42]

No less important, after the suppression of the revolt a group of surviving veterans reconstituted themselves into a small clandestine movement that maintained close contact with Ibn Hanafiyya, and after his death (sometime between 700 and 705) passed their loyalty to his son Abu Hashem. Widely known as the Hashemiyya, this group was to initiate the revolution that would sweep the Umayyads from power.

Precisely when and how the Abbasids managed to harness the Hashemiyya to their cause is not entirely clear. According to the traditional Arabic version, shortly before he died in 716 or 717, Abu Hashem transferred his right to the imamate, which he had inherited from his father, to Muhammad ibn Ali, then head of the Abbasid family. The two had allegedly grown close to each other while living in Damascus, where the sonless Abu Hashem came to regard the younger Muhammad as a son and groomed him for his future role as imam.[43] Yet recent research shows that it was not until the early 740s that the Abbasids, who resided at the time in the small village of Humayma in southern Transjordan, managed to gain control over the activities of the Hashemiyya. It has even been suggested that such control was never achieved and that the Abbasids rode to power on the back of the Hashemiyya's successful revolution.[44]

By this time, the Hashemiyya had established a firm foothold in the vast frontier province of Khurasan, at the northeastern tip of the empire in Central Asia (comprising territories that are today parts of Iran, Afghanistan, Kazakhstan, Uzbekistan, and Tajikistan). The province was uniquely suited for this revolutionary endeavor, and not only because of the widespread sympathy felt there for the unfortunate Mukhtar and for the Alid family more generally. It was in Khurasan that the apartheid wall built by the Arabs was being most comprehensively demolished and a mixing of colonizer and colonized was taking place. Unlike Iraq, where they had been settled in garrison towns, in Khurasan the Arabs were dispersed among the local population as a small and assimilating minority. They used Iranian servants, married local women, embraced Iranian habits and forms of dress, observed local festivals, and even adopted the Persian language for everyday use. In short, the Arabs developed a Khurasani identity that largely obliterated ethnic and tribal distinctions and made them feel at one with the indigenous population and sympathize with its cause. Moreover, these colonists, who had mostly arrived from Iraq, brought with them a deeply entrenched hostility toward the Umayyad dynasty, which they did not fail to spread among their Iranian neighbors.

Nor were the local Iranians hostile to the Arab colonists. Their daily lives were hardly affected by the nominal change of imperial masters since the existing Iranian rulers were left in place in return for the payment of tribute. There was no pressure to convert to Islam and the physical safety of the general population was significantly enhanced since the Arabs provided a better defense against external attacks by the neighboring Turkish tribes than had the declining Sasanid Empire. Paradoxically, the most intractable grievances emerged among the Iranian converts, disillusioned with the lack of improvement in their lot, and among the assimilated Arab colonists, who had lost their privileges as members of the ruling class and were forced to accept the authority of non-Arab, non-Muslim local rulers to whom they had to pay taxes. This created an explosive alliance of underdogs, both Iranians and Arabs, expressed in largely Shiite terms and aimed against the discriminatory imperial order.[45]

The timing of the revolution could not have been more opportune. By the early 740s the empire was clearly in the throes of over-extension. From their first days on the throne the Umayyads had relied on constant campaigning in order to keep the restless Arab tribes preoccupied and to ensure a steady flow of booty, on which the imperial economy was heavily dependent. It was during their reign that the empire reached the farthest frontiers of its expansion: the western lands of the Maghreb and Spain were conquered, together with vast territories in Central Asia and India, and the Muslims knocked at the gates of Constantinople and burst deep into France.

With the passage of time this policy of expansion increasingly taxed the empire's human and financial resources. Umar II, who recognized this reality, made preparations to relinquish the Arab conquests in Central Asia, which he deemed unworthy of the heavy expenditure of men and resources required to hold them against the Turks and the Chinese.[46] But his premature death prevented the implementation of this dramatic shift in thinking, and Hisham ibn Abdel Malik, who ascended the throne in 724, spent his nineteen-year reign in constant, and mostly futile, campaigning throughout his empire. This shattered the professional Syrian-Yemeni army, which had served as the mainstay of Umayyad rule since Mu'awiya's days. By the time of the Abbasid revolution, the once-formidable military district of Damascus had been reduced to a few thousand troops, and the situation in the neighboring Syrian provinces was not much better. To make things worse, the depleted Syrian army was spread thin across the empire, which further reduced its ability to protect the regime. At the time of Hisham's accession, there were Syrian troops only in Syria, Iraq, the Caucasus, and probably to a very limited extent in northern India. By the end of his reign, Syrian troops had almost completely disappeared from Syria itself and had instead been deployed in virtually every single province, from the Chinese frontier to Spain.[47]

Alarmed by the decline of their military might, especially in view of the ability of their Qaysi arch-enemies to preserve their strength owing to their far more limited involvement in imperial campaigning, the Yemenis sought to goad Walid II, who in February 743 succeeded Hisham, into far-reaching reforms that would equalize the position of the Mawali in the imperial order. As the caliph refused to do anything of the sort, they had him murdered only fourteen months after he took office and installed Yazid III in his place. This turned out to be a catastrophic move, which led in short order to the collapse of the Umayyad dynasty. Yazid died after a mere six months on the throne and was succeeded in December 744 by Marwan II, who peremptorily expelled the Yemeni leaders from Syria. This reopened the Pandora's box of Yemeni-Qaysi rivalry. In no time Syria was rocked by a string of uprisings while in Iraq the Yemenis collaborated for the first time with Shiite and Kharijite insurrections. These were all suppressed with great brutality, yet left the regime extremely vulnerable to the brewing revolution in the east, which now enjoyed the support of Khurasan's Yemeni tribes. In June 747 a young and obscure Mawla by the name of Abu Muslim, sent to Khurasan a year earlier to organize the revolution, raised the Abbasid black banner. By February 748 he had occupied the Khurasani capital city of Merv. Some ten months later, on November 28, 749, Abul Abbas, son of Muhammad ibn Ali, was proclaimed the first Abbasid caliph in Kufa's great mosque.

In a last-ditch attempt to save his throne, Marwan summoned his loyalists for the final battle, only to suffer a crushing defeat by the vastly outnumbered Abbasid armies on the left bank of the Greater Zab, a tributary of the Tigris, on January 25, 750. Vanquished but not broken, the indefatigable Marwan fled from place to place in a vain effort to rally support. He eventually surfaced in Upper Egypt and in early August 750 made his last stand. His head was sent to Abul Abbas and his tongue was reportedly fed to a cat.[48] The Umayyad dynasty was no more.

The Best of Times, the Worst of Times

The rise of the Abbasids was yet another crucial triumph for the periphery over the center. Emerging from a remote frontier province, a coalition of the empire's underdogs, Arabs and non-Arabs, marginalized and discriminated against on the basis of ethnicity, religion, tribal affinity, and geographic location, managed to overwhelm the imperial armed forces and to unseat the long-reigning dynasty. This resulted not only in the immediate shift of the metropolitan center of gravity from Damascus to Iraq, home to many of the region's ancient empires, but also in the gradual transformation of the empire's socio-political order.

It will be recalled that the Prophet Muhammad had envisaged the umma as a universal community free of racial distinctions, in which all Muslims would live side by side in peace and equality. In reality, the Islamic empire was an Arab military autocracy run by Arabs for the sole benefit of Arabs. It dissuaded non-Arabs from converting to Islam so as to keep them subjugated and in a position of inferiority, and treated those who nevertheless converted (not to mention non-Muslim subjects) as second-class citizens. Non-Arabs played no role in the making of imperial policies and had to endure numerous encroachments on their social and cultural identities, notably the superimposition of Arabic over their indigenous languages. But while Arabic remained the lingua franca under the Abbasids and the caliphate remained in Arab hands, they nevertheless lost their exclusive mastery of the empire, which was being transformed in a steady process of ethnic and cultural assimilation from an Arab into a truly Muslim entity. If by the end of the Umayyad era less than 10 percent of the empire's subjects had adopted Islam, within a century or two of the start of Abbasid rule most of these populations had been converted, thus blurring the dividing line between master and subject still further. "What held the empire together was no longer the 'Arab nation,' the Arabs in leading positions, but the dynasty as the administrator of Islamic unity, ultimately therefore Islam itself," wrote the historian Gustave von Grunebaum. "It is religion that lies open to all and, like the idea of the state in Rome, guarantees the universality of the spiritual and political structure."[1]

Increasing numbers of officials were drawn from among the Mawali, while the Khurasanis, and subsequently other ethnic groups, acted as the regime's military mainstay. Imperial Iranian ideals, norms, and practices penetrated the Abbasid court and bureaucracy. The administration was carefully organized into a string of separate departments (*diwans*), particularly for the army, finance and taxes, and the provinces. The postal system, which had been in existence since the Achaemenid Empire (558–331 B.C.E.) was reorganized and extended, with local directors acting not merely as postmasters but as the caliph's eyes and ears in the provinces. The growth of monarchical despotism, already noticeable in the days of the Umayyads, gained considerable momentum under the Abbasids and was starkly exemplified by the presence of the executioner by the side of the throne. Like the Iranian shahs, the caliph became increasingly inaccessible to his subjects, shielding himself behind a vast cohort of officials, ministers, and eunuchs, and leaving the daily running of the empire in the hands of the vizier, a chief executive answerable only to him. Even the new Abbasid capital, founded by the second caliph Mansur (754–75), was symbolically located near the ruins of the old Iranian capital of Ctesiphon, and Mansur ordered builders to use bricks from the ancient Iranian royal palace in the construction of one of his palaces. Named by its founder "The City of Peace," the Abbasid capital would come to be universally known by the name of the Iranian village on the ruins of which it was established: Baghdad.[2]

Having come to power with the stated objective of restoring Islam's true ways and of undoing the godless practices of their predecessors, the Abbasids were anxious to underscore the theocratic character of their rule. "It is through us that Allah guided the people after they had gone astray and showed them the light after their ignorance," proclaimed the first Abbasid caliph, Abul Abbas, in his inaugural speech on October 20, 749. "Allah put up with [the Umayyads] for a while until they angered Him; and when they did, He avenged Himself on them at our hands and returned our right to us." The caliph's uncle, Dawud ibn Ali, was even more forthright. The Umayyads had abused their power and strayed far from the right path, he claimed. But this dark period was over. The believers were now yet again "under the protection of Allah's Messenger and his family," who would govern in line with the Qur'an and the traditions set by Muhammad until the end of days.[3]

Abul Abbas and his half-brother and successor, Mansur, were too preoccupied with consolidating their grip on power and eliminating actual and potential enemies to concentrate on the religious aspects of their rule. But these came to the fore under the third caliph, Mahdi (775–85), and his grandson

Ma'mun (813–33), the first to style himself as imam, the community's religious leader and spiritual heir to the Prophet. Even so, prior to his accession Mansur had allegedly written down sayings and practices attributed to the Prophet, and Abul Abbas had purchased the supposed mantle of the Prophet, which quickly became the most ubiquitous symbol of the dynasty's religious prowess. It was worn by the caliph on his inauguration and on every ceremonial occasion thereafter, including for performances of prayer before the community. The frequent use of this sacred relic, which contrasted with the habit of some Umayyad caliphs of appearing in full military gear for the prayer service, was designed to buttress the exclusivity of the Abbasid claim to the succession. So was the adoption of the title "Allah's Caliph."

The Abbasids were, of course, not the first to have used this title: the caliph Uthman and the Umayyads had done so as well. Yet whereas the Umayyads had perceived the title in largely secular terms—as a means to convey the unlimited extent of their power—for the Abbasids it was a religious concept in accordance with their perception of themselves as representatives of "Allah's rule on earth" or even as "Allah's shadow on earth."

This claim to divine inspiration was exemplified in the strong messianic overtones of the throne names adopted by all Abbasid caliphs, and was accompanied by public indulgence of religious figures and institutions. Theologians and men of learning were welcomed into the Abbasid court and several caliphs took pleasure in attending religious discussions and having a theological education imparted to their sons. The relaxed Umayyad attitude to religious observance gave way to strict public enforcement of religious codes of behavior and zealous persecution of heretics. If in Umayyad times a wine party could have been held in a mosque, such behavior was inconceivable under the Abbasids.[4]

In reality, the substantive differences between the Abbasids and their predecessors were far smaller than might appear. For one thing, despite their manifest secularism, the Umayyads often sought to buttress their credentials through spectacular religious acts, such as the building of the Dome of the Rock in Jerusalem and the mosques of Damascus and Medina. For another, the Abbasids complied with the stipulations of the nascent religious law (Shari'a), the development of which they encouraged, only to the extent that it served their needs, and there was no shortage of theologians willing to bend the law in deference to those needs. Worse, in the privacy of their palaces the Abbasids indulged in the same vices—wine, singing girls, and sexual license—that had given the Umayyads their bad reputation. "They drink wine while imposing legal punishment upon the drinkers," the celebrated Kufan scholar and jurisprudent Sufian al-Thawri (d. 778) lamented to the future caliph Harun al-Rashid. He censured Harun's father, Mahdi, for his opulent style of pilgrimage and had no qualms about going to Mansur and deriding his viziers, and by implication the caliph himself, as "Pharaohs," a contemporary pejorative that was to regain its popularity among twentieth-century Islamic radicals. ("I have killed Pharaoh," boasted the militant young officer who assassinated the Egyptian president Anwar Sadat on October 6, 1981.)

Similarly scathing criticism was leveled at Ma'mun and his two immediate successors, Mu'tasim (833–42) and Wathiq (842–47), for their endorsement of the precepts of the philo-Hellenistic Mu'tazilite school of thought, notably its perception of the Qur'an as created rather than eternal, and for their strident efforts to enforce this dogma on the Muslim community at large through the repressive instrument known as the *mihna* (inquisition). "While his companions drink into the early hours of the morning they profoundly investigate the problem of whether the Qur'an is created," a contemporary poet acidly commented about the behavior of the chief Iraqi judge charged with the institutionalization of the new creed. Yet even when the caliph Mutawakil (847–61) abandoned the mihna and reestablished the orthodox dogma, this did not mean greater religious observance at the personal level. Mutawakil was known to be a heavy drinker, just as the caliph Qahir (932–34), who took strict measures against wine-drinkers and singing girls, was hardly ever sober.[5]

In short, for all their claims of religious piety, the Abbasids, like the Umayyads, were first and foremost imperial monarchs for whom Islam was a means to shore up their credentials and to create the most conducive sociopolitical environment for their reign. It was, moreover, a handy façade behind which they could fully enjoy the material fruits of imperial expansion. "We did not rebel in order to grow rich in silver and in gold," Dawud ibn Ali, uncle of the first Abbasid caliph, proclaimed on the occasion of his nephew's coronation. Yet it was precisely the ever-increasing pomp and circumstance of the caliphate that largely underpinned Abbasid prestige.[6]

As in countless other cases of imperial expansion throughout the ages, the quest for booty had been a central impetus behind the Islamic conquests, enabling the Arab aristocracy to live in great luxury. But nowhere was the splendor of the Islamic empire more extravagantly pronounced than under the Abbasids, not only during Harun's reign (786–809), widely considered the golden age of the Abbasid era, but continuing well after the caliphs had lost their prowess: the gem-studded golden dishes on the caliph's table, the thousands of gilded curtains at the royal palace, and the golden tree and the ruby-eyed golden elephant in the caliph's courtyard are only some of the more ostentatious possessions that bear witness to this extravagance.

This opulence extended well beyond the confines of the caliph's palace. The shifting of the imperial center of gravity to Iraq and the establishment of Baghdad as the new capital linked the empire with the farthest corners of the globe and underpinned a vast economic entity, the like of which had never existed in the ancient world. It was based on both extensive commercial exchanges within the empire and international trade on an unprecedented scale, especially in precious metals and luxury goods: gold and ivory, silk and porcelain, furs and skins, spices and aromatics, slaves and wild animals. By the ninth century the Abbasid Empire had developed into a leading world economic force, vastly superior to other powers in Asia and Africa, and even more so to Western Europe, which was in the throes of economic stagnation and contraction.[7]

This economic ascendancy, which was to last for some two hundred years, was accompanied by the creation of a network of cities in the Fertile Crescent with a highly developed urban life and a prosperous and intellectually curious bourgeoisie, highly receptive to foreign ideas and influences, mainly Hellenistic and Indo-Iranian. This in turn triggered one of the most momentous intellectual awakenings in world history, encompassing most spheres of intellectual and scientific activity, from astronomy, theology, philosophy, and medicine, to history, literature, and poetry.

There was, however, another side to the ledger. Abbasid extravagance was in stark contrast to the daily existence of most of the caliph's subjects. The empire might have been fabulously rich, but these riches were concentrated in the hands of the few at the expense of the many: at a time when the caliph could bestow dozens of thousands of dirhams on a favorite poet for reciting a few lines, ordinary Iraqi laborers were carrying home between one and two dirhams a month.[8]

Wastefulness and corruption permeated all walks of imperial life, from the caliph and military commanders to local officials and administrators. Since the caliphal court required vast amounts of money to finance its extravagant lifestyle, confiscation of funds and properties, both private and public, became a ubiquitous feature of royal life. The caliph Mu'tamid (870–92) even created a special ministry for the confiscation and distribution of the properties of those who had died without an heir. Although the ministry was eventually abolished, the practice remained widespread throughout the empire as government officials invariably exploited their positions for self-enrichment. Bribery was institutionalized and ingenious illegitimate techniques for tax evasion were devised at the expense of small businessmen and landowners.

The growing burden of taxation and the decline in availability of cultivable land, owing to the deterioration of the irrigation system in southern Iraq, drove large numbers of peasants to the cities. The authorities did their utmost to force them back to their communities, so as to prevent a decrease in payments of land tax, the main source of government income, but even so a restless proletariat developed in the cities, providing an audience for preachers and agitators of all hues. Violent clashes among local groups, and between these groups and the government, became commonplace. Growing lawlessness on the part of the troops led to the formation of citizen organizations for defense and reprisals, which were often transformed into robber gangs. Notable among these were the *Ayyarun*, thugs drawn from the lower reaches of society who made their living through extortion, racketeering, and robbery. Ready to sell their services to the highest bidder, groups of Ayyarun competed against each other to serve the rival Shiite and Sunni camps in their incessant squabbles in Baghdad and other Iraqi cities. At times the Ayyarun were recruited to the local security services as a means of controlling their bubbling aggressiveness; on other occasions they were hired by the upper classes to resist government policies.[9]

To make things worse, the imperial metropolis shamelessly plundered the natural resources of the provinces for its own use while disregarding these territories' interests and needs. This practice had already started at the time of the Prophet, when Medina thrived on the tribute of the rapidly expanding umma. It continued after the conquests and reached its apogee under the Abbasids: rice, grains, and fabrics arrived from Egypt, silver, copper, and iron from Iran, Afghanistan, and Central Asia, brocade, pearls, and weapons from Arabia. A special effort was made to obtain the largest possible quantities of gold. Aside from a steady stream of this precious metal from Sudan, bought from the unwitting locals for insubstantial amounts of bartered goods, the Abbasids removed huge quantities of gold from the palaces of the Iranian kings and nobility. In Egypt they went so far as to systematically plunder the pharaonic tombs, where they apparently found more gold.[10]

This economic exploitation, combined with the government's weakening control of the periphery, triggered rebellions throughout the empire. These often had a religious coloring. As early as 750 a peasant uprising took place in Upper Egypt, followed the next year by an insurrection in northern Iraq. Even in Khurasan, the foremost bastion of support for the Abbasid dynasty and the primary source of manpower and matériel for the imperial administration, there was a tremendous amount of opposition to the central government.[11]

One of the most serious revolts in the province, which threatened to sever Central Asia from the empire, was headed by a non-Muslim Iranian nobleman by the name of Babak who sought to break free from Abbasid colonial subjugation and establish his own kingdom. "Perhaps I shall not live long from this day," he reportedly wrote to his son, "[but] it is better to live one day as a leader than forty years as an abject slave." In late 816 or early 817 Babak rose in revolt, capitalizing on widespread resentment at Abbasid colonization of Armenia and Azerbaijan on the one hand, and the deteriorating economic conditions in the region on the other. Several expeditionary forces sent by the caliph were comprehensively routed and legions of peasants flocked to Babak's camp, enthused by his populist policy of breaking up large estates and distributing their lands among the needy. For twenty years the ambitious rebel managed to hold out against the imperial government, steadily expanding his domain and making alliances with local potentates. It was only in 837 that the caliph Mu'tasim, who four years earlier had succeeded his brother Ma'mun, finally managed to put down the revolt. To magnify the effect of his victory, the caliph paraded the captured rebel around his newly established capital of Samarra on the back of an elephant before ordering the executioner to dismember his body, rip open his stomach, and decapitate him. Babak is said to have endured these atrocities with such dignity that Mu'tasim might have pardoned him had he not endangered the empire's integrity to such an extent.[12]

No sooner had the dust settled on Babak's revolt than the imperial center was rocked by a similarly formidable social rising, this time by the empire's most despised class: the Zanj. Herded by the hundreds and thousands into labor camps in the salt flats near Basra, without their families or hope, and given meager rations of food, these black East African slaves had revolted previously during Umayyad times, and in the autumn of 869 they again rose in strength. Led by a charismatic Iranian Kharijite who claimed Alid descent and styled himself as the Mahdi, they managed to rout the local governors and to establish their own independent entity. Within a year the rebels were in control of much of southern Iraq and the western Iranian province of Khuzistan. In September 871 they occupied Basra, slaughtering most of its residents and carrying the rest off as slaves. For the next twelve years they continually terrorized the government and in 879 they nearly reached Baghdad. This was, however, the limit of their success. For all their efforts, the Zanj failed to win over other sectors of imperial society. A number of Bedouin tribes aside, neither the peasants nor the urban proletariat threw in their lot with the rebels. Religious resentment of the heretic Zanj, together with deep contempt among the indigenous population toward black Africans (nearly five hundred years later the great Muslim historian Ibn Khaldun would describe them as "close in their character to dumb animals"), left the rebels isolated. By the summer of 883 they had been crushed by the imperial armies. Their leader was killed and his head was sent on a pole to Baghdad.[13]

This violent record underscores yet another striking similarity between the Abbasids and their Umayyad predecessors: reliance on armed force as the primary means of dynastic survival. This was ominously foreshadowed by Abul Abbas's regnal title of *Saffah* ("bloodshedder"), which he invoked as early as his inaugural speech. "Oh people of Kufa," he said, "you have become the happiest of people through us and the most honored by us. We have raised your [annual] stipends by one hundred dirhams. Hold yourselves ready, for I am the ultimate bloodshedder and the destroying avenger."[14]

Abul Abbas was to earn his title. In an attempt to prevent any backlash from supporters of the fallen dynasty, the Abbasids embarked on a murderous spree. In Mecca and Medina scores of Umayyads were rounded up. Some were executed on the spot; the rest were arrested and murdered in detention. In the Iraqi garrison town of Wasit the governor laid down his weapons in return for a personal guarantee of safe conduct by the caliph, only to be treacherously murdered. In Palestine, the newly appointed governor of Syria invited a group of eighty prominent Umayyads to a banquet, slaughtered them all, then sat calmly among the corpses to finish his meal. Even the dead were not spared, as the remains of the Umayyad caliphs were exhumed and desecrated. Particularly gruesome treatment was meted out to Hisham (724–43). His corpse was discovered virtually intact; after being crucified and given 120 lashes, it was burned to ashes. Only the pious Umar II escaped desecration. Small wonder, then, that upon Mansur's death on October 7, 775, his body was interred in a secret location to prevent its future desecration.[15]

In fairness to the Abbasids, it should be said that they were only following in the footsteps of their fallen predecessors and that they murdered "only" those deemed most dangerous to their rule. It had been a common Umayyad practice to kill rebels and mutilate their bodies as a means to deter future insurrections. The renegades were habitually decapitated and their corpses crucified. The heads of the chief rebels were then displayed throughout the province before being sent to the caliph, where they were kept in a special storehouse in the royal palace, each in a separate basket.[16]

Having rid themselves of their enemies, the Abbasids turned on their allies and champions with similar savagery. First to fall was the Hashemiyya leader Abu Salama Khallal, who was instrumental in laying the ground for the revolt that carried the Abbasids to power. Appointed *Wazir Al Muhammad* (Vizier of the House of Muhammad) after the fall of Kufa, he antagonized the Abbasids by failing to act with sufficient swiftness and conviction to have Abul Abbas proclaimed as caliph. By some accounts, he even had serious doubts regarding Abul Abbas's suitability for this lofty position. Abu Salama paid dearly for his behavior: in March 750 he was assassinated while on his way home after an audience with the caliph. His death was conveniently attributed to the Kharijites.[17]

Next in line was Abu Muslim, to whom, more than anyone else, the Abbasids owed their throne. The dashing Mawla had established himself during the revolution as the undisputed master of most of Iran and the eastern provinces, and while he remained loyal to his suzerain, his autonomy was deeply resented by some members of the ruling family. "Commander of the Faithful, just give me an order and I will kill Abu Muslim," Mansur pleaded with Abul Abbas, "for his head is full of treachery." The caliph was reluctant to undertake such a gratuitous act. "My brother, you know the trials and tribulations he has gone through and what has been achieved because of him," he protested. Mansur remained unmoved. "That was only because of our revolution," he said. "Had you sent a cat, it would have taken his place and done what he had done for the revolution." "But how could we kill him?" "When he comes to see you, and you will be engaging him in conversation . . . I could sneak in unnoticed and deal him a blow from behind that would take his life."

As Abu Abbas remained unconvinced, it was left to Mansur to implement his plan after ascending the throne in June 654, but not before using Abu Muslim's military skills to crush a bid for the caliphate by an Abbasid rival. In February 655, after much hesitation and against the counsels of his advisers, Abu Muslim decided to accept Mansur's invitation for an audience. Upon arriving at the caliph's camp, he was warmly received by Mansur. "Go, Abdel Rahman, and make yourself comfortable," the caliph said. "Take a hot bath, for travel is a messy business. Then come back to me."

When the hardened Abu Muslim, who had reputedly put hundreds of thousands of people to death during the revolution, arrived for his meeting with Mansur the next morning he was confronted with a barrage of charges over trivial matters. As he was busy explaining himself, the caliph signaled to the guards, who promptly entered the room and killed Mansur's political savior. The caliph then summoned Abu Muslim's friends and associates on a false promise of remuneration and contemptuously threw the decapitated head of their fallen leader in front of them.[18]

A similar fate befell the Barmakids, an aristocratic Iranian family and the first vizierial dynasty in medieval Islam. As Mansur's vizier, Khaled Barmaki played a key role in the development of the Abbasid administrative system, and over the next four decades he and his descendants ran the imperial administration very much on their own since the caliphs who succeeded the austere and tough-minded Mansur preferred to indulge in the pleasures of royal life rather than shoulder its burdens. "I delegate to you the responsibility for my subjects," Harun told Khaled's son Yahya. "You may pass judgment as you like, appoint whom you like, for I shall not occupy myself with these matters together with you." Harun's lack of interest in public affairs ran so deep that he allowed Yahya and two of his sons—Fadl and Ja'far—to act as judges in his place, a hitherto unprecedented renunciation of the caliph's most sacred right that even the "godless" Umayyads had resisted. Yahya was also entrusted with the royal seal and was the first vizier to be given the title of Emir: an important innovation that effectively made the vizier the caliph's deputy.[19]

Yet all this was of no help to the Barmakids once Harun decided to dispose of his faithful servants. The family's property was confiscated and Yahya and three of his sons were thrown into prison, where the aged vizier and his illustrious son Fadl died some time later. Ja'far, a refined man of letters and culture, who had a particularly close relationship with Harun, was singled out for special treatment. He was executed in Kufa and his body was sent to Baghdad at the caliph's specific orders, where it was beheaded and dismembered. Ja'far's head was impaled in the city center and the two halves of his body were hung on either side of Baghdad's main bridge. The mutilated body remained on display for many months, while Ja'far's magnificent palace was subsequently expropriated by Ma'mun.[20]

The potential threat posed by Abu Muslim or the Barmakids was wholly personal and could readily be removed through their physical elimination, though Abu Muslim's murder triggered a string of uprisings in Khurasan that had to be summarily suppressed. Not so the Shiite danger. The Abbasids had come to power on the back of a demand to restore the caliphate to the House of Muhammad. Hypothetically, their claim to occupy this prestigious post might have appeared as good as that of any family branch, but in important respects it was far inferior to that of the House of Ali. It was Abu Talib, Ali's father, who had tended to the orphaned Muhammad and who had subsequently protected him as a prophet against Meccan enmity. Ali himself spent much of his childhood in Muhammad's household, was among the first converts to Islam, and married the Prophet's beloved daughter Fatima before becoming the last of the four "rightly guided" caliphs. By contrast, Abbas had apparently never converted to Islam and his relations with Muhammad were correct but not particularly warm.[21]

By way of circumventing this problem, Abbasid propaganda deliberately avoided allusions to the particular identity of the would-be caliph, and instead concentrated more broadly on the need to restore the caliphate to "the chosen one from the House of the Prophet." But knowing full well that for most the House of Muhammad was largely synonymous with Alid lineage, the Abbasids did their utmost to give their efforts a Shiite coloring. Hence their claim to be the rightful successors to Muhammad ibn Hanafiyya's imamate, and hence the portrayal of the revolt as an act of revenge for the martyrdom of Ali's son Hussein and the widely revered Yahya ibn Zaid, a descendant of Ali killed in the course of an anti-Umayyad revolt (743).[22]

Such pretenses could not have been further from the truth. Though they exploited the Shiites' machinery, ideological zeal, and above all widespread appeal to Khurasan's disenfranchised communities, the Abbasids had no intention of sharing power with their Alid cousins. Quite the contrary: because of the relative weakness of their claim to the caliphate they went out of their way, after seizing power, to garnish their own credentials and to deride those of the Alids. Gone was the claim to legitimacy by virtue of association with the Hashemiyya, to be replaced by inflated accounts of Abbas's importance in Islamic history and his close relations with the Prophet, who had allegedly promised him that "the rule will pass unto your descendants."[23] Abbas was portrayed as Muhammad's guide and counselor, a caring uncle, whereas Ali was said never to have been recognized as a lawful candidate for the caliphate, which is why he had been passed over in favor of the Umayyad Uthman in the succession of Umar. "Which is more closely related to the Prophet of God, his uncle or his nephew?" ran a typical piece of pro-Abbasid propaganda:

> The [Prophet's] daughter's children desire the rights of the caliphate but theirs is not even that which can be put under a nail;
> The daughter's husband [i.e., Ali] is not heir, and the daughter does not inherit the Imamate;
> And those who claim your inheritance will inherit only repentance.[24]

Such claims did little to endear the Abbasids to the Shiites, who believed that their former partners had deceitfully robbed them of the fruits of the revolution. In the autumn of 762, after years of covert agitation, two great-grandsons of Ali—Muhammad ibn Abdallah, known as "The Pure Soul," and his brother Ibrahim—rose in open revolt against the Abbasids. Although Mansur had sought for some time to lure the brothers into a direct confrontation, the uprising caught him totally off guard. With only one thousand soldiers at his immediate disposal (the rest were deployed throughout the empire), the caliph found himself in such desperate straits that for seven weeks he never changed clothes except to attend public prayers. So deep was Mansur's anxiety that he had a close relative of the brothers decapitated, then had his head paraded throughout Khurasan as that of the Pure Soul.

Fortunately for the caliph, the brothers showed a fatal lack of political and military experience and failed to coordinate their operations. Muhammad was the first to fall: the Abbasid force sent to the Hijaz cut off his supply routes before killing him in a quick and decisive battle. Ibrahim, who launched his revolt from Basra, was far more successful. At one point he managed to raise as many as 100,000 fighters and to occupy the garrison town of Wasit and the former Iranian province of Fars, in the process inflicting a crushing military defeat on the imperial armies. But he, too, was eventually defeated, having failed to sustain the cohesion and motivation of his troops.[25]

Other Shiite contenders were more fortunate. Twenty-four years after the suppression of the Pure Soul's revolt, a younger brother by the name of Idris participated in yet another abortive insurrection in Medina before escaping to Morocco. In 789 he established his own dynasty, the Idrisids, founding a capital at Fez two years later. He was poisoned at Harun's behest, but his dynasty survived for another 130 years and prepared the way for a string of local dynasties that rule Morocco to the present day and claim descent from the Prophet.

The success of the various Shiite sects, offshoots, and dynasties in establishing themselves at the empire's periphery from where they challenged the regime's legitimacy gave the Abbasids their worst recurring headache. One such sect was the Zaidiya, which viewed Zaid ibn Ali, a great-grandson of Ali killed in the course of an abortive rising in 740, as the rightful imam. In the ninth century they established an independent imamate in Daylam, the mountainous ridge at the southwestern tip of the Caspian Sea, and in 892 one of their leaders was invited by the local tribes to Yemen, where he established his own dynasty.

A far greater challenge to Abbasid rule came from the Shiite offshoot known as Ismailiya. With the coming to power of the Abbasids on the back of a movement associated with Muhammad ibn Hanafiyya, this branch of the House of Ali had outplayed its historic role, leaving the future role of challenger for the caliphate to the Fatimids. After the death of the sixth imam, Ja'far, in 765, most Shiites recognized the descendants of his younger son Musa up to the twelfth imam in the line, Muhammad ibn Hassan, who disappeared in obscure circumstances in 873–74 at the tender age of ten, and whose return is still awaited by the so-called Twelver Shi'a. By contrast, a minority group, which regarded Ja'far's eldest son, Ismail, who had died five years before his father, as the true imam, developed into a militant revolutionary movement known as Ismailiya.

Through extensive missionary activity the Ismailis managed to build on their humble beginnings to create a large and diverse constituency among the rural and urban communities in the Fertile Crescent. By the early tenth century they had set up an independent entity on the northeastern coast of the Arabian Peninsula (the so-called Qarmatian republic), which survived for nearly two centuries and served as a base for occasional raids on the pilgrims to Mecca. In 930 they even raided the city and stole the Kaaba's holy Black Stone (which they returned twenty-one years later). Far more important, the Ismailis managed to establish a firm foothold in the Maghreb and, in January 910, having brought most of the area under their sway, they crowned an alleged descendant of Ali as the first Fatimid caliph and Mahdi.

For nearly 250 years the Fatimids challenged the religious legitimacy of the Abbasids and tested the limits of their political control. As Shiite imams, they claimed universal authority over all Muslims. As quintessential imperialists who saw their ultimate goal as the substitution of their own reign for that of the Sunni caliphate of the Abbasids, they pushed their geographic and political boundaries as far as they could. In 969 they occupied Egypt, from where they quickly extended their rule to Palestine, Syria, and western Arabia. The holy cities of Mecca and Medina, heavily dependent on Egyptian grains for their sustenance, readily acquiesced in their new Shiite suzerain. For the first time since antiquity Egypt had regained its position as a pre-eminent imperial power, characterized for the most part by extraordinary religious tolerance and great economic prosperity.

Fatimid prestige reached its apogee in the late 1050s, when a rebellious Turkish general in the service of the Abbasid caliph captured Baghdad and for forty weeks proclaimed from its pulpits the sovereignty of the Fatimid caliphs. This, however, was a Pyrrhic victory. By 1060 the general had been killed, and soon afterward the Fatimids went into a steady decline as a prolonged economic and military crisis in Egypt made it possible for a string of local warlords to assert their independence throughout the empire. This process was eventually wrapped up by the celebrated Kurdish warrior Saladin, who went on to establish his own dynasty, the Ayyubis, which was to rule Egypt and much of the Levant for nearly a century (1171–1260).[26]

By now the Abbasid Empire had become a pale shadow of its former self. Theoretically the caliphs remained the nominal masters of vast territories between the Indus and the Atlantic. In practice they were hapless captives in a golden cage. In an imperial order bent on world domination yet riven by powerful centrifugal forces of regionalism and tribalism, it was only natural that the military should assume the role of power broker. It was the army that had created the empire in the first place and subsequently protected its integrity; as it was transformed in late Umayyad times from a "nation in arms" into a professional force, the generals were increasingly drawn into the political maelstrom. As early as 743, in the twilight of the Umayyad era, the army acted as kingmaker by murdering the caliph Walid II and installing Yazid III in his place. Although it would take some time for such activities to become common practice under the Abbasids, the army was deeply involved in dynastical politics from the very beginning. Even the appointment of the first Abbasid caliph can be considered a putsch of sorts—commanders of the Khurasani revolutionary army forced the dithering Abu Salama to have Abul Abbas proclaimed.[27] Several years later the military was instrumental in overriding Abul Abbas's own choice of successor by sealing the election of Mahdi as the third caliph at the expense of his cousin Isa ibn Musa.

Appointed by Abul Abbas as next in line to Mansur, Isa served Mansur loyally and efficiently for years, only to learn of the caliph's decision to appoint his own son Mahdi as his heir apparent. "O Commander of the Faithful, what

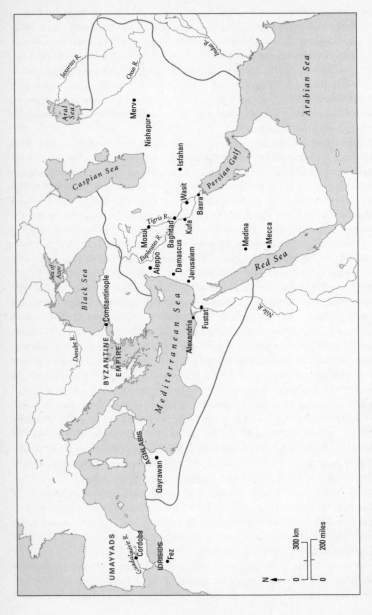

Map 3 The Abbasid Empire at its Height

about the oaths and the agreements that bind me and bind the Muslims in my favor?" he protested. "There is absolutely no way [I would accept] this." Since Isa would neither listen to reason nor be deflected by his public humiliation, the generals were brought into the picture. Mahdi was popular with the military, which had thrived under his father; its involvement now brought home to Isa that he had better renounce his right to the caliphate. He finally complied in return for a lavish compensation of ten million dirhams and a royal pledge to succeed Mahdi in due course, yet this was not good enough for the generals. In the autumn of 776, a year after Mahdi's accession, they detained Isa in Baghdad and forced him to make a public renunciation of his rights and to sign a written declaration to this effect.

The generals were far less successful a decade later when they backed the attempts of Hadi (783–86) to prevent his brother Harun from succeeding him to the caliphate. Many officers were disgraced, but the military made its peace with Harun and was instrumental in bringing about the demise of the Barmakids. It went on to play a key role in the bitter civil war between Harun's sons Amin and Ma'mun which raged for years and resulted in the fundamental restructuring of the imperial armed forces. Until then, the Khurasanis had been the regime's military mainstay, not unlike the role played by the Syrians under the Umayyads. Khurasani troops garrisoned the empire's various corners and formed the caliph's praetorian guard, while Khurasani military leaders were often made provincial governors, especially in such trouble spots as Armenia and Azerbaijan. With the foundation of Baghdad, many Khurasanis moved to the new capital, where they and their descendants became part of the imperial aristocracy known as the *Abna al-Dawla* (sons of the revolution or dynasty), constituting the backbone of the Abbasid standing army.[28]

The civil war shattered the armed forces, which fought on Amin's side and were decisively beaten. It also generated a deep schism between the Abna and the main body of Khurasanis who remained in their ancestral homeland and sided with Ma'mun, who had governed the province and used it as his operational base during the war and administrative center in its aftermath. A quintessential "peripheral," Ma'mun considered moving the imperial capital to Merv and remained deeply distrustful of the Abna. He made no attempt to restore their pre-eminence and instead sought to marginalize the military by building a new force based on peripheral ethnic groups, such as Turks and Iranians, who would owe their position solely to him and would thus render him their undivided loyalty. This tapped into a long-standing, if modest, trend dating back to late Umayyad and early Abbasid times, of using non-Arab Mawali forces to counterbalance the traditional tribal armies. As Mansur told his son Mahdi shortly before his death: "I have collected for you Mawali [in quantities], the like of which has not been collected by a caliph before me . . . Show favor to them and increase their number, because they are your source of power and reinforcement in emergency."[29]

These humble foundations were substantially expanded during the reign of Mu'tasim (833–42). Not only did the caliph establish a new army of slave-soldiers (Mamluks, Ghilman, or Mawali) in what heralded the dominant military institution in medieval Islam, but he also founded a new imperial capital,

Table 1 The Abbasid Dynasty

Accession date	
749	Abul Abbas
754	Mansur
775	Mahdi
785	Hadi (assassinated)
786	Harun al-Rashid
809	Amin (executed)
813	Ma'mun
833	Mu'tasim
842	Wathiq
847	Mutawakkil (killed by his soldiers)
861	Muntasir (killed by his soldiers)
862	Musta'in (killed by his soldiers)
866	Mu'tazz (killed by his soldiers)
869	Muhtadi (killed by his soldiers)
870	Mu'tamid
892	Mu'tadi
902	Muktafi
908	Muqtadir (killed by his generals)
932	Qahir (deposed and blinded)
934	Radi
940	Muttaqi (deposed and blinded)
944	Mustakfi (deposed and blinded)
946	Muti
974	Ta'i (deposed and imprisoned)
991	Qadir
1031	Qa'im
1075	Muqtadi
1094	Mustazhir
1118	Mustarshid (killed by political rivals)
1135	Rashid
1136	Muqtafi
1160	Mustanjid
1170	Mustadi
1180	Nasser
1225	Zahir
1226	Mustansir
1242–58	Musta'sim (executed by the Mongols)

Samarra, some eighty miles north of Baghdad, to isolate its members from society at large and thus ensure their absolute loyalty. This force was overwhelmingly populated by Turks, but also included Khurasanis, Iranians, Arabs, and Maghrebis. Forcibly uprooted from their native regions at a very young age and implanted in a totally alien environment, these slave-soldiers were trained and molded in a way that imbued them with unquestioning loyalty to their master. By making the Mamluks an aristocracy of only one generation, the government sought to prolong the life of this institution indefinitely without losing its military sharpness. This objective was further reinforced by the superior military quality of the peoples from which the Mamluks were drawn.[30] Yet it was precisely these qualities that were to turn them before too long into a sort of "Frankestein's monster" that would turn against its master whenever the latter appeared to neglect or endanger its vested interests.

In a treatise prepared for Mansur, the eighth-century Iranian historian and *littérateur* Ibn Muqaffa likened the caliph's excessive reliance on the military to riding on a lion's back. Mu'tasim carried off this hazardous exercise with great energy and considerable skill, but his son (and the second caliph after him) Mutawakil, paid with his life for crossing the Mamluks: on the night of December 10, 861, a group of Turkish soldiers burst into his palace as he was having a drink with his vizier and slaughtered them both. This ushered in a decade of political turbulence in which three of four reigning caliphs were murdered in rapid succession. But this wanton violence pales in comparison with the anarchy wrought by the Turks during the reigns of Muqtadir (908–32) and his immediate successors. Brought to power by the empire's leading bureaucrats who sought a compliant occupant for the caliphal palace, Muqtadir survived a number of coup attempts before being murdered by one of his generals at the end of an ignominious reign marked by drunkenness, promiscuity, and extravagance. He was succeeded by his brother, Qahir, who made strenuous efforts to project himself as an austere ruler of high morality. But after two years of drunken brutality he was forcibly deposed and blinded with red-hot needles. The generals replaced him with Radi, a son of the murdered Muqtadir, who for seven years was their hapless tool. Radi died peacefully in 940 and was succeeded by his brother, Muttaqi, who attempted to restore some of the caliph's lost powers, only to be forced to flee Baghdad. In 944, having declined an offer of refuge from the ruler of Egypt, Muttaqi rashly placed himself in the hands of the Turkish general Tuzun, who had been the cause of many of his troubles. He was peremptorily blinded and deposed, and Tuzun set another puppet caliph, Mustakaff, in his place. In the following year Tuzun died, but the caliph only passed from the hands of one master to another, as Baghdad was captured by the Buyids, an Iranian dynasty from the Caspian Sea province of Daylam which had gained control over most of Iran and Iraq.

The Buyid takeover affords yet another illustration of the perennial tension between center and periphery that had beset the Arab/Muslim empire from its inception. Just as the Arabs burst out from the margins of the Middle East to overwhelm the existing empires and the Abbasids emerged from the sidelines to storm the imperial metropolis, so they, in turn, fell victim to both the peripheral mercenary groups they had brought in to protect their rule and to the powerful centrifugal forces within the empire. Even under the Umayyads the empire had already become hopelessly over-extended, which is what made the Abbasid revolution possible in the first place. Under the Abbasids this process continued apace, with an ever-growing number of provinces drifting away from central control and coming under the sway of local dynasties. The empire became an agglomeration of entities united by the overarching factors of language and religion yet no longer having "a metropolis to look to, but rather a whole galaxy of regional centers, each developing its own political society and culture."[31]

First to go its own way was Spain, or Andalus as it was known to Arabs and Muslims after the name of the Vandal settlement in its south, the empire's westernmost outpost. The Berber chief Tareq ibn Zaid, a Mawla of Musa ibn Nusair, conqueror of northwestern Africa, had invaded the country in the spring of 711 at the head of seven thousand Berbers. After a short pause on the rock that still bears his name (*Jabel Tareq*, Gibraltar—the Mount of Tareq), he advanced deep into the hinterland and occupied the great cities of Cordoba and Toledo, the former capital of the Visigoth kingdom. He found there fabulous treasures, including a golden table, ornamented with jewels, which was said to have come from Solomon's Temple. This whetted his master Musa's appetite and the following year he set off for Spain. After a few months' siege he captured Seville, the largest city in the country, before taking Merida and Saragossa. City after city fell in rapid succession and by the summer of 714 the Muslim forces were in control of most of the Iberian Peninsula and even sent raiding parties across the Pyrenees as far as Avignon and Lyon. Drunk with success, Musa reportedly began to entertain megalomaniacal ideas of imperial expansion:

With powerful armament by sea and land he was preparing to re-cross the Pyrenees, to extinguish Gaul and Italy, the declining kingdoms of the Franks and Lombards, and to preach the unity of God on the altar of the Vatican. From there, subduing the Barbarians of Germany, he proposed to follow the course of the Danube from its source to the Euxine Sea, to overthrow the Greek or Roman empire of Constantinople, and, returning from

Europe to Asia, to unite his new acquisitions with Antioch and the provinces of Syria.

Whether or not word of these grandiose plans reached the caliph, he quickly summoned his chieftains to Damascus, where both narrowly escaped execution. Tareq was reduced to slavery again, while Musa was heavily fined. His son, whom he had left to govern Spain in his absence, was assassinated in Cordoba and his head was presented to the fallen leader. "I know his features," he exclaimed in response to the credulous question whether he recognized the features of the deceased, "and I imprecate the same, a juster fate, against the authors of his death." In the end, Musa was allowed to retire to Mecca, where he died impoverished and heartbroken,[32] yet it would not be long before the Muslims would cross the Pyrenees in strength. But for Charles Martel and the battle of Poitiers (732), Musa's imperial dream might well have come to fruition.

The Umayyads thus obtained a major foothold in Christian Europe, but their actual control over the province was always shaky given the formidable problems of communication. So much so that within a decade of the conquest of Spain the caliph Umar II had appointed a governor whose mission was to evacuate the Muslims from the peninsula.[33] It was paradoxically only after their fall from power that the Umayyads managed to assert their authority over the province. One of their few surviving princes, Abdel Rahman ibn Mu'awiya, grandson of the caliph Hisham, managed to escape the Abbasid bloodbath and to make his way to Spain, where he won the loyalty of the Berber and Arab colonists who had settled there following the conquest. In 756 he founded the Umayyad dynasty of Spain, where he ruled for the next thirty-two years without offering allegiance to the Abbasid caliph.

For nearly three hundred years the Umayyads reigned over a Spain divided from the rest of the Islamic world, leading it to political, economic, and cultural greatness. Unlike the Middle East and North Africa, where the vast majority of the subject peoples converted to Islam, substantial parts of Spain's indigenous population remained loyal to the Christian faith and to their native culture and language. Many of them also retained the hope of political deliverance, and the Christian states of León and Navarre, in the mountainous ridge of northern Spain, became springboards for a relentless campaign to expel the Muslim occupiers. Boosted by a persistent drive southward by the Franks, such hopes generated Muslim distrust of the Christian majority and resulted in their widespread exclusion from governmental posts.[34] These Muslim-Christian tensions were further exacerbated by the bitter enmity between Berbers and Arabs, manifested in frequent clashes, as well as by a series of social and religious grievances, which often took a violent form, and numerous squabbles among the unruly slave-soldiers, imported primarily from the Balkans and the Maghreb. Neither did the Arab colonists themselves enjoy a high degree of social cohesion, having imported the perennial rivalry between the two great tribal leagues of Qays and Yemen. Even so, the Umayyads managed to maintain their prowess until the eleventh century, when they suddenly disintegrated. What makes this decline all the more perplexing is that it came only decades after the fifty-year reign of Abdel Rahman III (912–61), the dynasty's most prominent scion, who took it to unprecedented peaks and who proclaimed himself "Caliph and Commander of the Faithful" in response to the Fatimid claims to the caliphate.[35]

The Islamic world was thus split into three imperial powers, the weakest of which was the Abbasid caliph. He had long lost control over his possessions west of Egypt. Domination of these territories had always been tenuous since the indigenous Berber population remained implacably hostile to Arab colonization and prone to violent resistance. In the early 740s they temporarily threw off Arab rule under the Kharijite banner and in 789 Morocco was effectively lost to the empire with the foundation of the Idrisid dynasty. Ifriqiya (modern Tunisia and eastern Algeria) followed suit eleven years later when Harun bowed to the inevitable and granted the right to hereditary rule in the province to Ibrahim ibn Aghlab, son of a Khurasani officer of Arab origin, for an annual tribute of forty thousand dinars. The Aghlabis ruled the area for a hundred years and their foremost imperial feat was the occupation of the island of Sicily, begun in 827 and completed some fifty years later. Their conquerors, the Fatimids, went on to occupy Egypt and to wrest the Levant from Abbasid rule, momentarily threatening Baghdad itself.

A no less lethal threat was developing in the empire's eastern backyard. Prior to his death, Harun envisaged the partition of the imperial domains between his two sons. Amin was to be caliph while Ma'mun, son of an Iranian slave woman, was to rule the eastern provinces as heir apparent in (somewhat ambiguous) subordination to his brother. This division proved a catastrophic blunder, sparking a vicious fratricidal war that set the empire on the path to irreversible decline. Yet its underlying rationale was not without merit: namely, that the eastern provinces, Iran in particular, could no longer be ruled directly from Baghdad.

Indeed, no sooner had the civil war ended than Ma'mun's leading general, Taher ibn Hussein, who had effectively won the war for his master and was rewarded with the governorship of Iran and the east, dropped the caliph's name from the Friday sermon, a defiant act that was tantamount to a declaration of independence. Ma'mun was taken aback by this act of insubordination, but there was little he could do. Babak's revolt in Azerbaijan was going from strength to strength and the caliph needed all the help he could get. Besides, one of Taher's sons was the caliph's commander-in-chief and so held his master captive to his whims. Ma'mun could also see the benefit in having an autonomous entity, officially subordinate to his authority, to defend the empire's eastern frontiers against the persistent pressure of neighboring infidel groups, such as the Turks. He therefore acquiesced in Taher's move, and when the general died shortly afterward (possibly by poisoning) he reaffirmed the hereditary rule of his descendants in Khurasan in return for recognition of the caliph's theoretical suzerainty.

The Taherids were merely local potentates seeking to carve out their own fiefdom. Yet by blatantly exposing the weakness of the imperial center they heralded the reassertion of Iranian nationalism and the attendant confinement of Abbasid rule to Iraq. The first Iranian popular movement was started by Ya'qub ibn Laith, from the eastern Iranian province of Sistan, who exchanged a career of banditry for revolutionary life. His charismatic personality and outstanding military skills won him massive popular support, and by 867 he had occupied Sistan and extended his power to Afghanistan in the east and to Kirman and Fars in the west, before then proceeding to destroy the Taherids and occupy their capital of Nishapur. This did not satisfy the ambitious Ya'qub, however, and in 876 he mounted an assault on Baghdad itself. The attack was beaten off and Ya'qub died three years later. Nonetheless, the caliph was sufficiently alarmed to grant the Saffarids, as the dynasty came to be called after its founder's original profession of coppersmith (*saffar*), the governorship of Sistan, Khurasan, and Fars. Not content with these substantial gains, the Saffarids invaded Transoxania, only to meet their match in an aristocratic Iranian dynasty, the Samanids, who brought Khurasan under their control and ran it from their capital of Bukhara, nominally as the caliph's viceroys but in reality as an independent regional dynasty.

Notwithstanding these setbacks, the Saffarids managed to maintain their position in Sistan for nearly six more centuries, thus highlighting the depth of popular support for their cause. In the short term, however, their defeat triggered prolonged turbulence in central and western Iran, from which Mardavij ibn Ziyar, a potentate from the Caspian Sea province of Daylam, emerged victorious. A ruthless megalomaniac who ruled his domain with an iron fist, Mardavij claimed to be none other than the biblical King Solomon, son of David, and spoke openly about reconstituting a great Zoroastrian Iranian empire. This grandiose plan failed to materialize as he was murdered by his Turkish mercenaries in 935 (his Ziyarid family managed to maintain its rule in the Caspian provinces until the late eleventh century).[36] All the same, three Daylamite brothers who rose high in his service exploited the ensuing vacuum to found their own dynasty.

The eldest of the three, Ali ibn Buya, better known as *Imad al-Dawla* ("Pillar of the Empire"), held Shiraz at the time of Mardavij's death and shortly afterward seized the entire province of Fars. His brother Hassan (*Rukn al-Dawla*, "Prop of the Empire") established himself after some setbacks as ruler of central Iran from Isfahan to Ravy (near today's Tehran), while the third brother, Ahmad (*Muizz al-Dawla*, "Fortifier of the Empire"), occupied parts of Khuzistan, and in December 945 entered Baghdad, where the caliph bestowed their honorary titles on the brothers.

For the next century, the Buyids were the empire's effective masters, appointing and deposing caliphs as they saw fit. As Twelver Shiites, they introduced traditional Shiite festivals (notably the annual commemoration of Hussein's martyrdom) and theological precepts into their domains. Yet they made no attempt to take over from the caliph or to replace him with a Shiite contender, thus underlining their highly pragmatic outlook. Since there was no question of a Shiite majority in the foreseeable future, the caliphal façade was indispensable for keeping the imperial fabric intact and the Buyids had no qualms about maintaining the pretense of subservience to their ostensible sovereign or boosting their legitimacy by accepting titles from him. They were not even deterred from backing the caliph against fellow Shiites: the fear of losing Syria to the Fatimids superseded all considerations of religious affinity.

At the same time, the Buyids evinced no great love for Arabs and Arabism. Mui'zz al-Dawla spoke no Arabic when he occupied Baghdad, and though subsequent generations of Buyids learned the language and patronized Arabic in their court, they did so out of necessity rather than conviction as their sentiments lay with Iran's glorious past and traditions. This was evidenced *inter alia* by their attempts to produce a genealogy linking them to the Sasanids, the prevalence of pre-Islamic Iranian customs and celebrations in the Buyid court, and the adoption of the old imperial title of *Shahanshah*, "King of Kings." This last measure was particularly galling to Arab Baghdad, and it was not until 1037, more than fifty years after its introduction, that the title's use was officially sanctioned by the caliph.

When in 1055 a Turkish strongman by the name of Tughrul Bey, head of the Seljuk clan of the Ghuzz tribes (or Turcoman as they were called by the Arabs), which had embraced Islam a few decades earlier, entered Baghdad after defeating the Buyids, he was received as a deliverer and invested with the title "Sultan of the East and the West." Yet it was not long before the caliphs realized that their new Sunni masters were not much better than their "heretic" predecessors. Though paying their dues to the caliph out of conviction rather than political expediency, and refraining from serial deposition of caliphs, the Seljuks left no room for doubt as to where the true source of power lay. They assumed the designation of "Allah's Shadow" that had hitherto been the caliph's sole prerogative and even robbed the Abbasids of their foremost symbol of religious prowess: the Prophet's mantle. It was hardly surprising, therefore, that when they were weakened by dynastic infighting, the caliphs attempted to reassert their independence. The caliph Nasser even managed during his long reign (1180–1225) to have the head of the Seljuk sultan of Iran impaled in front of his palace. Yet this flicker of independence proved short-lived. In 1258 the Mongol hordes stormed Baghdad and put the last Abbasid caliph, Mu'tasim, to death.[37]

The House of Islam and the House of War

"I was ordered to fight all men until they say 'There is no god but Allah.'"[1]
With these farewell words the Prophet Muhammad summed up the international vision of the faith he had brought to the world. As a universal religion,
Islam envisages a global political order in which all humankind will live under
Muslim rule as either believers or subject communities. In order to achieve
this goal it is incumbent on all free, male, adult Muslims to carry out an
uncompromising struggle "in the path of Allah," or jihad. This in turn makes
those parts of the world that have not yet been conquered by the House of
Islam an abode of permanent conflict (*Dar al-Harb*, the House of War) which
will only end with Islam's eventual triumph. In the meantime, there can be no
peace between these two world systems, only the temporary suspensions of
hostilities for reasons of necessity or expediency. In the words of Ibn Khaldun:

> In the Muslim community, the jihad is a religious duty because of the
> universalism of the Islamic mission and the obligation [to convert] every-
> body to Islam either by persuasion or by force . . . [By contrast] the other
> religions had no such universal mission and the holy war was [therefore]
> not a religious duty to them apart from self-defense.[2]

This dogmatic worldview has been matched by a good measure of tactical
pragmatism. Although Muhammad and his successors relinquished neither
their dichotomist view of international affairs nor their ultimate goal of world
domination, the Prophet was not deterred from crossing the religious divide
and aligning himself with non-Muslims whenever this suited his needs.[3] This
practice was widely developed by his successors who, as we have seen, were far
less interested in the mass conversion of the conquered populations than in
enjoying the material fruits of their subjugation. For them the triumph of
Islam was not so much a cultural and civilizational issue as it was a territorial
and political matter. The lands they occupied and ruled became an integral

part of the House of Islam whether or not most of their inhabitants became Muslims.

No matter how hard the caliphs professed their commitment to the pursuit of a holy war against the unbelievers, theirs was a straightforward act of empire-building rather than a "clash of civilizations." They were, of course, extremely proud of their religion and convinced of its superiority over all other faiths. Yet this did not prevent them from appropriating the intellectual property of other cultures and religions, and for good reason. At the time of the conquests the Arabs were a marginal group, lacking substantial material resources, with a dearth of bureaucratic and administrative experience and a limited literary and cultural tradition. It was only natural for them to take whatever they could from the great cultural and intellectual centers that had come under their rule in order to strengthen their own imperial prowess.

The Byzantine (and Iranian) bureaucratic and administrative systems thus remained in operation, especially in the fiscal and monetary fields, and were manned by former imperial officials. Roman and provincial legal norms and practices influenced the nascent Islamic law, and the Umayyad caliphs had a distinct penchant for emulating their Byzantine counterparts, so much so that a prominent student of Islam described the Umayyad caliphate as a Neo-Byzantine Empire.[4] This was illustrated *inter alia* by the adoption of the title "Allah's Caliph," which evoked the universal claim to power made by the Byzantine emperors (and the Iranian shahs). It was also manifested by the designation of a royal heir by the caliph himself, by the policy of glorification through monumental architecture, by the remarkable attention paid to the maintenance of the roads, to the extent of imitating the Roman milestones, and by the modeling of the earliest dinar on Byzantine coinage until it was withdrawn and replaced by a more "Islamic" design. Even the most extraordinary Umayyad acts of religious piety—the building of the Dome of the Rock and the mosques of Damascus and Medina—were inspired by the grand Byzantine monuments and were constructed with Byzantine help and building materials, notably gold and mosaic cubes, sent by the emperor at the caliph's request. When criticized for his shameless imitation of the Byzantine emperors, the first Umayyad caliph Mu'awiya (661–80) retorted that "Damascus was full of Greeks and that none would believe in his power if he did not behave and look like an emperor."[5]

The absorption of the conquered civilizations was thorough and comprehensive. Indian medicine, mathematics, and astronomy were eagerly studied, while Iranian administrative techniques, social and economic traditions, literary and artistic methods, and important elements of political thinking were adopted and acted upon. Yet the largest source of borrowing by a wide margin came precisely from that part of the world with which the House of

Islam was supposedly locked in a deadly civilizational confrontation—the West. Countless Hellenistic sciences and fields of learning were incorporated en masse into the nascent Islamic civilization: medicine and pharmaceutics, botany and zoology, mineralogy and meteorology, mathematics, mechanics, and astronomy, and, above all, philosophy. In all these spheres the Hellenistic heritage fused with local traditions and with foreign influences, especially from Iran and other Eastern countries. Even Arabic literature adopted many Hellenistic motifs and themes, as well as less readily discernible elements such as its stylistic and presentational patterns and emotional conventions.[6]

It is arguable, of course, that cultural and intellectual appropriation implies no affinity with those from whom you take and that the pretense to originality and uniqueness often results in the disparagement of one's intellectual and conceptual roots. Just as the early Christian church sought to consolidate its position by denigrating its Jewish origins, so Islam accused the "People of the Book," Jews and Christians, from whom it derived most of its ideas, of straying from the "right path" or even of tampering with the Holy Scriptures. Islam's wholesale incorporation of Hellenistic culture and science did not therefore mean acquiescence to Western civilization but rather an augmentation and refinement of its own edifice so as to maintain its supremacy. As far as Muslims were concerned there was no fundamental difference between the material and the intellectual properties of the vanquished peoples. Both were legitimate spoils of war that could readily be appropriated by the conquerors without attribution and regarded as an indigenous part of the House of Islam (Muhammad, for example, is said to have commended to his followers a prayer that is virtually identical to the Christian Paternoster, or Lord's Prayer).[7]

A similarly pragmatic approach characterized Islam's economic relations with Christendom. Born in a mercantile milieu, Islam had always been amenable to trade and commerce. Muhammad himself was a successful merchant, as were several of his early companions, and their favorable attitude to trade permeated the new religion from the start. Numerous sayings attributed to the Prophet sang the praises of commerce, while Islamic law and political practice took great care to protect the interests of Muslim merchants.[8] A clear line was thus drawn between the religious duty to fight unbelievers wherever they were, and the maintenance of economic relations with the non-Muslim world. In the words of the historian Daniel Dennett: "Neither in the Qur'an, nor in the sayings of the Prophet, nor in the acts of the first caliphs, nor in the opinions of Muslim jurists is there any prohibition against trading with the Christians or unbelievers."[9]

This approach generated in short order a thriving international trade as the Islamic empire happily interacted with "infidels" of all hues, from the Far East to the Atlantic. Pagan Africa was probably the most lucrative branch of this foreign trade for centuries, as Muslim merchants exchanged very cheap products against gold (as late as the eleventh century black African tribes were reportedly trading gold for an equal weight of salt). Yet there was also extensive trade between Muslims and their immediate European neighbors: Byzantium and the pagan peoples to its north. The magnitude of this trade is evidenced by the huge quantities of Islamic coins (dating from the end of the seventh to the beginning of the eleventh century) discovered in different parts of Russia, Finland, Sweden, and Norway, and it comprised a wide range of commodities including furs, skins, amber, timber, cattle, and weapons. The primary commodity by far was slaves, mainly from the pagan Slav peoples; the pervasiveness of this phenomenon is borne out by the fact that in a number of European languages, and also in Arabic, the word for slave is a derivative of "Slav."[10]

Muslim trade with Western Europe was more limited, but this had less to do with the creation of two implacably hostile civilizations on the opposite sides of the Mediterranean, as argued by the eminent Belgian historian Henri Pirenne,[11] than with the economic inferiority of Western Europe, which had not yet reached the level of manufacturing and production that would allow it to compete on an equal footing with the Islamic empire. As a result, the trade relations between the two systems bore some resemblance to the "colonial trade" of the nineteenth and twentieth centuries, except that in this case Europe held the status of colony, exporting raw materials and slaves in return for consumer goods.[12]

The Jews played a central role in this trade, on the European side. Owing to their exclusion from agriculture, the main occupation of the Christian majority, they became a largely commercial people. Their high level of literacy and knowledge of foreign languages, and their ability to communicate with co-religionists in the Islamic lands, made them uniquely suited to serve as a bridge between the two world powers, though their position was extremely tenuous and exposed to the rapacity of greedy potentates and fanatic mobs. The tenth and early eleventh centuries marked the high point of Jewish prominence in international trade, after which they went into rapid decline owing to the draconian religious persecution attending the crusades. Their position was largely taken over by the Italian commercial cities, especially Amalfi and Venice, which developed a thriving trade with the Maghreb based on the exchange of Eastern luxury goods (mainly spices, silk, and ivories) in return for timber, iron, agricultural products, and slaves. (Venice became the largest slave market in Central Europe, selling even Christian slaves to the Muslims.)

Particularly close relations were developed with the Fatimids, who in the tenth century conquered most of North Africa, Egypt, and the Levant. Keenly aware of the importance of international trade for the realization of their imperial ambitions, the Fatimids were especially dependent on the importation of timber and iron for shipbuilding, which the Italians gladly provided, together, perhaps, with direct naval support. In consequence, an extensive network of Italian merchant colonies was established in the Levant and North Africa under Fatimid protection, aside from a sizeable presence in Egypt itself, which contributed to Egyptian economic prosperity and self-sufficiency and was to survive the tumultuous period of the crusades and even the demise of the Fatimid dynasty.[13]

These trade relations created a strong convergence of interests that transcended the Muslim-Christian divide, and before long Italians and Muslims found themselves cooperating against co-religionists and compatriots. As early as 805, the Khurasani potentate Ibrahim ibn Aghlab, who five years earlier had been granted the province of Ifriqiya by the Abbasid caliph, signed a ten-year truce and trade agreement with the Byzantine ruler of Sicily, aimed at curbing the expansionist designs of Umayyad Spain and Idrisid Morocco. The treaty was extended for a further ten years by Ibrahim's successor Abdallah (812–17). Even when they embarked in 827 on an ambitious effort to occupy Sicily, the Aghlabis maintained a close relationship with the Italian cities, which for their part proved more than willing to fight their co-religionists. In 837 the duke of Naples appealed for Aghlabi support against a local potentate besieging his city; whereupon the Muslims made their first appearance on the Italian mainland, lifted the siege, and signed a treaty of friendship and trade with Naples. The thankful Neapolitans reciprocated by assisting the Muslim attack on the Sicilian city of Messina, and the entente between the two parties remained intact for over fifty years in the face of repeated attempts to wreck it by popes and emperors alike. Naples was joined by the cities of Amalfi and Gaeta, which allowed the Muslims to use their ports for raids on Sicily and the Italian mainland and served as markets for the disposal of the booty obtained in these raids.

This collaboration was briefly fractured in 846, when Naples and Amalfi rebuffed a Muslim attempt to seize some neighboring islands, and yet again in 849, when the two cities helped the pope to fight off a Muslim attack on Rome. But these cracks were quickly papered over, and in 876–77 the southern cities participated in the Muslim raids on the Roman littoral, with Naples serving as a base of operations. It was only with great effort and lavish financial inducements that the pope managed to detach momentarily most of the cities from their Muslim allies. But they refused to form an anti-Muslim front under papal leadership and realigned themselves with the Muslims whenever they saw fit. As a result, the Muslims entrenched themselves along the road to Rome, plundering and ravaging substantial parts of the countryside at will. It was as late as 915 that the pope finally managed to assemble an effective war coalition that routed the last remaining Muslim forces on the Italian mainland; even then, Amalfi refused to join the campaign while Naples and Gaeta connived to help the enemy escape. This was to no avail. The Muslims were hunted down and their imperial presence in Italy terminated, though attacks from Sicily and North Africa continued for another century, with the ad hoc connivance of local Italian cities.[14]

These were no isolated episodes of collaboration with the infidel. The highest reaches of the Islamic (and Christian) worlds were prepared to act in this way whenever it suited their needs. It is a well-known fact that the Umayyad caliphs Mu'awiya (661–80) and Abdel Malik (685–705) entered into agreements with the Byzantine emperor committing them to the payment of tribute. Both were involved in deadly fights for the leadership of the Islamic empire (Mu'awiya against Ali, Abdel Malik against Ibn Zubair) and were anxious to secure their rear from a Byzantine attack.[15] And while in this case the caliphs were prepared to pay a price in order to buy infidel neutrality at a critical juncture, other Muslim rulers were not deterred from direct collaboration with Christian powers against fellow Muslims. In the ninth century Spain's Umayyad dynasty established contacts with the Byzantines in order to neutralize Abbasid pressures. The Fatimids followed the same course for the same reason a century later.[16]

For their part, the Abbasids and the newly established Carolingian dynasty in France drew closer to each other in common enmity to Umayyad Spain and the Byzantine Empire. Contacts between the two powers were already established during the caliphate of Mansur (754–75), who sent a military force to restore Spain to Abbasid rule. The attempt failed miserably and the heads of the insurgents, together with the Abbasid insignia, were sent back to the caliph. Yet it was apparently conclusive enough to convince Pippin the Short, son of Charles Martel of Poitiers fame, of a congruence of interests with the Abbasids. Since his coronation in 752 Pippin had endeavored to follow in the footsteps of his illustrious father by eradicating the Muslim presence in southern France. During this struggle, which came to a head in 759, Pippin realized both the extent of the Umayyad threat to his position and the importance of Abbasid support, as Christian potentates in southern France sided with the Muslim invaders against him, while the Muslim governor of Barcelona, who remained loyal to the Abbasids, sought Pippin's protection against the newly installed Umayyad dynasty.

In 765 Pippin sent a diplomatic mission to Baghdad, which returned three years later accompanied by an embassy from the caliph and bearing many gifts. The envoys were given a personal audience with the Frankish king and were in turn sent back with lavish presents. But in 768 Pippin died and it was not until ten years later that his son and successor, Charlemagne, was tempted into invading Spain by the Muslim governor of Saragossa, who promised him the city, together with a number of neighboring towns, in return for help against the Umayyad emir. The invasion did not go as planned and Charlemagne was soon forced to return to France to suppress a local rebellion. Yet eight years later he again directed his attention southward and, as on the previous occasion, he did so at the instigation of a prominent Muslim figure. This time it was a brother of the Umayyad emir who in 785 offered to help Charlemagne to conquer Barcelona and the Ebro Delta in return for the right to the throne. Twelve years later the governor of Barcelona offered to surrender his city, while the ruler of Saragossa sent a similar offer to Charlemagne's son Louis I, the Pious, who governed the south of France on his father's behalf.

A man of grandiose imperial ambitions—his coronation by Pope Leo III on Christmas Day, 800, inaugurated the Holy Roman Empire—Charlemagne did not content himself with dealing with local Muslim potentates and opted instead for a direct relationship with his imperial peer, Harun al-Rashid, through the exchange of a number of missions. Muslim writers do not mention these, but according to Western sources the first mission left for Baghdad in 797, apparently with a view to establishing some bilateral cooperation and ensuring freedom of access and protection from molestation for pilgrims visiting the Holy Land, Jerusalem in particular. Two of the envoys died during the mission and the surviving member returned three years later with rich gifts, including fabrics, aromatics, and a rare white elephant. A second mission, sent in 802, was received with similar cordiality, while a priest was sent on another mission to the patriarch of Jerusalem. He returned a year later to Rome, accompanied by two Orthodox monks who reportedly brought with them the keys of the Church of the Holy Sepulcher, the standard of the city of Jerusalem, and some sacred relics, which they presented to Charlemagne. Meanwhile, Harun allowed the building of special facilities for Frankish pilgrims visiting Jerusalem's holy sites, and an embassy on his behalf visited the emperor in Italy.

It is difficult to assess the long-term consequences of these exchanges. They were ostensibly substantial enough to convince Pope Leo III to expedite the crowning of Charlemagne. It has also been suggested that the anxiety over the Abbasid-Carolingian entente played a role in the Byzantine decision to recognize Charlemagne as emperor—a bitter pill to swallow for a power that styled itself as the sole heir of the Roman Empire. Be that as it may, in 807 Charlemagne sent another mission to Harun. But the caliph died in 809, and it was his son and successor, Ma'mun, who apparently sent the reply that arrived in 813 via the Sicilian governor who had been acting as a middleman.

By this time mutual interest in cooperation had subsided, and the decline of the Carolingian Empire after Charlemagne's death in 814 meant that these initiatives were not followed up. Yet in 831, as he was about to renew hostilities against Byzantium, Ma'mun sent two ambassadors to Louis I in a move that indicated the pre-eminence of imperial interests in his overall strategy.[17]

This pattern of pragmatic cooperation across the religious divide was vastly expanded during the age of the crusades (1096–1291). On the face of it, these tumultuous events constituted the apogee of the millenarian Christian-Muslim clash of civilizations; the culmination of a long conflict between the church and civilization of the West and that of Islam, which began with the defeat of the emperor Heraclius in 636 by the caliph Umar. In practice, the crusades were as much prompted by earthly factors as by religious zeal. For ordinary peasants who took to the road, the crusades held the promise of relief from a grim and brutish existence; for the princes and feudal lords who led them, they presented an opportunity for self-aggrandizement and an outlet for the pressures of feudal overpopulation.

Even Pope Urban II, who stirred up this religious tidal wave, was not immune to such pragmatic considerations as the expansion of Rome's power and influence, and the diversion "against the pagans [of] the fighting which up to now customarily went on among the Christians."[18] No less important, in the mid-eleventh century a schism had evolved between the Western and Eastern churches, mainly over Constantinople's refusal to recognize papal supremacy, and the popes were eager to reassert their authority over Eastern Christendom. When in 1074, three years after the Seljuks had routed the Byzantines at the battle of Manzikert and conquered almost the whole of Anatolia, Emperor Michael VII offered to recognize the Roman primacy in exchange for military help, Pope Gregory VII expressed his readiness to lead a campaign that would expel the Muslim infidels from Anatolia. So enthusiastic was the pope about the idea that, when Michael VII was deposed, he promptly excommunicated his successors Nicephorus III (1078–81) and Alexius Comnenus (1081–1118). Yet in an ironic twist of history it was Alexius who breathed life into Gregory's idea by approaching Pope Urban II with a similar request for assistance.

A worthy heir to his formidable predecessor, Urban did not fail to seize the moment. Addressing a huge crowd of clergymen and laymen in the French town of Clermont on November 27, 1095, he made an emotive appeal for an organized campaign in the East. He told his listeners about the great suffering and abuse wrought by the Turks on the Byzantine Empire and Eastern Christendom, before breaking with the main gist of the emperor's appeal and urging a holy war for the liberation of Jerusalem and the Holy Sepulcher. "Jerusalem is the navel of the world," he said. "Enter upon the road to the Holy

Sepulcher; wrest that land from the wicked race, and subject it to yourself." Urban promised those who would leave their homes and families and join the crusade absolution for their sins and the promise of "everlasting life"; and for those who would not be won over by this heavenly reward, more earthly gains were on offer: "The possessions of the enemy, too, will be yours, since you will make spoil of their treasures and return victorious to your own."[19]

The response to Urban's appeal was overwhelming. Scores of people left their homes and marched eastward, reaching Constantinople on August 1, 1096, to Alexius's undisguised horror. The astute and vigorous emperor had been hard at work to resurrect the empire after the Manzikert catastrophe. He expected a small contingent of well-trained knights that would enable him to take on the Seljuks, not vast and disorderly hordes that seemed far more eager to plunder the people they had supposedly come to save than to fight on their behalf. Alexius thus ferried the crusaders as quickly as possible into Anatolia where the Seljuks summarily annihilated them. Yet in the following months substantial and orderly armies, led by a number of prominent princes, began arriving in Constantinople. In June 1097 they captured the Seljuk capital of Iznik, some eighty miles southeast of Constantinople, and a year later they took the ancient metropolis of Antioch in northern Syria. The climax of the campaign, commonly known as the First Crusade, was reached in mid-July 1099 with the conquest of Jerusalem after a five-week siege and the massacre of its entire population, Muslims and Jews, men, women, and children. Most of the crusaders then left the country and returned to Europe. Those who stayed behind were organized into four newly established entities: the principalities of Antioch and Edessa, the county of Tripoli, and the Latin Kingdom of Jerusalem, which exercised general sovereignty over the rest of the crusading states in the Levant.[20]

This created a lasting source of friction between the crusaders and the Byzantines, who hoped to regain the territories they had lost to Islam. (Alexius would not allow the princes to cross into Anatolia before exacting from most of them an oath of allegiance and a pledge to this effect.) As this did not happen, the emperor did not hesitate to collaborate with the Muslims against his co-religionists. Already before the crusaders reached Palestine, Alexius had written to the Fatimid caliph in Cairo to dissociate himself from the imminent invasion. He would rather have the Orthodox Christians under the tolerant rule of the Fatimids, with whom the Byzantines had maintained a close and generally friendly relationship over the past century, than under the control of the Franks (i.e., Catholics of varied European origin), whose mistreatment of the Antioch Christians revealed a deep animosity toward their Eastern co-religionists. This animosity was to mar Frankish-Byzantine relations for the next century, and to culminate in the massacre of Europeans in Constantinople in 1182 and the

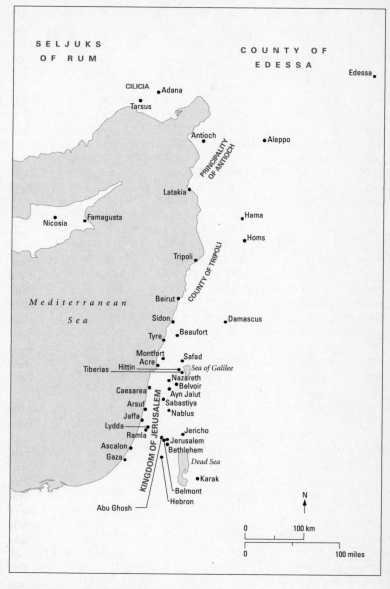

Map 4 The Crusading Kingdoms

sacking of the city twenty-two years later in the Fourth Crusade, which, according to a leading historian of the crusades, "was to lead in due course to the tragedy of 1453 [the fall of the Byzantine Empire], and at last to the Turks' hammering at the walls of Vienna."[21]

If the crusades were hardly a unified attack by the House of War on the House of Islam, the Muslim response was far more disjointed still. The two rival empires of the Shiite Fatimids and the Sunni Abbasids had vied for Islamic leadership for over a century. They feared and loathed each other as much as they feared and loathed the Christian powers, and this precluded any conceivable collaboration between them against the European invaders. The Seljuk Turks managed to bring most of the Levant and the Fertile Crescent under unified control, ostensibly on behalf of the Abbasid caliph. But the vast empire they conquered in the mid-eleventh century quickly dissolved into a number of smaller kingdoms, under the theoretical rule of the Seljuk sultan of Baghdad, which were further fragmented into a string of rival fiefdoms and principalities.

To ensure the continuity of their reign the Seljuk princes left their infants in the care of trusted military generals (*atabegs*) whom they deemed sufficiently strong and loyal to defend their rights. This gave the atabegs far greater power and prestige than ordinary generals and enabled many of them with the passage of time to substitute their own dynasties for those of their protégés. Finally, the traditional enmity between Syria and Iraq, and Damascus's reluctance to reconcile itself to the loss of its metropolitan status, made it a fertile ground for dissent. This enabled the Assassins (a word derived from the Arabic *Hashishiyyun*, users of hashish, as they were derisively called by their enemies), a militant sect that seceded from Fatimid Shiism in the late twelfth century following a dispute over the identity of the rightful caliph, to extend their propaganda and murderous activities from their base in the Iranian mountains to the Levant.[22]

The limited scale of the crusades, which affected only a fraction of the Middle East, paradoxically exacerbated Muslim fragmentation and disunity. The invasions were virtually confined to Palestine and parts of Syria, and even at their height meant little or nothing to Iraq and the caliphate, let alone to Iran, Central Asia, or even Upper Egypt. The political evolution of these lands was hardly influenced by the crusaders, with whom their inhabitants had no contact whatever. As a result, the crusades were seen not as a cataclysmic event but as yet another round in the intermittent fighting that had been raging between the Byzantine and the Islamic empires for centuries. Only a century earlier the Byzantines had temporarily regained substantial parts of the Levant, as far south as the Galilee, and the crusades appeared to be a repetition of this. So much so that an Iraqi poet lamenting the fall of Jerusalem in July 1099—more than two years after the arrival of the crusaders in the

Levant—substituted the Byzantines for the Franks as the city's conquerors, while the oral histories of the Anatolian Turks contained hardly a trace of the crossing of the Frankish armies.[23] There was no general fear of impending doom to Islam's collective existence, and the Muslim dynasts and potentates viewed the crusades in purely localized terms. As far as they were concerned, the Franks were not representatives of a hostile civilization that had to be fought to the death but a new factor in the existing network of local feuds and rivalries that had to be utilized to one's own advantage. The outcome was an intricate web of shifting alliances, based on the vicissitudes in the regional balance of forces and opportunities rather than on religious affiliation, which as often as not pitted Muslim and Christian against Muslim and Christian.

The first to attempt to exploit the new situation were the Fatimids. Having lost most of Palestine and Syria to the Seljuks in the 1070s, they viewed the crusades as a golden opportunity to recover these territories and to create a buffer zone between them and their Turkish enemies. In March 1098, at the height of the siege of Antioch, Fatimid envoys arrived at the camp of the crusaders with a proposal for the partition of the Levant, whereby Syria would go to the Franks and Palestine to Egypt. They were cordially received and after a few weeks' stay were sent home with lavish gifts, accompanied by a small Frankish delegation. Before long, however, the Fatimids realized that the delegates were not authorized to reach an agreement. They thus moved to reoccupy Palestine and much of Lebanon on their own, then offered to allow Christendom free access to Palestine's holy shrines provided the crusaders refrained from occupying it. This ran counter to the entire rationale of the crusades, and on July 15, 1099, the Franks took Jerusalem and defeated a Fatimid force that arrived in southern Palestine.

As the crusaders went from strength to strength, regional acquiescence in their permanent presence grew wider and deeper. Rather than prompting a general outcry for a holy war, the fall of Jerusalem drove numerous local potentates to seek an accommodation with the Franks. An emotional appeal to the Abbasid court by the qadi of Damascus, who made a special trip to Baghdad in August 1099 together with a number of refugees from the Jerusalem massacre, left many in the audience in tears, yet produced no concrete results. Though the caliph was apparently moved, there was nothing he could do since he was a puppet of the Seljuk sultans, whose incessant infighting left them totally indifferent to Muslim setbacks in the Holy Land. The despondent qadi thus left Baghdad empty-handed, having failed to get an audience with the sultan who was far away in Iran campaigning against his own brother. "The sultans were at loggerheads with each other," the great medieval historian Ibn Athir (d. 1233) commented wryly, "and this enabled the Franks to occupy the country."[24]

This indifference was not confined to Baghdad. The odd call for a jihad by the religious classes in Syria did not translate into concrete action.[25] Political life in the country was dominated by the fratricidal fighting between the two Seljuk brothers—Rudwan, the sovereign of Aleppo, and his younger brother, Duqaq, who reigned in Damascus—which fragmented Muslim power and facilitated the entrenchment of the Frankish presence in the Levant. Both brothers feared their Muslim rivals more than they feared the crusaders, and both pursued an overtly opportunistic policy that showed no preference for Muslim over Christian. As long as there was some likelihood of a Fatimid recapture of Palestine, Damascus adopted a strict policy of neutrality, which worked in favor of the crusaders by sparing them the need to protect their rear from a Muslim attack. Yet when in May 1104 the Franks consolidated their grip over the coastal plain by occupying the key port town of Acre, the Damascenes, fearing the disruption of their invaluable Mediterranean trading, quickly gave the Fatimid governors of the coastal towns indirect support by engaging the Franks in a series of minor clashes in the Galilee and the Golan Heights, northeast of Lake Tiberias. In 1108, having realized that these fears were grossly exaggerated, the Damascus atabeg Tughtigin, the city's effective master following Duqaq's death four years earlier, signed an armistice agreement with the Kingdom of Jerusalem, which made the Golan Heights a demilitarized zone and divided the revenues from their fertile agricultural lands: one-third to Damascus, one-third to the crusaders, and one-third to the local peasants who tilled the land. The following year a similar agreement was signed with regard to the Beqa Valley in eastern Lebanon.[26]

These arrangements were to remain intact until the collapse of the Latin Kingdom in 1187, although they did not prevent the signatories from attacking each other whenever this suited their needs. When in 1109 Tughtigin moved against the Franks of Tripoli in contravention of the agreement, King Baldwin I reassured him that the peace between them would remain unaffected. When four years later Baldwin violated the agreement Tughtigin joined forces with Mosul's powerful ruler Mawdud in attacking northern Palestine. Yet he had no intention of making Damascus a sidekick of its powerful Iraqi counterpart. He was apparently behind Mawdud's murder (in October 1113) by a member of the order of the Assassins, and the following year signed another truce agreement with Baldwin.[27]

The fear of domination had likewise driven Rudwan, as early as 1108, to appeal to the Norman prince Tancred for help against Mosul's atabeg Jawali, who for his part summoned the Edessa counts Baldwin II and Jocelin to his aid. The two had been captured in the spring of 1104, when the crusaders suffered a crushing defeat near the northern Iraqi town of Harran, and were released four years later by Jawali in return for a ransom and a pledge to help him whenever he so required. In a revealing indication of the instrumental nature of Christian-Muslim politics, Tancred and his uncle Bohemond, founder of the principality of Antioch, pocketed a hefty sum paid by the Mosul emir for the release of a prominent Seljuk princess, without making the slightest attempt to trade her for the two imprisoned counts.[28]

In the winter of 1110–11 Emperor Alexius sent an envoy bearing precious gifts to the Seljuk sultan in Baghdad to entice him into a joint attack that would drive the Franks out of the Levant. It is not clear whether the emperor received a formal reply, but in the summer of 1111 a large Seljuk force ventured from Mosul and attacked Edessa, before turning south and marching on Syria. To their frustration and disgust they found the gates of Aleppo locked and Rudwan adamant that he would have nothing to do with the anti-crusading campaign. Repeated pleas and threats followed to no avail. Even a threat to execute his son, whom he had left with the campaigners as a sign of goodwill, failed to persuade Rudwan. For his part Tughtigin was no more enthusiastic to host the Mosul army in Damascus. He therefore attempted to divert it to a reconquest of Tripoli while secretly conspiring with the Franks.[29]

In 1115 Tughtigin took a big step forward by joining a diverse war coalition comprising the atabeg of Aleppo, the powerful Turkish warlord Najm al-Din Ilghazi, and Roger of Salerno, the regent of Antioch. This crushed yet another anti-crusading campaign by the Seljuk sultan of Baghdad. Nevertheless, it did not prevent Ilghazi from declaring a jihad a few years later and killing Roger in a battle that came to be known in crusading history as the *Agera Sanguinis* (Field of Blood).[30]

These twists and turns illustrate the opportunistic nature of the Muslim-Frankish political and military interaction. There was no total war on either side, let alone an ideological one. Both were, of course, utterly convinced of the superiority of their respective religions but their actions were guided by a far more earthly combination of territorial and material ambition, military strategy, and political expedience, not dissimilar from that which character-ized the feudal wars in Europe and the incessant infighting among Muslim rulers. Fighting was in accordance with the conventions of the day, conceived as an armed duel between rival princes and warlords, whether Christian or Muslim. Those caught in the crossfire often paid the ultimate price: massacres, plundering, and enslavement. Those outside the eye of the storm were very much left to their own devices. "The soldiers engage themselves in their war, while the people are at peace and the world goes to him who conquers," commented the renowned Spanish-Muslim traveler Ibn Jubayr, who passed through Syria and Palestine at the end of the twelfth century. "Such is the usage in war of the people of these lands; and in the dispute existing between the Muslim Emirs and their kings it is the same, the subjects and the merchants interfering not. Security never leaves them in any circumstances, neither in peace nor in war."[31]

This limited warfare exemplified the general nature of the crusading enterprise. Unlike the early Islamic conquests the crusades were not a drive for world mastery but a limited endeavor geared toward a specific objective: the liberation of Jerusalem and the Holy Sepulcher from infidel rule. Pope Urban II had no clear idea about the most desirable form of future Christian control of these sites and the mechanics for its establishment, which allowed the various princes to carve out their own fiefdoms and principalities rather than return the conquered territories to their former master—the Byzantine emperor. These princes were not driven by a universal vision, or even a desire for a regional empire, but were typical feudal lords anxious to secure their new acquisitions. This required the odd act of local expansion, such as the occupation of the Palestinian ports and the routes linking them with the hinterland in order to ensure uninterrupted communication with the West, but not much more. The zeal for holy war was quickly extinguished. Instead the Frankish population in the Levant was assimilated into the wider Muslim environment, adopting local customs, laws, and institutions in a unique blend of East and West. "We who were Occidentals have now become Orientals," Fulcher of Chartres, the foremost contemporary chronicler of the First Crusade, famously wrote (as early as 1127) of the transformation undergone by those Franks who chose to remain in the Levant:

> He who was a Roman or a Frank has in this land been made into a Galilean or a Palestinian. He who was of Rheims or Chartres has now become a citizen of Tyre or Antioch. We have already forgotten the places of our birth; already these are unknown to many of us or not mentioned any more. Some already possess homes or households by inheritance. Some have taken wives not only of their own people but Syrians or Armenians or even Saracens who have obtained the grace of baptism . . .. Those who were poor in the Occident, God makes rich in this land . . .. Therefore why should one return to the Occident who has found the Orient like this?[32]

For its part the indigenous population viewed the crusaders as the latest in a long line of foreign occupiers (Arabs, Fatimids, and Turks) and adjusted accordingly. Muslims and Jews who had fled their homes in fear of massacres during the first years of crusader rule returned en masse as this murderous practice was suspended, together with fresh waves of immigrants who preferred the less cumbersome and more lightly taxed life under the Franks to Muslim rule.[33] Thus we have the contemporary Damascus resident Ibn Qalanisi (d. 1160), the earliest Arab historian to write about the crusades, relating the positive implications of Frankish occupation of a certain territory near Aleppo in April 1123: "Friendly relations were maintained on this footing, the provinces prospered on both sides, and the roads became safe for travelers between the districts of the two parties."[34]

Sixty-one years later Ibn Jubayr related a similarly idyllic picture of coexistence between Muslims and Christians in southern Syria and northern Palestine. "The cultivation of the vale is divided between the Franks and the Muslims," he said of the situation on the Golan Heights. "They apportion the crops equally, and their animals are mingled together, yet no wrong takes place between them because of it." In the Galilee Ibn Jubayr found

> continuous farms and ordered settlements, whose inhabitants were all Muslims, living comfortably with the Franks . . . They surrender half their crops to the Frank at harvest time, and pay as well a poll tax of one dinar and five qirat for each person. Other than that, they are not interfered with, save for a light tax on the fruits of trees. Their houses and all their effects are left to their full possession. All the coastal cities occupied by the Franks are managed in this fashion, their rural districts, the villages and farms, belonging to the Muslims.

To the deeply devout Spanish scholar this spectacle of Muslims preferring to live under Christian rule was highly offensive. "There can be no excuse in the eyes of God for a Muslim to stay in any infidel country, save when passing through it," he lamented.

> But their hearts have been seduced, for they observe how unlike them in ease and comfort are their brethren in the Muslim regions under their [Muslim] governors. This is one of the misfortunes afflicting the Muslims. The Muslim community bewails the injustice of a landlord of its own faith, and applauds the conduct of its opponent and enemy, the Frankish landlord, and is accustomed to justice from him.[35]

Of course, one should not read too much into a single account, made in a specific situation and at a given point in time, no matter how distinguished the author. Yet the fact that numerous Muslims would rather live under non-Muslim rule at a time when they could have readily chosen not to do so shows that the practical considerations of daily life far exceeded any ideological fervor.

These were the circumstances in which the Turkish atabeg of Mosul Imad al-Din Zangi and his son Nur al-Din Mahmoud set in train the process that was to culminate within a few decades in the destruction of the Kingdom of

Jerusalem by their vassal and successor Salah al-Din Yusuf ibn Ayyub, or Saladin as he is commonly known. It has long been a staple of Muslim and Western historiography that the three were selfless champions of Islam, leaders of a relentless jihad to drive the infidel from the House of Islam. Yet, as has been noted by a number of historians, these men were primarily driven by a desire to build up their own imperial domains and the fighting against the crusaders was incidental to this goal rather than its underlying impetus. All three applied the call for a jihad not only to the anti-Frankish campaigns but to their far more numerous and violent wars against Muslim rivals, and none had any qualms about signing repeated truce agreements with the crusaders. Nor did they enjoy the support of the Muslim population at large, let alone that of all Muslim rulers, many of whom fought alongside the Franks against these self-styled holy warriors.[36]

Zangi, for instance, began his career by helping his Seljuk sultan to crush an attempt by the Abbasid caliph, the nominal head of Sunni Islam, to reassert the power of the caliphate; for this he was rewarded with the governorship of Mosul. In 1128 he added Aleppo to his dominions, and for the next sixteen of the remaining eighteen years of his life (he was murdered in 1146 by a Frankish slave) Zangi strove to become the pre-eminent ruler in the Abbasid lands. Anti-Frankish campaigns occupied a marginal place in this overall effort, and it was only on Christmas Eve, 1144, that Zangi managed to occupy the city of Edessa.

This success won him a string of honorific religious titles from the caliph and is widely considered the key moment in the harnessing of the concept of jihad to the anti-crusading struggle.[37] Yet this shift stemmed from a rare power vacuum attending the accidental deaths a few months earlier of the Byzantine emperor and the king of Jerusalem rather than from a deliberate policy of jihad. The opportunistic nature of Zangi's anti-crusading policies had already been revealed seven years earlier by his reaction to a stinging attack by Damascus on the crusader principality of Tripoli. Instead of supporting his Muslim peer against their common enemy, Zangi sought to contain Damascus by besieging its dependency of Homs. Under no circumstances would he allow the Syrian capital to emerge triumphant, even if this meant extending indirect help to the infidel.[38]

Nur al-Din, who realized his father's dream to become the most powerful Muslim potentate in the Middle East, led a far more pious life (a heavy drinker, Zangi was assassinated as he lay intoxicated on his bed) and spent considerably more time campaigning against the crusaders. He also established a close relationship with the religious classes, which increasingly gave their blessing to his ambitions, and made the need for the liberation of Jerusalem a central theme of his religious propaganda. (He went so far as to order the construction of a pulpit destined for the al-Aqsa mosque, which was finished after his death and duly installed in Jerusalem by Saladin.)[39] Yet this still accounted for only a small fraction of his overall policies, which were largely focused on fighting rival Muslim potentates, at times with infidel support.[40] Nowhere was this subordination of religious dogmas to practical considerations of self-aggrandizement more clearly illustrated than in Nur al-Din's attitude to the rise of his renowned protégé and lieutenant—Saladin.

Born in the Iraqi town of Tikrit into a Kurdish officer family, Saladin grew up in the Lebanese town of Baalbek, where his father, Ayyub, was governor, first for Zangi and then for the princes of Damascus. In 1152, at the age of fourteen, he joined his uncle Shirkuh in the service of Nur al-Din, with whom he subsequently established a close and lengthy relationship. The breakthrough in his hitherto undistinguished career came in March 1169, when Saladin became vizier to the Fatimid caliph Adid by succeeding Sirkuh, who died that month after having occupied Egypt two months earlier. Upon Adid's death on September 12, 1171, Saladin terminated the Fatimid caliphate by ordering that the name of the Abbasid caliph be mentioned in the Friday sermons—for the first time since 969.[41] Shortly afterward all members of the Fatimid house were placed in luxurious incarceration, sexes separated, to spend the rest of their lives in total seclusion from the outside world.

By now Saladin had consolidated his grip on Egypt and substituted his own army for that of the Fatimids. On the face of it, he was a vassal of Nur al-Din under the nominal suzerainty of the Abbasid caliph, who formally invested the Turkish warlord with the right to rule over Syria and Egypt. But in practice he was Egypt's undisputed master and commander of one of the most powerful armies in the House of Islam. This generated a rift between the two men, as Saladin became increasingly defiant of his suspicious overlord, demonstratively failing to discharge long-overdue Egyptian monetary obligations to Syria. "By god we have no need for all this," an enraged Nur al-Din dismissed the fancy gifts sent by Saladin in tandem with a payment of 100,000 dinars. "This dispatch hardly amounts to one percent of the money we spent on fitting the troops sent to conquer Egypt."[42]

In the autumn of 1171 Saladin led his troops into Transjordan in a combined offensive with Nur al-Din against the great crusading castles of Karak and Shawbak, which controlled the routes linking Damascus with Egypt and the Hijaz, only to abandon the operation in mid-course on the pretext of internal disorders in Egypt. A second expedition to Transjordan a couple of years later was similarly suspended in a clear demonstration of Saladin's preference for a Frankish buffer zone over direct contiguity between his domains and those of his overlord. The fuming Nur al-Din announced his intention to go down to Egypt and drive his unruly subject from the country, sending a comptroller to audit Saladin's fiscal records while he mustered his troops for the confrontation. The threat seemed real enough to drive Saladin and his family to seek alternative safe havens, in Yemen and Nubia, for a rainy day. Had Nur al-Din not died on May 15, 1174, a showdown between him and Saladin would surely have ensued.[43]

"Nothing makes me so sad except the thought of what will befall my family on the part of Yusuf, the son of Ayyub." Nur al-Din's purported deathbed words proved prophetic.[44] No sooner had he passed away than Saladin moved to secure for himself Nur al-Din's vast empire, which rapidly broke up after his death. For twelve full years Saladin would occupy himself with this goal, paying scant attention to the jihad against the crusaders—so much so that his devoted secretary of state, Abdel Rahim Fadl, reproached him, saying: "How shall we turn aside to fight the Muslims, which is forbidden, when we are called to war against the people of war?"[45]

To the historian Hamilton Gibb, who takes at face value the pious portrayal of Saladin by his advisers and biographers, Imad al-Din al-Isfahani and Baha al-Din ibn Shaddad, this self-serving behavior was an inevitable outcome of the contemporary circumstances. "However unselfregarding [Saladin's] motives were," he argues, "the only way in which his object could be realized was by concentrating power in his own hands."[46]

To Saladin's contemporaries, the opposite of this assertion held true, namely that his elaborate holy-war propaganda was a fig leaf for an unabashed quest for self-aggrandizement. To the Zangids Saladin was a thankless usurper who exploited the power he had acquired in their service to disinherit them from their rightful possessions. To other local potentates he was a dangerous imperial contender who wanted to deprive them of their independence and who had therefore to be resisted by all means.

Such views were not so detached from reality. Had Saladin been truly alarmed by infidel presence in the midst of the House of Islam he would have supported Nur al-Din's operations in Transjordan, an important stepping stone for an assault on the Latin Kingdom. He could also have established an anti-crusading alliance with the Zangid princes and other warlords after Nur al-Din's death. That he instead chose to unify the region under his exclusive control, putting his family in the driver's seat and disparaging other Muslim contenders as enemies of Islam, indicated the supremacy of his imperial ambitions over his religious piety: nearly a decade before his death on March 4, 1193, and a few years before the capture of Jerusalem, he took the trouble to ensure the survival of his nascent empire by publicizing his last will and testament, which partitioned his territories among his three young sons.[47]

While he was busy fighting fellow Muslims for regional mastery, a fact that is deliberately omitted by his two official biographers, Saladin maintained a generally peaceful relationship with the crusader states, based on friendly correspondence and truce agreements. The intermittent clashes between them were largely sparked by Frankish violations of these agreements. At the same time he continued the profitable trade with the Italian city-states that had existed since Fatimid times, and cultivated the Byzantine Empire as a strategic counterweight to both Muslim and Christian potential rivals (in 1185 the two parties signed a formal treaty of alliance).[48]

Neither did Saladin attempt to undo the existing arrangements with the Franks in the territories that had come under his rule, such as the 1108 agreement between Damascus and the Latin Kingdom on the partition of the Golan Heights revenues. He was likewise intent on ensuring the smooth operation of the Levant trade, and it was the endangering of this trade by the prince of Karak, Reynald of Châtillon, that triggered the attack on the Karak castle in the summer of 1187, which set in train the process that led within a few months to the recapture of Jerusalem and the collapse of the Latin Kingdom.

This was not the first punitive action taken by Saladin against Reynald. As early as 1182 the reckless prince had attacked the rich caravans passing through his territory, in flagrant violation of a truce agreement signed two years earlier. He even launched a naval squadron in the Red Sea that harassed the sea traffic to Mecca and landed raiding parties on the Arabian coastline in an attempt to attack Islam's holiest cities. Saladin sent the Egyptian fleet to destroy the marauders, and in 1183 and 1184 besieged Karak for several months but failed to breach its formidable walls.[49]

This perhaps explains Saladin's reluctance to move against Reynald in early 1187, when the prince intercepted an exceptionally large caravan between Cairo and Damascus, and carried off substantial booty and a number of prisoners. Rather than retaliate for this act, Saladin attempted to secure the release of the caravan and compensation of its owners by diplomatic means. It was only when Reynald contemptuously dismissed this demand, which was backed by King Guy of Jerusalem, that Saladin mobilized his forces and declared a jihad. "The prince [Reynald], sovereign of the Franks at Karak, overwhelmed a large [Muslim] caravan and captured its members," ran the description of the medieval Egyptian historian Maqrizi (d. 1442) of the sequence of events leading up to this momentous watershed.

He refused to respond to the Sultan's wish for their release; therefore the Sultan prepared to attack him and wrote to the provinces to send troops against him. ... Al-Adel [Saladin's brother] marched from Cairo on the seventh of Muharram to Birkat al-Jubb. He moved on Karak, passing by Aylah [Eilat], and met the Sultan at al-Qaratayn. They both then returned to Karak which they invested during the month of Rabi al-Awwal [May

11–June 9] and reduced the garrison to sore straits. The Sultan then moved from Karak and lay before Tiberias. The Franks called a general muster of nearly 50,000 men in the Acre district, and raised the Crucifixion Cross above their heads.

On the twenty-third of Rabi al-Awwal [July 3, 1187] the Sultan took Tiberias by assault. The Franks were much enraged at this, and assembled their forces. The Sultan marched against them and on Saturday the twenty-fourth of this month [July 4, 1187] there took place the Battle of Hittin in which God gave victory to His creed.[50]

In other words, Islam's most celebrated triumph over the crusaders was not a result of a deliberate strategy of jihad or a concerted effort to uproot the infidel but a propitious coincidence. Had Reynald not raided a particular caravan at a specific moment in time, or had he agreed to release the prisoners and return the booty, this fateful encounter would have been postponed, if not averted altogether. Had the crusaders sent lighter forces to confront Saladin rather than the greatest army the kingdom had ever assembled, or adopted different battlefield tactics as suggested by some of their leaders, the consequences of the Hittin debacle would have been wholly different. Even at his moment of glory, Saladin hardly commanded most of the resources of the Muslim world. Not a few Muslim potentates were overtly hostile to him, including his nominal master—the Abbasid caliph Nasser. Although Saladin had taken care to gain the caliph's diploma of investiture for all his conquests, which he presented as being geared toward the ultimate goal of a holy war, Nasser remained unimpressed. Determined to restore the power of the caliphate vis-à-vis the numerous sultans ruling under its auspices, he viewed Saladin as yet another power-hungry overlord seeking to substitute his own house for the existing dynasties. Rather than congratulate Saladin on his spectacular achievement, the caliph sent him a scathing letter "rebuking him harshly and disapproving of his actions."[51]

Even Saladin's soldiers and commanders seemed to have lost their appetite for fighting shortly after the capture of Jerusalem on October 2, 1187. This was illustrated by the failure to capture Tyre in the winter of 1187–88, and the lackluster performance and increasing desertions in the war against the Third Crusade (1189–92), sparked by the fall of Jerusalem. When, on September 2, 1192, Saladin reached a truce agreement with King Richard the Lion-Heart of England, his troops were ecstatic. "The day when peace came was an auspicious day," wrote Maqrizi, "both sides showing universal joy and happiness after what had afflicted them for so long a war. The Frankish soldiers mixed with those of the Muslims, and a group of Muslims left for [Christian-held] Jaffa for trade. A great number of Franks entered Jerusalem to make the pilgrimage, and the Sultan received them with regard, giving them food and liberal hospitality."[52]

Reflecting neither a burning spirit of jihad nor an unwavering anti-Christian enmity, this behavior epitomized Saladin's career. For all his extensive holy-war propaganda, an essential component in a socio-political order based on the principle of religion, Saladin's attitude to the Frankish states was above all derived from his lifelong effort at empire-building. As long as they did not stand in the way of this endeavor he was amenable to leaving them in peace or even to maintaining a mutually beneficial economic and political relationship with them. But when a unique opportunity to land a shattering blow presented itself, he had no qualms about seizing the moment, just as he unhesitatingly ended hostilities when such action had outlived its usefulness. There was nothing personal about this behavior. It was strictly business.

"Now that we are done with the Franks and have nothing else to do in this country, in which direction shall we turn?" Ibn Athir has Saladin asking his brother Adel and his son Afdal prior to his death, before suggesting a possible course of action: "You [Adel] take some of my sons and a part of the army and advance to Akhlat [in present-day eastern Turkey]. When I have finished with Byzantium, I will join you and we will proceed into Azerbaijan, from where we will gain access to Iran. There is nobody there who can stop us."[53]

It is arguable that, for all his prodigious historiographical skills, Ibn Athir was a champion of the House of Zangi and therefore had a vested interest in presenting Saladin as a quintessential imperialist rather than a genuine holy warrior. Yet no such ulterior motives can be attributed to Saladin himself. In a letter to the caliph Nasser, after the death of Nur al-Din's son in 1181, he claimed to be the true heir to the Zangid legacy and espoused a grandiose imperialist design extending well beyond the liberation of Jerusalem and the destruction of the crusader states. Were he to be given possession of Mosul, Saladin hinted in an attempt to attract the interest of his suzerain, this would lead to the capture of Jerusalem, Constantinople, Georgia, and North Africa, "until the word of God is supreme and the Abbasid caliphate has wiped the world clean, turning the churches into mosques."[54]

In a conversation with his aide and biographer, Ibn Shaddad, eight years later, Saladin reiterated his imperial dream. "When God Almighty has enabled me to conquer the rest of the coast," he said, "I shall divide up the land [among my sons], make my testament, then cross this sea to their islands to pursue them until there remains no one on the face of the earth who does not acknowledge Allah—or I die [in the attempt]."[55]

The Last Great Islamic Empire

Saladin did not live to see his imperialist dream realized. In his last years he was forced to concede some of his gains to the Third Crusade and to acquiesce in the reconstitution of the Latin Kingdom, albeit on a more limited scale. After his death in 1193 the empire he had built was divided between members of his family, the Ayyubis, who maintained their rule in Egypt until 1250 and in Syria for a further decade. Lacking their great ancestor's expansionist drive and torn by fratricidal feuds, they spent most of their reign engaged in a rearguard action to secure their shrinking dominions. Their relations with the crusader states were largely peaceful, and they continued the thriving trade with the Italian city-states, in which the Frankish ports along the Mediterranean played an important role. In 1229, only forty-two years after Saladin's occupation of Jerusalem, his nephew surrendered the city to the Franks.[1]

It was thus left to the Ayyubis' formidable slave-soldiers, the Mamluks, who in 1250 ousted their masters in a military putsch, to deliver the *coup de grâce* to the independent Christian presence in the Middle East. In a series of brilliant campaigns, the general-turned-sultan Baybars I (1260–77) undermined the crusading infrastructure in the Galilee and the coastal plain. The process was completed in 1291 with the destruction of the last crusader strongholds and the displacement of their inhabitants.

There was, however, no great sense of exhilaration, no mass celebrations. The Frankish states had long been transformed from a Western bridgehead into an integral part of the Middle Eastern political landscape, largely alienated from their European roots. Their demise, received with indifference in Europe, was therefore no different from the decline and fall of numerous other Middle Eastern powers and dynasties. Nor was Baybars fired by a burning spirit of jihad. At the same time that he was fighting the Frankish states in the Levant he was also busy seeking alliances with the leading European powers. This practice was sustained by his successors, who maintained extensive commercial and diplomatic relations with the Europeans—

including the Kingdom of Aragon, which was actively eradicating the Islamic imperial presence in Spain.[2]

In line with the general pattern of Muslim-Christian relations during the preceding two centuries, the latest drive against the crusaders had less to do with the holy war against the infidel than with Mamluk imperial ambitions. Just as Saladin had portrayed the routing of his Muslim rivals as a prelude to a holy war against the Latin Kingdom, so the Mamluks destroyed the Ayyubi presence in Syria prior to turning on the Franks. In their quest for regional mastery they made no distinction between believer and non-believer. Both were equally legitimate targets whenever the need arose, and in the later part of the thirteenth century they could afford no hostile presence in their rear as they confronted a dangerous new invader from the east: the Mongol hordes.

These nomadic tribes, which had hitherto led a rather undistinguished existence on the fringes of eastern Asia, between Lake Baikal and the Altai Mountains, were transformed at the turn of the thirteenth century into an awesome military machine by one of their petty chiefs, who in 1206 took the title of Genghis Khan ("Universal Ruler"). Driven by an unwavering conviction of their God-given mandate to conquer and rule the world, the Mongols swept across the Asian steppes like wild fire, spreading death and destruction on an unprecedented scale. The first to feel their wrath was the Chin Empire in northern China. In 1211 the Great Wall was effortlessly breached and in the next five years the Mongols completed what has been estimated as the conquest of one hundred million people by one hundred thousand soldiers.

With this task accomplished, Genghis set his sights westward, smashed the Muslim forces in Central Asia, and reached as far as the Caucasus. The great commercial and cultural centers of eastern Islam were laid waste and their populations systematically exterminated. Khurasan and Iraq, the heart of the Islamic empire, were singled out for particularly brutal treatment: "Every town and every village has been several times subjected to pillage and massacre and has suffered this confusion for years, so that even though there be generation and increase until the Resurrection the population will not attain to a tenth part of what it was before." "I am the punishment of God," Genghis proudly proclaimed upon entering the city of Bukhara (1220). "If you had not committed great sins, God would not have sent a punishment like me upon you."[3]

Genghis died in 1227 and his vast empire, stretching from the Pacific to the Black Sea, was divided among his four sons. The best known of these successor kingdoms, or khanates as they were called, was the Golden Horde of the northern steppes, which quickly conquered most of Russia, Ukraine, southern Poland, Bulgaria, and Hungary up to the Adriatic Sea. Only the death of its khan in 1241 saved Europe from the Mongol yoke. Meanwhile another descendant of Genghis, Great Khan Mongke of Mongolia and northern China, set out to complete the conquest of Asia and appointed two of his brothers to command the ambitious campaign: Kubilai was to occupy China and Korea, Hulagu was to subdue "all the lands of the west."[4]

Hulagu set off from Mongolia in 1253, reaching the Middle East three years later, an inordinately long time by Mongol standards, a period that he used for meticulous preparations. His first target was the Assassins, who a few years earlier had sent hundreds of their killers to the Mongolian capital to murder Mongke. It was only after dealing with them that Hulagu moved against the Abbasid caliph. Summonses to submit were ignored, and on February 10, 1258, Baghdad fell to the Mongols. The terrified caliph, Mu'tasim, accompanied by his sons, ministers, and other members of his coterie, produced himself to Hulagu. He was forced to disclose his treasures and was ridiculed for having failed to put them to good use in the city's defense. Ten days later the hapless suzerain was taken to a neighboring village and executed, apparently by being rolled in a carpet and trampled to death by horses, as the superstitious Mongols would not shed royal blood by the sword.[5] Meanwhile Baghdad was thoroughly ravaged and plundered, with most of its inhabitants brutally slaughtered. So powerful was the stench of the unburied corpses that Hulagu was forced to withdraw temporarily from the city for fear of a plague.

Having dealt the *coup de grâce* to the clinically dead Abbasid Empire and deprived Islam of its titular figurehead, Hulagu crossed the Euphrates into northern Syria. After a fierce battle in January 1260 he occupied Aleppo and put its population to the sword. Shortly afterward, however, he was forced to return to Iran and to withdraw the bulk of his army from Syria to confront the attempt by the Golden Horde to exploit Mongke's sudden death for territorial gains in Central Asia. The depleted forces he left behind managed to take Damascus without a fight, but were destroyed in September 1260 by Baybars at the Galilean site of Ain Jalut (Goliath's Spring)—an often-overlooked historical turning point that probably saved the House of Islam from total collapse.

Five days after the battle the Egyptian sultan Kutuz (soon to be murdered and succeeded by Baybars) entered Damascus and within a month the Mongols had effectively lost control of Syria to the Mamluks. Although repeated incursions into Syria would continue into the second decade of the fourteenth century,[6] the battle of Ain Jalut irrevocably checked the Mongol westward advance, leaving them to concentrate on consolidating the territories under their control into a large autonomous kingdom (the so-called *ilkhanade*) comprising Iran, Iraq, the Caucasus, and Anatolia, under the aegis of the Great Khan of China.

Notwithstanding the horrific destructiveness of the Mongol irruption, probably the most devastating single blow to the House of Islam throughout the ages, its impact on the course of Middle Eastern history proved ephemeral. Like numerous barbarian invaders before them the Mongols brought no religious and cultural baggage of their own and so were quickly absorbed into the superior civilization they had conquered. Hulagu died a pagan in 1265, but his son Teguder (1282–84) became a Muslim, and during the reign of his great-grandson Ghazan (1294–1304) the Mongol ruling elite was converted to Islam and great efforts were made to reconstitute the wreckage left by their fearful ancestors.[7] Likewise, the Great Khan of the Golden Horde converted to Islam in the 1260s and by the early fourteenth century the entire khanate had been thoroughly Islamized. When a fresh wave of horrific Mongol campaigns was launched in the late fourteenth century by the Central Asian potentate Timur-i Lang (Timur the Lame, or Tamerlane in its Europeanized form), this was done in the name of Islam against its alleged enemies.

There was, however, one crucial and lasting consequence of the Mongol invasion. The rout and subjugation of the Seljuk sultanate of Rum, which had dominated most of Anatolia since the historic victory over the Byzantines at Manzikert (1071), triggered a mass migration of nomadic Turkish tribes to the mountainous ridges of western Anatolia to escape Mongol control. Here the émigré population was assimilated into the frontier society that had long existed along the Muslim-Byzantine fault line. This society was dominated by the distinct militant ethos of the *ghaza*, or holy war, reminiscent of Islam's earliest days, which combined the love of fighting and its spoils—booty, territory, and prestige—with unwavering religious commitment to world conquest through perpetual raiding and colonization of infidel dominions. Bands of *ghazis*, warriors for the faith, mushroomed throughout the country. They lived on the booty acquired in incessant fighting with their Byzantine counterparts, themselves mostly Turkish mercenaries.[8]

Now that the heathen Mongols had reduced the sultanate of Rum to vassalage, about a dozen small ghazi principalities (or *beyliks*) quickly stepped into the void, each named after its ruler. Officially they were subjects of the tottering Seljuk sultanate and its Mongol masters; in reality they were independent entities following their different paths to self-aggrandizement. The largest and strongest of them was the central Anatolian principality of Karaman, which controlled the former Seljuk capital of Konya, but the most vibrant were those of the far west, and none more so than the obscure little fiefdom named after its founder Osman Bey (1291–1326), or Ottoman as he would become commonly known.

On the face of it, the Ottoman position could not have been worse. Located on the farthest northwestern tip of Anatolia, not far from Constantinople, where Byzantine resistance was naturally at its most intense, the tiny principality seemed doomed to destruction. Yet it was paradoxically this inhospitable location that turned out to be the Ottomans' greatest asset and the springboard for their future transformation into a world power. Long after the rest of the beyliks had exhausted their expansive potential and settled for a short period of comfortable existence before degenerating into internal strife, the Ottomans were relentlessly fighting the Byzantine infidels. This frontier position imbued the Ottomans with a uniquely ferocious ghazi ethos that was to become the foundation stone of their corporate existence and to carry them to military and political greatness. As they saw it, the constant expansion of Muslim power was a predestined development in which they were chosen to act as Allah's Sword "blazing forth the way of Islam from the East to the West." This privileged role made it imperative for them to unify the House of Islam under their command and turned their fight against all Muslim rivals into a quintessential act of jihad.[9]

Osman himself rose from obscurity to widespread fame as early as 1301, when he routed a large Byzantine force south of Constantinople. Scores of volunteers from all over Anatolia flocked to his camp, eager to play an active role in what increasingly appeared as Islam's newest offensive against the Christian world. He bequeathed a militarily strong and substantially expanded beylik to his son Orhan (1326–60), who proceeded to eradicate the remnants of the Byzantine presence in Anatolia. In 1354 he obtained the first Ottoman foothold in Europe by crossing the straits and occupying the Gallipoli Peninsula. Shortly afterward the Ottomans stormed into southeastern Europe in the largest Muslim irruption since the invasion of Spain some 650 years earlier.

Orhan did not live to see his momentous move completed, but expansion continued apace under his son and successor, Murad I (1360–89), who quickly encircled Constantinople from the north by conquering the Thracian capital of Adrianople (Edirne) and adjacent territories. This brought the Ottomans into contact with the Bulgarians and the Serbs across the Balkan Mountains, and for the next two decades Murad steadily annexed their territories to his expanding domains. Fortunately for him, both countries were torn by domestic strife and thus could offer only desultory resistance. Many local potentates did not hesitate to seek Ottoman help, while the large peasant populations welcomed the Muslim invaders as providing relief from the oppressive yoke of their feudal lords. In 1385 Sofia fell to the Ottomans. The key Aegean port of Salonika followed two years later, and in June 1389 Murad scored his most spectacular success by crushing the Serbs in the battle of Kosovo. He was assassinated shortly afterward but his successor, Bayezid I (1389–1402), extended Ottoman rule to the Adriatic, and in September 1396 defeated a hastily organized crusade near the Bulgarian city of Nicopolis. On the heels of the advancing troops came waves of Turkish colonists who settled in the newly conquered Balkan territories, which were duly formed into the province of Rumelia ("the Roman lands").

Nothing could stop Turkish expansionism. Even the sudden emergence of Tamerlane's fearsome hordes, who routed Bayezid's armies and temporarily put the Ottomans' prospects in peril, failed to undermine their overall position. With the rapid disintegration of Tamerlane's empire after his death in 1405, the Ottomans recovered their lost territories and, on May 29, 1453, Mehmed II rode his white horse into Constantinople, making this proud city his new imperial capital and winning the honorific title of "The Conqueror."

For the West this was a dark moment. For Islam it was a cause for celebration. For nearly a millennium Constantinople had been the foremost barrier—both physically and ideologically—to Islam's sustained drive for world conquest and the object of desire of numerous Muslim rulers. Its fall at a time when the longest-surviving imperial Muslim outpost in Europe—Spain—was in its death throes could not but confirm the conviction of its conqueror of his predestination for world mastery. He was no longer a ghazi "blazing forth the way of Islam," or even the foremost sultan in the House of Islam. He was the head of a great empire stretching from the Black Sea to the very heart of Europe and the legitimate heir to the universal Byzantine Empire. Manifested by Mehmed's adoption of the title Sultan-i Rum—"Ruler of Rome" (or rather Byzantium)—and his determination to turn his new capital of Constantinople, or Istanbul as it would henceforth be called, into the leading world metropolis, this alleged continuity was to become a central component of the Ottoman claim to universal empire.

By the time of his death in 1481, Mehmed had completed the conquest of Greece, Serbia, and the Balkan territories south of the Danube, and had added the Crimean Peninsula to his domains, as the once-omnipotent Great Mongol Khan of the Golden Horde humbly accepted the status of Ottoman vassal. This effectively made the Black Sea an Ottoman lake and brought the important trade highway linking Russia and Central Asia with Europe under Ottoman control. Mehmed's grandson, Selim I (1512–20), extended the empire's rule to the Levant, Egypt, and the Hijaz, with its holy cities of Mecca and Medina. His great-grandson, Suleiman the Magnificent (1520–66), conquered Iraq and North Africa, brought most of Hungary under Ottoman rule, and established a firm foothold in southern Italy. In 1529 the Ottomans were knocking at the gates of Vienna. Even in remote Iceland the Lutheran Book of Common Prayer pleaded to God Almighty to save the people from "the terror of the Turk."[10]

For the first time since the early Abbasid era, most of the House of Islam was unified under a single imperial authority combining supreme religious and temporal power. As early as the end of the fourteenth century the Ottomans had styled themselves as caliphs, a claim that received a powerful boost once they had become "servitors of the two holy sanctuaries." The titular Abbasid caliphs, instated in Cairo after the Mongol destruction of the Baghdad caliphate to rubber-stamp Mamluk power, were driven out of office and the Ottoman sultans were recognized as caliphs throughout the Muslim world, aside from the Mughal emperors of northern India (1526–1858), who styled themselves as caliphs, if not Lords of the Universe, and Iran's Safavid dynasty (1501–1722), which adopted the Shiite creed and placed itself in lasting opposition to the Sunni Ottomans.

No sooner had the Ottoman Empire reached its apogee than it went into a prolonged and steady decline. Centrifugal pressures, degeneration, and bureaucratic and administrative mismanagement, all perennial problems that had plagued past Muslim empires, came to afflict the newest member of the imperial club. True to the Turkish proverb "the fish begins to stink from the head," decline spread from the top. Just as the spectacular Ottoman rise owed much to the ability to produce a long line of energetic and highly capable sultans, so its decline reflected a steep drop in the level of royal competence. Unlike their formidable ancestors, the sultans were far less interested in military campaigns and state affairs than in the majestic indulgences of hunting, the harem, and the heavenly promises held by drugs. Suleiman's son and successor was widely known as Selim "the Sot" (1566–74), while Selim's own son and heir, Murad III (1574–95), began his rule by having his five brothers strangled and was best known for his formidable procreative powers, fathering more than a hundred children.[11]

Rot pervaded the entire state apparatus. Bribery and favoritism, not merit, were the way to appointments and promotions. The armed forces, the cornerstone of the empire and the engine of its worldwide expansion, lost most of their celebrated qualities. As early as the fourteenth century, Murad and Bayezid had attempted to replace the existing ghazi system with Islamized slave-soldiers recruited from among the prisoners of war taken in the Balkan campaigns. This effort was interrupted by Tamerlane's invasion, but was renewed in earnest by Mehmed II in what heralded the basing of the armed forces on a hard core of elite slave-soldiers. Among these, the infantry corps of the Janissaries occupied pride of place. Drawn from carefully selected Christian boys from the subject populations of the Balkans who had been converted to Islam and brought up as a military elite totally loyal to the sultan, these warriors led the Ottoman armies to great successes. Yet by the seventeenth century they had degenerated into a self-indulgent hereditary caste that would go to almost any length to protect their privileged status, including the overthrow and murder of the sultan. All attempts at reform and modernization were summarily nipped in the bud.[12]

The economy underwent a gradual process of stagnation and decline as it had to support an increasingly expensive yet inefficient superstructure and pay for the rising cost of wars. The mainstay of the early Ottoman agrarian system, the fief-holding peasants who had cultivated the land and provided the empire with soldiers, arms, and horses in times of war, was progressively squeezed out of its livelihood. Leaseholders coalesced with landowners to create a new landed aristocracy that usurped functions and authority from the central government, with ordinary peasants having to pay the price of their caprices.

Trade relations with Europe further accelerated Ottoman economic decline. As the former was rapidly transformed from a net importer of manufactured goods to an exporter of produced commodities, the Ottoman Empire was beset by a huge trade deficit that drained it not only of raw materials and native industries but also of much of the gold and silver on which the imperial economy was heavily dependent. To make things worse, Western trade with the Ottoman Empire was legally regulated in the form of special concessions known as "Capitulations." These gave subjects of the Western powers extraterritorial privileges, allowing them to be ruled by the laws of their home countries while on Ottoman territory. Initially the capitulations were granted solely for the lifetime of the ruling sultan, but they gradually acquired permanence. Only in the nineteenth century did the sultans achieve an element of reciprocity in their commercial relations with the West, but even then the conceded benefits did not confer extraterritorial rights on the Ottoman subjects.

Neither was degeneration confined to the central government. It was acutely reflected throughout the empire, making central control over many of its possessions virtually impossible. Ottoman officials were both corrupt and hated. Anarchy and the reign of local chiefs and notables who disregarded the government's orders created widespread confusion, insecurity, and misery. Some of these declared their subservience to the sultan; others refused to recognize any Ottoman authority and openly defied the central government. The North African colonies were de facto independent, as was the European colony of Montenegro. Egypt was effectively run by Mamluk chieftains who paid little attention to the official rulers appointed by the sultan, while the Danubian principalities of Moldavia and Wallachia (modern-day Romania) were virtually autonomous, though formally ruled by a governor appointed by Istanbul. The Levant, split into countless power centers, was teeming with feuds among local chiefs and notables, and torn by ethnic and religious enmities. In the Arabian Peninsula, tribal rule was the only effective means of control, and Ottoman authority was repeatedly challenged by militant opponents such as the radical Wahhabi sect, established in the mid-eighteenth century by Muhammad ibn Abdel Wahhab and preaching a return to the "unspoiled" Islam of the seventh century. Even in Anatolia, from where the Ottomans had begun their world conquest, the empire's grip was far from complete. The malaise of the Ottoman Empire was vividly illustrated in 1757, when the sultan's sister was murdered during the hajj, the holy pilgrimage to Mecca.

External threats loomed increasingly large. The Habsburg dynasty, a traditional enemy of the Ottomans, vied with them for control over the Balkans, while Russia, the rising giant to the north, began expanding southward in search of territorial aggrandizement and a secure outlet to the Mediterranean. A grandiose Ottoman bid to arrest their declining fortunes broke against the walls of Vienna in September 1683, and from that moment onward the road downhill was rapid. In 1696 Tsar Peter the Great seized the port town of Azov, thus gaining the first, albeit temporary, Russian foothold on the Black Sea. In the peace treaty of Carlowitz of January 1699 the Ottoman Empire was forced, for the first time in its history, to cede extensive lands to the infidel. Less than a century later, another watershed in the Turkish decline was reached. On July 21, 1774, after a six-year war against Tsarina Catherine the Great, the Ottomans signed the treaty of Kuchuk Kainardji, which established Russia as the predominant naval power in the Black Sea, hitherto a Turkish lake, thereby giving it long-coveted access to the Mediterranean.[13] Nine years later Russia consolidated its Black Sea foothold by formally annexing the Crimea and extinguishing the Muslim Tatar khanate there.

This, however, was not the extent of Catherine's ambitions. An imperialist through and through, she aspired to nothing short of the dissolution of Turkey-in-Europe and the partitioning of its colonies among the European powers. Closest to her heart was the so-called "Greek Project," which envisaged the restoration under Russian protection of the Byzantine Empire with its original capital. Between 1788 and 1791 the Ottomans were confronted with a joint Russo-Habsburg offensive, which made major gains in the Balkans and ominously approached Istanbul. Fortunately for the sultan, the French Revolution and the rise of its extraordinary Corsican general, Napoleon Bonaparte, alarmed the European powers and diverted their attention from the east. In 1791 the Habsburgs made their peace with the Ottomans, and Russia contented itself the following year with far smaller territorial gains than it had originally envisaged.[14]

By the beginning of the nineteenth century, then, the Ottoman Empire had become a pale reflection of its former self. Confronted with widespread domestic instability and formidable external challenges, the Ottomans desperately vied to keep their heads above water. All attempts to reorganize and modernize the empire by equalizing the status of its non-Muslim subjects backfired as the Muslim populations were loath to compromise on their superior position in any way. A royal decree in 1839 (*Hatt-i Sherif of Gülhane*) triggered a violent revolt by the Muslim landowners in the provinces of Bosnia and Herzegovina, at the southwestern extreme of Turkey-in-Europe, which the authorities were unable to suppress for eleven years. The more far-reaching *Hatt-i Hümayun* of February 1856 sparked widespread riots throughout the Levant, which reached their horrific apogee in the spring and summer of 1860. Between twenty and twenty-five thousand Christians were brutally slaughtered in Lebanon and Damascus, while thousands perished of starvation and diseases and another hundred thousand were forcefully dislocated. Women were seized for harems; mothers were forced to sell their children. To this day the Maronites speak bitterly of the *Madhabih al-Sittin*, the Massacres of 1860.[15]

In a reflection of the wider Muslim resentment of the reforms, local Ottoman officials openly defied the decrees of their sublime suzerain. The governor of the province (*velayet*) of Damascus turned a blind eye to the atrocities perpetrated in his jurisdiction and forces under his command even took an active part in the massacres. In Lebanon, Ottoman troops were involved in the preparation and arming of the massacring Druze, while Turkish irregulars pillaged the hapless refugees. Small wonder that when the reforming sultan Abdul Mejid died in June 1861, Muslims in Syria burst out with cries of "Islam is saved."[16]

These numerous strands of hostility epitomized the hopelessness of the Ottoman reformers. Theirs was a Catch-22 situation. Whatever course of action they chose, they were bound to antagonize some of their subjects. The preservation of the tottering empire required tighter central control; the prevention of the religious, social, and economic cauldron from boiling over necessitated greater local freedoms. Even in the best of cases, such incompatible objectives are very difficult to reconcile. In non-consensual, multi-ethnic and multi-denominational empires, the chances of such reconciliations being achieved are virtually nil. All that can realistically be hoped for is a working balance between the constituent elements that will keep the empire going. In the Ottoman case, because of the stark reality of the empire's weakness, the gap between the imperial dream and the actual process of fragmentation was too wide to bridge through reform. Rather than putting the Ottoman house in order and reconciling its many differences, the reforms accelerated separatism and deepened existing schisms.

"We have on our hands a sick man—a very sick man. It will be . . . a great misfortune if, one of these days, he should slip away from us, especially before all necessary arrangements were made."[17] This stark prognosis, made by Tsar Nicholas I in 1853, was to become the standard metaphor of the Eastern

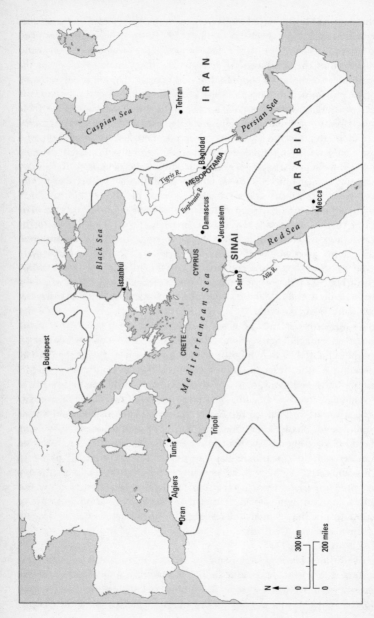

Map 5 The Ottoman Empire in the Late Eighteenth Century

Question, as Ottoman-European relations during the century preceding the destruction of the Muslim empire are commonly known. To many European contemporaries the question was not whether the Ottoman Empire would succeed in arresting its steady decline and fragmentation, but rather when it would actually gasp its terminal breath and what consequences this would entail for the balance of power on the continent. To latter-day historians, the story is similarly straightforward. Having long coveted the territories of the declining Ottoman Empire, the European powers exploited its entry into World War I in order to "fall upon the carcass" and carve up the defunct Muslim empire among themselves. As a veteran observer of Middle Eastern affairs put it: "So, the statesmen of Europe having decided in their wisdom that the Ottoman Empire was sick, therefore the Ottoman Empire had to die. This is the Eastern Question in a nutshell."[18]

The reality, however, was quite different. The Eastern Question was *not* an extended period "during which European powers slowly picked the Ottoman Empire to pieces,"[19] but one during which they tried to shore up the last great Muslim empire. To the Ottomans, it was the final hope of preserving their imperial status. To the Europeans, these were the high days of imperialism. The Ottomans created an empire among empires, and, apart from their strategic, economic, and political interest in Ottoman survival, the European powers were loath to knock a fellow empire out of existence, or rock the international imperial boat. This enabled the Ottomans to use their artificial resuscitation by Europe to gain an additional lease of life and even to outlive (if by a slim margin) their two formidable imperial rivals: the Habsburgs and the Romanovs.

Neither was the Ottoman Empire a passive spectator of European events. It was certainly "sick," and seriously so, but it would not just lie down and die. Instead, it would do whatever it took to survive, be that skillfully pitting its enemies against one another or using European support to arrest, and if possible reverse, domestic disintegration and external decline. The first such instance occurred in the late eighteenth century when Sultan Selim III (1789–1807), threatened by Napoleon Bonaparte's invasion of Egypt, turned to the European powers for help and was saved. Three decades later the Ottoman Empire crossed another threshold by using infidel Europe to escape certain destruction at the hands of one of its Muslim subjects, Egypt's governor Muhammad Ali, who sought to substitute his own empire for that of the Ottomans.

When in the early 1830s a large army headed by Muhammad Ali's illustrious son Ibrahim Pasha occupied most of the Levant and Anatolia all the way to the town of Kutahia, less than two hundred miles from the Ottoman capital, the sultan turned for help to the bête noire of the Ottoman Empire:

Russia. This was not a request Tsar Nicholas I had expected yet it was one he could not refuse. Not only did the Egyptian advances threaten the privileges granted to Russia by a succession of favorable treaties with Istanbul since 1774, but Muhammad Ali was viewed as a dangerous source of regional instability. Were the Ottoman Empire to collapse, a great-power struggle was certain to ensue in Russia's backyard. Hence, in April 1833 the Russians landed a task force near Istanbul and dispatched a naval squadron to the straits. This convinced the Egyptian pasha that the occupation of the Ottoman capital was no longer feasible, and that he had better strike a deal with the sultan. In the Peace of Kutahia, signed on May 5, 1833, Muhammad Ali received the governorships of Crete and the four Syrian provinces of Aleppo, Tripoli, Damascus, and Sidon, for which he was to pay an annual tribute, and was granted the right to collect taxes in Adana, in Anatolia. The Egyptian forces retreated behind the Taurus Mountains and the Russians withdrew from the Bosphorus.

Six years later, when an Ottoman attempt to drive the Egyptians from the Levant was defeated by Ibrahim, it was Britain's turn to act as the sultan's savior. With France breaking ranks with its peers and effectively siding with Muhammad Ali in a bid to consolidate its grip over Algiers, which it had occupied in 1830, the rest of the European powers convened in London and in July 1840 signed a series of defense agreements with the Ottoman Empire against "all aggression" by Muhammad Ali. The rebellious governor was offered the hereditary vice-royalty of Egypt under Ottoman suzerainty and, for his lifetime, the title of the pasha of Acre and the administration of the southern part of Syria. Were he to fail to accept within ten days, the lifetime concessions would be withdrawn; were he to procrastinate for a further ten days, he would lose the hereditary tenure of Egypt as well.[20]

As Muhammad Ali ignored these demands, the British fleet subjected Beirut to heavy bombardment, while Ottoman troops supported by British and Austrian marines attacked the Egyptian forces in Lebanon. On October 4, the port of Sidon fell, and soon afterward Beirut surrendered. When the British fleet appeared in Alexandria on November 15, Muhammad Ali understood that the game was up. By this time France had rejoined the pro-Ottoman great-power consensus, and the embittered pasha was not inclined to risk the future of his dynasty by taking on the combined powers of Europe. On November 27, he signed a convention on the evacuation of the Levant which recognized him as Egypt's hereditary governor. By February 1841, Ibrahim's forces had returned to Egypt.

No sooner had Sultan Abdul Mejid (1839–61) saved his empire from imminent destruction by a rebellious subject than he exploited European fears over Ottoman survival to escape his ill-conceived jihad against Russia. The conflict was sparked by the sultan's decision, in December 1852, to give Catholics custody of the holy shrines in Jerusalem, a rejection of the Orthodox demand for this privilege. Viewing this move as a denial of the religious rights of the Orthodox subjects of the Ottoman Empire, who, under the treaty of Kuchuk Kainardji, had been placed under Russian protection, Tsar Nicholas I demanded that the sultan rescind his decision and, moreover, place his Orthodox subjects under a Russian protectorate. As Abdul Mejid would not subordinate some ten million of his subjects to Russian rule, on May 27, 1853, the Russians broke diplomatic relations with the Ottoman Empire and warned that unless their demands were accepted within eight days, they would invade the Danubian principalities of Moldavia and Wallachia.[21]

The tsar was bluffing. War was the last thing on his mind. When in August 1853 the European powers devised a compromise proposal, Nicholas gave his assent within four days. The sultan, by contrast, equivocated for three weeks before rejecting the proposal. In a last-ditch attempt to prevent war, Nicholas agreed to give the sultan guarantees against Russian aggression provided the religious status quo of the Ottoman Orthodox was secured.

To no avail: Istanbul was set on a showdown. On September 25, 1853, the Ottoman Grand Council solemnly decided to wage a jihad and the sultan ratified the decision four days later. On October 4, the official declaration of war was conveyed to Russia with a demand that it withdraw from the principalities within a fortnight. When the ultimatum was rejected, an Ottoman force crossed the Danube, while other forces confronted the Russians in Erzurum and Kars, southeast of the Black Sea.

News of the conflagration was received with dismay by the European powers, which blamed the Ottomans for starting the conflict and feared an uncontrollable escalation. A peace proposal was thus announced on December 5, 1853, calling upon the tsar to respect Ottoman territorial integrity and to avoid weakening the sultan's control of his Christian subjects, and urging the sultan to abide by his earlier commitments to protect those subjects. The tsar accepted the plan within days, but as the European chancelleries sighed with relief at the prospect of the imminent suspension of hostilities, news of the sinking of a sizeable Ottoman flotilla by Russian ships near the Black Sea port of Sinope turned the tables on them.

Why this military encounter, which was neither significant enough to decide the Russo-Ottoman war nor to endanger seriously Ottoman prospects of survival, was to exert such a profound impact on the course of European history remains a mystery. The annals of history are littered with events that have been blown out of proportion, and the greater the event, the greater still the clamor. When the Ottoman cabinet was told of the Sinope debacle, its immediate reaction was one of complete disinterest; when news of the "massacre of Sinope" reached London and Paris, thousands of miles away from the scene of the events, the public cried out for war.

On January 4, 1854, the British and French fleets entered the Black Sea to protect the Ottoman Empire. The following month Russia broke off diplomatic relations with the two powers, and on March 12, following Russia's rejection of an ultimatum to withdraw from the Danubian principalities, Britain and France signed a defense alliance with the Ottoman Empire. When Nicholas responded by sending his troops across the Danube, Britain and France declared war on Russia on March 28. The Crimean War had begun.

By the time the guns fell silent in January 1856, after nearly two years of one of the bloodiest conflicts in modern European history, the Ottoman Empire had emerged as the war's undisputed winner. Having triggered a conflict they could not afford, the Ottomans effortlessly convinced the Europeans to fight it on their behalf, for the chain of events they had set in motion did the work for them. Consequently, the Ottoman Empire appeared to fight the Crimean War as a fully fledged member of a great-power coalition, rather than as the protected party it actually was. The postwar Congress of Paris, where the Ottoman Empire gained a collective guarantee for its security and was introduced into the prestigious great-power club, formally institutionalized this equality.

Nonetheless, the Ottomans failed to hold on to these gains. A general revolt in their Balkan provinces culminated in the spring of 1877 in yet another war with Russia, which ended in a crushing defeat and the imposition of draconian peace terms that virtually squeezed the Ottomans out of the Balkans.[22] This, however, did not end European interest in the continued survival of the Ottoman Empire. When in 1912–13 Istanbul was about to be overrun by a war coalition of the Balkan states seeking the termination of the Ottoman imperial presence in Europe, the great powers once more stepped in. The Russian foreign minister, Sergei Sazonov, offered to mediate between the warring parties and warned the Balkan states not to march on Istanbul, while the British foreign secretary, Sir Edward Grey, devised a compromise formula that led to the end of the war in May 1913. The Ottoman Empire had been saved yet again.

This is not to say that the Europeans did not encroach on Ottoman territories. One should recall the French occupation of Algeria (1830) and Tunisia (1881) and the Italian conquest of Libya (1911–12). But such nibbling at the edges of the empire was not uncommon among fellow imperialists, and had little effect on the Ottoman heartland. The only substantial great-power infringement on Ottoman territorial integrity—the British occupation of Egypt in 1882—was born of chance, not design, and was neither a premeditated act of imperial aggrandizement nor an attempt to sunder the Ottoman

Empire. Rather, in a vivid illustration of the limits of great-power control over Middle Eastern dynamics, the largest empire on earth found itself sucked into an undesirable regional crisis that it had done little to create and over which it exercised little control.

At the heart of the crisis was a group of Egyptian officers, headed by Colonel Ahmad Urabi, who since the fall of 1881 had challenged the authority of the country's ruler, Tawfiq Pasha, and his imperial master, the Ottoman sultan Abdul Hamid II. Initially, the anti-imperialist British prime minister William Ewart Gladstone paid little attention to the Egyptian imbroglio, and it was only in mid-May 1882, when the Egyptian situation seemed to be spiraling out of control, that an Anglo-French naval squadron arrived off Alexandria in a show of support for Tawfiq. This stirred a wave of anti-Christian violence that claimed the lives of fifty Europeans and caused a general uproar in London. Yet Gladstone kept his nerve, advocating the resolution of the crisis through a concerted diplomatic effort that would allow the sultan to reassert his authority over Egypt. An international conference thus convened in Istanbul on June 23 to discuss the Egyptian situation, with the participation of the great European powers.

The sultan, however, preferred to stay away from this multilateral effort on his behalf. Instead he sent his private secretary, Reshid Bey, to the British ambassador to Istanbul, Lord Dufferin, with the astounding proposal of giving Britain the exclusive control and administration of Egypt, with the sultan reserving to himself only those rights of suzerainty that he possessed at the time.

Had Britain been on the lookout to extend its imperial control over Egypt, as is widely believed,[23] there could have been no better opportunity to achieve it. Yet military intervention, let alone Egypt's physical occupation, was anathema to Gladstone and most of his ministers. Without much ado, Dufferin declined the offer. "Britain's principal aims are the maintenance of the sultan's existing rights and of the *status quo*," he said. "If the sultan were to hand over Egypt to us as a gift, with all Europe consenting, I doubt whether the British Government would accept such a burden and responsibility."

Reshid was evidently disheartened. He pleaded with Dufferin to convey the request promptly to his superiors, and to hand the official reply in person to the sultan. This came within a day. Gladstone and his foreign secretary Lord Granville found the idea so ludicrous that they dismissed it without consulting their fellow ministers. "We wish to see the sultan's sovereignty maintained without any limitation excepting those which have been conceded by the Firmans," Granville wrote to Dufferin. "Our wish for the present is that the Sultan should by sending troops to support the authority of the Khedive, free His Highness from the risk of the continuance or renewal of the military pressure which has been exercised against him, and restore the normal status quo."[24]

Confronted with Britain's refusal to occupy Egypt on his behalf, Abdul Hamid continued to equivocate. When on July 6 the international conference requested that Ottoman troops be sent to Egypt, the sultan refused, against the view of his ministers; a desperate offer by one of his most illustrious generals to go to Egypt, if only as the head of a battalion, also failed to do the trick. Even when on July 12, a day after the British squadron had bombarded the naval fortifications in Alexandria, Gladstone urged the sultan to exploit this extraordinary window of opportunity, Abdul Hamid could not bring himself to clinch the deal that might have saved his most prized Arabic-speaking province.[25] He dragged the negotiations out for months, constantly changing tack in accordance with the latest advice from his court. Particularly influential there was the xenophobic sheikh Abul Huda Sayyadi, an Arab from the province of Aleppo who arrived in Istanbul in 1878 to establish himself in the role of Abdul Hamid's Rasputin. He worked indefatigably to prevent an agreement with "infidel" Britain and warned the sultan of the (supposed) backlash it would cause among Muslim communities.

On September 15 Abdul Hamid invited Dufferin to his palace, and for eleven hours haggled with him over the amendments he wished to introduce into the Anglo-Ottoman agreement. Yet even at this stage the sultan failed to make up his mind. At 1.15 a.m. Dufferin's young secretary and brother-in-law, Arthur Nicolson, who waited with him for Abdul Hamid's reply, observed "the sinister figure of the sultan's astrologer [Abul Huda] creeping across the anteroom toward his master's room." Half an hour later the ambassador was duly informed that "His Majesty was unable to approve the compromise agreed to and further discussions would be required."

Unbeknown to Abdul Hamid, he had missed his last chance. As the distraught Dufferin arrived at the embassy, he was handed a ciphered telegram from the foreign minister Lord Granville stating that a British force had routed Urabi's army. The following day Gladstone outlined his ideas for an Egyptian settlement. British forces were to be withdrawn as soon as possible and Egypt set on the road to self-rule. Egyptian military and police forces were to be reorganized, self-governing institutions developed, and privileges enjoyed by the Europeans, such as exemption from taxation, terminated. The sultan's suzerainty over Egypt would be retained, albeit on a more restricted basis: he would still receive tribute, but he would not nominate the Egyptian ruler or command the service of Egyptian troops.

Dufferin was accordingly instructed to inform Abdul Hamid that "Her Majesty's Government contemplated shortly commencing the withdrawal of the British troops from Egypt." In a circular to the great powers on January 3,

1883, Granville promised that Britain would withdraw from Egypt "as soon as the state of the country, and the organization of proper means for the maintenance of the Khedive's authority, will admit of it." This promise was to be repeated sixty-six times between 1882 and 1922, when Egypt became an independent state.[26]

Table 2 The Ottoman Dynasty

Accession date	
1291	Osman I
1326	Orhan
1360	Murad I (assassinated)
1389	Bayezid I (died in captivity)
1402	Mehmed I (killed contending brothers in internecine strife)
1421	Murad II (abdicated the throne to his 12-year-old son Mehmed II)
1444	Mehmed II The Conqueror
1446	Murad II (second reign)
1451	Mehmed II The Conqueror
1481	Bayezid II (abdicated the throne)
1521	Selim I The Grim
1520	Suleiman I The Magnificent
1566	Selim II The Sot
1574	Murad III
1595	Mehmed III
1603	Ahmed I
1617	Mustafa I (deposed)
1618	Osman II
1622	Mustafa I (restored and subsequently deposed)
1623	Murad IV
1640	Ibrahim (deposed and murdered)
1648	Mehmed IV (deposed)
1687	Suleiman II
1691	Ahmed II
1695	Mustafa II (deposed)
1703	Ahmed III (abdicated the throne)
1730	Mahmud I
1754	Osman III
1757	Mustafa III
1774	Abdul Hamid I
1789	Selim III (murdered by rebellious troops)
1807	Mustafa IV (deposed)
1808	Mahmud II
1839	Abdul Mejid I
1861	Abdul Aziz (deposed)
1876	Murad V (deposed)
1876	Abdul Hamid II (deposed)
1909	Mehmed V
1918	Mehmed VI (deposed)
1922–24	Abdel Majid II (caliph only; deposed)

That despite such extensive support the Ottoman Empire steadily contracted, was mostly owing to internal fragmentation and decay, not external threats. However adept they were in manipulating European interests to their advantage, the Ottomans could not perform miracles. Like the other imperial powers, the Ottomans never found an adequate response to the ultimate challenge to empire of modern times: the rise of nationalism. In a relentless process of de-colonization, which was to afflict the Western empires in the mid-twentieth century, nationalism squeezed the Ottomans out of their European provinces, making Turkey-in-Europe the most violent area of the continent between the Napoleonic upheavals and World War I.

It was indeed the desire to redress these imperial setbacks that largely accounted for the Ottoman decision to enter World War I. This was by far the single most important decision in the history of the modern Middle East, and it was anything but inevitable. The Ottoman Empire was neither forced into the war by a last-ditch attempt to ensure its survival, nor manipulated into it by an overbearing German ally and an indifferent, or even hostile, British policy. Rather, it found itself in the highly enviable position of being courted by both warring camps: the Central Powers (notably Germany and Austro-Hungary) wished for its participation, the Anglo-Franco-Russian Entente hoped that it would stay out.

As early as August 7, 1914, about a month after the outbreak of hostilities, the foreign secretary, Edward Grey, disavowed any idea of "injuring Turkey" and emphatically denied Ottoman allegations of a British plan to alter the status of Egypt—which officially remained an Ottoman province. When a week later the first lord of the admiralty, Winston Churchill, sent a personal letter to the minister of war, Enver Pasha, to warn him of the folly of an alliance with Germany, Grey inserted an unequivocal piece of reassurance: "If Turkey remains loyal to her neutrality, a solemn agreement to respect the integrity of the Turkish Empire must be a condition of any terms of peace that affect the Near East."[27]

Approached by Sazonov with a proposal for a tripartite declaration to the same effect, Grey gave his immediate consent. "As soon as French and Russian Ambassadors are similarly instructed," he wrote to the British chargé d'affaires in Istanbul on August 16, "you are authorised to declare to [the] Turkish Government that if Turkey will observe scrupulous neutrality during the war England, France, and Russia will uphold her independence and integrity against any enemies that may wish to utilise the general European complication in order to attack her." Two days later Grey reassured the Ottoman ambassador to London that his empire's territorial integrity "would be preserved in any conditions of peace which affected the Near East, provided she preserved a real neutrality during the war." On the same day, August 18, the British, French, and

Russian ambassadors to Istanbul gave the grand vizier a tripartite guarantee of Ottoman territorial integrity in return for Ottoman neutrality. Five days later, at Ottoman request, the Triple Entente put this guarantee in writing.[28]

The significance of this proposal cannot be overstated. The Ottoman Empire was effectively offered a defense pact—*and assured postwar survival*—at no price at all. Still the Ottoman leadership failed to seize the moment. Why? Because the triumvirs who had dominated the empire's political scene since seizing power in a violent putsch in January 1913—Minister of the Interior Talaat Pasha, Minister of War Enver Pasha, and Minister of the Marine Djemal Pasha—were avowed admirers of Germany and were convinced of its ultimate triumph in the conflict.

Within days of the assassination of the Austro-Hungarian heir apparent, Archduke Franz Ferdinand, in Sarajevo on June 28, 1914, Enver reportedly made his first secret overture to Berlin for an alliance,[29] and on August 2 the German ambassador to Istanbul and the grand vizier affixed their signatures to the secret alliance treaty.[30] To German dismay, however, instead of declaring war on Russia as required by the newly signed agreement, the Ottoman Empire mobilized its forces and proclaimed a position of armed neutrality. While this proclamation was evidently phony—the alliance treaty had legally made the Ottoman Empire a combatant in the European conflict—the agreement's secretive nature allowed Enver to extract material and political benefits simultaneously from Germany, which was keen to see the treaty's immediate implementation, and from the Entente powers, whose eagerness to keep the Ottoman Empire out of the war made them susceptible to believing the most incredible Ottoman lies.

Even when, on October 29, two German cruisers attacked the Black Sea port of Sebastopol, while Ottoman torpedo boats attacked Russian vessels in Odessa in a blatant act of aggression that could have constituted a perfectly legitimate *casus belli* against the Ottoman Empire, the Entente *still* sought to avoid war. Repudiating the absurd Ottoman apology, which blamed Russia for the attack and offered to settle the matter amicably, Sazonov gave Istanbul a last chance to avert war: the immediate dismissal of all German military officers in the Ottoman army and navy as required by its proclamation of neutrality. London and Paris followed suit. The British ambassador to Istanbul pleaded with his superiors to exercise the utmost restraint, for there was still a chance that the anti-German faction, which he wrongly believed to exist within the Ottoman government, would prevail. But he was instructed by Grey to warn the Ottoman leaders that unless they promised, within twelve hours, to divest themselves "of all responsibility for these unprovoked acts of hostility by dismissing the German military and naval missions," he would have to leave Istanbul with the staff of the embassy.[31]

The Entente was asking for the impossible. The Ottomans had attacked Russia not with the intention of averting war but in the hope of triggering it. For months Enver and his associates had been patiently laying the groundwork for what they saw as a historic chance to reverse centuries of Ottoman decline and to reach new imperial vistas, and they were not going to let this golden opportunity slip from their grasp—as their proclamation of war attested: "Our participation in the world war represents the vindication of our national ideal. The ideal of our nation and people leads us toward the destruction of our Muscovite enemy to obtain a natural frontier to our empire, which should include and unite all branches of our race."[32]

The Price of Empire

Nearly a century after the Ottomans' disastrous decision to enter World War I on what turned out to be the losing side, culpability is still apportioned to the European powers for having supposedly driven the hapless Muslim empire into this world conflict.[1] With the passage of time, moreover, and in contrast to their scathing indictment of the legacy of Western imperialism, scholars and pundits have come to idealize the Ottoman colonial order as a shining example of tolerance vis-à-vis colonial subjects. "The multi-ethnic Ottoman Turkish Empire," wrote American journalist Robert Kaplan,

> was more hospitable to minorities than the uni-ethnic democratic states that immediately succeeded it. The Ottoman caliphate welcomed Turkish, Kurdish, and other Muslims with open arms, and tolerated Christian Armenians and Jews . . . Ottoman toleration was built on territorial indifference. Because the same loosely administered imperial rule extended from the Balkans to Mesopotamia, and as far south as Yemen, minorities could live anywhere within this space without provoking issues of sovereignty. Violent discussions over what group got to control which territory emerged only when the empire came to an end, after World War I.[2]

The American academic Edward Said was similarly impressed by Ottoman colonialism—so much so that he advocated the destruction of the State of Israel and the relegation of its Jewish population to a minority group on the lines of the Ottoman colonial model. "I don't find the idea of a Jewish state terribly interesting," he argued.

> We can find other models from the past other than the separationist, partition model . . . in a funny sort of way, it worked rather well under the Ottoman Empire with its [religiously based] *millet* system . . . Of course, there were inequities. But they lived without this ridiculous notion that

every *millet* has to have its own state . . . What they had then seems a lot more humane than what we have now.[3]

It is doubtful whether the former Ottoman subjects would share this view. The imperial notion, by its very definition, posits the domination of one ethnic, religious, or national group over another, and the Ottoman Empire was no exception. It might have tolerated the existence of vast non-Muslim subject populations in its midst, as did earlier Muslim (and non-Muslim) empires, but only provided that these acquiesced in their legal and institutional inferiority in the Islamic order of things. Whenever these groups dared to question this status, let alone attempt to break free from the Ottoman colonial yoke, they were brutally suppressed.

The simmering tension between the Ottomans and their more nationally aware subjects first boiled over in Greece, when in January 1822 a newly convened National Assembly adopted a constitution, elected the first president of the Hellenic Republic, and issued a Declaration of Greek Independence: "The Greek nation calls Heaven and Earth to witness that in spite of the dreadful yoke of the Ottomans, which threatened it with destruction, it still exists."[4]

To Sultan Mahmud II (1808–39), the declaration was an unabashedly treacherous act. The Greeks were the most privileged and prosperous of his Christian subjects, enjoying a high degree of autonomy and achieving pride of place in the empire's administrative and commercial life, and the sultan saw no conceivable reason for them to bite the hand that fed them. As far as he was concerned, the Greeks were a subject people, had always been and would always be. The notion of an independent Greek nation-state on a par with its imperial master was not only an unspeakable affront to Ottoman-Muslim dignity but also a subversive ideal that could undermine the very foundations of the Ottoman colonial order:

Whereas it has become a sacred duty upon all and every member professing the Mahomettan Faith, from first to last to form themselves in one body [i.e., the universal umma] . . . the encouragement of such idle reports [that is, nationalist sedition] would, God forbid, be a means of operating with those very purposes which are peculiar to the infidel race, and be the cause of rendering dissension permanent among the Mussulmans: which is unworthy of man professing the true Faith . . . We are true believers, and all in strict union together.[5]

Before long, the Ottoman-Greek confrontation deteriorated into an endless exercise in violence. Almost immediately the Greek rebels embarked on wanton massacres of their hated Muslim masters, with the Ottomans responding with ferocious attacks on Greek quarters in the towns of Anatolia. In Istanbul itself, the sultan shocked all of Christendom, especially Orthodox Russia, by having the venerable patriarch, Gregorius V, publicly hanged at dawn on Easter Day.[6] It mattered not that Gregorius had preached restraint to his congregation; as far as the sultan was concerned, the patriarch, as the head of the Orthodox millet, was the guarantor of the community's loyalty. Having failed to deliver this, he had to pay the ultimate price.

As his forces failed to subdue the uprising, Mahmud II was gradually pushed to approach the Egyptian governor Muhammad Ali, promising him the island of Crete in return for his services. The ambitious viceroy agreed and sent his son Ibrahim Pasha to crush the Greek revolt. This Ibrahim did with great enthusiasm, sending a bag of rebels' ears to Istanbul to prove his efficiency. He was then ordered to move against the Greek mainland, after Muhammad Ali had extracted further concessions from the sultan. By early June 1827 the Greek garrison in Athens had been forced to surrender.

This alarmed the European powers, which feared the all-out destruction of the Greeks, and on February 3, 1830, after three more years of bloodshed and mayhem, an international conference in London ceremoniously declared that "Greece shall form an independent State."[7] Greece's new government was to be a monarchy, and its territorial integrity would be guaranteed by Britain, Russia, and France. On May 7, 1832, the three powers, together with Bavaria, signed a convention that named Prince Otto of Bavaria the king of Greece, and provided for a much-needed loan for the new monarch, who arrived in Athens in February 1833.

This was a truly revolutionary development for the Ottoman Empire, signaling the first loss of territory to the rising force of nationalism and the onset of a steady process of decolonization that was to squeeze it out of its European provinces by the end of the nineteenth century. The next chapter in this saga unfolded in the Danubian principalities of Moldavia and Wallachia in the summer of 1848, when a revolutionary government adopted a constitution that abolished feudal rights and social distinctions and declared an independent Romania, comprising the two principalities. And while the Ottomans managed to arrest this development temporarily with the support of the European powers, which were equally anxious to stem the mounting tide of nationalism before it wrecked their own empires, by the mid-1870s the Danubian crisis had been fully rekindled, this time developing into a string of revolts across the Balkans.

The Balkan powder keg was sparked in July 1875 by a peasant uprising in the province of Herzegovina, at the southwestern extreme of the Ottoman Empire in Europe, which spread rapidly to engulf the neighboring province of

Bosnia. "Dead bodies were lying in various corners unburied; and we noticed the head of a boy in one of the streets blackening in the sun," the British consul in Sarajevo reported of a typical "battlefield" scene: "A little Turkish girl was brought to us, wounded in the throat, and we were told that an insurgent was on the point of cutting off her head when she was snatched from him. . . . as far as could be ascertained some fifty or sixty persons perished on both sides during the attack [on the previous day]."[8] Ottoman efforts to suppress the insurrection triggered a cycle of violence, and before long the turmoil in Bosnia–Herzegovina was reverberating throughout the region. In Serbia and Montenegro nationalist passions were flying high. In the port town of Salonika, foreign consuls were murdered. A revolt in Bulgaria in September 1875 invoked the Bosnian insurrection as "the spark which will set the whole Balkan Peninsula in flames . . . [and will] lay the Turkish monarchy in ruins."[9] This prognosis proved somewhat premature, as the revolt was brutally suppressed, but a year later the Bulgarians rose again in the Balkan Mountains, supported by Serbia and émigré revolutionaries. The Ottoman authorities responded heavy-handedly, and the uprising deteriorated into a bloodbath. Massacres of Bulgarians and the destruction of villages by Turkish irregulars and equally gruesome atrocities by the rebels became commonplace. By June 1876 the Ottomans had suppressed the uprising, only to be confronted with Serb and Montenegrin declarations of war.

Unlike Bosnia and Herzegovina, the Serb and Montenegrin move was no spontaneous and poorly organized insurrection but a carefully planned revolt by the two most powerful South Slav nations, determined to substitute their own regional empire for the existing colonial subjugation. Yet the Ottomans had no intention of simply packing their bags and leaving. The graver the threat to their empire, the harsher their response became. Although Montenegro scored some initial successes, Serbia was soon brought to its knees. Rumors of a Serbo-Russian alliance, setting off loud alarm bells in Istanbul, turned out to be baseless. Not only had Russia not been consulted on the war, it would also not support the insurgents and made it eminently clear that if Serbia committed aggression against the Ottoman Empire, Russia would abandon it to its fate. At a meeting on July 8, a week after the Serbian declaration of war, the Russian and Habsburg foreign ministers decided not to intervene in the new conflict and agreed that none of the belligerents would be allowed to reverse the status quo ante bellum in the event of victory. This meant that the Serbo-Montenegrin dream of a South Slav empire could not be achieved, and in September 1876 the Ottomans routed the Serbs and advanced on Belgrade.

Had the Ottomans stopped at this point and accepted a European pacification plan for the region, they would have retained their Balkan provinces. Yet intoxication with their Serbian exploits, exacerbated by the deeply troubled personality of the new sultan, the thirty-five-year-old Abdul Hamid II, who, on August 31, 1876, replaced his half-brother, Murad V, on the throne, precluded such an eventuality. Notwithstanding his pledges of reform, which had helped him to gain power in the first place, Abdul Hamid was imbued with pan-Islamic ideals: religious conservatism, not Western-type reform, was for him the key to restoring imperial glory. Suspicious to the point of paranoia, the new sultan lived in constant fear of domestic conspiracies and foreign machinations. He surrounded himself with an elaborate system of spies and double agents, going so far as to have all the water pipes in his palace disinterred under his own watchful eyes and replaced with new ones, running closer to the surface, to ensure that any attempt to use them for bad purposes would be instantly detected.

Aggravated by these psychological pressures, Abdul Hamid's near-messianic commitment to the preservation of Ottoman Islamic order was to have a profound impact on the domestic and foreign affairs of the empire for more than three decades. In the turbulent months of 1876 and 1877, it undermined the international efforts toward a peaceful resolution of the Balkan conflict and landed the Ottoman Empire in a disastrous war with Russia, brought to an end by the March 1878 peace treaty of San Stefano, which effectively squeezed the Ottoman Empire out of the Balkans.

Although these setbacks were somewhat reversed by a great-power congress that convened in June 1878 in the German capital of Berlin, half a millennium of Ottoman imperialism in Europe was to all intents and purposes at an end as the Muslim empire was forced to give up most of its European colonies aside from a tenuous foothold on the continent. The independence of Romania, Montenegro, and Serbia, proclaimed in San Stefano, was reaffirmed, while eastern Rumelia south of the Balkan Mountains, where the Ottomans had established their initial colonial presence, was placed under a Christian governor and made semi-autonomous. Greece received Thessaly and part of Epirus, Bosnia and Herzegovina passed to Austro-Hungarian control, and Russia received southern Bessarabia and the Asiatic territories of Kars, Ardahan, and the port of Batum on the Black Sea. Only in Macedonia and a smallish Bulgaria, completely severed from the Aegean, did the Ottomans manage to maintain a semblance of their former imperial rule.

The sixty-year orgy of bloodletting and mayhem attending the Ottoman Empire's rearguard action to keep its reluctant European subjects under its domination pales in comparison with the treatment meted out to the foremost nationalist awakening in Turkey-in-Asia: that of Armenia.[10]

By the second half of the nineteenth century the Armenian population of the Ottoman Empire totaled some two million, three-quarters of whom resided in so-called Turkish Armenia, namely, the velayets of Erzerum, Van, Bitlis, Sivas, Kharput, and Diarbekir in eastern Anatolia. The rest, about half a million Armenians, were equally distributed in the Istanbul–eastern Thrace region and in Cilicia, in southwestern Anatolia.[11]

As a result of Russian agitation, European and American missionary work, and, not least, the nationalist revival in the Balkans, a surge of national consciousness began to take place within the three Armenian religious communities—Gregorian, Catholic, and Protestant. In the 1870s Armenian secret societies sprang up at home and abroad, developing gradually into militant nationalist groups. Uprisings against Ottoman rule erupted time and again; terrorism became a common phenomenon, both against Turks and against non-compliant fellow Armenians. Nationalists pleaded with the European chancelleries to enforce Ottoman compliance with the 1878 Berlin Treaty, which had obliged the empire to undertake "improvements and reforms demanded by local requirements in the provinces inhabited by the Armenians, and to guarantee their security against the Circassians and Kurds." But the great powers were reluctant to weaken the Ottoman Empire in any way, and Abdul Hamid made the best of this reluctance. In a brutal campaign of repression in 1895–96, in which nearly 200,000 people perished and thousands more fled to Europe and America, Armenian resistance was crushed and the dwindling population cowered into submission.

But not for long. Armenian nationalism continued to breathe beneath the embers, and by the early 1910s, despite years of cultural repression, including a ban on the public use of the Armenian language and a new round of horrendous massacres (in the spring of 1909), it had been fully rekindled. In April 1913, for example, Armenian nationalists asked Britain to occupy Cilicia, from Antalya to Alexandretta, and to internationalize Istanbul and the straits as a means of "repairing the iniquity of the Congress of Berlin," which had stipulated Ottoman reforms "in the provinces inhabited by the Armenians." At about the same time, a committee of the Armenian National Assembly, the governing body of the Apostolic Ottoman Christians, submitted to the Russian embassy in Istanbul an elaborate reform plan for Ottoman Armenia.[12]

Bowing to international pressure, in February 1914 the Ottoman authorities accepted a Russo-German proposal for the creation of two large Armenian provinces, to be administered by European inspector-generals appointed by the great powers. This was a far cry from the Armenians' aspirations for a unified independent state, yet it was the most significant concession they had managed to extract from their suzerain, and most of them were anxious to preserve this gain, come what may. Hence, when the Ottoman Empire entered World War I the Armenians immediately strove to demonstrate their loyalty: prayers for an Ottoman victory were said in churches throughout the empire, and the Armenian patriarch of Istanbul, as well as several nationalist groups, announced their loyalty to the Ottoman Empire and implored the Armenian masses to perform their obligations to the best of their ability.

Not all Armenians complied with this wish. Scores of Ottoman Armenians, including several prominent figures, crossed the border to assist the Russian campaign. Others offered to help the Entente by different means. In February 1915, for example, Armenian revolutionaries in the Cilician city of Zeitun pledged to assist a Russian advance on the area, provided they were given the necessary weapons; to the British they promised help in the event of a naval landing in Alexandretta.[13]

Although these activities were an exception to the otherwise loyal conduct of the Armenian community, they confirmed the Ottoman stereotype of the Armenians as a troublesome and treacherous people. This view was further reinforced by a number of crushing defeats in the Caucasus, in which (non-Ottoman) Armenians were implicated in the Russian war effort. Above all, as the largest nationally aware minority in Asiatic Turkey, the Armenians consti-tuted the gravest internal threat to Ottoman imperialism in that domain; and with Turkey-in-Europe a fading memory and Turkey-in-Africa under Anglo-French-Italian domination, the disintegration of Turkey-in-Asia would spell the end of the Ottoman Empire, something that its rulers would never accept.

Before long the Ottoman Armenians were subjected to the kind of retribu-tion that had been inflicted on rebellious Middle Eastern populations since Assyrian and Babylonian times: deportation and exile. First the Armenians had to be rendered defenseless; then they were to be uprooted from their homes and relocated to concentration camps in the most inhospitable corners of Ottoman Asia. The Armenians' towns and villages would then be populated by Muslim refugees, their property seized by the authorities or plundered by their Muslim neighbors.

Whether or not there was a premeditated genocidal master plan, something that contemporary Ottoman leaders and latter-day Turkish politicians and academics would persistently deny, is immaterial. It must have occurred to the Ottoman leadership that the destruction of such a pervasive nationalist move-ment would inevitably entail suffering on an enormous scale, and that the forceful relocation of almost an entire people to a remote, alien, and hostile environment amid a general war was tantamount to a collective death sentence. In the end, whatever their initial intention, the Ottoman actions constituted nothing short of genocide.[14]

The first step in this direction was taken in early 1915, when the Armenian soldiers in the Ottoman army were relegated to "labor battalions" and stripped of their weapons. Most of these fighters-turned-laborers would never get the opportunity to toil for their suzerain: they would be marched out in droves to secluded places and shot in cold blood, often after being forced to dig their own graves. Those fortunate enough to escape summary execution were employed as laborers in the most inhumane conditions.

At the same time, the authorities initiated a ruthless campaign to disarm the entire Armenian population of all personal weapons. This sent a tremor throughout Armenia: the 1895–96 massacres had been preceded by similar measures, and most Armenians had no illusions regarding the consequences of surrendering their arms while their Muslim neighbors were permitted to retain theirs. Nonetheless, the community's religious and political leaders persuaded their reluctant flock to do precisely that in order to avoid harsh retaliation by the government. But even this was not a simple task. The Ottoman authorities demanded that the Armenians produce a certain number of weapons, regardless of the actual number of arms-bearers, thus putting many Armenians in an impossible position: those who could not produce arms were brutally tortured; those who produced them for surrender, by purchase from their Muslim neighbors or by other means, were imprisoned for treachery and similarly tortured; those found to have hidden their arms were given even harsher treatment.

With the Armenian nation rendered defenseless, the genocidal spree entered its main stage: mass deportations and massacres. Having ethnically cleansed Cilicia by the autumn of 1915, the authorities next turned their sights to the foremost Armenian settlement area: the velayets of eastern Anatolia. First to be cleansed was the zone bordering Van, extending from the Black Sea to the Iranian frontier and immediately threatened by Russian advance; only there did outright massacres often substitute for otherwise slow deaths along the deportation routes or in the concentration camps of the Syrian desert.

The main executioner was Djevdet Pasha, the brother-in-law of the minister of war, Enver Pasha, who, in February 1915, was made governor of Van. A sadist known throughout Armenia as the "horseshoer of Bashkale" for his favorite pastime of nailing horseshoes to the feet of his victims, Djevdet inaugurated his term in office by slaughtering some eight hundred people—mostly old men, women, and children. By April the death toll had risen to ten thousand, and in the following months the population of the Van zone would be systematically exterminated. In the western and northwestern districts of Ottoman Armenia, depopulated between July and September, the Turks attempted to preserve an appearance of a deportation policy, though most deportees were summarily executed after hitting the road. In the coastal towns of Trebizond, for example, the authorities sent Armenians out to sea, ostensibly to be deported, only to throw them overboard shortly afterward. Of the deportees from Erzerum, Erzindjan, and Baibourt, only a handful survived the initial stages of the journey.

The Armenian population in western Anatolia and in the metropolitan districts of Istanbul was somewhat more fortunate, as many people were transported in (grossly overcrowded) trains for much of the deportation route, rather than having to straggle along by foot. In Istanbul, deportations commenced in late April, when hundreds of prominent Armenians were picked up by the police and sent away, most of them never to be seen again; some five thousand "ordinary" Armenians soon shared their fate. Though the majority of the city's 150,000–strong community escaped deportation, Armenians were squeezed out of all public posts, with numerous families reduced to appalling poverty. Deportations in Ankara began toward the end of July; in Broussa, in the first weeks of September; and in Adrianople, in mid-October. By early 1916 scores of deportees, thrown into a string of concentration camps in the Syrian desert and along the Euphrates, were dying every day of malnutrition and diseases; many others were systematically taken out of the camps and shot.[15]

The Ottoman authorities tried to put a gloss of legality and innocence on their actions. The general deportation decree of May 30, 1915, for example, instructed the security forces to protect the deportees against nomadic attacks, to provide them with sufficient food and supplies for their journey, and to compensate them with new property, land, and goods necessary for their resettlement. But this decree was a sham. For one thing, massacres and deportations had already begun prior to its proclamation. For another, the Armenians were never informed of its existence, hence could not even hypothetically have insisted on its observance. Most important, as is overwhelmingly borne out by the evidence, given both by numerous first-hand witnesses to the Ottoman atrocities and by survivors, the rights granted by the deportation decree were never honored.

Take the provisions for adequate supplies for the journey and compensation for the loss of property, for example. After the extermination of the male population of a particular town or village, an act normally preceding deportations, the Turks often extended a "grace period" to the rest of the populace, namely, women, children, and the old and the sick, so they could settle their affairs and prepare for their journey. But the term normally given was a bare week, and never more than a fortnight, which was utterly insufficient for all that had to be done. Moreover, the government often carried away its victims before the stated deadline, snatching them without warning from streets, places of employment, or even their beds. Last but not least, the local authorities prevented the deportees from selling their property or their stock under the official fiction that their expulsion was to be only temporary. Even in the rare cases in which Armenians managed to dispose of their property, their Muslim neighbors took advantage of their plight to buy their possessions at a fraction of their real value.[16]

Nor did the deportees receive even a semblance of the protection promised by the deportation decree. On the contrary, from the moment they started on their march, indeed even before they had done so, they became public outcasts, never safe from the most atrocious outrages, constantly mobbed and plundered by the Muslim population as they straggled along. Their guards connived at this brutality. There were, of course, exceptions in which Muslims, including Turks, tendered help to the long-suffering Armenians; but these were very rare, isolated instances.

Whenever the deportees arrived at a village or town, they were exhibited like slaves in a public place, often before the government building itself. Female slave markets were established in the Muslim agglomerations through which the Armenians were driven, and thousands of young Armenian women and girls were sold in this way. Even the clerics were quick to avail themselves of the bargains of the white slave market.

Suffering on the deportation routes was intense. Travelers on the Levantine railway saw dogs feeding on the bodies of hundreds of men, women, and children on both sides of the track, with women searching the clothing of the corpses for hidden treasure. In some of the transfer stations, notably Aleppo, the hub where all convoys converged, thousands of Armenians would be left for weeks outdoors, starving, waiting to be taken away. Epidemics spread rapidly, chiefly spot typhus. In almost all cases the dead were not buried for days, the reason being, as an Ottoman officer cheerfully explained to an inquisitive foreigner, that it was hoped the epidemics might get rid of the Armenians once and for all.

Independent estimates of the precise extent of the Armenian genocide differ somewhat, but all paint a stark picture of national annihilation of unprecedented proportions. In his official report to the British parliament in July 1916, Viscount Bryce calculated the total number of uprooted Armenians during the preceding year as 1,200,000 (half slain, half deported), or about two thirds of the entire community. Johannes Lepsius, the chief of the Protestant Mission in the Ottoman Empire who had personally witnessed the atrocities and had studied them thoroughly, put the total higher, at 1,396,000, as did the American Committee for Armenian and Syrian Relief, which computed the number of deaths at about 600,000 and of deportees at 786,000. And Aaron Aaronsohn, a world-renowned Zionist agronomist who set up the most effective pro-Entente intelligence network in the Middle East during World War I, estimated the number of deaths at between 850,000 and 950,000.[17]

Mishandling the Great Game

For all their waning fortunes, at the dawn of the twentieth century the Ottomans could still boast a vast, albeit steadily shrinking empire. Their Iranian neighbors to the east had no such luck. While the Turkish leadership was daydreaming about new expansionist plans, Iran, which for centuries had nibbled at the Ottoman Empire's eastern frontier, was a spent force that had been partitioned into spheres of influence between Russia and Britain. This decline is generally considered a corollary of Iran's unavoidable involvement in the Anglo-Russian struggle for hegemony in Central Asia, commonly known as the Great Game. In fact, it was precisely this great-power rivalry that had ensured Iran's territorial integrity, perhaps even preventing its total disintegration. This was because both Russia and Britain preferred the preservation of a stable Iranian buffer over direct contiguity between their respective empires. Had it not been for the Great Game, Iran would have succumbed to the wide gap between its imperial ambitions and its internal centrifugal pressures—tribal, ethnic, linguistic, and religious—well before the twentieth century.

These ambitions tapped into an imperial Iranian ethos dating back to antiquity. Until its destruction by Alexander the Great, the Achaemenid dynasty (558–331 B.C.E.) reigned over most of the ancient Middle East, including Egypt, as well as parts of Eastern Europe. Iran then went through nearly a millennium of imperial rule by the foreign Parthians (250 B.C.E.–228 C.E.) and the native Sasanids (242–642 C.E.), before surrendering to the rising force of Islam. It did not take long, however, for Iranian imperial traditions and influences to be incorporated into the Islamic imperial edifice, and by the ninth century Iranian dynasties had become the effective masters of the eastern part of the Abbasid Empire. This process reached its apogee with the Buyid takeover of the empire in the mid-tenth century. Even after the overthrow of the Buyids by the Seljuk Turks, Iran retained its imperial status. The Seljuk sultanate, before its dissolution into a number of rival kingdoms, was largely modeled on the Iranian-Islamic pattern and acted as a medium for the transfer of Iranian cultural and administrative influences all the way to Anatolia. The Mongol irruption dealt a devastating blow to the resurgence of Iranian identity, but after they were converted to Islam the Mongols were gradually won over by Iranian cultural and political ideas. At the same time, the mass dislocation they occasioned shattered Iranian society, which was largely deprived of its traditional means of livelihood and state protection, and drove it into the arms of religious and mystical movements and orders, which took over many functions hitherto provided by the central government. One of these groups, founded in the thirteenth century by a Kurdish religious preacher who advocated a return to Islam's original ways, was to culminate in 1501 in the establishment of Iran's first modern imperial dynasty, the Safavid, which would reign until 1722.

The dynasty's first monarch, Ismail Shah, was a formidable ruler, whose political and military prowess was matched only by his youthfulness (he was fourteen upon taking the throne) and his megalomania (he was convinced he was the "hidden imam," the reembodiment of Caliph Ali). During his twenty-three years on the throne, Iran's countless power centers were brought under central government control and vast territories that had belonged to the Sasanid Empire were restored. He even managed to take Baghdad, but was eventually defeated by the Ottomans, who temporarily occupied the Safavid capital of Tabriz. Ismail's most important accomplishment by far was to make Shiism Iran's official state religion and to undertake the forceful conversion of the country's overwhelmingly Sunni population. This move, taken against the advice of some of the shah's counselors who feared a violent backlash, irrevocably set Iran on a distinct path of development, separate from the Sunni world and largely antagonistic to it.

After a few decades' lull under Ismail's ineffectual successors Safavid expansion was resumed by Abbas Shah (1587–1629), who drove the Ottomans from Azerbaijan and extended Iran's imperial reach as far as the key Armenian town of Kars. He also consolidated Iran's control over the Persian Gulf and expelled the Portuguese from the island of Hormuz at the southern mouth of the Gulf. His reign marked the apex of Safavid power and cultural prowess. After his death the empire went into rapid decline, and in 1722 Afghan rebels sacked the Iranian capital and brought about the Safavid dynasty's ignominious collapse.[1]

Iran's imperial fortunes were temporarily revived by Nadir Shah (1736–47), an able general who ascended the throne following the Safavid collapse. Having expelled the Afghans from Iranian territory, he successfully campaigned against the Ottoman and Russian empires and defeated India's Mughal sultan, carrying off much booty. This whetted Nadir's appetite. He began viewing himself as the head of an Iranian-dominated universal Islamic empire, and even adopted a virulent anti-Shiite stance so as to make himself acceptable to Sunni Muslims. Yet his phenomenal cruelty—Nadir was notorious for piling his victims' skulls into large pyramids, second in size only to those erected by the omnipotent Tamerlane some 350 years earlier—bought him the hatred of his subjects and culminated in his assassination. This threw Iran into fratricidal strife, from which it recovered only half a century later when Agha Muhammad, leader of the Qajar tribe, defeated his main rivals and established his own ruling dynasty with Tehran as its capital.

The domestic challenges confronting the new dynasty were daunting. Iranian society was a mosaic of contrasts and contradictions: between Muslims and non-Muslims, Shiites and Sunnis, rich and poor, urban and rural, settled and pastoral, tribal and non-tribal communities, and so forth. The medieval fabric of parochialism, in which local affinities and loyalties lay with tribe, clan, and the like, together with Iran's inhospitable geographical terrain, remained a powerful barrier to the enforcement of central authority. The Safavids managed somewhat to overcome these obstacles by using the newly imposed Shiite creed as a unifying force, but this instrument had largely run out of steam by the time of their demise. The wholesale conversion of the population to Shiism by Ismail Shah was by no means complete, leaving substantial parts of Iranian society, such as the Central Asian Muslims, Kurds, Arabs, and Afghans, largely untouched. Once Iran slid into anarchy, the antagonisms between the Shiite majority and the Sunni minority quickly resurfaced.

The fusion of religious and temporal authority in the person of the shah, which had enabled the Safavids to keep their subjects in constant awe, gave way to a system in which state and mosque drew increasingly apart. The shah no longer exercised absolute power over religious appointments and endowments, and the clerics, the *ulama*, quickly filled the vacuum. They controlled the religious, judicial, and educational institutions, cultivated ties with *bazaar* merchants and artisans, and exploited the collapse of the powerful group of local administrators (*sayyeds*) to amass fabulous wealth. Some of them even used theology students and urban thugs as private armies. In short, the ulama developed into an influential political player, which the Qajars could only ignore at their peril.[2]

In these circumstances, the Qajars saw the reassertion of the imperial dream as a trump card that would help unify a fragmented Iranian society and provide an outlet for the release of internal pressures. Their first target was Afghanistan, once a part of the Safavid Empire and now for the first time in its modern history a sovereign entity ruled by an indigenous dynasty. Another prominent target was the Caucasian principalities, especially Georgia, which had drifted away from Iranian control in the chaotic aftermath of Nadir Shah's assassination and which, in 1783, had concluded a treaty of alliance with Russia. In 1795 Agha Muhammad occupied the Georgian capital of Tbilisi, which he then subjected to wholesale pillage before being forced to withdraw in the face of the approaching winter, carrying off with him some fifteen thousand enslaved women and children. The shah was fortunate enough to escape Russian retribution owing to the death of Catherine the Great in November 1796, but his policy backfired by driving the fearful Georgians into the Russian sphere. In December 1800 Tsar Paul I acquiesced in desperate Georgian pleas and signed a decree incorporating the kingdom into the Russian Empire. The following summer Georgia's fate was sealed when Paul's successor, Alexander I, announced its annexation to Russia in the name of "humanity." This made Russia a direct neighbor of Iran, a development that caused great alarm in Tehran but also fueled irredentist aspirations.[3]

It was at this juncture that the Qajars plunged themselves into the evolving Anglo-Russian competition in Central Asia. Fath Ali Shah, who in 1797 succeeded his uncle Agha Muhammad, recognized the importance of British India as both a counterweight against Russian expansionism and a sponsor of Iran's imperial aspirations. This view found favor with the shah's coterie—sons, advisers, and ministers—who quickly embraced the British connection as a means to enhance their personal standing and to fill their pockets with generous bribes.[4]

The Iranian display of interest was warmly welcomed by British India. Marquis Richard Colley Wellesley, the elder brother of the Duke of Wellington and governor-general of India, whose claims to fame include not only the doubling of the territories under the control of the East India Company during his time in office but also his rumored habit of wearing his decorations on his pajamas, viewed collaboration with Iran as a strategic asset against a common enemy: Afghanistan. The Afghan threat to India dated back to its establishment as an independent kingdom by Ahmad Khan (1743–73) and escalated under the reign of Zaman Shah (1793–1800), who attacked Punjab and seemed poised to march on Delhi itself.[5] Wellesley was not the only one to show interest in Afghanistan. The French general Napoleon Bonaparte, who in 1798 invaded Egypt and quickly ventured into the Levant, aimed at nothing short of the occupation of India and sought to collaborate with Tsar Paul I to this end.

In 1799 Wellesley sent envoys to Tehran to strike a deal on the defense of India. In January 1801, after protracted talks lubricated by the lavish use of gifts and bribes, Iran signed its first-ever treaty with a European power. This provided for British military support in the event of an Afghan or French attack on Iran, and for Iranian support against an Afghan invasion of India. In addition, the two signatories undertook to ensure that France would not expand its influence in Iran.[6]

To the shah's exasperation the agreement was stillborn. British India's strategic outlook was not shared by decision-makers in London, the Foreign Office in particular, who viewed the Ottoman Empire, rather than Iran, as the key to the protection of Britain's imperial interests in the East. In a moment of anxiety during Napoleon's Middle Eastern expedition, London appeared willing to go along with it anyway; but with the disappearance of the French threat to India on the one hand, and the diminution of Afghan militancy following the death of Zaman Shah on the other, the gap between London and India widened again. When in 1804 a Russo-Iranian war broke out and the shah approached Britain for military support, London refused to do anything that could damage its relations with Russia at a time when the anti-Napoleonic struggle in Europe was at its height. Some in London could even see an advantage in the consolidation of Russian power in the Caucasus as a barrier against French penetration of the region.[7]

The embittered shah felt he had no choice but to approach Napoleon. The newly crowned emperor for his part sought to transform Iran (and Turkey) into a base for an attack against India and Russia, and so the two empires signed a defense alliance on May 4, 1807. France undertook to "direct every effort toward compelling Russia to withdraw from Georgia and Persian [Iranian] territory" and to provide the military aid necessary to this end, while Iran undertook to "sever all diplomatic and commercial relations with England, to declare war at once on the latter power, and to commence hostil-ities without delay." It also pledged to persuade "the Afghans and other peoples of Qandahar to add their armies to his [i.e., the shah's] fighting England", and to allow the French army to cross Iranian territory in the event of an attack against India.[8]

No sooner had the ink dried on the agreement than it fell prey to Napoleon's shifting priorities. The Tilsit treaty of July 1807, which terminated the war between France and Russia, put an end at a stroke to Napoleon's Asian grand design, so instead the emperor attempted to mediate an Iranian-Russian peace settlement, only to be rebuffed by the shah who insisted on the surrender of Georgia to Iran. As the Russians had no intention of making any such concessions, Fath Ali reverted to his first choice: Britain. This time London was sufficiently alarmed by the French threat to India to come to terms, and between 1809 and 1814 the two countries signed three agreements extending military and financial support to Iran if it was attacked by a European power, and precluding British interference in any war between Iran and Afghanistan.[9]

Before long, British support spilled over to other spheres. A handsome subsidy provided for nearly 10 percent of the shah's regular income, British doctors treated the Iranian monarch, and the young princes traveled to England for their education. So keen was Fath Ali to cultivate the alliance that in December 1812 he offered Britain the opportunity "to do in Persia [Iran] exactly as if it belonged to you." Iran would provide 200,000 troops for Britain to train and deploy as it saw fit, the government of India could send an army to Iran of whatever size it chose, and the British could build forts wherever they wished. If they so desired, they could even have the strategic island of Kharg.[10]

By now the Russians had crushed the Iranian army, commanded by the overconfident heir apparent Abbas Mirza, and the shah hoped that his spectacular offer would shore up his empire's crumbling military position. To his deep dismay, rather than extending their protective wing over their Iranian allies, the British now pressured them into an agreement with Russia. This culminated in the October 1813 treaty of Gulistan which included a number of painful concessions, such as recognition of Russia's sovereignty over "all the territory between the Caucasus and the Caspian Sea," including Georgia, and its exclusive right to sail warships on the Caspian. As the shah would not reconcile himself to these losses, another Russo-Iranian war broke out in 1826, resulting in the even more humiliating treaty of Turkmanchai (February 1828), which reaffirmed Russia's annexation of Erevan and Nakhechevan and gave it extraterritorial rights in Iran.[11]

With their imperial ambitions in the Caucasus thwarted, the Iranians turned again to Afghanistan. Ascending the throne in 1834, Muhammad Shah attempted to regain the Afghan khanate of Herat, to no avail. Twenty years later, Muhammad's successor, Shah Nasser al-Din (1848–96), sent his troops to Herat once more in an attempt to exploit a window of opportunity opened by Britain's involvement in the Crimean War. He was to be painfully disillusioned. Despite its reluctance to weaken Iran in any way that could increase its susceptibility to Russian power and influence, Britain considered the invasion alarming enough to warrant an immediate declaration of war. In December 1856 British forces invaded Iran, and before the year was over they had captured the southern islands of Kharg and Bushir and continued their advance northward. In early March 1857, the heavily fortified town of Muhammara fell after an hour's fighting, with thirteen thousand panic-stricken Iranians being pursued as they fled by forty-five British cavalrymen. Ahwaz was captured on April 1, and the following day Iran signed a peace treaty renouncing all its territorial claims to Afghanistan.

It would take more than two decades for British foreign policy to swing back in Iran's favor. In 1879, following a serious deterioration in Anglo-Afghan relations resulting in two wars, the foreign secretary, Lord Salisbury, offered Nasser al-Din the coveted territories of Herat and Sistan, together with a handsome subsidy. In return, Iran was to allow the presence of British officers in Herat, in order to enable the construction of a railroad from Kandahar to Herat, and was to undertake, under British supervision, projects for internal reform and for improving transportation from the Gulf inland.

This was music to the shah's ears, and it also whetted his appetite. Hoping to extract further concessions from Britain, he indulged in "an almost interminable series of discussions on points of detail and changes of wording, and when matters appeared almost ripe for the signature of the Convention, the Persian Government announced suddenly, in February 1880, that they were not prepared to proceed further unless the arrangement was made permanent."[12]

This proved a critical mistake. In April 1880 the anti-imperialist Gladstone returned to power and Britain reverted to a policy of aloofness. Nasser al-Din thus missed a golden opportunity for territorial aggrandizement that was never to present itself again. When Salisbury succeeded Gladstone as prime minister in June 1885, he no longer backed his earlier efforts to make Iran a bastion against Russian expansionism with generous territorial concessions. "It is to the interest of this country that the integrity of Persia should be maintained, that its resources should be developed, and that its Government should be strong, independent, and friendly," he instructed his new ambassador to Tehran, Sir Henry Drummond Wolff. "It is to the promotion of these objects that your attention should be directed." The ambassador did precisely that, and in October 1888 gave a formal guarantee for the preservation of Iran's territorial integrity against any foreign power.[13] The shah reciprocated by opening the Karun River to commercial steamers of all nations and gave Baron Julius von Reuter a concession to establish the Imperial Bank of Persia, which for sixty years would have the right to issue notes of legal tender in Iran and to engage in any operations on its own account or for others in the fields of finance, commerce, and industry.

Now that Britain had extracted handsome economic concessions there, Russia sought to make the best possible gains for itself and to curb the rise of British influence in Iran. One such gain was the concession to open the Discount and Loan Bank of Persia, which was effectively a branch of the Russian Ministry of Finance and part of the Russian central bank. With no real stockholders or need to show profit, the bank made loans on convenient terms to Iranian princes, officials, clerics, and merchants—to the degree that it was widely joked that Russia had bought off the entire ruling elite. In 1887 the shah, who was far from enthusiastic about having trains in Iran, pledged not to give any concession for a railroad or a waterway without prior consultation with Russia. Three years later he acquiesced in yet another Russian demand that no railroad be built on Iranian territory for ten years.

For the shah and his court these concessions were highly valuable. Nasser al-Din was, of course, not the only avaricious ruler in Iran's modern history, but his exploitation of great-power competition for the purpose of self-enrichment is legendary. Keenly aware that Britain and Russia would pay dearly to buy their way into Iran, he developed the tendering of concessions into a highly lucrative industry. One famous concession provided for the construction of telegraph lines throughout the country (by the end of 1864 the first single-wire line was ready, and the Indo-European Telegraph was inaugurated the following year), another empowered Reuter to develop Iran's economy and industry, including granting the rights to mine, construct railways, and found a bank.[14] Although this concession was quickly withdrawn following widespread opposition in Iran and Russia, the shah retained the lavish bribes.

As concession-hunters flocked to the imperial court, the shah's men were swimming in ever-growing bribes—none more so than Mirza Ali Asghar Khan, better known as Amin al-Sultan ("Trusted of the Sovereign"), the grand vizier and holder of several key ministerial posts. They also secured a steady flow of cash from the development of a semi-annual auction of offices in which governorships went to the highest bidders, a practice that proved catastrophic to the empire's economic well-being.[15]

To make things worse, the shah's insatiable thirst for money led to the rapid expansion of foreign presence and influence in Iran, which in turn generated a wave of xenophobia. Nasser al-Din's three visits to "infidel" Europe during the 1880s did little to endear him to his subjects. Aside from sparking a charge that Iran had been relegated to "Farangistan," the land of the Franks, their exorbitant cost at a time when the empire was on the brink of bankruptcy fueled widespread discontent.

Things came to a head in March 1890, when the shah gave a certain Major Gerald Talbot, a close friend of the ambassador, Drummond Wolff, a fifty-year monopoly over the manufacturing, trade, and export of tobacco and its products throughout the Iranian Empire, in return for an annual lump sum of £15,000 and a quarter of the annual net profits.[16] Like the Reuter concession two decades previously, the Tobacco Régie affected virtually every single individual throughout the empire. Many Iranians smoked heavily and no fewer depended on the tobacco industry for their livelihood. In no time there was a public uproar against the concession. Initially this was seen as a minor outburst by "the very lowest classes with a sprinkling of the better-class people." But by 1891 the protest had developed into a mass movement headed by the ulama and the bazaaris. Anger was vented in all directions as people went on the rampage in the major cities. Merchants burned their entire stock to avoid selling to the tobacco company. Those who used tobacco were subjected to violent reprisals, those who continued to work for the Régie were declared "unclean" and ran the risk of being murdered. Europeans, many of whom had absolutely nothing to do with the concession, were harassed and humiliated. Religious leaders accused the shah of selling Muslims like slaves to the Christians and placards threatening an imminent jihad if the Régie were not immediately withdrawn appeared in several cities.

On January 4, 1892, all shops in the Tehran bazaar closed down and the agitated mob, led by the clerics, made its way to the royal palace. An attempt by the shah's favorite son and minister of war, Kamran Mirza, to disperse the demonstrators failed miserably and the prince beat a hasty and undignified retreat in the course of which he fell on his face in the mud. The terrified shah sent for his elite Cossack Brigade (established in 1882 and commanded by a Russian officer), only to realize to his horror that it had decided to side with the clerics. As the mob closed on the palace, the shah backed down and abolished the tobacco concession out of "love for his people." The clerics rejoiced. This was the first time in Iran's modern history that they had managed to impose their will on the shah through a popular uprising. It would not be the last.[17]

To recover from this humiliation, the shah retreated into his harem, doting on cats and marrying a long succession of wives. There was no real government in Iran, with corruption as prevalent as ever. The minister of post busied himself with stealing parcels suspected of containing valuables, while the minister of war filled his pockets with money destined for his soldiers. When the Imperial Tobacco Corporation of Persia demanded £500,000 in compensation for the cancellation of the concession, and the shah declared himself willing to compromise on £300,000, Amin al-Sultan expressed his readiness "to again urge upon the Shah to accept the terms of the Company on condition that the £15,000 should be made over to him which he had paid in cash to the Shah for the shares to that amount allotted to H.M."[18] The vizier made good his promise, convincing the shah to pay the requested £500,000 in cash. A loan was quickly arranged from the Imperial Bank of Persia, and as one loan led to another Iran yet again found itself on the brink of bankruptcy.

A sense of foreboding doom permeated the empire. Mas'ud Mirza Zell al-Sultan, the shah's eldest son, repeatedly talked about partitioning Iran after his father's death between himself and his brother, Crown Prince Muzaffar al-Din. The shah's brother compared Iran to a "lump of sugar in a glass of water" gradually melting away. Even Amin al-Sultan became sufficiently alarmed to plead with Britain to prevent the bartering-away of Iran by the shah, who "resisted any attempt to improve the country and refused to take any thought for what might happen after his own death."[19]

His concern was justified. When on May 1, 1896, Nasser al-Din was assassinated in the midst of preparations to celebrate his fiftieth anniversary on the throne, his successor, Muzaffar al-Din, proved disastrous. Illiterate, sickly, and completely under the spell of his courtiers, the new shah immersed himself in the minutiae of his daily existence, paying little attention to public affairs. A central goal from his first days in power was to travel to Europe in the grand style of his predecessor, and to obtain the enormous sums of money needed for this trip he was prepared to mortgage ever-growing segments of the Iranian economy to foreign powers. Belgian administrators flocked to the empire to restructure the customs system, and a Belgian national was even made minister of customs. Russia obtained a number of lucrative concessions, including a customs treaty that removed tariffs on cotton cloth, thereby ruining most Iranian cloth manufacturers. Britain also reaped handsome gains, including a sixty-year exclusive concession for petroleum, gas, and asphalt throughout the entire empire, excluding the five northern provinces.

When Muzaffar al-Din eventually went on his coveted European trip in 1902, it proved a catastrophic drain on the treasury. The ten million roubles borrowed from Russia in April had evaporated into thin air by the end of the year. The shah's desperate attempts to secure another loan were given the cold shoulder by the Russian finance minister, who insisted that "money would be employed for definite public purposes, and not squandered amongst the courtiers and H. H.'s own worthless dependants."[20] A £300,000 loan from the British-controlled Imperial Bank gave the shah a vital respite but did nothing to stem the tidal wave of xenophobic and anti-government sentiment engulfing the empire. The ulama resented the government's half-hearted attempts at reform, while the bazaaris protested against the favoring of foreign interests and demanded the removal of Belgian customs officials. Secret societies distributed inflammatory leaflets in the major Iranian cities, and attacks on foreigners and minority groups—Christians, Jews, and Bahais[21]—became a common sight. The Bahais in particular were earmarked for harsh treatment: hundreds of men, women, and children were massacred in Yazd at the instigation of the local governor and their property destroyed or pillaged. The British consular agent in Yazd even reported that the governor had a Bahai fired from a cannon "to appease the crowd."[22]

Anarchy was contagious. In Azerbaijan the governor and heir to the throne, Muhammad Ali Mirza, relied on criminal elements to maintain his hold on the province, appointing a notorious local brigand, condemned to death a year earlier but pardoned by the prince-governor, as commander of the cavalry. An unholy alliance was contrived among leading ulama, courtiers, and secular reformers to bring about the downfall of Amin al-Sultan, blamed for Iran's ills.

They did not have to work very hard. The grand vizier's fortunes were rapidly waning. When, after dreaming that this loyal servant had saved him from drowning, the shah ordered his favorite astrologer to be paid a £3,000 annual pension plus a large lump sum, Amin al-Sultan lost his temper and complained that "he had raised large sums to pay for the Shah's tours and toys, but must protest against paying for his dreams."[23] Six months later, in September 1903, he found himself out of office.

Any hopes that the vizier's downfall would calm the situation were soon disappointed. His successor to the premiership, Majid Mirza Ain al-Dawla, grandson of Fath Ali Shah and Muzaffar al-Din's son-in-law, was a corrupt and brutal bigot who drew pleasure from punishing convicts by driving horseshoes into their bare heels. Not only did he do nothing to curb the insatiable greed of the shah and his coterie, he was also an active member of this corrupt system, amassing an enormous fortune for himself. The powerful forces of decay and fragmentation that had been operative throughout the nineteenth century were now quickly brewing into a revolution.

In December 1905 several Tehran merchants were publicly flogged for raising the price of sugar, and the entire bazaar was closed in protest. When ordered to reopen their shops or have their goods confiscated, some two thousand merchants, together with a number of ulama, took sanctuary in the Imperial Mosque, the traditional form of protest in Iran. Supported by the vengeful Amin al-Sultan and the crown prince, they demanded the dismissal of Ain al-Dawla and other ministers, the sacking of the governor of Tehran, the removal of the Belgians from the customs offices, and the foundation of a "House of Justice" comprising merchants, landowners, and clergy. In January 1906 the shah acceded to these demands and the crisis seemed to have abated.

When the shah subsequently reneged on his word, expelling a number of prominent ulama from Tehran, a fresh wave of popular discontent engulfed the capital. Recognizing that sanctuary in mosques and shrines was no longer respected, on July 19, 1906, merchants, guild members and clerics took refuge at the "infidel" British embassy. Within a couple of weeks nearly fourteen thousand protesters were camping in the embassy's gardens. Their demand now grew from the dismissal of Ain al-Dawla to the formation of a representative assembly, or *majlis*. Nudged by the British, the ailing shah (he suffered a stroke in the spring) peremptorily dismissed Ain al-Dawla and called for a majlis to be introduced.

Parliamentary elections were held in October 1906, and on December 30 the shah, his prime minister, and the crown prince signed the empire's constitution. Yet the "constitutional revolution" quickly ran into a dead end. The majlis was beset by internal antagonisms from the outset, notably between the constitutionalists, who favored secular legislation and a modern constitution, and the religionists, who supported the formation of a theocratic consultative body. Local political groups defied the authority of the majlis and the central government, with local governors exercising arbitrary power across the country. Land taxes went unpaid. Smuggling flourished. The Belgian customs regime frequently turned over revenues to ministers rather than using them for the repayment of loans. Yet again the specter of bankruptcy loomed large. In these circumstances it was widely agreed that the detested Amin al-Sultan had to be recalled from his Swiss exile to save the day. He returned in March 1907 and was about to arrange a new loan with Russian, French, British, and German backing when he was assassinated by a religious militant. It was widely rumored that the driving force behind the killing was none other than the shah.[24]

This suggestion was not wholly unfounded. Muhammad Ali Shah, who ascended the throne following Muzaffar al-Din's death on January 8, 1907, was a bitter enemy of constitutionalism and representative rule. He may have sworn to uphold the constitution, but had never seriously intended to keep his word. He was supported by a number of high-ranking ulama who had initially seen the majlis as an opportunity to increase their political power but were subsequently disillusioned as the liberals gained the upper hand there. He was also backed by the Russian government, which believed that Iran "was not yet ready for a constitution, and that the Shah, and only the Shah, was the foundation stone of order in his country," and by the French, who were convinced that "the anti-Government party in Persia was under the active control and direction of the British Minister."[25]

Unfortunately for the shah, Russia was going through its own cycle of cataclysmic upheavals. It had suffered a humiliating defeat by Japan, had experienced its own revolution, and had had its resources—political, military, and economic—strained to the limit. In Britain, too, important changes were taking place. The long reign of the Conservatives had come to an end, and the new foreign secretary, Sir Edward Grey, like his monarch, King Edward VII, advocated a quick rapprochement with Russia that would bring an end to the Anglo-Russian Great Game.

This policy shift was unacceptable to both the British ambassador to Tehran, Sir Cecil Spring-Rice, and British India which sympathized with the Iranian constitutionalists and the more pragmatic clerics. "I venture to observe that it would in my opinion be a grave error to attribute the popular movement in Persia to such a slight or accidental cause as the intrigues of a foreign Legation," Spring-Rice wrote to Grey.

I think that European nations should be prepared to face in Persia, what they are beginning to experience elsewhere, a national and religious movement, formless perhaps and misdirected, but of great vigour and intensity. And owing, perhaps, to the superior mental attainments of the Persian race, I think it is not improbable that the leaders of the movement here, especially as they are in close touch with the Russian Mussulmans already represented in considerable numbers in the Duma, may occupy a prominent, perhaps a dominant position in the future development of the national and constitutional movement among Mussulman peoples. Should the movement be really of this nature, we cannot make it our tool, and we cannot wish to make it our enemy.[26]

These words fell on deaf ears. By this time—and completely unknown to Spring-Rice or the Iranians—the British and Russian governments were busy ironing out their long-standing disputes in Asia. In addition to Afghanistan and Tibet, their nascent agreement included the Iranian question, which in the view of both powers contained the seeds of a potential future confrontation between them. In Grey's words: "The inefficiency of Persian Governments, the state of their finances, the internal disorders, not only laid Persia open to foreign interference, but positively invited and attracted it. . . . Unless the mists of suspicion were dissolved by the warm air of friendship, the increasing friction would cause Britain and Russia to drift toward war."[27]

And so, on the very same day as Amin al-Sultan's assassination, August 31, 1907, an Anglo-Russian deal was reached in St. Petersburg on the partitioning of Iran, while paying lip service to its "integrity and independence." Russia would dominate the northern part of the country, including Tehran and Tabriz. Britain would control the south, with a neutral buffer zone established in the center.[28]

Although Grey presented the agreement as a "real gain" that prevented further Russian advances in the direction of India, the Indian government was deeply disappointed.[29] No less embittered were the Iranian constitutionalists, who viewed the British move as an act of betrayal. How could it be that after all their moralizing and encouragement, the British had turned their backs on Iran? Yet the Iranian authorities had only themselves to blame. Having thrust their empire for over a century into the midst of great-power competition, for reasons of political and territorial aggrandizement and financial self-enrichment, they had now fallen victim to that very competition. Had the Qajars shunned the Anglo-Russian rivalry, and had they put their house in order and ensured its political and economic stability, Iran might have well been left in peace. As it was, Iran came to be viewed by both Britain and Russia as a dangerous vacuum that could draw them into an undesirable confrontation that had therefore to be filled without delay. The stark reality of weakness behind the imperial dream exacted yet another casualty.

The Rise of the Arab Imperial Dream

The fall of the Ottoman Empire, which ended at a stroke thirteen hundred years of Islamic imperialism, was not a necessary, let alone an inevitable, consequence of World War I. It was a self-inflicted disaster by a short-sighted leadership blinded by imperialist ambitions. Had the Ottomans heeded the Entente's repeated pleas for neutrality, their empire would most likely have weathered the storm. But they did not, and this blunder led to the destruction of the Ottoman Empire by the British army and the creation of the new Middle Eastern state system on its ruins. Yet even this momentous development was not inevitable, and its main impetus came not from the great powers but from a local imperial aspirant: Hussein ibn Ali of the Hashemite family, the *sharif* of Mecca and custodian of Islam's two holiest shrines.

As late as June 1915, nearly a year after the outbreak of World War I, an interdepartmental British committee regarded the preservation of a decentralized and largely intact Ottoman Empire as the most desirable option.[1] But four months later, the British high commissioner in Egypt, Sir Arthur Henry McMahon, had been sufficiently impressed by Hussein's promises to raise the Arabic-speaking Ottoman subjects in revolt against the sultan to accept his vision of a successor empire and to agree to his main territorial demands, albeit in a tentative and highly equivocal fashion.

Hussein's achievement was nothing short of extraordinary. Notwithstanding his pretense to represent "the whole of the Arab Nation without any exception,"[2] the sharif represented little more than himself. The minimal backing he received from a few neighboring tribes had far less to do with a yearning for independence than with the glitter of British gold and the promise of booty. Hussein could not even count on the support of his own local constituency. As late as December 1916, six months after the sharif and his two prominent sons, Abdallah and Faisal, launched what came to be known euphemistically as "The Great Arab Revolt," the residents of Mecca were "almost pro-Turks,"[3] and it would not be before the winter of 1917 that the pendulum would start swinging in the Hashemite direction.

Unlike Turkey-in-Europe, where the rise of nationalism dealt a body blow to Ottoman imperialism, there was no nationalist fervor among the Ottoman Empire's Arabic-speaking subjects. One historian has credibly estimated that a mere 350 activists belonged to all the secret Arab societies operating throughout the Middle East at the outbreak of World War I, and most of them were not seeking actual Arab independence but rather greater autonomy within the Ottoman Empire.[4] To the vast majority of the eight to ten million Arabic-speaking Ottoman subjects the message of these tiny societies meant nothing. They remained loyal to their imperial master to the bitter end and shunned the sharifian revolt altogether. Between 100,000 and 300,000 of them even fought in the Ottoman army during the war. As Lawrence of Arabia put it in a 1915 memorandum on the conditions in Syria:

> Between town and town, village and village, family and family, creed and creed, exist intimate jealousies, sedulously fostered by the Turks to render a spontaneous union impossible. The largest indigenous political entity in settled Syria is only the village under its sheikh, and in patriarchal Syria the tribe under its chief. . . . All the constitution above them is the artificial bureaucracy of the Turk. . . . By accident and time the Arabic language has gradually permeated the country, until it is now almost the only one in use; but this does not mean that Syria—any more than Egypt—is an Arabian country.[5]

These realities were of little import for Hussein and his sons. For all the rhetoric of Arab independence in which they couched their communications with the British, the Hashemites were no champions of national liberation but imperialist aspirants anxious to exploit a unique window of opportunity to substitute their own empire for that of the Ottomans. Hussein had demonstrated no nationalist sentiments prior to the war, when he had generally been considered a loyal Ottoman apparatchik, and neither he nor his sons changed in this respect during the revolt. They did not regard themselves as part of a wider Arab nation, bound together by a shared language, religion, history, or culture. Rather, they held themselves superior to those ignorant creatures whom they were "destined" to rule and educate. In the words of a senior British official who, in January 1918, held several conversations with Hussein: "Arabs as a whole have not asked him to be their king; but seeing how ignorant and disunited they are, how can this be expected of them until he is called?"[6]

What the Hashemites demanded of the post-war peace conference, then, was not self-determination for the Arabic-speaking subjects of the defunct

Ottoman Empire but the formation of a successor empire, extending well beyond the predominantly Arabic-speaking territories and comprising such diverse ethnic and national groups as Turks, Armenians, Kurds, Greeks, Assyrians, Chechens, Circassians, and Jews. As Hussein told Lawrence of Arabia in the summer of 1917: "If advisable we will pursue the Turks to Constantinople and Erzurum—so why talk about Beirut, Aleppo, and Hailo?" Abdallah put it in similar terms when demanding that Britain abide by the vast territorial promises made to his father: "it was ... up to the British government to see that the Arab kingdom is such as will make it a substitute for the Ottoman Empire."[7]

This regal mindset was vividly illustrated by the frequent Hashemite allusions to Islamic imperial glory, rather than to national rights, which served as justifications for their territorial claims. Thus, for example, Hussein based his objection to British attempts to exclude Iraq from the prospective empire on the fact that "the Iraqi vilayets are parts of the pure Arab Kingdom, and were in fact the seat of its government in the time of Ali Ibn-Abu-Talib, and in the time of all the khalifs [caliphs] who succeeded him." Similarly, Abdallah rejected the French occupation of Syria not on the ground that this territory had constituted an integral part of the "Arab homeland" but because it was inconceivable for the Umayyad capital of Damascus to become a French colony.[8]

Had the British officials in Cairo recognized how meager was the sharif's political and military power base, they would undoubtedly have shunned his grandiose demands, as indeed was their initial inclination. In the event, they were lured by Hussein's false pretenses, but even then they were wise enough to make their territorial and financial largesse contingent on his harnessing the entire "Arab nation" to the Entente's cause and its subsequent liberation of the Arabic-speaking Ottoman provinces. In McMahon's words:

> It is most essential that you should spare no effort to attach all the Arab peoples to our united cause and urge them to afford no assistance to our enemies. It is on the success of these efforts and on the more active measures which the Arabs may hereafter take in support of our cause, when the time for action comes, that the permanence and the strength of our agreement must depend.[9]

Needless to say, the Hashemites never came remotely close to fulfilling this fundamental condition, on which the entire deal was predicated, as the overwhelming majority of Arabs remained loyal to their Ottoman suzerain to the very end. Nevertheless, the failure to deliver on their part of the bargain did not prevent the Hashemites from enjoying the deal's abundant fruits (they were, as it happens, generously rewarded in the form of vast territories several times the size of the British Isles) while nonetheless complaining of being "robbed" of the fruits of victory promised to them during the war. Thus arose the standard grievance leveled by Arab intellectuals and politicians at the Western powers, Britain in particular, and thus emerged the imperialist theory of pan-Arabism (or *qawmiya*), with the avowed aim of redressing this grievance, which dominated Middle Eastern political discourse for most of the twentieth century.[10]

Giving the notion of the territorial nation-state short shrift as a temporary aberration destined to wither away before long, pan-Arabism postulates the existence of "a single [Arab] nation bound by the common ties of language, religion and history . . . behind the facade of a multiplicity of sovereign states." The territorial expanse of this supposed nation has varied among the exponents of the ideology, ranging from "merely" the Fertile Crescent to the entire territory "from the Zagros Mountains in the east to the Atlantic Ocean in the west, and from the Mediterranean shores and the Anatolian hills in the north to the Indian Ocean, the sources of the Nile, and the Great Desert in the south."[11] But the unity of the Arabic-speaking populations inhabiting these vast territories is never questioned. In the words of Nuri Said, Faisal's comrade-in-arms and a longtime prime minister of Iraq:

> All Arabs and particularly those of the Near and Middle East have deep down in their hearts the feeling that they are "members one of another." Their "nationalism" springs from the Muslim feeling of brotherhood enjoined on them by the Prophet Muhammad in his last public speech. It differs therefore from a great deal of European nationalism and patriotism. Although Arabs are naturally attached to their native land their nationalism is not confined by boundaries. It is an aspiration to restore the great tolerant civilization of the early Caliphate.[12]

This doctrine had already been articulated before World War I, most notably by the Syrian political exiles Abdel Rahman Kawakibi (d. 1902) and Najib Azuri (d. 1916). But it is highly doubtful whether these early beginnings would have ever amounted to anything more than intellectual musings had it not been for the huge ambitions of Hussein and his sons. It was only after the Hashemites had gained access to the great-power decision-making process as representatives of the "Arab nation," and, moreover, had been given control over the newly established Arab states in the wake of the war, that the pan-Arab ideal began to be inculcated into the Arab masses, transcending in the process the Hashemite imperial dream, which focused on the Fertile Crescent to the total exclusion of Egypt and North Africa.

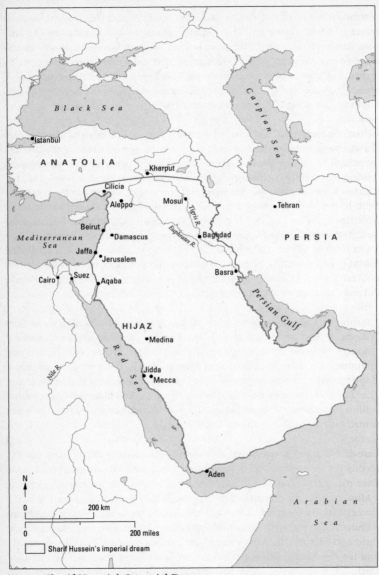

Map 6 Sharif Hussein's Imperial Dream
From Efraim and Inari Karsh, *Empires of the Sand: The Struggle for Mastery in the Middle East, 1789–1923* (Cambridge, Mass.: Harvard University Press, 1999).

Substituting empire-building for national unity, successive pan-Arab ideologues and politicians have delved into the region's millenarian imperial tradition. At times the justification for Arab unification has been based on the more recent imperial past. The Iraqi case for the annexation of Kuwait in August 1990, for instance, was predicated on Kuwait at times having been part of the Ottoman velayet of Basra. Baghdad presented the annexation as a rectification of a historic wrong (European disruption of the alleged unity of the Arab world in the wake of World War I) and claimed this event would "return the part and branch, Kuwait, to the whole root, Iraq."[13] Likewise, Abu Khaldun Sati al-Husri, perhaps the foremost theoretician of pan-Arabism, lauded the Egyptian president Gamal Abdel Nasser (1954–70) as "one of the greatest [leaders] in modern Arab history, rivaled perhaps only by Muhammad Ali the Great of Egypt and Faisal I of the Arab Revolt."[14] The trouble is, neither of these leaders was a nationalist: both were aspiring imperialists seeking to substitute their empires for that of the Ottomans. The Albanian Muhammad Ali did not even speak Arabic and did not identify himself as an Arab.

On other occasions, the invocation of former glories harks back to the distant pre-Islamic Arab past. In an attempt to prove the historic continuity of an "Arab nation" from antiquity to the present day, the Palestinian intellectual and political leader Yusuf Heikal traced Arab imperial greatness to the ancient Fertile Crescent peoples such as the Hittites, Canaanites, and Amourites, ignoring the fact that these diverse groups never constituted a single people, let alone an Arab one. So did Sami Shawkat, the influential director-general of education in Iraq during the 1930s. "The history of our illustrious Arab nation extends over thousands of years, and goes back to the time when the peoples of Europe lived in forests and over marshes, in caves and in the interstices of the rock," he boasted. "In the same way we find that everything makes us lift our heads high when we consider the histories of the Semitic empires formed in the Fertile Crescent—the Chaldean, the Assyrian, the African, the Pharaonic, or the Carthaginian." Having appropriated the imperial exploits of these distinct non-Arab peoples for the pan-Arab narrative he was attempting to construct, Shawkat proudly concluded that "the civilizations of the world at the present time are based on foundations laid by our ancestors."[15]

Most commonly, however, the origin of the "Arab nation" is traced to the advent of Islam and the earliest Arab and Islamic empires. This is not difficult to understand, given that it was the Arabs who had revealed this religion to the world and had practiced it for longer than anyone else. Kawakibi went so far as to lament the conversion to Islam of non-Arab communities and nations which, in his opinion, had both corrupted their adoptive religion and deprived the Arabs of their Islamic birthright: the caliphate.[16] The Hashemite claim to represent the "whole of the Arab Nation without any exception," and

Britain's willingness to acquiesce in it, were likewise based on Sharif Hussein's impressive religious credentials as a member of the Prophet's family and custodian of Islam's two holiest shrines.

It is true that great efforts were subsequently made to dilute the role of religion in pan-Arab identity. Faisal claimed that "we are Arabs before being Muslims, and Muhammad is an Arab before being a prophet," while Husri defined an Arab as any Arabic-speaking member of the "Arab country", regardless of his religion. In his opinion, it was not Islam that constituted the defining principle of the "Arab nation", but the other way round: Arab unity was a *sine qua non* for Islamic universalism. This is because no great world religion, with the partial exception of early Islam, had ever succeeded in unifying diverse multilingual societies, while the idea of Arab unity was "a social force drawing its vitality from the life of the Arabic language, from the history of the Arab nation, and from the connectedness of the Arab countries." And although pan-Arabism had remained dormant for centuries, it was released with renewed vigor in the early twentieth century and was destined to restore the Arab nation's "ancient glory to its rightful place in the history of the modern world."[17]

For all its professed secularism, however, pan-Arabism has not only been forced to claim allegiance to the religious beliefs and traditions to which most Arabs remain attached to date, but has effectively been Muslim in its ethos, worldview, and imperialist vision. Hence Nuri Said's perception of pan-Arabism as the "aspiration to restore the great tolerant civilization of the early Caliphate," and hence the interconnectedness between the Arab and Islamic factors in Nasser's thinking and the constant deference to Islam of Christian pan-Arabists. The prominent Christian intellectual Qustantin Zuraiq, for example, declared it the duty of every Arab, whatever his religion, to sanctify the memory of Muhammad and to interest himself in Islam, while the celebrated Christian academic Edward Said reminisced that although he was "almost Western" in his education and knowledge, he never felt during his childhood years in Cairo that he was a member of a minority and regarded his heritage as "Arab-Islamic." Michel Aflaq, founding father of the secularist Ba'th party, which was to hold power in Syria and Iraq for decades, went a step further by equating Islam and pan-Arabism and urging Christian Arabs to "preserve Islam as they would preserve the most precious element in their Arabism."[18]

It is often easier to unite people through a common hatred than through a shared loyalty. Pan-Arabism, like other "pan" movements, has had its share of villains and aggressors, which it has borrowed from the House of Islam's millenarian struggle against the House of War, again substituting Arab unity for Islamic imperial power. The crusades, a secondary issue for Muslims during medieval times, have accordingly been elevated to the top of this "hate list" as the first alleged incursion of Western imperialism into the "Arab father-land." Saladin, a quintessential imperialist seeking territorial and political self-aggrandizement, became the ultimate role model for generations of pan-Arab leaders. The fact that the Arabs played no role whatsoever in expelling the crusaders, which was exclusively accomplished by the Turks (the scourge of pan-Arabists), and that Saladin himself was a Kurd, did little to dampen the myth of a united Arab nation resisting a concerted foreign assault. "Our difference with the West is an essential and primary one," wrote the Egyptian weekly *Ruz al-Yusuf* in the early 1950s. "Its roots go back in the past as far as the crusades. . . . the battle with the West has been going on, and it can only lead to one of the two conclusions that allow of no compromise: our defeat or that of the West."[19]

Nasser elaborated still further on the nature of this supposed historic confrontation. "In the days of our forefathers the name they adopted for deception and treachery was the Crusades," he argued.

The deception was in the name of religion, but religion had no connection whatsoever with that aggression, for the Crusades represented nothing else than Imperialism, domination and despotism in every sense of these terms. The Arab people, Moslems and Christians alike, all stood fast and firm against those imperialistic invasions. They were never deceived by the name under which the expeditions went. Indeed, the unity of the Arab people was the only way to victory at the time.

Having painted a false picture of the crusades and the regional responses to them, Nasser proceeded to draw the implications of this momentous event for the twentieth-century Middle East. In his view, since the modern European powers considered Arab unity the nemesis of the crusaders, they had exploited World War I to break this unity by carving out artificial states from the defunct Ottoman Empire. To add insult to injury, these powers had implanted a neo-crusading Jewish bridgehead in the midst of the "Arab nation" so as to keep it divided and subservient to the whims of world impe-rialism. "Names have changed since, but the aims remained the same—colonization, domination and despotism," Nasser maintained, evoking the standard Hashemite anti-British charge.

After . . . World War [I], during which England promised to give us our inde-pendence, Britain and Imperialism wanted to suppress Arab nationalism by other means. Imperialism signed a pact with Zionism and the result was the Balfour Declaration. . . . The battle was continued, Brethren, to deal the deathblow to our Nationalism, this time under a new name, a substitute for "the Crusades," which was "the mandate." Palestine was placed under mandate, for no other purpose than the destruction of Arab nationalism in a new way.[20]

This account crystallizes the core of the pan-Arab rejection of the Jewish right to statehood: not concern for the national rights of the Palestinian Arabs but a desire to fend off a perceived encroachment on the pan-Arab imperial patrimony. "Centuries ago the Crusaders established themselves in our midst against our will, and in 200 years we ejected them," Abdel Rahman Azzam, the first secretary-general of the newly established Arab League, told Jewish officials who came to him in September 1947 to plead for peace. "We will try to rout you. I am not sure we will succeed, but we will try. We succeeded in expelling the Crusaders, but lost Spain and Persia, and may lose Palestine."[21] In other words, Palestine was not perceived as a distinct entity deserving of national self-determination but as an integral part of a unified regional Arab order, no element of which should be conceded at any cost.

The group that posed this perceived threat to the resurgent Arab imperial dream was the Jewish national movement commonly known as Zionism. Since the Roman destruction of Jewish statehood in the land that has subsequently come to be known as Palestine, exile and dispersion have become the hallmark of Jewish existence. Even in its ancestral homeland the Jewish community was relegated to a small minority under a long succession of imperial occupiers—Byzantines, Arabs, Seljuk Turks, crusaders, Mamluks, and Ottoman Turks—who inflicted repression and dislocation upon Jewish life.

This forced marginalization notwithstanding, not only was the Jewish presence in Palestine never totally eliminated, but the Jews' longing for their ancestral homeland, or Zion, occupied a focal place in their collective memory for millennia and became an integral part of Jewish religious ritual. Moreover, Jews began returning to Palestine from the earliest days of dispersion, mostly on an individual basis, but also on a wider communal scale. The expulsion of the Jews from Spain in 1492, for example, brought in its wake a wave of new immigrants; an appreciable influx of East European Hasidim occurred in the late eighteenth century, and of Yemenite Jews a hundred years later.

In the 1880s, however, an altogether different type of immigrant began arriving: the young nationalist who rejected diaspora life and sought to restore Jewish national existence in the historic homeland. Dozens of committees and societies for the settlement of the Land of Israel mushroomed in Russia and Eastern Europe, most notably *Hibbat Zion* ("Love of Zion"). By 1890 this group comprised some fourteen thousand members, about one-fifth of whom had already emigrated to Palestine.

In August 1897 the First Zionist Congress was held in the Swiss town of Basle, under the charismatic Theodor Herzl, a young and dynamic Austro-Hungarian journalist. A milestone in modern Jewish and Middle Eastern history, the congress defined the aim of Zionism as "the creation of a home for the Jewish people in Palestine to be secured by public law." It also established institutions for the promotion of this goal. By the outbreak of World War I in 1914, the Jewish community in Palestine (or the *Yishuv* as it was commonly known) had grown to some 85,000–100,000 people, twice its size at the turn of the century and four times its size in the early 1880s.[22]

This physical expansion reflected the broader development of the Yishuv into a cohesive and organized national community, with its own economic, political, and social institutions. The "old" agricultural settlements of the late nineteenth century were flourishing, while a string of new villages was vigorously following suit. An influx of capital from the diaspora allowed the development of the urban sector and laid the foundations of an industrial infrastructure; and while half of Palestine Jewry still lived in Jerusalem, the Jewish population in Jaffa and Haifa grew rapidly, and in 1909 Tel Aviv was established as the first modern Hebrew city. The Hebrew language had been revived and was rapidly establishing itself as the national language of the community.

Palestine at the time did not exist as a unified geographical entity; rather, it was divided between the Ottoman province of Beirut in the north and the district of Jerusalem in the south. Its local inhabitants, like the rest of the Arabic-speaking communities throughout the region, viewed themselves as subjects of the Ottoman Empire rather than members of a wider Arab nation, and extended the sultan their unconditional loyalty during the war. Not even the repressive Ottoman measures in the Levant from the autumn of 1915 onward could turn the local population against their suzerain. Not before the summer of 1917, after the British advance from Egypt into Palestine had driven home the reality of Allied successes, would mutterings of discontent begin to be heard. But even these were owing to the serious shortages of food, fodder, and wood caused by the Ottoman setbacks rather than to identification with the Hashemite "Great Arab Revolt." According to Colonel Richard Meinertzhagen, the director of the intelligence section of the Egyptian Expeditionary Force, on December 1, 1917, when British forces entered Ramleh, some twenty miles south of Jaffa,

> a large batch of Turkish prisoners were being marched through the village but they were not preceded by their British Guard. The Arabs, thinking that it was the return of the Turkish Army, turned out in force, yelling with delight and waving Turkish flags; it was not till the end of the column

appeared and they saw the British soldiers with fixed bayonets that they realized their mistake and great was their confusion. Their faces fell with a bump and they slunk disconsolate to their hovels.

As late as the end of August 1918, less than a month before the end of hostilities in the Middle East, a British report stated that

> the Muslim population of Judea took little or no interest in the Arab national movement. Even now the Effendi class, and particularly the educated Muslim-Levantine population of Jaffa, evince a feeling somewhat akin to hostility toward the Arab movement very similar to the feeling so prevalent in Cairo and Alexandria. This Muslim-Effendi class which has no real political cohesion, and above all no power of organization, is either pro-Turkish or pro-British.[23]

In these circumstances, the growing Jewish presence in Palestine encountered no widespread opposition beyond the odd local dispute. Even the Balfour Declaration of November 1917, in which the British government endorsed "the establishment in Palestine of a national home for the Jewish people" and pledged to "use its best endeavors to facilitate the achievement of this object," generated no immediate antagonism. It took one full year for the manifestation of local opposition to emerge in the form of a petition by a group of Arab dignitaries and nationalists proclaiming their loyalty to the Arab kingdom established in Damascus in the wake of the war, and headed by Sharif Hussein's third son, Faisal.

It was indeed the Hashemite imperial dream that placed the "Palestine Question" on the pan-Arab political agenda as its most celebrated cause. To begin with, there was the claim that the territory was included in the prospective Arab empire promised by McMahon to Hussein in their wartime correspondence. Actually, McMahon excluded Palestine from such an empire, a fact already acknowledged by Hussein in their correspondence and by Faisal shortly after the war.[24] This nevertheless did not prevent successive generations of pan-Arabists and their Western champions from charging Britain with a shameless betrayal of its wartime pledges.

This claim received its initial firepower from the grandiose ambitions of Faisal and Abdallah. Already during the revolt against the Ottoman Empire, Faisal had begun toying with the idea of establishing his own Syrian empire, independent of his father's prospective regional empire. In late 1917 and early 1918 he went so far as to negotiate this option with key members of the Ottoman leadership behind the backs of his father and his British allies. As his terms were rejected by the Ottomans, Faisal tried to gain great-power endorsement for his imperial dream by telling the post-war Paris Peace Conference that "Syria claimed her unity and her independence", and that it was "sufficiently advanced politically to manage her own internal affairs" if given adequate foreign and technical assistance.[25]

By way of promoting his Syrian ambitions, Faisal was not averse to courting the Zionist movement. In January 1919, shortly before giving evidence to the peace conference, he signed an agreement with Chaim Weizmann, head of the Zionists, expressing support for "the fullest guarantees for carrying into effect the British Government's Declaration of 2 November 1917", and for the adoption of "all necessary measures ... to encourage and stimulate immigration of Jews into Palestine on a large scale."[26]

When his efforts to gain international recognition for his imperial dream came to naught, Faisal quickly reneged on this historic promise. On 8 March 1920 he was crowned by his supporters as King Faisal I of Syria, "within its natural boundaries, including Palestine," and the newly installed monarch had no intention of allowing the Jewish national movement to wrest away any part of his kingdom. The coronation was thus followed by riots in Palestine as rumors spread regarding the country's imminent annexation to Syria. These culminated in early April 1920 in a pogrom in Jerusalem in which five Jews were killed and more than two hundred were wounded.

Although in July 1920 Faisal was overthrown by the French, his brief reign in Syria delineated the broad contours of the nascent Arab-Israeli conflict for decades to come. It did so by transforming a bilateral dispute between Arabs and Jews in Palestine into a pan-Arab-Jewish conflict, and, moreover, by making violence the primary instrument for opposing Jewish national aspirations. In May 1921 Arab riots claimed a far higher toll than they had in the whole of the previous year—some ninety dead and hundreds wounded. In the summer of 1929, another wave of violence resulted in the death of 133 Jews and the wounding of hundreds more.

Neither did Faisal abandon the "Greater Syrian" dream after his expulsion from Damascus. Using his subsequent position as the first monarch of Iraq, he toiled ceaselessly to bring about the unification of the Fertile Crescent, including Palestine, under his rule. This policy was sustained, following Faisal's untimely death in September 1933, by successive Iraqi leaders, notably by Nuri Said, who in 1943 published a detailed plan for pan-Arab unification that envisaged Syria, Lebanon, Palestine, and Transjordan as "reunited into one state".[27]

This scheme was vigorously opposed by Abdallah, who sought to transform the emirate of Transjordan, which he had ruled since the spring of 1921, into a "Greater Syrian" empire comprising Syria, Palestine, and possibly Iraq and Saudi Arabia. He was to nurture this ambition until the late 1940s, when it was dealt a mortal blow by the establishment of the State of Israel, and by the latter's ability to withstand the pan-Arab assault of May 1948; he never tired of reiterating his vision to whoever was prepared to listen. As late as May 11, 1948, three days before the proclamation of Israel and its subsequent invasion, Abdallah sought to convince the prominent Jewish leader Golda Meir to give up the idea of Jewish statehood. "Why are you in such a hurry to proclaim your state?" he asked. "Why don't you wait a few years? I will take over the whole country and you will be represented in my parliament. I will treat you very well and there will be no war." Meir's categorical rejection of the idea failed to impress the king. Even as she was taking her leave, Abdallah repeated his request that she consider his offer, "and if the reply were affirmative, it had to be given before May 15."[28]

The Arab states were no more amenable to Abdallah's imperial dream than the Jews. In early December 1947, shortly after the UN General Assembly had decided to partition Palestine into two states—one Jewish, one Arab—the Arab League rejected Abdallah's request for it to finance Transjordan's occupation of Palestine.[29] This rejection, however, was less motivated by concern for the protection of the Palestinian Arabs than by the desire to block Abdallah's incorporation of Palestine, or substantial parts of it, into his kingdom. So was the subsequent pan-Arab invasion of the newly proclaimed State of Israel in May 1948. This, on the face of it, was a shining demonstration of pan-Arab solidarity. In reality, it was a wholesale "scramble for Palestine" in the classic imperialist tradition. Had the Jews lost the war, their territory would not have been handed over to the Palestinian Arabs. Rather, it would have been divided among the invading Arab forces, for the simple reason that none of the region's Arab regimes viewed Palestine as a distinct entity and most of them had their own designs on this territory.

The eminent Arab-American historian Philip Hitti described the common Arab view to an Anglo-American commission of inquiry in 1946: "There is no such thing as Palestine in history, absolutely not."[30] A similar view was voiced by the Jerusalem newspaper *al-Wahda* (Unity), mouthpiece of the Arab Higher Committee, the effective "government" of the Palestinian Arabs, which in the summer of 1947 advocated the incorporation of Palestine (and Transjordan) into "Greater Syria." So did Fawzi Qauqji, commander of the pan-Arab force that invaded Palestine in early 1948. He expressed the hope that the UN partition resolution of November 1947 "will oblige the Arab states to put aside their differences and will prepare the way for a greater Arab nation." As late as 1974, the Syrian president Hafiz Assad still referred to

Palestine as being "not only a part of the Arab homeland but a basic part of southern Syria";[31] there is no evidence to suggest that he had changed his mind by the time of his death on June 10, 2000.

The British, who had ruled Palestine since the early 1920s under a League of Nations mandate, recognized this fact. As one official observed in mid-December 1947, "it does not appear that Arab Palestine will be an entity, but rather that the Arab countries will each claim a portion in return for their assistance [in the war against Israel], unless King Abdullah [sic] takes rapid and firm action as soon as the British withdrawal is completed." A couple of months later, the British high commissioner for Palestine informed the colonial secretary that "the most likely arrangement seems to be Eastern Galilee to Syria, Samaria and Hebron to Abdullah [sic], and the south to Egypt."[32]

This observation proved prescient. Neither Egypt nor Jordan ever allowed Palestinian self-determination in the parts of Palestine conquered by them during the 1948 war. Upon occupying the biblical lands of Judea and Samaria, Abdallah moved quickly to erase all traces of corporate Palestinian identity. On April 4, 1950, the territory was formally annexed to Jordan, to be known henceforth as the West Bank (of the Hashemite Kingdom of Jordan). Its residents became Jordanian citizens, and they were increasingly integrated into the kingdom's economic, political, and social structures. For its part, the Egyptian government showed no desire to annex the Gaza Strip but instead ruled the newly acquired area as an occupied military zone. This did not imply support of Palestinian nationalism, however, or of any sort of collective political awareness among the Palestinians. The refugees were denied Egyptian citizenship and remained in squalid, harshly supervised camps as a means of tarnishing the image of Israel in the eyes of the West and arousing pan-Arab sentiments. "The Palestinians are useful to the Arab states as they are," President Nasser candidly responded to an inquiring Western reporter in 1956. "We will always see that they do not become too powerful. Can you imagine yet another nation on the shores of the eastern Mediterranean!"[33]

Nasser's total lack of empathy with the Palestinian tragedy was indicative of the wider Arab attitude. Like the "Great Arab Revolt" of World War I, the lack of real pan-Arab solidarity manifested itself in deep animosity between the Palestinians and their would-be saviors, as the pan-Arab volunteer force that entered the country in early 1948 found itself at loggerheads with the community it was supposed to defend. Denunciations and violent clashes were common. The local population often refused to provide the foreign force with the basic necessities for its daily upkeep and military operations, while the army personnel for their part abused their Palestinian hosts, of whom they were openly contemptuous. When an Iraqi officer in Jerusalem was asked to explain his persistent refusal to greet the local populace, he angrily retorted that "one doesn't greet these dodging dogs, whose cowardice causes poor Iraqis to die."[34]

The Palestinian refugees fleeing to the Arab states were likewise derided as a cowardly lot who had shamefully deserted their homeland while expecting others to fight for them. In Syria, Lebanon, and Transjordan there were repeated calls for the return of the refugees to Palestine, or at the very least of the young men of military age, many of whom had arrived on the pretext of volunteering for the pan-Arab force assembled to fight in Palestine. When occasional restrictions in Syria and Lebanon on the entry of males between the ages of sixteen and fifty drove Palestinians to Egypt, they were often received with disdain. "Why should we go to Palestine to fight while Palestine Arab fighters are deserting the cause by flight to Egypt?" was the local reaction in Alexandria upon the arrival of several refugee ships from Haifa in late April 1948.

The Palestinians did not hesitate to reply in kind, blaming the Arab states, rather than Israel, for their disaster. In a letter to the Syrian representative at the UN, Jamal Husseini, vice-president of the Arab Higher Committee, complained that "the regular [Arab] armies did not enable the inhabitants of the country to defend themselves, but merely facilitated their escape from Palestine." The prominent Palestinian leader Emile Ghoury was even more forthright. In an interview with the London *Telegraph* in August 1948, he blamed the Arab states for the creation of the refugee problem; so did the organizers of protest demonstrations that took place in many West Bank towns on the first anniversary of Israel's establishment.[35] During a fact-finding mission to Gaza in June 1949, Sir John Troutbeck, head of the British Middle East office in Cairo and no friend to Israel or the Jews, was surprised to discover that while the refugees

> express no bitterness against the Jews (or for that matter against the Americans or ourselves) they speak with the utmost bitterness of the Egyptians and other Arab states. "We know who our enemies are," they will say, and they are referring to their Arab brothers who, they declare, persuaded them unnecessarily to leave their homes. . . . I even heard it said that many of the refugees would give a welcome to the Israelis if they were to come in and take the district over.[36]

The prevailing conviction among Palestinians that they had been, and remained, the victims of their fellow Arabs rather than of Israeli aggression was grounded not only in experience but in the larger facts of inter-Arab politics. During the decades of Palestinian dispersal following the 1948 war, the Arab states manipulated the Palestinian national cause to their own ends. So they did with regard to pan-Arabism's most cherished ideal of Arab unity.

Over the past eighty years Arab leaders have had many opportunities to undo the much-maligned international order established on the ruins of the Ottoman Empire—only to miss them all. The Iraqi and Transjordanian branches of the Hashemite dynasty, for instance, could have promoted the unification of their respective kingdoms rather than undermining each other's regional position. So, later on, could the avowedly pan-Arabist Ba'thist regimes in Syria and Iraq. But just as King Faisal and his Iraqi successors would not acquiesce in Abdallah's supremacy, and vice versa, so Saddam Hussein would never accept Assad as *primus inter pares.* In the late 1950s Syria did not wish to foot the bill for Nasser's high pan-Arab ideals by becoming an Egypt-dominated province in the United Arab Republic. Nor did Kuwaitis relish their designated role under Saddam Hussein's boot.

All this means that, for all its stated universalism, pan-Arabism has effectively been a euphemism for the imperialist ambitions of successive Arab dynasties and rulers, with its precepts often phrased and rephrased in accordance with self-serving goals. As the British official reported after his January 1918 meetings with Hussein: "It is obvious that the King regards Arab Unity as synonymous with his own Kingship."[37]

Even Abdel Rahman Kawakibi, widely considered the first exponent of the pan-Arab concept, was not above tailoring his argument to the needs of his paymaster, the Egyptian ruler Abbas Hilmi (1892–1914), who toyed with the idea of wresting the caliphate from the Ottoman sultan. For a handsome monthly allowance of fifty Egyptian pounds, Kawakibi became Abbas's propagandist, praising the Egyptian ruling family and deriding their Ottoman suzerain. He even went on a six-month mission to the Arabian Peninsula and the Muslim parts of India and East Africa to promote Abbas's claim to the caliphate.[38]

In his book *Umm al-Qura* (*The Mother of All Cities*—i.e., Mecca), Kawakibi blamed the Ottoman Empire for the ills of Islam, challenged its right to hold on to the caliphate, and called for the appointment of an Arab caliph, residing in Mecca, as spiritual head of an Islamic union. The emphasis on a spiritual caliph, in contrast to the millenarian Muslim conception of this figure as the umma's spiritual and temporal leader, seems to reflect an ulterior motive. The Ottoman sultan, whose right to the caliphate Kawakibi attempted to discredit, was the head of the most powerful Islamic empire on earth. The Egyptian ruler, whose right to the caliphate Kawakibi sought to establish and whom he praised in his book for his "religious fervor and Arab zeal," was the titular head of an Ottoman province that had been under British occupation since 1882.[39] The restoration of an Arab caliphate in the traditional sense—as a political and territorial empire—was totally inconceivable; the attainment of Arab spiritual pre-eminence seemed a more feasible objective.

If a pioneering intellectual figure of Kawakibi's stature could bend his argument to political ends, it was only natural that the actual imperial aspirants should do the same. Thus we find Faisal telling the Paris Peace Conference that few nations in the world were as homogeneous as the Arabs and that "personally he was afraid of partition. His principle was Arab unity"—then making the contradictory assertion that "the various provinces of Arab Asia—Syria, Irak, Jezireh, Hejaz, Nejd, Yemen—are very different economically and socially," and that "the object of all Arab hopes and fears" was a confederation of independent states—not a unitary empire.[40]

This doublespeak reflected the opportunistic nature of Faisal's imperial dream. As his father's representative at the peace conference, he had to pay the necessary lip service to Hussein's demand for a pan-Arab empire. At the same time, Faisal was acting as a free agent seeking to carve out his own Syrian empire. As he put it on one occasion, since Syria was "merchandise which has no owner," it was only natural for him to "try to appropriate it before the others."[41] The hopes and wishes of the governed, needless to say, counted for nothing, not least since there was tough opposition in the Levant to Hashemite domination in general, and to Faisal's personal rule in particular. It was the "white man's burden," Hijaz-style.

An Arab Caesar

As Hashemite ambitions faded away, following Abdallah's assassination in 1951 and the overthrow of the Iraqi monarchy seven years later, Cairo became the standard-bearer of the Arab imperial dream. This, on the face of it, was a rather surprising development. Physically detached from the eastern part of the Arabic-speaking world, with an illustrious imperial past dating back to Pharaonic times and followed by prolonged rule by non-Arab Islamic dynasties (Tulunids, Fatimids, Ayyubis, Mamluks, Ottomans, and Muhammad Ali's line), Egypt was excluded by early pan-Arabists from the envisaged Arab empire because "Egyptians do not belong to the Arab race."[1] For their part, generations of Egyptian intellectuals and politicians had looked down on the rest of the Arabs, using the term "Arab" in a derogatory fashion to denote a shiftless and uncultured nomad, someone to be viewed with contempt by a people with a millenarian tradition of settled cultivation. "If you add one zero to another, and then to another, what sum will you get?" said Saad Zaghlul, the doyen of modern Egyptian nationalism, dismissing the ideal of Arab unity.[2]

It was only in the 1930s that pan-Arab ideologues came to consider Egypt an integral and important part of the "Arab nation." Sati al-Husri even argued that, by virtue of its size, geographic location, and illustrious past, Egypt was destined to spearhead the Arab quest for unity. This theme struck a responsive chord among intellectuals and politicians within Egypt, where King Farouq (1937–52), himself of non-Arab stock, invested considerable energies in establishing himself as the leader of all Arabs, if not the caliph of all Muslims.[3] Yet it would not be until Gamal Abdel Nasser's rise to absolute power in the mid-1950s that Egypt became synonymous with the Arab imperial dream.

Son of a local postal clerk, Nasser was born in a small provincial town on January 15, 1918, but was sent to be educated in Cairo, where in 1937 he joined the military academy. He served as a staff captain in the 1948 Palestine war, after which he began conspiring with a group of fellow officers to topple the monarchy, which had ruled Egypt since the early nineteenth century. This was achieved by the military putsch of July 23, 1952, euphemized in Egyptian and Arab historiography as the "July Revolution." Two years later, Nasser removed General Muhammad Naguib, appointed by the conspirators as the country's president, to become Egypt's unassailable dictator, consolidating the national decision-making apparatus into his own hands with the support of a docile inner circle.[4]

Tall, charismatic, larger than life, Nasser was held in fascination and awe by his Egyptian subjects and the masses throughout the Arab world. For them he was not just another ruler. He was a hero of mythic proportions who could do no wrong, a link between a glorious past and a bright future, the embodiment of the Arab imperial dream. Nasser did not fail to give his audience its full value for money. From a publicity-shy, stiff, almost reclusive staff officer, he recast himself into a fiery speaker capable of extemporaneously captivating mass audiences for hours. "We shall all defend our pan-Arab identity and our Arabism and work until the Arab nation extends from the Atlantic Ocean to the Persian Gulf," he screamed at the top of his voice as he proclaimed the nationalization of the Suez Canal on July 26, 1956, a move that instantaneously transformed him into a pan-Arab idol. "Our battle is against imperialism and its stooges, our battle is against Israel, created by imperialism to destroy our pan-Arabism just as it has destroyed Palestine."[5]

This is not how things had appeared just four years earlier, in the wake of the 1952 putsch. "Apart from getting rid of the King and his corrupt associates, the Free Officers had few plans," recounted Muhammad Hassanein Heikal, longtime editor of the influential Cairo daily *al-Ahram* and Nasser's close friend and collaborator.

> They knew that they had to operate in three fields; they had to do something about the country's social and economic problems; they had to tackle the problem of the army; and they then had to pursue more purposefully than those they had supplanted the goal of complete independence. But there had been little or no preliminary debate or decisions on any of these topics.

Nasser himself admitted at the time that "I really have no plans . . . no foreign policy, I just react to what the British do."[6]

Upon his arrival in Egypt in July 1953, Miles Copeland, a former CIA operative who developed a warm and close relationship with Nasser, could not find a single member of the military junta who showed the slightest interest in Egypt's pan-Arab leadership. Even when this group later rallied behind Nasser's imperial ambitions, it would do so only to the extent that these served purely Egyptian interests. "Whenever any of us is doing something constructive," a prominent Egyptian told Copeland, "he is at that moment a Syrian or an Egyptian or a Lebanese . . . When he is doing something *destructive* he is an Arab."[7]

Nasser shared this skeptical attitude toward wider Arab solidarity. Like most Egyptians, his basic loyalties and affinities were parochial and his knowledge of Arab life outside his own country wholly derivative. He had not visited any Arab state or interacted with non-Egyptians prior to the 1952 coup, and although he frequented a number of Arab capitals during the 1950s this was hardly in circumstances that would teach him much about these societies. As late as 1958, when he became president of the newly established Egyptian-Syrian union, Nasser knew fewer than half-a-dozen Syrians. "I am Egyptian," he argued. "Egypt means the Bible, it means the very essence of all religions. . . . I love the word 'Egypt.'"

This glorification of Egypt contrasted starkly with Nasser's perception of the rest of the Arab world as an unpleasant amalgam of disparate groups and communities with little in common: "Iraqis are savage, the Lebanese venal and morally degenerate ['I picture Beirut as being one big night club,' he once told Copeland], the Saudis dirty, the Yemenis hopelessly backward and stupid, and the Syrians irresponsible, unreliable and treacherous."[8]

The Palestinians fared no better with him at the helm. During his years in power Nasser never allowed Palestinian self-determination in the Gaza Strip, conquered by Egypt during the 1948 war. Instead he ruled the newly acquired area as an occupied military zone with the local population kept under tight control, denied Egyptian citizenship, and subjected to severe restrictions on travel. In 1954–55, Nasser was receptive to a secret Anglo-American plan to have Israel's southern part, or the Negev, ceded to Egypt. Had this been realized, the future development of Palestinian nationalism would have been dealt a mortal blow, as a third of Palestine would have become part of Egypt.

In contrast to his scathing opinion of his Arab peers, Nasser initially viewed Israel and Zionism with deep respect. During the 1948 war, while encircled with his unit in the southern village of Faluja, he struck up a close friendship with an Israeli liaison officer by the name of Yeroham Cohen. According to Cohen, in their conversations Nasser was highly appreciative of the Zionist success in terminating Britain's presence in Palestine through a combined military and political struggle. He was also impressed by certain aspects of Israeli society, especially the kibbutzim and their "progressive" way of life. Showing little interest in other Arab states, Nasser argued that Egypt had yet to confront the formidable tasks of expelling the British and building a modern and progressive society.[9]

In *The Philosophy of the Revolution*, a programmatic little book published under his name in September 1954, Nasser fondly recalled his wartime conversations with Cohen on "the struggle of Israel against the English, and how [it] organized the underground resistance movement against them in Palestine, and how [the Israelis] were able to muster world public opinion."[10] Years after the war Nasser openly admitted to an American official that while he and his fellow officers had been "humiliated" by the Israelis during the 1948 war, their main grievance was directed "against our own superior officers, other Arabs, the British and the Israelis—in that order."[11] "Britain is the main cause of the Palestine catastrophe," he said in a public speech in Alexandria in December 1953. "The Arabs tend to forget this fact and blame Israel and the Jews, but they are afraid to acknowledge that Britain is the cause."[12] In line with this thinking, both Nasser's published war memoirs and *The Philosophy of the Revolution* are conspicuously free of anti-Israel invective.

This benign disposition disappeared overnight when Nasser embraced the pan-Arab cause. Suddenly the national movement that had been admired for its anti-imperialist struggle was transformed into the bridgehead of "world imperialism"—not only in the Middle East, where it allegedly sought to destroy pan-Arab unity by expanding from the Nile to the Euphrates, but also in the Third World. "It is noticeable that before the [imperial powers] quit any country in Africa," argued Nasser, "they ensure for Israel and the Israeli economy a place in that country."[13] Steadily inflating Israel from a puppet of world imperialism into a demonic force in its own right, and making it a regular theme in his public statements, Nasser went so far as to recommend *The Protocols of the Elders of Zion*, a virulent anti-Semitic tract fabricated by the Russian secret police at the turn of the twentieth century, as a useful guide to the "Jewish mind."[14]

This policy shift reflected a deliberate and opportunistic calculation rather than a genuine change of heart. Given Nasser's scornful view of his fellow Arabs on the one hand, and of inter-Arab collaboration during the 1948 war on the other, it was only natural for him to be deeply suspicious of anything that smacked of pan-Arabism. He viewed the Arab League as a fraudulent imperialist creation and had its veteran secretary-general Abdel Rahman Azzam removed from office.[15] Yet being the inveterate political animal that he was, Nasser quickly recognized the immense potential of pan-Arabism and its most celebrated cause, the "Palestine Question," for his domestic and international standing. "Formerly I believed neither in the Arabs nor in Arabism. Each time that you or someone else spoke to me of the Arabs, I laughed at what you said," he confided to a close friend at the end of 1953. "But then I realized all the potential possessed by the Arab states! That is what made me change my mind."[16]

What was this vast potential that captured Nasser's imagination? Strategic pre-eminence for one. By his own account, Nasser was an avid student of strategy who had long recognized the importance of "Greater Syria" for Egypt's geopolitical standing. In thinking along these lines Nasser was taking his cue from the two great nineteenth-century imperial aspirants— Muhammad Ali and his illustrious son Ibrahim—who sought to establish Egypt at the pinnacle of a new regional empire. But while the latter were hardened men of the sword who fought their way to an empire, occupying the Levant and marching on Istanbul, Nasser preferred to achieve his goal through less risky means, such as virulent propaganda, political manipulation, and subversion of rival Arab regimes. "Those who delude themselves into believing that [Arab] unity can be achieved with honeyed words alone should open their eyes and see the Egyptian army of today," he told the Egyptian general staff in March 1957. "But the army is not the only means. . . . There is this irregular war which costs us little, but which costs our enemies much."[17]

Aside from its strategic gains, pan-Arabism held great economic promise. As the most populous Arab country by a wide margin, Egypt's demographic prowess had long been matched by its economic weakness, first and foremost its lack of natural resources and an adequate labor base to service its burgeoning population. It was therefore evident to Nasser that if Egypt were to play an international role commensurate with its size it had to tap the economic resources of the wealthier Arab states, especially the oil producers among them. "Oil [is] a sinew of material civilization without which all its machines would cease to function," he argued in *The Philosophy of the Revolution*, adding that "half the proved reserves of oil in the world lie beneath Arab soil." This, in his view, placed the Arabs in a unique position to influence world affairs:

So we are strong. Strong not in the loudness of our voices when we wail or shout for help, but rather when we remain silent and measure the extent of our ability to act; when we really understand the strength resulting from the ties binding us together, making our land a single region from which no part can withdraw, and of which no part, like an isolated island, can be defended without defense of the whole.[18]

Nasser's emphasis on the indivisibility of the "Arab region" is not difficult to understand. Had he promoted a vision of the Middle East where, as in other parts of the world, states pursue their distinct national interests and are the sole beneficiaries of their natural resources, there would have been no way for Egypt to access Arab oil and its attendant economic and political gains. But if the Arabic-speaking countries constituted "a single region from which no part can withdraw," then Egypt would not only have the legitimate right to share their fabulous wealth but would also be able to become the region's leader. "With the inclusion of Iraq in an Egyptian-Syrian union, the unified state would secure the oil wells and pipelines east of Suez," Nasser enthused to the Syrian and Iraqi negotiators during the ill-fated talks on a trilateral union in 1963. "Its possibilities would be greater than France, commanding a population of fifty million."[19]

More immediately, pan-Arabism proved an invaluable weapon in Nasser's effort to overthrow Naguib. The elderly general had not participated in the 1952 putsch but was installed by the junta as head of state owing to his popular appeal, only to disappoint his benefactors by refusing to content himself with the titular figurehead role assigned to him. Nasser's attempt to remove Naguib from the presidency (in February–March 1954) unleashed a tidal wave of public resentment, and the ambitious colonel was forced to bide his time in anticipation of the right moment. By raising the pan-Arab banner, which harped simultaneously on the dominant political and intellectual ideology in the Arab world and the age-old Egyptian ambition for regional mastery, Nasser not only gave his personal standing vis-à-vis Naguib a major boost but also carved out for himself the political role he had been searching for since the 1952 coup. This laid the groundwork for his future rise as the foremost Arab leader, if not the embodiment of the Arab imperial dream.

Pan-Arabism was also instrumental in curbing the power and influence of the militant religious organization the Muslim Brothers, the main opponent of Nasser's personal rule during the 1950s and the early 1960s, by fusing pan-Arab and Islamic motives and creating pan-Islamic institutions to promote the regime's agenda. Foremost among these was the Islamic Congress, established in August 1954 in collaboration with Saudi Arabia and Pakistan, and headed by Anwar Sadat, one of Nasser's closest friends since his cadet days and his successor as Egyptian president. Officially designed to promote Islamic values and education, the congress quickly became a tool of Egyptian policy, mainly in Black Africa. A "Voice of Islam" radio station was established to broadcast Egyptian propaganda, and Egyptian teachers and experts were sent to spread Nasser's word across the Islamic world.[20]

On the Arab front, pan-Arabism proved useful in discrediting Nasser's rivals as "enemies of the Arab nation", and in enhancing Egypt's position in the struggle for regional leadership, especially vis-à-vis its main hegemonic rival, Iraq. The two countries had been contenders for regional mastery since antiquity, and their rivalry was resumed in earnest following the collapse of the Ottoman Empire as Egypt sought to contain repeated attempts by the Hashemites, in control of Iraq and Transjordan, to unify the Fertile Crescent, or most of it, under their rule. Even the Egyptian participation in the 1948 war was motivated by the desire to prevent Transjordan's King Abdallah from making Palestine part of the "Greater Syrian" empire he had been striving to create throughout his political career.

Now that Prime Minister Nuri Said was moving toward a regional defense pact with Turkey and Pakistan under Anglo-American auspices that could enhance Iraq's regional standing, Nasser quickly cried foul in the name of pan-Arab solidarity. "Every Arab now realizes the glaring fact that the West wants to settle in our land forever ... so that it may colonize, enslave and exploit it," lamented Cairo's *Voice of the Arabs*, while Nasser himself spelled out the alternative to the crystallizing regional pact. "The weight of the defense of the Arab states falls first and foremost on the Arabs and they are worthy of undertaking it," he stated. "The aim of the Revolution Government is for the Arabs to become one Nation with all its sons collaborating for the common welfare."[21] This claim failed to prevent Iraq from forming an alliance with Turkey in February 1955, acceded to shortly afterward by Britain, Iran, and Pakistan in what came to be known as the Baghdad Pact. But it did goad two of Iraq's neighbors—Syria and Saudi Arabia—into forming a tripartite alliance with Egypt in March 1955 as a counterweight to the pact.

His fiery rhetoric notwithstanding, Nasser was hardly a deep thinker. His ideas were derivative, amounting to little more than a rendition of the standard pan-Arab narrative about past glory and the alleged disruption of Arab unity by Western imperialism in the wake of World War I. His speeches were highly repetitive, comprising the same elements and the same arguments often presented in the same order. These would normally start with a blistering attack on "imperialism" and its alleged desire to subjugate the "Arab nation," before proceeding to applaud Egypt's heroic struggle for self-liberation, deride Nasser's Arab rivals as "imperialist stooges," castigate Israel as an imperialist creation designed to destroy pan-Arabism, and promise Egyptians and Arabs years of hard struggle.

The Philosophy of the Revolution is similarly a work of little originality. Aside from being ghostwritten by Heikal, who apparently inculcated Nasser with much of his pan-Arab ideological baggage, its themes and ideas are wholly consistent with the language and vocabulary of the Arab imperial dream, combining an admiring view of Islam's earliest epoch with the standard call for the restoration of the Arabic-speaking world's supposed unity. Even the book's celebrated vision of Egypt playing a leading role in three concentric circles—the Arab, the African, and the Islamic—breaks no new intellectual ground. With Islam constituting the linchpin of the Middle Eastern social and political order for over a millennium, its appropriation in the service of Nasser's ambitions was a natural, if not a self-evident, move. The perception of Egypt as the cornerstone of a unified Arab regional order can be traced back to Muhammad Ali's attempt to substitute his own empire for that of the Ottomans, while Nasser's African orientation dates back to Muhammad Ali's grandson Ismail Pasha, who sought to establish Egypt as a great empire in the Black Continent. On a more immediate level, Nasser's vision was influenced by Ahmad Hussein, spiritual father of the Young Egypt Society (*Misr al-Fatat*), a nationalist-fascist organization in which the young Nasser was schooled in the early 1930s. Hussein had advocated the transformation of Egypt into "a great empire comprising Egypt and the Sudan, allied to the Arab states, and leading the Muslim world."[22]

Nasser's enormous impact on the Arab imperial dream, though, lay not in the theoretical refinement of the ideal but in its unprecedented inculcation among the Arabic-speaking populations of the Middle East. Day by day, from dawn to dusk, eleven powerful transmitters were broadcasting militant Egyptian propaganda to each of the Arab states, extolling the virtues of pan-Arab unity and deriding its supposed enemies. Addressing the proverbial "Arab street" rather than the ruling elites, these broadcasts often urged their listeners to rise up against their leaders or to assassinate them. Jordan's King Hussein, Saudi Arabia's King Saud, and the Lebanese president Camille Chamoun, all bitter enemies of Nasser, were singled out for special vilification. So were Israel and the Western nations. Englishmen and Frenchmen were "imperialists and bloodsuckers," Americans "pythons, white dogs, and pigs." Listeners were regularly fed the most outlandish lies and conspiracy theories, thinly disguised as "news reports." They were informed of regular murders of Egyptians in the United States, of bombings of Arabs that had never occurred, of demonstrations and riots in Arab towns that existed on no map, and so on and so forth.[23]

While this propaganda made a deeper impression on the Arab masses than previous attempts to spread the imperial message, it was clearly driven by opportunistic self-interest rather than genuine conviction and was heightened or toned down in accordance with Nasser's shifting priorities and needs. There was nothing ideological about Nasser's imperialist ambitions. They were purely personal, and he pursued them with persistent aggressiveness, artfully substituting Egyptian interests and personal ambition for the general Arab good. "The pages of history are full of heroes who created for themselves roles of glorious valor which they played at decisive moments," Nasser wrote in *The Philosophy of the Revolution*.

It seems to me that within the Arab circle there is a role, wandering aimlessly in search of a hero. And I do not know why it seems to me that this role, exhausted by its wanderings, has at last settled down, tired and weary, near the borders of our country and is beckoning to us to move, to take up its lines, to put on its costume, since no one else is qualified to play it.[24]

"I do not think of myself as a leader of the Arab world," he added a few years later. "But the Arab peoples feel that what we do in Egypt reflects their collective hopes and aspirations."[25]

This recalls Sharif Hussein's 1918 comment that although the Arabs as a whole had not asked him to be their king, he was the only one who stood sufficiently above his peers to become king of pan-Arabia. Though Nasser, unlike Hussein, did not frame his ambition in such blatantly personal terms but rather spoke about Egypt as the only entity capable of leading the Arabs, there is little doubt that he viewed himself as the personification of Egypt. Openly contemptuous of political parties and institutions, Nasser argued from the moment of his political ascent that his mandate came from the people, which made him answerable only to them. Since the "people" could hardly express its wishes in the repressive police state that he created—with its terrifying security services, draconian legislation, outlawed political parties, and state-controlled media—Nasser quickly identified Egypt with his own persona, in speech and in thought, personalizing the national interest and nationalizing his personal interest.

While presenting his anti-Western policy as a Manichean struggle over Arab destiny, Nasser did not shy away from improving Egypt's relations with Britain and the United States whenever it suited his needs. In November 1954, at the height of his campaign to forestall the creation of the Baghdad Pact, he signed a $40 million economic assistance agreement with the United States. Nasser even implied that his virulent anti-Western rhetoric was a retaliation for what he considered an Anglo-American violation of a "gentleman's agreement" to place Egypt—that is, himself—in the driver's seat of inter-Arab politics, and their preference for his nemesis, Iraq's Nuri Said, in this role.[26]

The July 1956 nationalization of the Suez Canal offers a similarly vivid illustration of Nasser's instrumentalism. This clear act of self-interest, which enhanced Egypt's regional prestige and gave its fledgling economy a much-needed boost in the form of toll revenues worth in excess of 10 percent of the Egyptian national budget, was usefully transformed into an altruistic pan-Arab move aimed at eliminating the remnants of Western colonialism in the region. Nasser repeated the same trick four months later by presenting Egypt's crushing defeat by Israel in the Sinai Peninsula, and its rather lackluster military performance against a combined Anglo-French landing in Port Said, as a heroic defense of the "Arab nation" against Western imperialism. What his account blatantly ignored was that it was the United States that had saved Nasser's regime from assured destruction by forcing the invading forces to cease hostilities before achieving their objectives.

Nasser's approach to the organizations and institutions charged with promoting the pan-Arab cause was no less indicative of his equation of Arab unity with his own pre-eminence. The Arab League, originally viewed by Nasser as a corrupt and inept organization, was quickly transformed into an extension of Egyptian will, with many of its existing officials, including the secretary-general, being replaced by Egyptian nationals. The international confederation of Arab trade unions, established in Damascus in March 1956 (with headquarters in Cairo) to promote the "unity of the Arab Nation" and ensure "a better life for workers in the Arab fatherland," was firmly controlled by Egyptians and used to service Egyptian interests in flagrant violation of its constitution. So were the Afro-Asian solidarity committee and the Islamic congress, which, rather than advancing their lofty ideals of international and religious solidarity, provided a vehicle for Nasser's ambitions in Africa and the Islamic world.[27]

Even the cherished goal of Arab unification—a shibboleth of pan-Arabism—was no more than a tool to promote Nasser's imperial dream. For all his hyped rhetoric about unification's many virtues, Nasser would not tolerate such a development unless it was associated with his own leadership. When in the summer of 1961, following the proclamation of Kuwaiti independence, Iraq demanded the incorporation of the emirate into its territory on account of its having been a part of the Ottoman velayet of Basra, Nasser had no qualms about collaborating with the "reactionary regimes" of Jordan and Saudi Arabia, which he had long been seeking to subvert, to prevent an Iraqi action against Kuwait. There was absolutely no way that he would allow Egypt's perennial rival to regional mastery to take any credit for promoting the ideal of pan-Arab unification.

Unification, when it came, would be on Nasser's terms, and in his own time. Upon forming the 1955 alliance with Syria and Saudi Arabia, he adamantly refused to make the deal any more binding than the minimum required for the immediate goal of undermining the Baghdad Pact. "We had a hand in preparing the draft of the Egyptian-Syrian-Saudi pact, conceiving it as a first step towards a federation of the three countries," recalled Michel Aflaq, a Ba'th founding father.

But the pact remained a dead-letter. It foundered in interminable discussions stretching over months on the question of a common defense budget and a common general staff. Egypt objected that she was poor and could not pay. Saudi Arabia was ready to pay but was reluctant to abandon any sovereignty. All parties were reticent when it came to discussing economic coordination.[28]

At a time when he was feigning poverty to Syria, Nasser found the necessary funds for a large-scale arms deal with the Soviet Union (with Czechoslovakia acting as a front) designed to enhance Egypt's regional standing. "To those who ask me whether I prefer the United States or Russia, I say that I prefer Egypt," he argued. "Our actions should be prompted solely by our country's interests."[29]

When Nasser eventually established a union with Syria in February 1958, it entailed the imposition of Egypt's domination over Syria rather than a partnership between equals, with power and authority concentrated in Nasser's hands and in Cairo more generally. All political parties in Syria were dissolved, and in October 1958 Nasser announced a new cabinet for the entire United Arab Republic (UAR), as the merger was called, in which fourteen ministries out of twenty-one, including the most important ones, were headed by Egyptians. The Syrian armed forces were subordinated to their Egyptian counterparts, the Syrian high court was replaced by a council of state on the Egyptian model, and laws governing a state of emergency were unified with those in Egypt, which, in turn, gave Nasser draconian powers. (One such law, passed in 1957, imposed the death penalty for such offenses as sabotage, libel, distributing secret leaflets, and insulting the president of the Egyptian republic.) The largely unregulated Syrian economy was gradually molded along the lines of its centrally controlled Egyptian counterpart. Most of the ministries concerned with economic affairs (such as finance, economics, communications, supply, public works, rural affairs, etc.) were united and placed under the authority of Cairo-based ministers.[30]

There is little doubt that the Egyptian-Syrian merger was not Nasser's ultimate ambition but rather a stepping stone to his imperialist ambitions. The UAR would bring together the entire Arab nation "whether they like it or not," he boasted shortly after unification, "because this is the will of the Arab people." And the Egyptian weekly *Akhar Sa'a* published a map envisaging the newly established union after thirty years: Lebanon and Israel had disappeared as political entities, and the Arab world and portions of Black Africa were included within the shaded area of the new Egyptian empire.[31]

This was not to be. By the end of 1958, the euphoria stirred by the UAR's creation had all but died away. In mid-July, some seventeen hundred US marines landed in Lebanon to shore up the government against a pro-Nasserite rebellion, and their number quickly grew to fourteen thousand. Another two thousand British paratroopers were airlifted from Cyprus to Jordan to protect King Hussein against Egyptian-Syrian subversion. Although it would take several months to stabilize the situation in the two countries, their imminent submergence under the tidal wave of Nasserism was irrevocably checked. Even what fleetingly seemed like Nasser's greatest triumph—the overthrow of the

Iraqi monarchy in a bloody coup on July 14, 1958—only served to confirm the decline of his imperial dream. The putsch's leader, Brigadier Abdel Karim Qassem, was vehemently opposed to subordinating Iraq to its historic nemesis. Within days of the coup Qassem turned down an Egyptian invitation to participate in the celebrations on the sixth anniversary of the July 1952 "revolution." This inaugurated a long and bitter enmity with Nasser that proved more damaging to the Egyptian dictator than his past tussles with Nuri Said. While Said was a quintessential representative of the *ancien régime* who could readily be discredited as a "reactionary," Qassem was made of the same fabric as Nasser: a "progressive anti-imperialist" officer who had toppled a reigning monarchy—and who was consequently far less vulnerable to Egyptian delegitimization tactics.

No less galling for Nasser were the fissures in the UAR itself. Within months of unification there were mutterings of discontent in the Syrian military, as well as reported strikes and demonstrations in Syrian cities. To make things worse, sharp disagreements ensued between Nasser and the Ba'th, which had spearheaded the Syrian drive toward unification but was subsequently forced to disband along with all other Syrian parties. By the autumn of 1959 disillusionment with the union throughout Syria was running high, and Nasser appointed Field Marshal Abdel Hakim Amer, his close associate and second-in-command, as the country's effective ruler. As Amer failed to contain the crisis—in December 1959 all Ba'th ministers resigned their posts in protest over their growing marginalization—Nasser was forced to increase his reliance on Colonel Abdel Hamid Sarraj, the young and brutal head of Syrian military intelligence and the chief enforcer of the union in Syria. In early 1960, to Amer's exasperation, Sarraj was appointed minister of the interior and set about rewarding his benefactor by unleashing a ferocious campaign of repression. This did not help either, and in August 1961 Nasser kicked Sarraj upward by making him vice-president and commander-in-chief, and moving him to Cairo. The embittered Sarraj complied, but not before warning that his removal would open the door to the union's break-up. His words proved prophetic. On September 28, 1961, a group of Syrian officers mounted a coup, expelled Amer from Damascus, and announced Syria's secession from the union.

The Syrian move could not have been more traumatic for Nasser. Although restiveness in the UAR's Northern Region, as Syria was named after unification, had been steadily mounting for years, and the possibility of a coup by disgruntled Syrian officers was occasionally mooted, the Egyptian dictator could not bring himself to entertain the possibility of the collapse of his imperial dream. Even when he received news of the putsch on the morning of September 28, Nasser refused to accept this fateful development for what it was, instead denouncing it in a radio broadcast as a treacherous act by a "small force" that would shortly be crushed. When in the afternoon hours the rebels reached an agreement with Amer to maintain the union in return for having their grievances redressed, notably the "Egyptianization" of the Syrian armed forces, Nasser dismissed the deal out of hand. "The United Arab Republic cannot be based on bargaining," he announced. "It is not possible for us to bargain over our Arabism."[32]

Given this mindset, it is hardly surprising that Nasser never blamed himself, let alone his imperialist ambitions, for the breakup of the union. Not prone to self-criticism in the first place (the handful of members of the Egyptian leadership who dared to question the slightest aspects of his personal rule were peremptorily removed from power with some placed under arrest), Nasser would not acknowledge that it was the high-handed Egyptian domination that had largely bred Syrian separatism. Neither did it occur to him that this very domination, and the Syrian response, provided further proof of the supremacy of local patriotism over the flimsy ideal of the "Arab nation." For if all Arabs were equal members of the same nation, there would have been no room for the subordination of some of them merely on account of geographical origin.

Immersing himself in the same kind of conspiratorial thinking that his awesome propaganda machine had been spreading for years, Nasser quickly castigated the secessionists as traitors who took their orders from Western imperialists, their Middle Eastern bridgehead (Israel), and local lackeys such as Jordan's King Hussein and the Iranian shah, Muhammad Reza Pahlavi. If the Egyptian regime had erred in the running of the union, such errors were not the product of excessive domination but rather of naïve goodwill. "We trusted the forces of reaction, and were deceived by them," Nasser told Egyptians a few days after secession, promising to redouble his efforts "against the forces of reaction, exploitation, and imperialism, in order to establish social justice, to protect socialism, and to protect Arab nationalism."[33]

This was easier said than done. For nearly a decade Nasser had been going from strength to strength, skillfully turning setbacks and defeats into shining victories and establishing himself in the eyes of the Arab masses as the embodiment of their imperial dream. Now that his most cherished gain had been embarrassingly snatched from his fingers, he needed a quick success to redeem his hitherto invincible image. This was seemingly found in the most unlikely corner of the Arab world: the remote and feudal state of Yemen. In September 1961 the long-reigning imam died. Shortly afterward the military stormed the royal palace and executed those members of the royal family they had managed to capture. They failed, however, to find the imam's son and successor, who fled to the mountains from where he waged a sustained guerrilla campaign, with Saudi arms and money, against the military junta.

As the fighting dragged on inconclusively, Nasser attempted to regain his lost prestige by shoring up a "revolutionary" regime against a "reactionary" challenger, conveniently overlooking the fact that only a few years earlier he had himself welcomed this feudal monarchy into the Egyptian-Syrian union. Before long, however, it transpired that Nasser had bitten off more than he could chew. What was arguably conceived as a brief and cheap operation became a prolonged and costly foreign venture as the Egyptian forces, untrained and ill-equipped for mountain warfare, were bogged down in the rugged terrain. Repeated attempts to achieve a decisive military outcome through air support and the use of poison gas did little to dent the royalist position, and the number of Egyptian troops in Yemen increased steadily: from thirteen thousand by the end of 1962, to forty thousand in 1964, to seventy thousand in 1965. But still they could not win the war, and the frustrated Nasser began to look for alternative issues that could extricate him from what was rapidly turning into yet another embarrassing setback.

This brought him in no time to the "Palestine Question." The issue had constituted an integral part of inter-Arab politics since the mid-1930s, with anti-Zionism forming the main common denominator of pan-Arab solidarity and its most effective rallying cry. Having ignored it in his early days, Nasser endorsed this problem with great zeal in the mid-1950s as a corollary of his imperial dream. Now that this dream lay in ruins following the collapse of the UAR and his inconclusive entanglement in Yemen, Nasser reintroduced the Palestine Question as the trump card in reviving his political fortunes. "Arab unity or the unity of the Arab action or the unity of the Arab goal is our way to the restoration of Palestine and the restoration of the rights of the people of Palestine," he argued. "Our path to Palestine will not be covered with a red carpet or with yellow sand. Our path to Palestine will be covered with blood."

"When we speak of Israel, we must think of 1948 and what happened in 1948": Nasser invoked the traumatic historical memory of the Palestine war to underscore his demand for pan-Arab unity.

> There was no Arab unity and no line for concerted Arab action. There was no plan for a unified Arab objective. . . . The Arab countries were defeated because they were seven countries fighting against one country, namely Israel. . . . In order that we may liberate Palestine, the Arab nation must unite, the Arab armies must unite, and a unified plan of action must be established.[34]

By way of transforming these high principles into concrete plans, in January 1964 Nasser convened the first all-Arab summit in Cairo to discuss ways and means to confront the "Israeli threat." A prominent item on the agenda was the adoption of a joint strategy to prevent Israel from using the Jordan River waters to irrigate the barren Negev desert in the south of the country. A no less important decision was to "lay the proper foundations for organizing the Palestinian people and enabling it to fulfill its role in the liberation of its homeland and its self-determination." Four months later, a gathering of 422 Palestinian activists in East Jerusalem, then under Jordanian rule, established the Palestine Liberation Organization (PLO) and approved its two founding documents—the organization's Basic Constitution and the Palestinian National Covenant.

At a stroke Nasser had managed to restore his lost prestige and influence. He was yet again the undisputed leader of the Arab world, the only person capable of making the Arabs transcend, however temporarily, their self-serving interests for the sake of the collective good. He was nowhere near his cherished goal of promoting the actual unification of the Arab world under his leadership, as he had seemingly been in 1958. Yet he had successfully hijacked pan-Arabism's most celebrated cause and established a working relationship with his erstwhile enemies in Amman and Riyadh. In a second summit meeting in Alexandria in October 1964, the heads of the Arab states accepted Nasser's long-term anti-Israel strategy. This envisaged the laying of the groundwork for a decisive confrontation with Israel through the patient buildup of Arab might in all areas—military, economic, social, and political—and the simultaneous weakening of Israel through concrete actions such as the diversion of the Jordan River estuaries. The PLO was authorized to create an army of Palestinian volunteers, to which the Arab governments were pledged to give support, and a special fund was established for the reorganization of the Lebanese, Syrian, and Jordanian armies under a united Arab command.

Nasser's strategic planning was thrown into disarray before too long by an unexpected sequence of events that led within a few weeks to the third Arab-Israeli war since 1948. The event that set in train this escalation was a Soviet warning (in early May 1967) of large-scale Israeli troop concentrations along the border with Syria aimed at launching an immediate attack.[35] The previous month the Israeli Air Force had shot down six Syrian fighters, and the Syrians demanded Egyptian military support in accordance with the defense pact signed between the two states in November 1966. This placed Nasser in a dilemma. Since he had little sympathy for the radical Ba'th regime, which had seized power in a military coup in February 1966, his main aim in mending the fences with Damascus, after years of alienation, was to gain the maximum control over the impetuous Syrians. Now all of a sudden his plan soured. Instead of enabling him to assert his authority over his junior partner, the defense pact threatened to force him into a crisis not of his own making. To calm things down, Nasser sent his prime minister and air-force commander to Damascus for consultations, yet took no concrete action on Syria's behalf.

Once the Soviets had warned of an imminent Israeli attack, however, Nasser could no longer remain aloof. As standard-bearer of the Arab imperial dream he had no choice but to come to the rescue of a threatened Arab ally, tied to Egypt in a bilateral defense treaty, especially when the rival regimes in Jordan and Saudi Arabia were openly ridiculing his failure to live up to his high pan-Arab rhetoric. On May 14, the Egyptian armed forces were placed on the highest state of alert and two armored divisions began moving into the Sinai Peninsula, formally demilitarized since the 1956 Suez war. That same day, the Egyptian chief of staff, Lt.-General Muhammad Fawzi, arrived in Damascus to get a first-hand impression of the military situation and to coordinate a joint response in the event of an Israeli attack. To his surprise, Fawzi found no trace of Israeli concentrations along the Syrian border or troop movements in northern Israel. He reported these findings to his superiors, but this had no impact on the Egyptian move into Sinai, which continued apace. "From that point onward," Fawzi was to recall in his memoirs, "I began to believe that the issue of Israeli concentrations along the Syrian border was not . . . the only or the main cause of the military deployments which Egypt was undertaking with such haste."[36]

Within less than twenty-four hours, Nasser's objective had been transformed from the deterrence of an Israeli attack against Syria into an outright challenge to the status quo established in the wake of the 1956 war. With Fawzi's reassuring findings corroborated both by Egyptian military intelligence and by a special UN inspection,[37] and the Israelis going out of their way to reassure the Soviets that they had not deployed militarily along their northern border,[38] Nasser must have realized that there was no imminent threat to Syria. He could have halted his troops at that point and claimed a political victory, having deterred an (alleged) Israeli attack against Syria. But his resolute move had catapulted him yet again to a position of regional pre-eminence that he was loath to relinquish. At a stroke he had managed to undo one of Israel's foremost gains in the 1956 war—the de facto demilitarization of the Sinai Peninsula—without drawing a serious response from Jerusalem. Now that the Egyptian troops were massing in Sinai, Nasser decided to raise the ante and eliminate another humiliating remnant of that war, for which he had repeatedly been castigated by his rivals in the Arab world: the presence of a United Nations Emergency Force (UNEF) on Egyptian (but not on Israeli) territory as a buffer between the two states.

As the UN observers were quickly withdrawn and replaced by Egyptian forces, Nasser escalated his activities still further. Addressing Egyptian pilots in Sinai on May 22, he announced the closure of the Strait of Tiran, at the southern mouth of the Gulf of Aqaba, to Israeli and Israel-bound shipping. "The Gulf of Aqaba constitutes our Egyptian territorial waters," he announced to the cheers of an ecstatic audience. "Under no circumstances will we allow the Israeli flag to pass through the Aqaba Gulf." The following day the Egyptian mass media broke the news to the entire world.

Did Nasser consider the possibility that his actions might lead to war? All the available evidence suggests that he did. Initially, when he briefly believed in the imminence of an Israeli attack against Syria, he could not have taken for granted that the Egyptian deployment in Sinai would have deterred such an action, in which case he would have been forced to come to Syria's defense. Moreover, the demilitarization of Sinai was seen by Israel as vital to its national security, which made its violation a legitimate *casus belli*. But then, Nasser was being rapidly entrapped by his imperialist ambitions. He began deploying his troops in Sinai out of fear that failure to do so would damage his pan-Arab position beyond repair. He kept on escalating his activities, knowing full well that there was no threat of an Israeli attack against Syria, because of his conviction that the continuation of the crisis boosted his pan-Arab standing.

It is true that the lack of a prompt and decisive Israeli response to the Egyptian challenge, together with the quick realization that there were no Israeli concentrations along the Syrian border, might have convinced Nasser that the risks were not so great, and that war was not inevitable. Yet when he decided to remove UNEF and to close the Strait of Tiran, Nasser undoubtedly knew that he was crossing the threshold from peace to war. "Now with our concentrations in Sinai, the chances of war are fifty-fifty," he told his cabinet on May 21, during a discussion on the possible consequences of a naval blockade. "But if we close the Strait, war will be a one hundred percent certainty." "We all knew that our armaments were adequate—indeed, infinitely better than in the October 1973 War," recalled Anwar Sadat, who participated in that crucial meeting. "When Nasser asked us our opinion, we were all agreed that the Strait should be closed—except for [Prime Minister] Sidqi Sulayman, who pleaded with Nasser to show more patience. . . . [But] Nasser paid no attention to Sulayman's objections. He was eager to close the Strait so as to put an end to the Arab maneuverings and maintain his great prestige within the Arab world."[39]

The die was cast. Having maneuvered himself yet again into the driver's seat of inter-Arab politics, Nasser could not climb down without risking a tremendous loss of face. He was approaching the brink with open eyes, and if there was no way out of the crisis other than war, so be it: Egypt was prepared. Daily consultations between the political and military leaderships were being held. The Egyptian forces in Sinai were being assigned their operational tasks. In a widely publicized article in *al-Ahram* on May 26, the newspaper's editor-in-chief, Nasser's mouthpiece Muhammad Hassanein Heikal, explained why war between Egypt and Israel was inevitable. A week later, at a meeting with the armed forces' supreme command, Nasser predicted an Israeli strike against Egypt within forty-eight to seventy-two hours at the latest.[40]

The coming of war is seldom a happy occasion. It is often fraught with misgivings and apprehensions. But if doubts assailed Nasser's peace of mind, he gave them no public expression. The Egyptian war preparations were carried out in a confident and even extravagant fashion, in front of the watching eyes of the world media. The closer Nasser came to the brink, the more aggressive he became. "The Jews have threatened war," he gloated in his May 22 speech, "we tell them: You are welcome, we are ready for war." Four days later he took a big step forward, announcing that if hostilities were to break out, "our main objective will be the destruction of Israel." "Now that we have the situation as it was before 1956," Nasser proclaimed on another occasion, "Allah will certainly help us to restore the status quo of before 1948."[41]

Once again imperialist winds were blowing. "This is the real rising of the Arab nation," Nasser boasted, while the few skeptics within the Egyptian leadership were being rapidly converted to belief in victory over Israel. In the representative words of Naguib Mahfuz, Egypt's foremost writer and winner of the 1988 Nobel Prize, "When Nasser held his famous press conference, before the June 1967 war, and spoke with confident pomp, I took our victory over Israel for granted. I envisaged it as a simple journey to Tel Aviv, of hours or days at the most, since I was convinced we were the greatest military power in the Middle East."[42]

By this time, the conflict was no longer about the presence of UN forces on Egyptian soil or freedom of navigation in the Gulf of Aqaba, let alone the alleged Israeli threat to Syria. It had been transformed into a jihad to eradicate the foremost "remnant of Western imperialism" in the Middle East. "During the crusaders' occupation, the Arabs waited seventy years before a suitable opportunity arose and they drove away the crusaders," Nasser said, styling himself as the new Saladin: "recently we felt that we are strong enough, that if we were to enter a battle with Israel, with God's help, we could triumph."[43]

Nasser's militancy was contagious. The irritating chorus of criticism had fallen silent. His former Arab rivals were standing in line to rally behind his banner. On the morning of May 30, King Hussein, who at the beginning of the crisis still mocked Nasser for "hiding behind UNEF's apron," arrived in Cairo where he immediately signed a defense pact with Egypt. He returned to Amman later that day accompanied by Ahmad Shuqeiri, head of the PLO and hitherto one of the king's arch-enemies. The following day an Egyptian general arrived in Amman to command the eastern front in the event of war. On June 4, Iraq followed suit by entering into a defense agreement with

Egypt, and Nasser informed King Hussein that their pact now included Iraq as well. By this time, Arab expeditionary forces—including an Iraqi armored division, a Saudi and a Syrian brigade, and two Egyptian commando battalions—were making their way to Jordan.[44] The balance of forces, so it seemed to the Arabs, had irreversibly shifted in their favor. The moment of reckoning with the "Zionist entity," as they pejoratively called Israel, had come. "Have your authorities considered all the factors involved and the consequences of the withdrawal of UNEF?" the commander of the UN force, General Indar Jit Rikhye, asked the Egyptian officers bearing the official demand. "Oh yes sir! We have arrived at this decision after much deliberation and we are prepared for anything. If there is war, we shall next meet at Tel Aviv."

The Iraqi president, Abdel Rahman Aref, was no less forthright. "This is the day of the battle," he told the Iraqi forces leaving for Jordan. "We are determined and united to achieve our clear aim—to remove Israel from the map. We shall, Allah willing, meet in Tel Aviv and Haifa."[45]

After the war Nasser would emphatically deny that he had any intention to attack Israel, a claim that was quickly endorsed by numerous apologists seeking to present the Egyptian leader as the hapless victim of an uncontrollable chain of events. Some went so far as to portray Nasser as a mindless creature thriving on hollow rhetoric and malleable in the extreme: "retired members of the old Revolutionary Command Council wander in and out of meetings and give their opinions; Nasser butts in and nobody pays much attention to him; he takes journalists seriously and revises his intelligence estimate on the basis of their remarks; he is influenced by the casual conversation of diplomats."[46]

Aside from doing a great injustice to Nasser—the charismatic dictator who had ruled Egypt autocratically for over a decade and mesmerized millions throughout the Arab world—this description has little basis in reality. As evidenced both by Nasser's escalatory behavior during the crisis and by captured military documents revealing elaborate plans for an invasion of Israel, the Egyptian president did not stumble into war but orchestrated it with open eyes. He steadily raised his sights in accordance with the vicissitudes in the crisis until he set them on the ultimate objective: the decisive defeat of Israel and, if possible, its destruction.

Yet for all his militant zeal, Nasser had weighty reasons to forgo a first strike at this particular time. His war preparations had not been completed: the Egyptian forces in Sinai were still digging in; the Arab expeditionary forces to Jordan had not yet been fully deployed; and coordination of the operational plans of the Arab military coalition required more time. Nasser also feared that an Egyptian attack would trigger a US military response that might neutralize the new Arab political and military superiority over Israel, which had been gained by the most remarkable demonstration of pan-Arab unity since the 1948 war.[47]

Nasser's fears of American intervention were compounded by the nature of the Egyptian operational plan, which envisaged deep thrusts into Israel's territory. An armored division was to break out of the Gaza Strip and capture some border villages inside Israel, while another armored division was to cut off the southern Negev from the rest of Israel, thereby achieving the long-standing Egyptian objective of establishing a land bridge with Jordan.[48] Given Nasser's belief in the US commitment to Israel's territorial integrity, such plans could hardly be implemented if Egypt were to take the military initiative. Their execution as an act of self-defense in response to an Israeli attack was a completely different matter, however.

This explains Nasser's readiness to play the political card, such as his decision to send his vice president, Zakaria Muhieddin, to Washington. He had no intention whatever of giving ground; the move was aimed at cornering Israel and making it more vulnerable to Arab pressure and, eventually, war. Robert Anderson, a special American envoy sent to Egypt to defuse the crisis, reported to President Lyndon Johnson that Nasser showed no sign of backing down and spoke confidently about the outcome of a conflict with Israel.[49]

Anderson was not the only person to have heard this upbeat assessment. Nasser's belief in Egypt's ability to absorb an Israeli strike and still win the war was widely shared by the Egyptian military and was readily expressed to the other members of the Arab military coalition. In his May 30 visit to Cairo, King Hussein was assured by Nasser of Egypt's full preparedness against an Israeli air strike: no more than 15–20 percent losses would be incurred before the Egyptian air force dealt a devastating blow to Israel. The other members of the Jordanian delegation heard equally confident words from Abdel Hakim Amer, Nasser's deputy and commander of the Egyptian armed forces.[50] When the Egyptian Foreign Minister, Mahmoud Riad, asked Amer about the armed forces' state of readiness, he was told that "if Israel actually carried out any military action against us I could, with only one third of our forces, reach Beersheba."[51]

The most eloquent public exposition of this euphoric state of mind was provided by Muhammad Heikal's May 26 article on the inevitability of war. "Egypt has exercised its power and achieved the objectives of this stage without resorting to arms so far," he wrote:

> But Israel has no alternative but to use arms if it wants to exercise power. This means that the logic of the fearful confrontation now taking place between Egypt which is fortified by the might of the masses of the Arab nation, and Israel which is fortified by the illusion of American might,

dictates that Egypt, after all it has now succeeded in achieving, must wait, even though it has to wait for a blow. This is necessitated also by the sound conduct of the battle, particularly from an international point of view. Let Israel begin. Let our second blow then be ready. Let it be a knockout.[52]

A Reckoning of Sorts

This was not quite the knockout Nasser had in mind. Instead of dealing Israel a mortal blow he saw his air force destroyed on the ground within three hours of the outbreak of hostilities on June 5, 1967, and his army crushed and expelled from Sinai over the next three days. As Syria, Jordan, and Iraq attacked Israel, their armies were similarly routed. By the time the war was over, after merely six days of fighting, Israel had extended its control over vast Arab territories about five times its own size, from the Suez Canal, to the Jordan River, to the Golan Heights.

The Arab world was stunned. For the first time since the 1948 "catastrophe" a pan-Arab coalition had been defeated by Israel, and in an even more humiliating manner. Then, only half of Palestine had been lost. Now the land was lost in its entirety, together with Egyptian and Syrian territories. In 1948 the dividing line between victor and vanquished was often blurred. While the Arabs failed to achieve their main objective of destroying the newly established State of Israel, all belligerents won victories and suffered defeats as the war dragged on intermittently for over a year. In 1967, owing to the war's swift and decisive nature, there was no doubt as to which side had lost. On June 4, the ecstatic Arab leaders were confidently predicting Israel's imminent collapse and promising their subjects the spoils of victory. A week later they were reconciling themselves to a staggering military defeat, the loss of vast territories, and international humiliation.

Not surprisingly, the Arab regimes lost no time in shrugging off responsibility. Bitter recriminations took place among former war allies. The most implausible conspiracy theories were put forward. The Israelis didn't actually win the war, ran a popular theory. It was the United States that won it for them, both by arming Israel to its teeth (in reality, France was Israel's main arms supplier at the time) and by destroying the Egyptian air force on its behalf. It has even been suggested that the war was a devious ploy by the US administration to divert public opinion from its own unwinnable war in Vietnam.[1]

Yet the magnitude of the defeat was far too large to be shrugged off with the customary blame placed on external powers and their regional lackeys, and a painful process of reckoning ensued, not only among intellectuals and political dissidents,[2] but also among some of the leaders responsible for the 1967 debacle. One person who needed no encouragement to question the Arab imperial dream was Jordan's King Hussein. From his early days on the throne, he had effectively disowned his family's aspirations to head an Arab empire, instead focusing on the consolidation of his own domestic position in the face of Nasser's sustained campaign of subversion during the 1950s and early 1960s. Hussein had no desire to take on Israel, and his impetuous decision to join Nasser's bandwagon in the fateful summer of 1967 stemmed from his reluctance to miss out on what seemed at the time an imminent pan-Arab triumph over Israel. When defeat came, the king quickly blamed it on pan-Arab ideals and rhetoric, which in his opinion bore little relation to reality and "enabled the Arabs to goad each other on to their destruction."[3]

Nasser was more cautious. On the face of it, he remained as ardent a pan-Arabist as ever. At an Arab League summit convened in the Sudanese capital of Khartoum between August 29 and September 1, 1967, to discuss the consequences of the defeat, he presided over the drawing-up of a militant final communiqué that underscored the Palestinians' right to regain the whole of Palestine—that is, to destroy the State of Israel—and spelled out what came to be known as the "Three Nos": no negotiation, no recognition, and no peace with Israel. In private, however, Nasser recoiled from his imperial dream. He had always championed the pan-Arab cause, not out of belief in the existence of an Arab nation and its manifest destiny but as a tool for self-aggrandizement. Now that his delusions of grandeur had been shattered, his defiant public rhetoric became a mere fig leaf for an attempt to regain the Egyptian territories lost in the war. "Those who knew Nasser realized that he did not die on September 28, 1970, but on June 5, 1967, exactly one hour after the war broke out," Anwar Sadat wrote in his memoirs. "That was how he looked at the time, and for a long time afterwards—a living corpse. The pallor of death was evident on his face and hands, although he still moved and walked, listened and talked."[4]

This change of heart was illustrated as early as July 1967, when Nasser rejected a Syrian proposal to merge the two states on the grounds that the liberation of the occupied territories constituted a more pressing need than Arab unity.[5] For a person who had built himself into the living symbol of pan-Arab unity this was a major reordering of priorities. So was his grudging acceptance of UN Security Council Resolution 242 of November 22, 1967, which established the principle of "land for peace" as the cornerstone of future Arab-Israeli peace negotiations, accepted Israel's right to a peaceful and secure existence, and left the door open to Israel's retention of some land by requiring its withdrawal "from territories occupied in the recent conflict." (The absence of the definite article "the" before "territories"—which, had it been included, would have required a *complete* Israeli withdrawal—was no accident and reflected the contemporary awareness, even by the Soviet Union, the Arabs' main patron, of the existential threat posed by its pre-1967 bound-aries.)[6] When urged by his peers to show greater commitment to the pan-Arab cause, Nasser exploded. "You issue statements, but we have to fight," he told an all-Arab summit in Cairo in September 1970. "If you want to liberate, then get in line in front of us . . . but we have learnt caution after 1967, and after the Yemenis dragged us into their affairs in 1962, and the Syrians into war in 1967."[7]

This was Nasser's final pan-Arab stand. On September 28, shortly after seeing off his last distinguished guests, King Faisal of Saudi Arabia and the emir of Kuwait, he suffered a fatal heart attack. His death at such a critical juncture, with Jordanians and Palestinians immersed in mutual bloodletting that would be immortalized as Black September, and pan-Arab solidarity at one of its lowest ebbs, could not have been more symbolic. The person who had carried the Arab imperial dream to unprecedented heights left the political arena in discord.

Yet it is doubtful whether this disillusionment would have resulted in a complete break with pan-Arabism had he lived longer. About a month before his death, Nasser confided in King Hussein that since the Arabs were in no position to destroy Israel by force of arms in the foreseeable future they should adopt a phased strategy that would first regain the territories lost in the 1967 war before launching the final drive to total victory. "I believe that we now have a duty to remove the aggressor from our land and to regain the Arab territory occupied by the Israelis," he said. "We can then engage in a clandestine struggle to liberate the land of Palestine, to liberate Haifa and Jaffa."[8]

It was thus left to Nasser's successor to give the imperial dream a cere-monial burial. On the face of it, Sadat seemed the unlikeliest person for this daunting task. Though a member of the junta that overthrew the monarchy in July 1952, he had never played a key role in Egyptian political life. His appointment as vice-president came entirely by default as Nasser made his deputy and heir apparent, Abdel Hakim Amer, the fall guy for the 1967 defeat. Few expected Sadat to last in office more than a few months.[9]

They were wrong. Behind the affable, harmless appearance lay a formi-dable, if highly unconventional, individual determined to leave his imprint on Egypt's destiny. Impatient with routine, disdainful of dogmatism, careless of small detail, Sadat was a man of grand vision. Endowed with a strong penchant for the theatrical, he reveled in surprising and confounding friends and foes alike. By the time of his assassination by an Islamic militant in October 1981, Sadat had altered the course of Middle Eastern history beyond recognition.

While paying homage to Nasser's pan-Arab legacy (in April 1971 he even announced the formation of an Egyptian-Syrian-Libyan federation), from his first moments in power Sadat adopted an "Egypt first" approach, which subordinated pan-Arab considerations to the Egyptian national interest. In December 1970 he expressed his readiness to recognize Israel "as an independent state" within internationally agreed and secure borders on the basis of a complete withdrawal from Egyptian lands—not from the other Arab territories occupied in the 1967 war.[10] Two months later, in a written response to the UN special envoy, Gunnar Jarring, he confirmed that "Egypt will be ready to enter into a peace agreement with Israel" in return for a complete Israeli withdrawal from its territory, as well as the Gaza Strip. He reiterated this position at a Cairo meeting with US secretary of state William Rogers, going so far as to tell his distinguished guest of his "full understanding for Israel's problems," including its "need for security."[11]

For the first time since Israel's creation in 1948, an Arab state publicly agreed to enter into an official peace treaty with the Jewish state, and not just any state but the largest and most powerful of them all. This is not to say that Sadat accepted the legitimacy of Israel, as opposed to merely recognizing the fact of its existence. His perception of peace at the time differed root and branch from the terms of the treaty he would sign toward the end of the decade. It precluded normal diplomatic relations even after the attainment of a comprehensive settlement to the Arab-Israeli conflict and demanded that Israel "put an end to immigration" and "cut its links with world Zionism."[12] Nevertheless, Sadat broke the most sacred pan-Arab taboo by publicly acquiescing in the existence of a non-Arab political entity on what Arabs had unanimously held to be an integral part of their patrimony. And he did so not because of a yearning for peaceful coexistence with the Jewish state but because of a desire to break with the Arab imperial dream, which he viewed as detrimental to Egypt's national interest by unnecessarily draining its human and material resources and preventing it from addressing its own weighty problems. Yet before making this historic break Sadat felt compelled to go to war one more time, in October 1973, in order to buttress his leadership credentials in the Arab world and to force Israel to take his proposals seriously.

Like the June 1967 conflict, the October 1973 war was a watershed in Middle Eastern history. It was the first all-out war in which the Arabs managed to score impressive military gains. Although the end of hostilities found the Israeli army closer than ever to Damascus and Cairo, the initial Arab successes shattered Israeli self-confidence. The line of defense along the Suez Canal, the embodiment of their military prowess in the minds of many Israelis, collapsed like a house of cards. The Golan Heights, the shield of northern Israel, proved no barrier to a surprise Syrian attack.

The echoes of the war reverberated well beyond the Middle East. On October 23, as Israeli forces that had crossed the canal were busy encircling the Egyptian Third Army, the Soviets threatened military intervention unless Israel halted its advance. The US responded with a nuclear alert, thus triggering the most serious direct superpower confrontation since the 1962 Cuban Missile Crisis. The war also witnessed the first use of oil as a political weapon as the Arabs accompanied their military campaign with the manipulation of oil supplies to the West. Posted oil prices rose from $3.01 to $5.12 a barrel in mid-October, before skyrocketing to around $20 in November. The industrialized world braced itself for a bleak economic future.

The Arabs were elated. For many of them the war was a moment to treasure, a glorious break with a painful past, redemption of lost pride and trampled dignity, "a new era of unity of ranks and purpose."[13] In fact, the October war was never really the demonstration of unity it was perceived to be. Each of the Arab belligerents fought for different reasons and with different goals in mind, which were diametrically opposed to those of its war allies. For Sadat the war was a means to reach the negotiating table with an improved bargaining position, for the Syrians it was the first step to the "restoration of the usurped Palestinian rights," a standard euphemism for the destruction of the State of Israel.[14]

Iraq reluctantly sent an armored division to the Syrian front, only to withdraw it at the first available opportunity, while King Hussein had attempted to prevent the war altogether by alerting the Americans and the Israelis to the Arab war preparations. He had never hidden his view that war would be catastrophic for Jordan and limited his participation to the dispatch of an armored brigade to Syria after seeking Israel's acquiescence in such a move. "Only in the Middle East is it conceivable that a belligerent would ask its adversary's approval for engaging in an act of war against it," the US secretary of state Henry Kissinger commented on the episode.[15]

Neither were the rest of the Arab states united behind the war. The efforts of the Egyptian chief of staff, Saad al-Din Shazly, to convince the Arab League to increase its contributions to the Arab military buildup met with a cold reception. When in late August 1973 Sadat informed King Faisal of his decision to launch war in the near future together with the Syrians, the king expressed his skepticism. "Mr. President," he said, "this Hafiz al-Assad is first of all a Ba'thist and second an Alawite. How can you enter with him upon war and feel secure?"[16]

While Sadat was less concerned than the Saudi monarch over the religious and sectarian background of his war ally, he had no qualms about breaking ranks with Assad during the war by confronting him with a fait accompli and accepting a ceasefire. Once the guns had fallen silent, Sadat moved quickly to reap the war's political gains by signing two disengagement agreements with Israel: in January 1974 and September 1975.

The first agreement provided for the redeployment of Egyptian and Israeli forces from the positions they held at the end of the October war and enabled Egypt to retain a military presence on the east bank of the Suez Canal—a significant psychological and economic achievement. The second, and far more ambitious, treaty contained a mutual recognition that "the conflict between them and in the Middle East shall not be resolved by military force but by peaceful means", and a commitment to the peaceful pursuit of a comprehensive settlement on the basis of Security Council Resolution 338 of October 22, 1973 (a follow-up to Resolution 242). Israel agreed to withdraw its forces to the eastern side of the Mitla and Gidi passes, some thirty miles east of the canal, and to return the oilfields on the southwestern coast of the Gulf of Suez, while Egypt agreed to the passage of "non-military cargoes destined for or coming from Israel" through the Suez Canal (something that four years earlier Sadat had made conditional on the resolution of the Palestinian problem).[17]

More than any other event until then, the 1975 agreement represented the demise of the imperial dream. Here was its foremost champion over the past two decades agreeing in all but name to end the state of belligerency with the Arab world's nemesis. By committing itself to peace with Israel on the basis of Resolutions 242 and 338, Egypt effectively recognized its right to existence, something that was anathema to most Arabs. By precluding the use of force in the quest for a settlement, Egypt distanced itself from the pan-Arab struggle against Israel. What Sadat seemed to be telling his fellow Arabs was that the old way of thinking on the conflict was passé. There was no military solution to this historic feud, only a political one. Israel was in the Middle East to stay and the Arabs had better disavow their unrealistic dream of a unified regional order and follow Egypt's lead in rolling Israel back to the 1967 borders. "You know nothing of the Arabs," Sadat reprimanded his foreign minister, Muhammad Ibrahim Kamel, who sought to dissuade him from opting for a separate peace with Israel.

I know them all too well. If they are left to themselves, they will never solve the problems, and Israeli occupation will be perpetuated. Israel will end by engulfing the occupied Arab territories, with the Arabs not lifting a finger to stop them, contenting themselves with bluster and empty words, as they have done from the very beginning. They will never agree on anything.[18]

This was no personal whim of a capricious president. In charting his daring course Sadat tapped into the growing disenchantment among Egyptians with pan-Arab ideals in general, and the Palestinian cause in particular. After four bitter wars and untold human and material losses, doubts had begun to surface as to whether the "full liberation of Palestine from Zionist occupation" was at all feasible, and whether it justified such an exorbitant price. Egyptians looked around and felt betrayed and exploited. While their Arab brothers had offered little more than fiery rhetoric and meager financial contributions, they had served as pan-Arabism's sacrificial lamb. Military expenditure topped a quarter of national income while revenues were rapidly drying up. The Suez Canal was closed, its once-thriving cities turned into ghost towns by the war of attrition waged during Nasser's last years (1969–70). Many of Egypt's best and brightest were drawn away from the economy into military service, while hard-currency earnings were down as tourists kept away.

Capitalizing on this growing disenchantment, Sadat embarked on a sustained attempt to discredit the Arab imperial dream and its hitherto untouchable idol—Gamal Abdel Nasser. In the wake of the 1973 war, Nasser's domestic and international legacy was systematically undone as intellectuals, journalists, and political victims of his regime lined up to expose the hitherto undisclosed side of the Nasserite era. Egyptians learned that Nasser's socialist programs had been ill-conceived and poorly managed, bankrupting the state and its citizens alike. They were informed of the repressive nature of the Nasserite police state, where paralyzing fear ensured submission and where arbitrary arrests, imprisonment without trial, torture, and execution were common practices. Nasser's pan-Arabism came under heavy fire for having substituted one imperial master for another by making Egypt fully subservient to Soviet expansionist designs. It was only Sadat's expulsion of the Soviet forces from Egypt in July 1972 and, even more so, the 1973 crossing of the Suez Canal that had made Egypt the true master of its own fate.

In discrediting his predecessor's legacy, Sadat found a staunch ally in the religious opposition in general, and the Muslim Brothers in particular. Brutally repressed by Nasser for nearly two decades, with thousands of its members imprisoned and many executed, the Brothers welcomed Sadat's rise to power, and for good reason. A devout Muslim himself, Sadat sought to nail religious colors to his still-uncertain mast as a counterweight to leftist and Nasserite influences. He released thousands of Islamic religious activists from jail, legalized the Muslim Brothers' activities, reinstated many activists in their previous positions, and compensated others for their lost income. The Shari'a (Islamic law) became "a main source of all state legislation" in the 1971 constitution, and *the* main one in 1980. Even the October 1973 war was rife with emotive religious themes, being launched in the holy month of Ramadan and codenamed Badr, after the Prophet Muhammad's first victory over his Meccan opponents. The Brothers reciprocated by unleashing their ire on Nasser and his legacy. They condemned his version of socialism as inefficient and corrupt, equated his secularism with atheism, derided his pan-Arabism as detrimental to the cause of Islam, and deplored his domestic policies as dictatorial.

This process was not confined to the eradication of Nasser's legacy but also included the demolition of his character. From the omnipotent, larger-than-life, infallible father of the nation, the late president was reduced to a pathetic figure who had embroiled Egypt in catastrophic adventures abroad, and whose paranoiac preoccupation with his personal rule had clouded his political judgment and compromised his personal integrity. A flood of behind-the-scenes revelations portrayed Nasser as a corrupt arch-manipulator who would not hesitate to betray his comrades-in-arms and to abuse state resources. He was even accused of siphoning off millions of dollars from Arab donations to the Egyptian war effort, into secret bank accounts abroad.[19]

The renowned novelist Tawfiq al-Hakim launched a particularly devastating assault on Nasser's personality and the damage it had wrought on Egypt. In a series of novels and plays, notably *The Return of Consciousness*, meaningfully echoing the title of his earlier great patriotic novel *The Return of the Spirit*, one of Nasser's favorites, Hakim accused the late president of suffocating all manifestations of independent thinking and self-criticism in Egypt, thus leading to a complete loss of collective consciousness. "This was perhaps the first time in the modern history of Egypt," he argued,

> that an idolized person had appeared who wanted his will to have, throughout the Arab countries, a degree of holiness, greatness and power which not even God's prophets and messengers possessed. . . . He had made us feel by every possible means that in Egypt and even in the whole Arab world there could only be found one single intelligence, one single power, and one personality, namely Abdel Nasser. Without him there would be nothing, no men, no intelligence, and no power that could be relied on; the only thing ahead would be ruin. Thus it was with Fascism, Hitlerism, and Nasserism; all of them stand on a single base, which is the elimination of minds and wills other than the mind and the will of the leader.

The external consequences of Nasser's hubris, according to Hakim, were no less detrimental. His imperial dreams had made him a destructive force—"destructive of himself, of Egypt, and of the Arabs." The unnecessary military catastrophes in which he embroiled Egypt, from the 1956 Suez war, to the Yemeni civil war, to the 1967 war, depleted the nation's human and material resources and prevented it from addressing its real problems. "We do not know exactly how much they cost us either in thousands of lives or in thousands of millions of Egyptian pounds," Hakim lamented.

> However, according to what has been mentioned and published, our losses in the recent wars alone are evaluated at about four billion pounds . . . had this amount been spent on the villages of Egypt, which number about four thousand, the share for each village would have been a million pounds. Such a sum would completely re-create the villages and raise them to the level of the villages of Europe. But our Egyptian villages have remained in their sad condition, and our poor peasants in their ignorance, disease, and poverty.

What made Nasser's blunders all the more galling, according to Hakim, was his total hostility to the idea of accountability. Unlike other historical figures who paid the price of their failure to the full, no matter how successful they had been before, Nasser "remained to disavow his defeat, to make his marshal [i.e., Amer] pay the price for him by committing suicide, and to dispatch his commanders to the courts and put the responsibility on them." This refusal to face reality, however, was an assured recipe for a continued malaise. Just as the struggle against the British had been necessary for Egypt to redeem its soul, so the disavowal of Nasser's legacy was now vital if the country wanted to regain its self-consciousness and revive its past glory.[20]

Old habits die hard. When in September 1978, after thirteen days of tough bargaining at the US presidential retreat of Camp David, Anwar Sadat and the Israeli prime minister, Menachem Begin, signed agreements on the "Framework for Peace in the Middle East" and on the "Framework for the Conclusion of a Peace Treaty Between Egypt and Israel" (widely known as the Camp David Accords), many Arab states demanded a harsh retribution. This was carried into effect on March 27, 1979, a day after the signing of an Egyptian-Israeli peace treaty. An Arab League summit in Baghdad severed diplomatic and political relations with Egypt, suspended its League member-ship, and moved the organization's headquarters from Cairo to Tunis. Egypt was also expelled from the League's associated economic institutions, funds, and organizations, and was subjected to a comprehensive economic boycott.

Sadat was livid. Once again he felt aggrieved by the attitudes of small-minded and shortsighted detractors who had failed to grasp the true meaning of his actions. Aside from serving Egypt's national interest, and by extension that of the Arab world, the Camp David Accords also laid the groundwork for a comprehensive settlement that would allow the Arabs to regain the territo-ries lost in the 1967 war. "How can there be a separate agreement, when I am committed in the process of self-rule in the West Bank and Gaza during the five-year transitional period and a solution to the Palestinian question in all its aspects?" Sadat blustered, predicting that "those ignorant dwarfs" who were now ostracizing him would soon be toeing the Egyptian line.[21] This prognosis proved prophetic. Not only did the radical Arabs fail to subvert the Egyptian-Israeli peace, but as the 1980s drew to a close Egypt had regained its focal role in the Arab world, without renouncing its peace treaty with Israel, with former detractors seeking its friendship and protection.

The most important single development contributing to this strategic change was the advent of the Islamic Republic in Iran in 1979 and the eruption of the Iran-Iraq war a year later. Tehran's relentless commitment to the substitution of its militant brand of Islamic order for the existing status quo, its reluctance to end the war before the overthrow of the Ba'th regime in Baghdad, and its campaign of subversion and terrorism against the Arab monarchies of the Persian Gulf convinced these neighboring states that the danger of Iranian imperialism exceeded by far the Israeli threat and that there was no adequate substitute to Egypt at the helm of the Arab world.

Nowhere was this reality better understood than in Iraq. In March 1979 Vice-President Saddam Hussein, shortly to become the country's ruler, triumphantly hosted the Baghdad summit that expelled Egypt from the Arab League. A year later he was pleading with the excommunicated Sadat for military support. As Egypt developed into an important military and economic patron, with more than one million Egyptians servicing the overextended Iraqi economy, Saddam would tirelessly toil to pave the way for its reincorporation into the Arab fold, regardless of its peace treaty with Israel. "Arab solidarity would never be the same without Egypt," he argued emphatically. "It is simply too large and important to be left outside the Arab camp."[22] In saying this, Saddam made a mockery of his self-professed pan-Arab ideals and brought the Arab world a step closer to acquiescence in the hitherto blasphemous idea of peace with Israel.

Neither was Saddam deterred from "supping with the devil" whenever his interest so required. In February 1985 he offered Israel, through American and Swiss middlemen, some $700 million over ten years in return for its consent to the laying of an Iraqi oil pipeline to the port of Aqaba, on the Jordanian-Israeli border. Although the initiative failed to materialize, in subsequent years Saddam attempted to buy weapons from Israel, especially its homemade Drone, a sophisticated unmanned reconnaissance mini-aircraft, and Soviet weaponry captured in Arab-Israeli wars. These secret overtures were accompanied by public expressions of support for peace negotiations between the Arabs and Israel. Saddam even went so far as to claim that "no Arab leader looks forward to the destruction of Israel", and that any solution to the conflict would require "the existence of a secure state for the Israelis."[23]

Iraq's ostensible moderation was welcomed by the Arab Gulf monarchies, which increasingly looked to Egypt as the only possible counterweight to the lethal Iranian threat. In August 1981, to Sadat's obvious delight, Crown Prince Fahd of Saudi Arabia put forward a peace plan which implicitly recognized Israel's right to a secure existence. In June 1982, during a condolence visit to Riyadh following the death of King Khaled, Husni Mubarak, who had assumed the Egyptian presidency in October 1981 after Sadat's assassination, held intensive talks with the newly installed King Fahd in what was widely seen as a prelude to an Egyptian-Saudi rapprochement. Three months later, an Arab League summit in the Moroccan town of Fez adopted a somewhat modified version of the Fahd plan. Rather than detaching Egypt from its peace treaty with Israel, the Arab world was slowly but surely edging in the direction of its largest member, whose absence from its ranks was becoming increasingly hard to bear.

This apparent process of Arab pragmatism gained further momentum by the Israeli invasion of Lebanon in June 1982 with the aim of eliminating the PLO as an independent political actor, breaking the Syrian stranglehold over Lebanon, and installing a Christian-dominated regime in Beirut. Within a few weeks the Israelis had advanced as far north as Beirut, and by September 1982 had compelled the evacuation of PLO forces and its leadership from the city.

On the face of it, such a development should have unified the Arabs against their Israeli nemesis. In reality, as on numerous past occasions, the latest Israeli-Palestinian confrontation only served to confirm the hollowness of pan-Arab solidarity, since none of the Arab states came to the rescue of the Palestinians. Even Syria, which was also on the receiving end of the Israeli invasion, failed to cooperate with the PLO and instead used the war as a means to make the Palestinian organization fully subservient to its will. When PLO chairman, Yasser Arafat, failed to play the role assigned to him by Assad, he was summarily expelled from Damascus and was confronted with an armed revolt against his authority by pro-Syrian elements within the PLO. In November 1983, having returned to Lebanon with some of his troops, Arafat and his loyalists found themselves besieged by the Syrian army in the northern town of Tripoli. A month later, a humiliating exodus of PLO forces from Lebanon took place—for the second time in a year—only this time from Tripoli rather than from Beirut, and under Syrian, rather than Israeli, pressure.

The other Arab radicals were no more sympathetic to the Palestinians. Libya's eccentric ruler, Muammar Qaddafi, urged them to martyr themselves in Beirut rather than evacuate the city. Saddam was even behind the attempt on the life of the Israeli ambassador in London, which was made by the-then Baghdad-based Abu Nidal terrorist group and which sparked the Israeli invasion. Given the tyrannical nature of Saddam's regime, it is inconceivable that Abu Nidal could have carried out such an operation without his host's approval. It was also common knowledge at the time that any Palestinian attack on Israeli targets was bound to lead to a general conflagration. Israel had publicly announced its determination to remove the Palestinian military threat to its civilian population in the Galilee, and was impatiently looking for an excuse to make good on its promise.

As a result, Arafat saw no choice but to seek Egyptian protection. In December 1983, shortly after his second expulsion from Lebanon, he arrived in Cairo, for the first time in six years, for a dramatic meeting with Mubarak. This was a diplomatic and public-relations coup for the Egyptian president, and in subsequent years Egypt would increasingly become the PLO's main patron, shielding it from Syrian pressure and providing a vital channel to the US administration. This facilitated the PLO's 1988 acceptance of General Assembly Resolution 181 of November 29, 1947, calling for the creation of Jewish and Arab states in Palestine, as well as of Security Council Resolution 242 of November 22, 1967.

The end of the Cold War and the consequent superpower collaboration delivered a body blow to the tottering Arab imperial dream. Special dissatisfaction with the thaw in superpower relations was voiced in Damascus, which did not attempt to disguise its abhorrence of the "new political thinking" announced by Mikhail Gorbachev upon his rise to power in 1985. In a clean break with the traditional Soviet policy of unmitigated support for the Arabs, Gorbachev adopted an even-handed approach to the Arab-Israeli conflict in an attempt to turn Moscow into an impartial broker to both parties in the conflict. This change of heart was accompanied by unprecedented criticism of Syria's quest for "strategic parity" with Israel, a visible drop in Soviet arms transfers to Damascus, and a perceptible improvement in Soviet-Israeli relations, including the initiation of a mass exodus of Soviet Jews to Israel. This last development was particularly galling to the Arabs. With up to one million Soviet Jews expected to emigrate to Israel during the 1990s and some ten thousand a month already arriving, the Arabs suddenly had to contemplate Israel's demographic position being strengthened rather than weakened over the long term.

With the crumbling of East European communism added to Gorbachev's "new thinking," the radical regimes in the Middle East were convinced that, to their detriment, the old rules of the game had been irrevocably reversed. Since the Soviet Union was no longer the superpower it had previously been, and since unreserved support from the East European states could no longer be taken for granted, the commonplace conclusion in the Middle East was that the region had been left to the mercy of the only remaining superpower, the United States, and its "lackeys"—first and foremost, Israel.

This gloomy assessment led to the further weakening of the Arab militant camp, illustrated most vividly by the completion of Egypt's reincorporation into the mainstream of Arab politics. As early as November 1987 an Arab League summit in Amman allowed member states to re-establish diplomatic relations with Egypt. All Arab states quickly seized the opportunity, with the exception of Libya, Syria, and Lebanon, which had by now become a de facto Syrian province. Once Arab radicalism had been further afflicted by the momentous events in Eastern Europe, the Arab world made the decisive leap. In May 1989 Egypt took part in the all-Arab summit in Casablanca for the first time since its expulsion from the Arab League a decade earlier. Four months later Qaddafi paid an official visit to Egypt, and in December 1989 President Assad, who for more than a decade had spearheaded the Arab campaign against the separate Egyptian-Israeli peace, swallowed his pride and restored full diplomatic relations with Egypt.

A circle had been closed. Within a decade of making peace with Israel, Egypt had regained its central place in the Arab world. Its policy, denounced by nearly every Arab chancellery in 1979, had become the mainstream line. Its former detractors were now seeking its friendship and protection. The imperial dream, which, like the legendary phoenix, had risen time and again from the ashes of the 1967 defeat despite repeated batterings, appeared to have been laid to rest at last. Or had it? Just as the Middle East seemed to be coming to terms with its diversity after one of the most violent decades in its modern history, it was yet again thrown into disarray. In the early morning hours of August 2, 1990, Iraqi forces invaded Kuwait in strength, and within twelve hours had occupied the tiny emirate. Six days later Kuwait officially became Iraq's nineteenth province.

The invasion once again brought the old Middle Eastern skeletons out of the closet. Confronted with an unexpected regional and international backlash to his predatory move, Saddam invoked all the slogans that had previously been used to inflame Arab sentiments. He was at once an ardent pan-Arabist and a pious Muslim, a champion of the Palestinian cause and a modern-day Saladin, a fellow native of the town of Tikrit. The occupation and annexation of Kuwait, Saddam insisted, had been done for the noblest of causes—to eliminate the "traces of colonialism" in the Middle East so as to expedite the unification of the Arab nation; to promote the liberation of Palestine and Jerusalem, Islam's third-holiest site, from Jewish-Zionist occupation; and to redistribute the mammoth Gulf wealth among the poor and needy Arabs.

These lofty claims had little to do with reality. The invasion of Kuwait was an outcome of Saddam's chronic political insecurity. Saddam was very much the creation of the imperial Arab dream of the 1950s and 1960s, and the cruel Iraqi school in which he had learned to survive and defeat all opponents. His sense of insecurity reflected the internal hostility his repressive government had generated, reinforced by a paranoiac perception of being the special target of hostile foreign powers. At the start of 1990 his anxiety was further aggravated by the fear of the democratic fallout from the collapse of communism and—even more so—the severe economic difficulties resulting from the war with Iran. For nearly a year he pressured Kuwait to bail Iraq out of its economic predicament. He demanded that the emirate write off its wartime loans to Iraq, reduce its oil production quota to allow prices to rise, and give Iraq a handsome annual subsidy of some ten billion dollars. When the Kuwaitis failed to give in to his extortionist tactics, Saddam decided to invade.

During these long months of secret pressure, Saddam made no mention of Palestine or other pan-Arab themes. Once confronted with a firm international response, however, he immediately opted to "Zionize" the crisis. His "peace initiative," as he called it, consisted of a comprehensive solution for "all issues of occupation, or the issues that have been depicted as occupation, in the entire region." The first item on his list: "the immediate and unconditional withdrawal of Israel from the occupied Arab territories in Palestine, Syria, and Lebanon." After this and other problems had been satisfactorily settled, he proclaimed, "an arrangement for the situation in Kuwait" could be reached.[24]

By linking his Kuwaiti venture to the Palestinian problem, Saddam aimed to portray himself as the champion of the pan-Arab cause. If, as he claimed, the "restoration of Kuwait to the motherland" was the first step toward "the liberation of Jerusalem," how could any Arab leader be opposed to it? What is more, with the Arab world behind him, how could the Western powers think of opposing him by force of arms? As Saddam told Arafat, who came to Baghdad to express his support for the Iraqi invasion: "It's obvious that as soon as I'm attacked I'll attack Israel. Israeli involvement in the conflict will change everyone's attitude in the Arab world, and the aggression against Iraq will be seen as an American-Zionist plot."[25]

The problem with this logic was that the Arab states refused to play along. They dismissed Saddam's "peace plan" as the ploy it obviously was, and had no compunction about fighting alongside the West to liberate Kuwait. Neither did the anti-Iraq coalition collapse when Saddam, in a desperate bid to widen the conflict, fired thirty-nine Scud missiles at Israel—a development cheered on by the Palestinians and by demonstrators in marginal states such as Yemen but otherwise greeted with conspicuous calm by the proverbially restive Arab "street." There was, moreover, a tacit alliance of sorts between Israel and the Arab members of the anti-Iraq coalition: the Israelis kept the lowest profile possible, even refraining from retaliating against Iraq's missile attacks, while the Arabs highlighted the hollowness of Saddam's pan-Arab pretensions and participated in the war operations against Iraq. This would make it easier for the US to kick off the Madrid peace process shortly after the war.

The Americans were also aided in their peace efforts by the PLO's catastrophic decision to align itself with Saddam during the crisis. Arafat had been striving for decades to entangle the Arab states in a war with Israel on the Palestinians' behalf. Now that the most powerful Arab state was apparently prepared to place its massive war machine in the service of the Palestinian cause, the temptation was too great for Arafat to resist, even if the price was the sacrifice of the ruling Kuwaiti family, or the potential elimination of Kuwait as an independent state.

This folly cost the PLO dearly. The Gulf monarchies were neither forgiving nor forgetful. As the primary financiers of the Palestinian cause they felt betrayed by their beneficiaries; as hosts to a large population of Palestinian workers they felt threatened. "You Palestinians seem to be completely unaware of everything the Kuwaitis have done for you," King Fahd blustered at Arafat, shortly after the Iraqi invasion. "You've never done anything in return for the trust and the help they've given you." The Syrian minister of defense, Mustafa Tlas, was no less scathing. "The entire world knows that Saudi Arabia and the Gulf states are those which helped the Palestinian resistance and provided it with money and weapons," he argued shortly after the 1991 Gulf war.

> We helped them too, and in the end Arafat turned his back on Syria, Egypt, and Saudi Arabia, and spoke only on the help given [to the Palestinians] by Saddam. Arafat also turned his back on Kuwait and the ruling al-Sabah family, where the Fatah movement was born, nurtured and financed. But Arafat coveted another two billion dollars so as to add them to the billions he holds overseas.[26]

If this was indeed one of Arafat's objectives, he had seriously miscalculated the situation. Not only did the PLO fail to make any financial gain as a result of the Iraqi misadventure, but it also lost $133 million in annual contributions as the Gulf states suspended their financial support for the Palestinian organization. Following the liberation of Kuwait, most of the 400,000 Palestinians who had been living and working in the emirate were expelled, creating a major humanitarian crisis and denying the PLO the substantial income regularly received from the earnings of those workers. With the additional loss of funds and investments in Kuwaiti banks, the total amount forfeited by the PLO as a direct result of the Gulf crisis was in excess of ten billion dollars, bringing the organization to the verge of bankruptcy.[27]

Starved of financial resources, ostracized by its Arab peers, and increasingly overpowered in the West Bank and Gaza by the Hamas militant Islamic movement, the PLO was desperate for political rehabilitation (in an Arab League summit in mid-1991, the organization was not even allowed to raise the Palestinian issue)—and Arafat for a personal comeback. Fortunately for Arafat, a lifeline was suddenly offered from the least expected source: the Israeli government headed by Yitzhak Rabin.

Brought to power in July 1992 for the second time in twenty years on a straightforward peace platform, the seventy-year-old Rabin, who as chief of staff had masterminded Israel's 1967 victory, was well aware that this was his last chance to go down in history as Israel's greatest peacemaker, and was therefore prepared to secure his legacy regardless of the costs, even if this meant breaking the taboo to which all Israeli governments had long subscribed: negotiating directly with the PLO without the organization first abandoning its formal commitment to Israel's destruction. This led in short order to secret Israeli-Palestinian talks in the Norwegian capital of Oslo, which culminated on September 13, 1993, in the signing on the White House lawn of a bilateral "Declaration of Principles on Interim Self-Government Arrangement" (DOP). This provided for Palestinian self-rule in the entire West Bank and Gaza Strip for a transitional period not to exceed five years, during which Israel and the Palestinians would negotiate a permanent peace settlement. During this interim period the territories would be administered by a Palestinian council, to be freely and democratically elected after the withdrawal of Israeli military forces both from the Gaza Strip and from the populated areas of the West Bank.

With the subsidence of the initial euphoria it gradually transpired that for Arafat and the PLO leadership the Oslo process had been a strategic means not to a two-state solution—Israel and a Palestinian state in the West Bank and Gaza—but to the substitution of a Palestinian state for the State of Israel. Reluctant to accept the right of the Jewish people to self-determination in its ancestral homeland, they had viewed Israel as an artificial alien entity created by Western imperialism, and implanted in the midst of the Arab world in order to divide and weaken it. This linked the Palestinian problem to the Arab imperial dream and transformed it into something far more profound than an ordinary territorial dispute between two parties: a Manichean struggle between the "Arab nation" and the "neo-crusading entity." In Arafat's words:

Our ancestors fought the crusaders for a hundred years, and later Ottoman imperialism, then British and French imperialism for years and years. It is our duty to take over the banner of struggle from them and hand it on untarnished and flying as proudly as ever to the generations that come after us. We shall never commit a crime against them, the crime of permitting the existence of a racialist state in the heart of the Arab world.[28]

As early as August 1968, Arafat had defined the PLO's strategic objective as "the transfer of all resistance bases" into the West Bank and the Gaza Strip, occupied by Israel during the June 1967 war, "so that the resistance may be gradually transformed into a popular armed revolution." This, he reasoned, would allow the PLO to undermine Israel's way of life by "preventing immigration and encouraging emigration ... destroying tourism ... weakening the Israeli economy and diverting the greater part of it to security requirements ... [and] creating and maintaining an atmosphere of strain and anxiety that will force the Zionists to realize that it is impossible for them to live in Israel."[29]

The Oslo accords enabled the PLO to achieve in one fell swoop what it had failed to attain through many years of violence and terrorism. Here was Israel, just over a decade after destroying the PLO's military infrastructure in Lebanon, asking the Palestinian organization, at one of the lowest ebbs in its history, to establish a real political and military presence—not in a neighboring Arab country but right on its doorstep. Israel was even prepared to arm thousands of (it was hoped, reformed) terrorists, who would be incorporated into newly established police and security forces charged with asserting the PLO's authority throughout the territories. As the prominent PLO leader Faisal Husseini famously quipped, Israel was willingly introducing into its midst a "Trojan Horse" designed to promote the PLO's strategic goal of a "Palestine from the [Jordan] river to the [Mediterranean] sea"—that is, a Palestine in place of Israel.[30]

Arafat admitted as much as early as September 13, 1993, when he told the Palestinian people, in a pre-recorded Arabic-language message broadcast by Jordanian television at about the same time as the peace treaty-signing ceremony was taking place on the White House lawn, that the DOP was merely part of the implementation of the PLO's "phased strategy" of June 1974. This stipulated that the Palestinians should seize whatever territory Israel was prepared or compelled to cede to them and use it as a springboard for further territorial gains until achieving the "complete liberation of Palestine."[31]

During the next seven years, until the September 2000 launch of his terrorist war, euphemistically titled the "al-Aqsa Intifada" after the mosque in Jerusalem, Arafat would play an intricate game of Jekyll-and-Hyde politics. Whenever addressing Israeli or Western audiences he would habitually extol the "peace of the brave" he had signed with "my partner Yitzhak Rabin," while at the same time denigrating the peace accords to the Palestinians as a temporary measure to be abandoned at the first available opportunity, and indoctrinating his people, and especially the youth, with an abiding hatred of the state of Israel, Jews, and Judaism.

Neither did Arafat confine himself merely to disparaging the Oslo accords and his peace partner. From the moment of his arrival in Gaza in July 1994, he set out to build an extensive terrorist infrastructure in flagrant violation of the accords and in total disregard of the overriding reason he had been brought to the territories, namely to lay the groundwork for Palestinian statehood. Arafat refused to disarm the militant religious groups Hamas and Islamic Jihad as required by the treaties and tacitly approved the murder of hundreds of Israelis by these groups. He created a far larger Palestinian army (the so-called police force) than was permitted by the accords. He reconstructed the PLO's old terrorist apparatus, mainly under the auspices of the Tanzim, which is the military arm of Fatah (the PLO's largest constituent organization and Arafat's own alma mater). He frantically acquired prohibited weapons with large sums of money donated to the Palestinian authority by the international community for the benefit of the civilian Palestinian population and, eventually, resorted to outright mass violence. He did so for the first time in September 1996 to publicly discredit the newly elected Israeli Prime Minister Benjamin Netanyahu, and then again in September 2000 with the launch of his war of terror shortly after Netanyahu's successor, Ehud Barak, had offered the creation of an independent Palestinian state in 92 percent of the West Bank and the entire Gaza Strip, with East Jerusalem as its capital. "Since [the caliph] Umar and Saladin we haven't given up our original rights in Jerusalem and al-Aqsa, our Jerusalem, our Palestine," a typical commentary by the official Palestinian television station ran, supposedly putting the conflict in a broader historical context. "If time constitutes the [criteria of] existence, then Israel's temporary existence is only fifty-two years long while we, the Palestinian Arabs, have lived here for thousands of years, and we, the indigenous population, will eventually expel the invaders, however long it takes."[32]

What made Arafat's war all the more significant for the future of the Middle East was not the fact of its occurrence or even its exceptional ferocity but rather the response of the Arab states. Notwithstanding the general loathing of Arafat by his Arab peers (he had been *persona non grata* in Syria since the early 1980s and in the Gulf states after the 1990–91 Gulf crisis, while President Mubarak addressed him as a "dog" at a public event that was covered worldwide), none of these leaders dared voice public criticism of Arafat's actions, despite their private disapproval. Instead, all of them without exception, including Egypt and Jordan—the two Arab states at peace with Israel— unequivocally blamed the Jewish state for the violent outburst.

This position, however, had far less to do with sympathy for the Palestinian struggle than with the continued resilience of the imperial dream. None of the Arab states took concrete measures to help the Palestinian struggle, with the partial exception of Saddam Hussein, who remunerated families of suicide bombers to the tune of $25,000. Yet as before, anti-Zionism proved the main common denominator of pan-Arab solidarity and its most effective rallying cry, thus underscoring Arab reluctance to accept the legitimacy of a non-Arab state on the part of the Arab imperial patrimony.

Peace, according to the great seventeenth-century philosopher Baruch Spinoza, is not merely the absence of war but rather a state of mind: a disposition to benevolence, confidence, and justice. From the birth of the Jewish national movement, that disposition has remained conspicuously absent from the minds of Arab and Palestinian leaders. Even Anwar Sadat, the man who went farther than any other Middle Eastern leader in accepting the existence of a sovereign Jewish state, could tell his foreign minister during the Camp David summit of September 1978, a few days before concluding his historic agreement with Prime Minister Begin, that "we are dealing with the lowest and meanest of enemies. The Jews even tormented their Prophet Moses, and exasperated their God."[33] While one can only speculate about Sadat's own ultimate intentions—he was assassinated in October 1981 by a religious zealot—there is little doubt that his successor, Husni Mubarak, has never had any desire to transform the formal Egyptian peace with Israel into a genuine reconciliation. For Mubarak, peace is of no value in and of itself; rather, it is the price Egypt has had to pay for such substantial benefits as US economic and military aid. As he candidly explained the nature of the Egyptian-Israeli peace:

> Against us stood the most intelligent people on earth—a people that controls the international press, the world economy, and world finances. We succeeded in compelling the Jews to do what we wanted; we received all our land back, up to the last grain of sand! We have outwitted them, and what have we given them in return? A piece of paper! . . . We were shrewder than the shrewdest people on earth! We managed to hamper their steps in every direction. We have established sophisticated machinery to control and limit to the minimum contacts with the Jews. We have proven that making peace with Israel does not entail Jewish domination and that there is no obligation to develop relations with Israel beyond those we desire.[34]

Over the decades, Mubarak has reduced interaction with Israel to the minimum level, while simultaneously transforming the Egyptian army into a formidable modern force. He has also fostered a culture of virulent anti-Semitism in Egypt, a culture whose premises he himself evidently shares, turning his country into the world's most prolific producer of anti-Semitic ideas and attitudes. These are voiced openly by the militant religious press, by the establishment media, and even by supporters of peace with Israel. In numberless articles, scholarly writings, books, cartoons, public statements, and radio and television programs, Jews are painted in the blackest terms imaginable.

The traditional "blood libel," that medieval fabrication according to which Jews use Gentile blood, and particularly the blood of children, for ritual purposes, is still in wide circulation in today's Egypt, together with a string of other canards whose tenor may be glimpsed in the title of an 1890 tract recently reprinted by the Egyptian Ministry of Education: *Human Sacrifice in the Talmud*. Jews have been accused of everything from exporting infected seeds, plants, and cattle in order to destroy Egyptian agriculture, to corrupting Egyptian society through the spread of venereal diseases and the distribution of drugs. Similarly popular are *The Protocols of the Elders of Zion*, a virulent anti-Semitic tract fabricated by the Russian secret police at the turn of the twentieth century, which may be in wider circulation in Egypt than anywhere else in the world. In 2002, during the holy month of Ramadan, the state-controlled Egyptian television ran a drama series based on the *Protocols*. A few months later, a copy of the *Protocols* was saliently displayed alongside a Torah scroll in an exhibition at the new Alexandria Library.

This is the view of "peaceful coexistence" as practiced by the largest and most powerful Arab state, which has been at peace with Israel for nearly three decades. It is hardly surprising, then, if other Arab players, with the partial exception of Jordan, have similarly never felt the need to acknowledge the Jewish state's legitimacy, and have declined even the most tempting offers in exchange for normalized relations. Four successive Israeli prime ministers, from Yitzhak Rabin to Ehud Barak, were willing to return the Golan Heights to Syria in exchange for peace. Hafiz Assad rejected every proposal. He did so not because of petty squabbles over a few hundred yards of territory around Lake Tiberias, as was widely believed at the time, but because of a fundamental reluctance to acquiesce formally in the very existence of the "neo-crusader state," whose fate, Assad never tired of reiterating, would eventually be that of the medieval crusader kingdom before it. "I regret to say that some of us, as Arab citizens, are seeking the shortest, easiest, and least difficult roads, which at the same time are the most prone to failure," lamented the Syrian president, whose office was adorned with a huge picture of Saladin.

We view the matter from the perspective of the future of the nation and not that of the next few hours, months, or years in which we shall live. . . . If we, as a generation, fail to do and to achieve what must be done, there will be future generations that will deal with this issue in the proper manner. . . . What I am saying here is not new. I am just reviewing some facts in our history. Let us go back to the crusaders' invasion. Although they fought us for two hundred years, we did not surrender or capitulate. They, too, were a big power and had scored victories, while we had been defeated. After two hundred years, however, we triumphed. Why are we now expected either to score a decisive victory in approximately thirty years or completely surrender?[35]

The Tail That Wags the Dog

In a blistering attack on the Israeli-Palestinian peace accord of September 1993, the American academic Edward Said ridiculed "the fashion-show vulgarities of the White House ceremony" which cast President Bill Clinton in the role of "a twentieth-century Roman emperor shepherding two vassal kings through rituals of reconciliation and obeisance."[1] Said failed to mention that the agreement was reached in secret Israeli-Palestinian negotiations in the Norwegian capital of Oslo, at a time when the formal and highly publicized peace process under American auspices, launched at the 1991 Madrid conference, was virtually deadlocked. Not only was the US administration conspicuously absent from the Oslo talks, but it was barely aware of their existence. When news of the agreement broke, Secretary of State Warren Christopher was stunned—just as he had been seventeen years earlier, as deputy secretary of state, on the occasion of Anwar Sadat's visit to Jerusalem, another product of secret Arab-Israeli talks from which the Americans had been excluded. For his part, President Clinton quickly capitalized on this unexpected breakthrough to boost his popularity by hosting the signing ceremony.

If anyone was shepherded to the White House lawn, as might well have been the case, it was the host of the party rather than his two guests. Far from representing an imperious American dictate, the Israeli-Palestinian deal was the culmination of regional dynamics and processes that had long been in operation, and over which the United States, or for that matter any other foreign power, had little if any influence, in line with the millenarian pattern of Middle Eastern relations with the outside world.

As we have seen, even when they were thrown onto the defensive in the late seventeenth century and subsequently confronted with external penetration of the Middle East itself, the Muslim powers never abandoned their imperial dreams. The Ottoman and the Qajar empires manipulated the European great-power rivalry to their advantage, though in the end both made tragic errors of judgment that led to their undoing. Time and again the Europeans found themselves drawn into regional conflicts to prevent the disintegration of the Ottoman Empire, often at no obvious advantage to themselves. Even the chain of events culminating in the destruction of this empire and the creation of the modern Middle East was not set in train by secret diplomacy bent on carving up the region but rather by the catastrophic decision of the Ottoman leadership to throw in its lot with Germany, despite repeated pleas by the Anglo-French-Russian Entente to remain aloof.

Likewise, it was Sharif Hussein of Mecca who drove British officialdom to seriously entertain the idea of the destruction of the Ottoman Empire. The tentative and qualified promises made to him by the British high commissioner in Egypt, Sir Arthur Henry McMahon, were to exert a considerable influence on the course and outcome of great-power negotiations on the future shape of the Middle East by forming the basis of the 1916 Anglo-French-Russian understanding known as the Sykes–Picot agreement.

In the historiography of the modern Middle East this agreement has gained lasting notoriety as "a startling piece of double-dealing", negotiated behind Hussein's back with a view to robbing the Arabs of their rightful war spoils and disrupting the natural development of the Middle East through its arbitrary partition into wholly artificial entities. Actually, if anyone was perfidious, it was Hussein and his sons, who initiated negotiations with Britain's Cairo Office on the false claim that they represented the "whole of the Arab Nation without any exception." In addition, they fantastically inflated their military strength and made a string of promises (notably, to detach the Arab forces in the Ottoman army from their imperial master) that they knew they could never make good. They also secretly dealt with the Ottomans behind Britain's back, both before the proclamation of the revolt and in the later stages of the war.[2]

In contrast, there was nothing deceitful about the Anglo-French talks. The two participants were war allies engaged in a mortal struggle over their destiny, and it was only natural for them to coordinate their strategies, especially since this was officially required by the September 1914 Declaration of London. If anything, France could lodge a complaint against Britain for breaching the terms of their wartime alliance by making unauthorized promises to a minor third party that had not even decided to ally itself with the Entente. It was precisely to answer this potential grievance that the British initiated the talks with the French: not to renege on their tentative understanding with Hussein but to give it the widest possible international recognition. In the words of a veteran observer of the Middle East: "It seems clear now that the intention of the British government, when it made the Sykes–Picot agreement, was to reconcile the interests of France with the pledges given to the Sharif Hussein."[3]

From the beginning of the talks, the British tried to convince their skeptical ally of the merits of both an Arab revolt and the establishment of an independent Arab state, or rather an empire. They succeeded. The Sykes–Picot agreement contained a commitment "to recognize and protect an independent Arab State or a Confederation of Arab States—under the suzerainty of an Arab chief" stretching over the vast territory from Aleppo to Rawandaz and from the Egyptian-Ottoman border to Kuwait.[4] This commitment represented a clear victory for Britain's championing of Arab independence and unity over French opposition. In other words, the Sykes–Picot agreement was a tool of unification rather than the divisive instrument it is now commonly thought to have been, and no fundamental contradiction existed between its territorial provisions and those of the Hussein–McMahon correspondence.[5]

Just as Sykes–Picot was a direct corollary of the Hashemite imperial dream, so the main factor to wreck this agreement was none other than its intended victim: the collapsing Ottoman Empire, which was to be stripped not only of its vast Arabic-speaking provinces, but also of most of the Turkish homeland itself. Istanbul and the straits were to go to Russia, together with most of Turkish Armenia, while the rest of Anatolia, apart from a tiny Turkish state in the eastern and north-central parts, was to be divided between France and Italy.[6]

This stark prospect gave rise to a new and vibrant brand of Turkish nationalism, ready to disown the Ottoman imperial legacy but never to accept the partition and subjugation of the Turkish homeland. The person who, almost single-handedly, was to produce this historic turning point in Turkish and Middle Eastern history was the dashing war hero General Mustafa Kemal, later known as Kemal Atatürk. In a sustained campaign in 1920–22 that combined astounding battlefield victories with shrewd diplomatic maneuvers Kemal drove the foreign powers out of Anatolia, thus undoing the humiliating treaty of Sèvres, imposed on Turkey by the great powers in August 1920, and laying the groundwork for the treaty of Lausanne of July 1923. This recognized Turkish sovereignty over the whole of Anatolia, together with parts of eastern Thrace. Kurdistan and Armenia, envisaged as independent states by the treaty of Sèvres, were effectively incorporated into Turkey and the Soviet Union. For its part, Turkey renounced all rights and titles over Egypt and Sudan, a clear act of disengagement from its imperial past.

By now Kemal had formally separated the sultanate from the caliphate. The former, representing temporal power, was abolished; the latter was retained as a purely spiritual post. Once he had secured Turkey's independence and international standing, Kemal pressed ahead with the country's transformation from an empire into a nation-state: in October 1923 Ankara was made

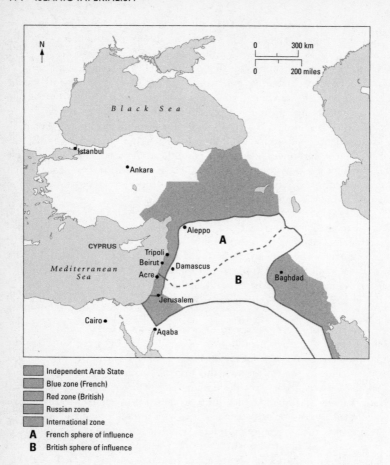

Map 7 The Sykes–Picot Agreement
From Efraim and Inari Karsh, *Empires of the Sand: The Struggle for Mastery in the Middle East, 1789–1923* (Cambridge, Mass.: Harvard University Press, 1999).

the new capital, and two weeks later a Western-type constitution was promulgated, declaring Turkey a republic and investing sovereignty in the people and its representative—the Grand National Assembly. Kemal was elected the republic's first president. Five months later, on March 3, 1924, the Turkish parliament drove the final nail into the coffin of the country's imperial past, if not Islam's millenarian imperial legacy, by abolishing the caliphate. "To labour for the maintenance of the Ottoman dynasty and its sovereign would have been to inflict the greatest injustice upon the Turkish nation," Kemal explained a few years later. "As for the Caliphate, it could only have been a laughing-stock in the eyes of the really civilised and cultured people of the world."[7]

Turkey's retreat from empire was accompanied by a wider regional transformation. The political system devised by the Sykes–Picot agreement, which substituted the Arabs, or rather the Hashemites, for the Turks, or rather the Ottomans, as the new imperial masters, gave way to a wholly different international order based on the novel ideal of the nation-state. This development, however, was nothing like the caricature portrayed by the standard historiography, according to which "Middle Eastern countries and frontiers were fabricated in Europe."[8] Rather it was the aggregate outcome of intense pushing and shoving by a multitude of regional and international bidders for the Ottoman war spoils, in which the local actors, despite their marked inferiority to the great powers, often had the upper hand.

Take the creation of the Kingdom of Iraq from the defunct Ottoman velayets of Basra, Baghdad, and Mosul. On the face of it this was a purely British decision taken by the cabinet in March 1921 on the recommendations of a special conference, held earlier that month in Cairo with the participation of the new colonial secretary, Winston Churchill, and his advisers. But, in fact, it was the culmination of a sustained effort by Faisal, the celebrated hero of the "Great Arab Revolt," to substitute Iraq for his Syrian kingdom from which he had been expelled by French forces in the summer of 1920.

It was Faisal's erstwhile champions—Lawrence of Arabia, who at Churchill's request joined the colonial office as an adviser on Arab affairs, and Hubert Young, another veteran of the revolt—who engineered the departmental consensus in this regard. Churchill had already been won over to the idea of Faisal's kingship before taking up his new post on February 15, 1921, while the Colonial Office itself was persuaded later that month. The issue was finally sealed at an interdepartmental conference on February 26. In addition to Lawrence and Young, the meeting was attended by two other veterans of the revolt—colonels Kinahan Cornwallis and Pierce Joyce—as well as Sir Arnold Wilson, the future British commissioner in Iraq and a new convert to Faisal's cause. Not only was there no objection to Faisal's ascent to the Iraqi throne, but the Foreign Office representative reassured his colonial office counterparts "that the difficulty of getting the French to agree was not insuperable and that if they were faced with a fait accompli no trouble was likely to ensue."

The Cairo Conference thus did little more than rubberstamp this collective recommendation. "I think we shall reach unanimous conclusion among all authorities that Faisal offers hope of best and cheapest solutions," Churchill cabled the prime minister, David Lloyd George, on March 14, after two days of deliberations. "I have no doubt personally Faisal offers far away best chance of saving our money. Please therefore endeavour to telegraph to me as soon as you possibly can that I am free to make plans on [the] basis of [this] formula."[9]

No sooner had Churchill resolved the Iraqi problem than he found himself forced to accommodate another member of the Hashemite family: Faisal's elder brother, Abdallah. Though the brightest and most politically astute of Hussein's sons and the main instigator of the Hashemite revolt, Abdallah had found himself marginalized by his younger brother, who, largely owing to Lawrence's exertions on his behalf, managed at first to carve out for himself the most coveted imperial prize: Syria. Once Faisal had been driven from Damascus, Abdallah, who had earmarked Iraq for himself, knew that it was only a matter of time before his brother would elbow him out by substituting this country for his lost Syrian kingdom. In a bid to forestall this eventuality, at the end of September 1920 Abdallah left Mecca at the head of several hundred tribesmen for the small oasis town of Ma'an at the northern tip of the Hijaz, arriving there in mid-November. Ostensibly, Abdallah was responding to appeals by Syrian nationalists to help them drive the French out of Syria on behalf of his deposed brother; in reality, he was positioning himself as a key player in the scramble for the defunct Ottoman Empire.

The ploy had the desired effect. The British grudgingly began to view Abdallah as Transjordan's potential ruler. Even Lawrence, who had developed an aversion to Abdallah during the revolt, joined Young in arguing, shortly before the Cairo Conference, that "we are prepared to allow Abdallah to consolidate his position in this region, provided he is ready to act in general accordance with the advice of our political officers." In Lawrence's and Young's view, it might even be possible at some future point to indicate to the French that if they wished to set Abdallah up in Damascus, "such a solution will have our cordial approval and will be particularly agreeable to us as an unmistakable sign of Franco-British solidarity in Arabian policy." "We see no menace to French interests in this," they reasoned. "On the contrary; Abdallah, like Faisal, will be much less dangerous as a settled ruler than as a freelancer."[10]

This logic was fully endorsed by the Cairo Conference. At a Jerusalem meeting with Abdallah on March 28, 1921, Churchill proposed that Transjordan be constituted as an Arab province of Palestine, under an Arab governor acceptable to Abdallah and subordinate to the high commissioner for Palestine. This, however, was not good enough for Abdallah who had gone to such great lengths in order to make himself an imperial ruler and a key player in regional affairs, not merely a subordinate provincial governor. If a certain territory had to be incorporated into another as a province, then it should be Palestine into Transjordan, under his headship, and not the other way round.

Churchill explained that since Britain was the mandatory power for Palestine, the Arab governor of Transjordan would have to recognize its authority and would be expected to refrain from any anti-French activities. At the same time he reassured Abdallah that "Trans-Jordania would not be included in the present administrative system of Palestine, and therefore the Zionist clauses of the mandate would not apply." As Abdallah indicated his readiness to accept the proposal, provided it was acceptable to his father and brother, Churchill offered the ultimate carrot. "The French authorities in Syria were not at the moment pursuing a Sherifian policy and it was not for His Majesty's Government to press them to do so," he said. "At the same time it appeared to him that if an example was set in the British sphere and at the same time His Majesty's Government could point to the admirable results achieved there by themselves, the French might possibly come round to the British way of thinking."[11]

This was just what Abdallah wanted to hear. In contrast to his opposition to Transjordan's westward expansion, Churchill effectively signaled Britain's possible acquiescence in Hashemite domination of Syria, this time under Abdallah's, rather than Faisal's rule. True, this was a long shot that might or might not pay off, but Abdallah felt that it was infinitely better to have a bird in the hand rather than two in the bush. Hence, in his second meeting with Churchill he went out of his way to reassure his interlocutor of his determination to prevent any anti-French activities in Transjordan; and when in their third meeting the colonial secretary suggested that "the Emir himself should remain in Trans-Jordania for a period of six months to prepare the way for the appointment, with his consent, at the end of that time of an Arab Governor under the High Commissioner," Abdallah readily accepted, his only request being "that he might be regarded as a British officer and trusted accordingly." The relieved Churchill was only too happy to comply.[12]

"The Emir Abdallah has promised to work with us and for us to do his best to restrain the people from anti-French action and to form, with our assistance, a local administration which can later be handed over to a native Governor of less consequence than himself," Churchill reported on the meeting.

His position will be informal, and no question either of governorship or sovereignty is raised. He must be given a very free hand, as he has a most difficult task to perform. Not only has he been checked in mid-career in his campaign against the French, but he has been asked to execute a complete *volte-face* and to take active steps to nullify the effects of his previous policy.[13]

Churchill could not have been more mistaken. Far from being checked in mid-career, let alone forced to execute a complete about-face, Abdallah had resurrected his imperial dream. Like Faisal, he had managed to recover from what was seemingly a virtually impossible position. In the summer of 1920 both brothers were very much a spent force. Spurned by his former British allies and his father alike after his ignominious expulsion from Damascus, Faisal was desperately seeking his place in the sun. Abdallah, who had suffered a crushing defeat in May 1919 at the hands of rival Arabian potentates, was similarly deprecated by the British, ridiculed in Arabia, and disfavored by his father. Eight months later both brothers had talked the largest empire on earth into enthroning them in the newly created Iraqi and Transjordanian states, thus making them key figures in the post-war Middle East and the natural contenders for the realization of the Arab imperial dream.

If the great powers could hardly impose their will on the Middle East at a time when the indigenous actors were at the weakest point in their modern history, it was only natural that the local states became less susceptible to external influences as they consolidated their domestic and international positions. Their bargaining power was substantially enhanced during the Cold War era, when global polarization and the nuclear balance of terror constrained great-power maneuverability. For all their exertions, neither the United States nor the Soviet Union, the two powers that had supplanted the traditional European empires after World War II, had a decisive say in their smaller allies' grand strategies. Time and again they were powerless to contain undesirable regional developments, whether it was Egypt's defection to the American camp in the mid-1970s or the 1979 Islamic revolution in Iran, and were forced to acquiesce in actions with which they were in total disagreement.

This is not to say that the US and the USSR slavishly followed the wishes of their junior partners. Rather, whatever success they had was due largely to the convergence of their own wishes with indigenous trends. In the late 1970s, it was the determination of Sadat and Israeli prime minister, Menachem Begin, to end the long-standing enmity between their peoples that rendered American mediation effective. But when the Carter administration attempted to sustain the momentum and bring the Palestinians into the picture, it ran into the brick wall of PLO rejectionism. "This is a lousy deal," Yasser Arafat told Edward Said, who had passed him the administration's offer. "We want Palestine. We're not interested in bits of Palestine. We don't want to negotiate with the Israelis. We're going to fight."[14]

Twenty-one years later, Arafat aborted two more presidential attempts to mediate a peace with Israel by rejecting, in July and December 2000, Bill Clinton's proposals for the creation of an independent Palestinian state in the West Bank and the Gaza Strip, with East Jerusalem as its capital. Even after Israel had confined Arafat to his Ramallah compound following the launch of his terror war in September 2000, and after President George W. Bush had urged the Palestinians to substitute a new and democratic leadership for Arafat's corrupt and oppressive regime, there was little Washington could do to enforce this vision; Bush was forced to watch helplessly as his own preferred candidate, Mahmoud Abbas (Abu Mazen), was unceremoniously subverted by Arafat, who maintained his unassailable hold on power until his death on November 11, 2004.

It was indeed on the cardinal issues of war and peace that superpower influence proved least effective. Just as the United States could not force its Arab allies and Israel to accept its position on a political settlement, so the Soviets failed to persuade most of their Arab partners to disavow their total rejection of Israel. Just as Israel launched the 1967 Six-Day War without Washington's blessing when it saw its existence threatened, so Egypt's war of attrition (1969–70) and October war (1973), Syria's military intervention in Lebanon (1976), and the Iraqi invasions of Iran (1980) and Kuwait (1990) took place against Soviet wishes and advice. Only in terminating hostilities did superpower intervention seem to carry any weight, if of a very limited kind and mostly where Israel was concerned.[15]

The Soviets failed to convince Sadat to accept a ceasefire on the first day of the October 1973 war, or to force Assad to stop his offensive against the PLO in the summer of 1976. Both superpowers toiled for about a year at the end of the 1980s to bring Iran to accept a UN ceasefire resolution, and even then the Iranian decision was more a result of the total collapse of national morale and a string of successful Iraqi offensives than of superpower pressure.

Consider, for example, Soviet-Arab discourses on the role of armed force in resolving the Arab-Israeli conflict. During the twenty-five-year period from the 1967 war to the disintegration of the USSR in 1991, the Soviets sought to convince their Arab allies of the merits of a peaceful resolution to the conflict, based on Security Council Resolution 242 of November 1967 and negotiated under the auspices of the United Nations and the active supervision of the two superpowers.[16] But their pleas fell on deaf ears. Violently opposed to Israel's right to exist, Syria and the PLO dismissed the idea of a political settlement and voiced their commitment to the continuation of the "armed struggle."[17]

Even Egypt, Moscow's foremost Middle Eastern ally, despite accepting Resolution 242, launched a war of attrition against Israel in April 1969.

The Soviets pleaded with Nasser to forgo the use of force and then, once hostilities broke out, to stop fighting and reach a negotiated settlement. They even threatened him with military sanctions—to no avail. Not only did these pressures fail to impress Nasser, but during a secret visit to Moscow at the end of January 1970 he managed to implicate the Soviets in his war by threatening to step down in favor of a pro-American president unless Soviet air-defense units were immediately sent to Egypt to neutralize Israel's overwhelming air supremacy.[18]

An even more pronounced demonstration of the limits of Soviet influence was afforded by the outbreak of the October 1973 war. When in 1971 Sadat began to threaten Israel with war unless there was progress toward a negotiated settlement, the Soviets were greatly alarmed. For over a year they denied Egypt vital arms supplies, thus frustrating its war preparations and forcing Sadat to postpone his campaign. The Egyptian retribution was not long in coming: in July 1972 Sadat expelled the Soviet units placed in Egypt in 1970 at Nasser's request.

This move caught the Soviets off guard. Notwithstanding their reluctance to introduce these units into Egypt in the first place and their consequent unease about keeping them there, this was certainly not the way they envisaged their departure. They therefore tried to cut their losses by resuming arms deliveries to Egypt, though not on the scale or at the pace desired by Sadat. At the same time they intensified their efforts to prevent a regional conflagration. But now they resorted to friendly persuasion rather than arm-twisting, trying to demonstrate to the Arabs the hazards of war and the benefits of a negotiated settlement. A special effort was made to alert the US administration to the inflammability of the Middle Eastern situation through a steady stream of public and private warnings. Secretary-General Leonid Brezhnev conveyed an exceptionally stark warning to President Richard Nixon during their summit meeting in California in June 1973. Foreign Minister Andrei Gromyko made similar warnings in his address to the UN General Assembly on September 25, 1973, and during his meeting with Nixon in the White House three days later. When these warnings fell on deaf ears, the Soviets made a last-ditch attempt to alert the Israelis to the imminent war by demonstratively withdrawing their civilian dependants from Egypt and Syria on October 4, two days before the outbreak of hostilities. Alas, the Israelis failed to read the writing on the wall.[19]

The Soviets were no more successful in bringing their Arab allies to the negotiating table than they had been in preventing them from waging war. Convinced that the key to a political settlement lay in Washington rather than Moscow, Sadat began extricating Egypt from the Soviet orbit in the early

1970s. The breach between the two countries rapidly widened in the wake of the October war as Egypt tied its fortunes to the United States, and was made unbridgeable in March 1976 when Egypt unilaterally abrogated its 1971 Friendship and Cooperation Treaty with the Soviet Union and terminated Soviet naval services in Egyptian ports.

Syria, by now Moscow's primary Middle Eastern ally, proved no more cooperative a partner. Ignoring repeated Soviet pleas, it refused to attend the Arab-Israeli peace conference convened in Geneva in December 1973. Shortly afterward, much to the Soviets' dismay, it opted for an American-sponsored disengagement agreement with Israel and, moreover, accompanied the negotiations with a war of attrition on the Golan Heights.

Although the Syrians would eventually adopt the Soviets' preferred way to a settlement, namely a multilateral peace conference, they would remain adamantly opposed to Moscow's perception of what the essence of such a settlement should be, which was predicated on the right of all regional states, Israel included, to a secure existence. As a result, a delicate "balance of toler-ance" evolved from the mid-1970s whereby the two allies agreed to disagree. The Syrians supported the convocation of an international conference on the Middle East, but continued to reject Israel's right to exist. The Soviets made no bones about their acceptance of Israel, yet refrained from overtly pressuring Syria to accept this position. They reluctantly signed a bilateral treaty with Syria in October 1980, yet told Damascus not to interpret it, or for that matter their military and political support, as an endorsement of its political stance.[20]

Even Mikhail Gorbachev, the first Soviet leader to attempt an even-handed approach to the Middle East conflict, which put the Arab and the Israeli causes on a par and called for a solution based on a "balance of interests among all sides,"[21] was forced to recognize the limits of Soviet influence. He went to far greater lengths than his predecessors in opposing Syria's intransigence, repeat-edly declining its requests for state-of-the-art weaponry and seeking to isolate it in the Arab world by supporting the conservative Arab regimes. He even restored diplomatic relations with Israel (severed since the 1967 war) and allowed a mass exodus of Soviet Jews to Israel. When Assad questioned the prudence of these actions he was bluntly told to seek a peaceful solution with Israel since "reliance on military force in settling the Arab-Israeli conflict has completely lost credibility." The quest for "strategic parity" with Israel, the cornerstone of Syria's regional policy since the mid-1970s, drew particularly scathing criticism for "diverting attention from the question of achieving security and peace in the Middle East."[22]

While there is little doubt that this approach heightened Assad's sense of vulnerability, it also intensified his hostility toward Gorbachev and left him impervious to his requests. When in 1988 the PLO ostensibly recognized

Israel's existence and declared Palestinian independence, Syria denounced the move as a sellout and refused to recognize the proclaimed Palestinian state; its response to the 1993 Israel-PLO agreement was even more scathing.

America's relations with its Middle Eastern allies were just as complex. Neither its most spectacular success in the post-1967 era (the winning-over of Egypt from Moscow) nor its most disastrous setback (the fall of the Iranian shah and the consequent loss of Iran) was primarily of its own making. It was Sadat's deep animosity toward the Soviet Union (significantly exacerbated by its attempts to prevent the October war) and his belief in America's leverage over Israel and its ability to relieve Egypt's economic plight that produced his change of heart, and it was he who was the driving force behind the improving relationship. Sadat sent his first signal to the US administration in July 1972, when he expelled the Soviet units from Egypt. He sent another in February 1973 by dispatching his national security adviser, Hafiz Ismail, for talks with Nixon and Kissinger. As the administration would not take the hint, Foreign Minister Ismail Fahmy turned up in Washington shortly after the October war with the explicit message that Sadat meant business. To underscore Egypt's strategic and political value to its would-be ally, Sadat gave the green light for ending the Arab oil embargo that had been imposed on the United States and several West European states during the October war. As architect and direct beneficiary of the embargo, he sought to cash in on its suspension now that his brainchild had outlived its usefulness.

Another example of a mutually beneficial alignment in which the junior partner called most of the shots, with the benevolent consent of the senior counterpart, was afforded by the US-Iranian relationship in the decade preceding the Islamic revolution of January 1979. Although Iran had been a longtime associate of the United States, it was only in the late 1960s and early 1970s that it established itself as America's closest Middle Eastern ally. The process started during the Johnson presidency, when Iran began receiving large quantities of sophisticated weaponry, and gained considerable momentum in 1972, when Nixon gave Shah Muhammad Reza Pahlavi a blank cheque to buy whatever conventional weaponry he wished.[23] The shah took the administration at its word, and Iran evolved into the most lucrative market for American military and civilian goods. Between 1972 and the shah's downfall in January 1979, the value of United States military sales to Iran amounted to some $20 billion, and included the highly advanced F-14 aircraft, attack helicopters, M-60A main battle tanks, and various types of missiles. In the summer of 1976 the two countries worked out a five-year trade program that provided for the purchase of $50 billion worth of American goods, including $10 billion worth of military equipment. On the eve of the revolution, the number of Americans working in Iran exceeded 27,000.[24]

This state of affairs gave the shah ever-growing leverage over the United States. He was no longer the young malleable ruler of 1953, reinstated through Western cloak-and-dagger operations, but rather a confident autocrat, keeping his subjects in permanent awe and pursuing a grandiose imperial vision, as evidenced by the celebration of his fifty-second birthday in October 1970. Perhaps the biggest birthday extravaganza in modern times, the party was timed to coincide with the 2,500th anniversary of the founding of the first Iranian empire by the Achaemenids. As his soldiers, dressed as warriors from different imperial epochs in Iran's history, marched across the ruins of Persepolis Palace, the shah vowed his allegiance to the imperial legacy of Cyrus the Great, the Achaemenid monarch who had subdued proud Babylon, in front of his worldwide assembly of guests:

> To you Cyrus, Great King, King of Kings, from Myself, Shahanshah of Iran, and from my people, hail! . . . We are here at this moment when Iran renews its pledge to History to bear witness to the immense gratitude of an entire people to you, immortal Hero of History, founder of the world's oldest empire, great liberator of all time, worthy son of mankind.[25]

For all their pomposity, these were no empty words. Since the late 1960s Iran had been rapidly establishing itself as the pre-eminent power in the Persian Gulf. As a result of a series of significant events—the announcement in 1968 of Britain's intention to withdraw from its military bases east of Suez, the diminution of a direct Soviet threat following the significant improvement in Iranian-Soviet relations beginning in the early 1960s, and rising oil revenues—Muhammad Reza felt able to embark on an ambitious drive aimed at reviving Iran's imperial glory. To justify this policy, the shah claimed that the responsibility for maintaining Gulf security lay solely with the local states and that no external powers were to be allowed to interfere in the affairs of the region. As the largest and most powerful Gulf country, he believed Iran had a moral, historical and geopolitical responsibility to ensure peace and stability in the region, not only for the local benefit but also for the good of the world. As his self-confidence grew still further, the shah cast his imperial sights well beyond the Persian Gulf. "World events were such that we were compelled to accept the fact that the sea adjoining the Oman Sea—I mean the Indian Ocean—does not recognize borders," he stated. "As for Iran's security limits—I will not state how many kilometers we have in mind, but anyone who is acquainted with geography and the strategic situation, and especially with the potential air and sea forces, knows what distances from Chah Bahar this limit can reach."[26]

While the shah's imperial ambitions would have been less tenable without American aid and support, his dependence on the United States was more than matched by Washington's need for Iran. As early as 1967, Secretary of Defense McNamara wrote to President Johnson that "our sales have created about 1.4 million man-years of employment in the US and over $1 billion in profits to American industry over the last five years."[27] As bilateral trade would soon enter the multibillion sphere, Iran's stability and well-being—or more precisely, the survival of the Pahlavi dynasty—would become an American concern of the first order.

But this was not all. Iran's unique geopolitical location, with the Soviet Union to the north and the world's largest oil deposits to the south, made it invaluable to US strategic interests. As the Americans desperately sought to extricate themselves from the Vietnamese quagmire and to avoid similar future entanglements, they appreciated any local power that could protect their interests in this part of the world. In July 1969, during a visit to the island of Guam, Nixon announced what came to be known as the Nixon Doctrine. He reaffirmed America's unwavering commitment to its treaty obligations, but made it clear that "as far as the problems of international security are concerned . . . the United States is going to encourage and has a right to expect that this problem will increasingly be handled by, and the responsibility for it taken by, the Asian nations themselves."[28]

As an astute politician, well versed in the art of political survival, the shah fully exploited this doctrine. He supported American allies and actions world-wide and cultivated a well-oiled lobby in the United States to convince the American public of Iran's strategic importance. At the same time, he did not shy away from exploiting America's Achilles' heel—its obsessive fear of communist expansionism. In June 1965 the shah made a state visit to Moscow which culminated in a large-scale commercial agreement and, no less impor-tant, a $110 million arms deal. In the next few years, Iran's relations with the Soviet Union and communist bloc countries improved further, lending greater credence to the shah's occasional threats to seek Soviet arms and mili-tary equipment. And even if some American officials doubted the shah's "Soviet Option," they could hardly ignore his threat to take his business else-where in the West. The United States was, after all, Iran's foremost, but not exclusive, arms supplier. Large quantities of British, French, and Italian weapons poured into the Iranian armed forces. Were the United States to reduce its share in Iran's military buildup, its Western competitors were certain to fill the gap.

In these circumstances the Americans were happy to allow the shah to dictate the general direction of the bilateral relationship. They ignored virulent anti-American attacks by Iran's domestic media on account of the shah's vocal international support for American policies; they tolerated the shah's persistent striving for higher oil prices, lauding instead his refusal to participate in the 1973–74 Arab oil embargo and his attempts to preserve stability in the world oil market; they conveniently overlooked their own long-standing opposition to nuclear proliferation and agreed to sell Iran eight large nuclear power plants for civilian purposes; and they supported the shah's subversive activities in Iraq in the early 1970s through the Kurdish uprising in the north of the country, then looked the other way when he betrayed the Kurds to the Iraqi regime once they had outlived their usefulness to him.[29]

So entrenched had the idea of this Iranian-American symbiosis become that successive US administrations came to view Iranian interests as indistinguishable from their own. The shah was seen as a permanent part of the Middle Eastern political landscape, something that had always been there and would remain long into the future. No indications to the contrary, however ominous, were allowed to shatter this illusion.[30]

Upon entering the White House in January 1977, Jimmy Carter was presented with a rosy picture of the domestic situation in Iran. "At age fifty-seven, in fine health, and protected by an absolute security apparatus," read a Department of State memorandum, "the Shah has an excellent chance to rule for a dozen or more years, at which time he indicated that the Crown Prince would assume the throne."[31] Actually, the shah's health was anything but fine. He was suffering from terminal cancer, diagnosed a few years earlier by French physicians. But what the French had known for quite some time remained unknown to the American intelligence and foreign-affairs community, despite the shah's supreme importance for the US national interest.[32] Small wonder that the administration remained largely oblivious to the gathering storm in Iran until it was too late.

In a memorandum to secretary of state Cyrus Vance in July 1977, his assistant for Near Eastern and South Asian affairs, Roy Atherton, assessed that "there is less chance of a dramatic shift in direction in Iran than in most other countries."[33] Reports by the CIA throughout the summer and autumn of 1977 were similarly sanguine. They anticipated "no radical change in Iranian political behavior in the near future" and estimated that, if anything, "we are looking at evolution not revolution." In line with the standard fallacy of attributing Middle Eastern developments to external influences rather than to indigenous dynamics, these assessments adopted an exceedingly optimistic tone: "The Shah seems to have no health or political problems at present that will prevent him from being the dominant figure in Iran into and possibly throughout the 1980s. His style of rule and his general policies will probably remain the same unless dramatic developments in the international environment force him to make a change."[34] It was only on November 9, 1978, that the US ambassador to Iran, William Sullivan, sent Washington a dramatic memorandum urging his superiors to start "thinking the unthinkable," namely what was to be done in the event of the shah's fall from power. This new perspective was shared by a handful of State Department analysts; the CIA reached the same view a fortnight later.[35]

Others remained hopeful almost to the end. Secretary of State Vance, for instance, could not bring himself to admit that the game was over. On November 16, when the shah declared martial law in a last-ditch attempt to arrest collapse, the US Department of State endorsed the move on the understanding that "military rule is only temporary and he [the shah] intends as rapidly as possible to move the country towards free elections and a new civilian-directed government." Zbigniew Brzezinski and his National Security Council staff were equally unaware of the real nature of the Iranian upheaval. Until the situation exploded in their face in January 1979, they were convinced that a tough, no-nonsense policy, either by the shah or by a successor military government, could save the day.[36] At no stage of the crisis, not even when it was over, did the administration realize that what had just happened in front of its very eyes was a revolution in the grand style of the French or the Russian, not merely turbulence on a large scale.

As a tearful shah fled Iran on January 16, 1979, and a buoyant Ayatollah Khomeini made a triumphant return home after fifteen years of exile, the supremacy of indigenous dynamics in Middle Eastern affairs and the limits of superpower influence were confirmed yet again. While the Carter administration undoubtedly mismanaged the crisis on a grand scale, the fact is that the United States was reacting to events that were not of its own making and over which it had but limited control. The Iranian revolution was a volcanic eruption of long-suppressed popular passions and desires. Putting this particular genie back into the bottle was well beyond America's power. All the administration could realistically do was to try to limit the damage to US interests to the barest minimum. As it was, the perennial constraints on superpower regional policy came to the fore in a particularly devastating way. The Cold War mentality, competing international priorities, bureaucratic infighting, inability to transcend cultural barriers—all these factors coalesced to produce a setback that even a decade of bitter regional conflict (the Iran-Iraq war, that is) and momentous global changes would fail to redress.

Neither could American post-Cold War pre-eminence prevent the repetition of similarly catastrophic blunders. As a superpower with a global array of interests, yet with a limited capacity for comprehending the social, cultural, and political underpinnings of these interests, the United States had often failed to identify unfavorable regional developments before their escalation into fully fledged conflicts. This tendency has not disappeared following the end of the Cold War, as starkly demonstrated by the 9/11 attacks.

As Iraqi troops were massing along the Kuwaiti border during July 1990, after a year of sustained pressure on the emirate to help finance Iraq's rehabilitation following the Iran–Iraq war, the Americans were fixated on Europe. This had been the case since the revolutions of 1989 had brought the East European communist regimes tumbling down. Now they were busy working with the Europeans to construct a new set of security arrangements that would allow conflicts on the continent to be handled in a sensitive and efficient manner. The general mood was euphoric. A brave new world was around the corner. No minor disputes between Third World autocrats would be allowed to spoil this moment of celebration.

This is not to say that the administration was completely unaware of the mounting tensions in the Gulf. American spy satellites picked up the movement of Iraqi troops toward the Kuwaiti border almost immediately, but it was believed that their purpose was intimidation rather than imminent action.[37] When the American ambassador, April Glaspie, reported back to Washington after her disastrous meeting with Saddam on July 25, 1990 that "his emphasis that he wants a peaceful settlement is surely sincere," there was a general sigh of relief and the administration returned to other business.

This rosy assessment was hardly supported by developments on the ground. Intelligence reports continued to tell of a rapidly expanding military buildup. By July 27, eight divisions of some hundred thousand men from the best Iraqi units were poised on the shared border. Senior officials in Washington still judged this to be more consistent with intimidation than with preparations for an actual invasion, which would have required far heavier communications traffic, more substantial artillery stocks and munitions, and more of a logistics "tail." This view was reinforced by a personal message from the Egyptian president Husni Mubarak to President George Bush, assuring the administration that there was no problem and encouraging the United States to keep a low profile. A message was then sent from Bush to Saddam, ensuring him of US affability and asking for an Iraqi quid pro quo. The Americans also decided to heed Arab advice to keep themselves detached from a problem that the Arabs now intended to solve among themselves.

This approach did little to calm the situation, and by the end of July Saddam had stepped up the military pressure on Kuwait by moving forward his artillery, logistics support, and aircraft. This apparently indicated that he had already made up his mind to invade, come what might. His public readiness to continue a dialogue with Kuwait was largely a smokescreen, aimed at gaining international legitimacy for the impending military action.

In conversation with the Arab League secretary-general, Chadly Klibi, the Iraqi foreign minister, Tariq Aziz, unequivocally stated that the Kuwaiti royal family must go.

Unfortunately, this was treated in Washington with the disbelief that commonly accompanies a warning that another government is about to break a fundamental international norm. The prevailing view—shared by the Kuwaitis, the other Arabs, the British, and even the Israeli intelligence services, which had long been warning of Saddam's aggressive intentions—was that Iraq's objective was still only intimidation and that, if military action was taken, it would probably be confined to seizing some disputed oilfields in northern Kuwait or possibly the strategically located Warba and Bubiyan islands that Iraq had long coveted.

The problem with this view was that these objectives had never figured prominently in Saddam's public or private utterances, where the immediate Iraqi demand was cash. Nevertheless, this notion of a limited strike was critical to American policy. If it had been appreciated that the logic of Iraqi military action had been to take all of Kuwait, that might have required a firmer American response; the thought that it was geared only to more limited objectives produced reticence instead.

Could the United States, and the West in general, have prevented the invasion? Probably not. The intensity of Saddam's anxiety over the future of his personal rule, and his conviction that the incorporation of Kuwait's wealth into the Iraqi finances provided the best guarantee for his political survival, meant that only a recognition that an invasion would lead to his certain undoing could have averted such a move. Since the Americans and the Europeans had failed to grasp Saddam's predicament, the need for such drastic measures never crossed their minds. Yet even if they had interpreted the situation correctly they would still have been dependent on their key regional allies such as Saudi Arabia and Egypt. The US administration therefore had little choice but to take its cue from those most directly involved with efforts at mediation, who also failed to identify the real nature of the problem at hand. The result was an incoherent and ineffectual policy combining mild warnings to Iraq with attempts to sustain good relations with a state that, on the most favorable interpretation, was engaged in extortion and stood in opposition to a number of major US foreign-policy goals. The unfortunate message this conveyed was one of indifference and weakness, which in turn encouraged Saddam to believe that he could invade Kuwait with impunity.

Just as America's position as "the only remaining superpower" did not deter Saddam from invading Kuwait, so it also failed to induce him to withdraw peacefully from the emirate afterward. Given the seriousness of Saddam's economic plight and the commitment which he had made by the invasion, a

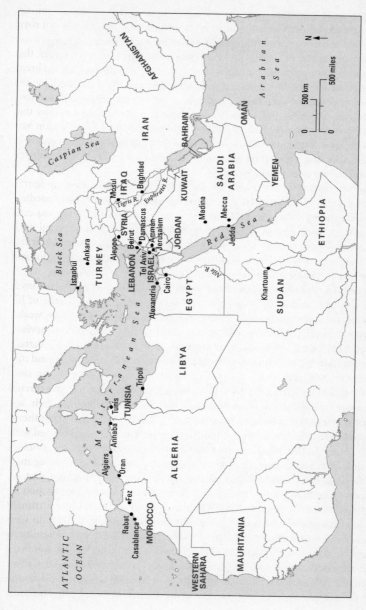

Map 8 The Contemporary Middle East

peaceful Iraqi departure was never a viable option. It was infinitely more difficult for Saddam to withdraw than it would have been for him not to invade in the first place. An unconditional withdrawal, or even withdrawal with a face-saving formula that did not involve the retention of the invasion's financial and economic gains, was totally unacceptable. Not only would such an outcome have failed to redress the economic problems which had driven Saddam into Kuwait, and which were then made worse by the international sanctions against Iraq which had followed, it would have also constituted an enormous loss of face. Only the credible threat that the retention of Kuwait would lead to his certain demise could have driven Saddam out again without war; but this was a message the United States, as leader of a variegated international coalition, could not convey.

Neither did the various carrots offered to Saddam, some of them by the US administration itself, do the trick. Four basic types of concession were on offer: a possible change of regime in Kuwait; serious negotiations with the Kuwaitis on economic and territorial questions; progress on other regional issues, such as the Arab-Israeli conflict; and a promise that Iraq would not be attacked and that American forces would leave the region following the evacuation of Kuwait. For example, on September 24, the French president François Mitterrand implicitly recognized the legitimacy of some of Iraq's territorial claims to Kuwait and suggested that the resolution of the Kuwait crisis be followed by a comprehensive peace conference on the Middle East. In the following months, France would offer Saddam several ladders for a climb-down; the last such attempt was made on January 15, 1991, a few hours before the expiry of the UN ultimatum to Iraq to leave Kuwait. It was contemptuously rebuffed by Saddam.

A request by Jacques Poos, Luxembourg's foreign minister and the European Union's rotating president, to visit Baghdad in January 1991 on behalf of the EU was similarly dismissed out of hand, as was his suggestion to meet the Iraqi foreign minister, Aziz, in Algeria. The UN secretary-general, Javier Pérez de Cuéllar, discovered no greater Iraqi flexibility, either in his meeting with Aziz in August 1990 or in a subsequent meeting with Saddam himself in January 1991. Even the Americans were showing signs of flexibility. In September 1990 Under-Secretary of State Robert Kimmitt hinted that the US would not be opposed to Kuwait being forced to negotiate with Iraq, once the latter had withdrawn. Later that month, in his address to the UN General Assembly, President Bush stated that Iraq's unconditional withdrawal from Kuwait would pave the way "for all the states and peoples of the region to settle the conflict that divides Arabs from Israel." Moreover, in an about face in America's long-standing opposition to an international conference on the Middle East, on December 5, 1990, the US ambassador to the United Nations,

Thomas Pickering, indicated his government's readiness to consider such a conference should Iraq withdraw from Kuwait.

That Saddam failed to pick up these offers of concessions, and many others of a similar kind, was a clear indication of both his lack of interest in withdrawal and the weakness of the anti-Iraq international coalition. Saddam wanted a political solution all right; but only one that would allow him to retain the financial fruits of his aggression. Had the international coalition acquiesced in Iraq's *complete* satellization of Kuwait—the invasion's original objective—Saddam might well have withdrawn, even though this process would inevitably have taken an exceedingly prolonged period of time. Since this was a non-starter, even for the most appeasing members of the coalition, an Iraqi withdrawal was not on the cards: the gap between the two sides was simply too wide to bridge. A worldwide coalition thus failed to coerce a local dictator into reneging on his aggression and was forced to resort to arms to this end; and although the war ended in a resounding victory, its very occurrence, not to speak of Saddam's survival for another twelve years, underscored the limits of American, and for that matter great-power, influence in the "New World Order."

Renewing the Quest for Allah's Empire

As the Arab imperial dream stumbled from one setback to another, the political scene was set for a resurgence of the factor that had dominated Middle
Eastern history for well over a millennium: religion. Not that the fall of the
Ottoman Empire and the subsequent abolition of the caliphate had failed to
trigger an immediate jockeying for the revival of this lofty post. Yet there was
no suitable candidate at hand. Sharif Hussein considered himself the religious
and temporal head of the new empire he sought to establish, but his religious
pretensions were anathema to most Arabic-speaking Ottoman subjects, while
his political ambitions were largely thwarted by the simultaneous quest of his
two sons, Faisal and Abdallah, for their own regional empires. When he had
himself proclaimed caliph, following the abolition of the caliphate in March
1924, Hussein received no more support from the Arab and Muslim masses
than he had for his World War I revolt. Likewise the caliphate was coveted by
a string of Egyptian rulers, descended from Muhammad Ali, from Abbas
Hilmi (1892–1914), to Fuad (1917–36), to Farouq (1937–52). Yet their claims
had never been widely accepted, while Farouq increasingly concentrated on
pursuing the Arab imperial dream, or at least on denying it to the Hashemites,
rather than promoting its wider Islamic version.[1]

The quest for Allah's empire thus passed from the monarchs to political
activists and ideologues, or Islamists as they are now commonly known, who
set their sights far higher than their predecessors. For the monarchs, the
caliphate meant little more than added legitimization of their ambitions for a
regional empire. They had little interest in the deeper inculcation of Islam's
precepts in their Muslim subjects, let alone in spreading Allah's message
beyond the House of Islam. The Islamists, by contrast, modeled themselves on
Islam's early conquerors, and aspired to nothing less than the substitution of
Allah's universal empire for the existing international system. "The power to
rule over the earth has been promised to *the whole community of believers*,"
argued the prominent Islamist Abul Ala Mawdudi (1903–79), founder of the

fundamentalist Jamaat Islami in Pakistan. "A state of this sort cannot evidently restrict the scope of its activities. Its approach is universal and all-embracing. Its sphere of activity is coexistent with the whole of human life." This universal state, or rather world empire, was to be established through a sustained jihad that would "destroy those regimes opposed to the precepts of Islam and replace them with a government based on Islamic principles . . . not merely in one specific region . . . but [as part] of a comprehensive Islamic transformation throughout the entire world."[2]

This was also the view of Hassan al-Banna, an Egyptian schoolteacher and sometime watch-repairer who probably did more than any of his contemporaries to transform Islamism from an obscure intellectual phenomenon into a mass movement that would exert a profound and lasting impact on the development of Arab and Muslim societies.

Born in 1906 in a small north Egyptian locality, Banna moved to Cairo in 1923 to train as a schoolteacher, and quickly immersed himself in religious activity. He used to go about the city wearing a long red cloak that partially hid his face, and boasted of making an average of fifteen hundred speeches a year. This might well have been true as Banna, a highly gifted orator, rented three of the largest cafés in Cairo and mesmerized his audiences with vivid descriptions of the torments of hell. In 1927, having graduated from the training college, he took a teaching position in the port town of Ismailiya, on the Suez Canal, where the following year he established the Society of the Muslim Brothers.[3] The organization's stated objectives were individual moral purification and collective political and social regeneration through the establishment of a truly Islamic government in Egypt, as a springboard for universal expansion "until the entire world will chant the name of the Prophet [Muhammad], Allah's prayers and blessings be upon him."[4]

This message struck a responsive chord among Egyptians. By the late 1940s, the Muslim Brothers had established some two thousand branches throughout the country, boasting about one million members and sympathizers. To this must be added the society's branches in Syria, Jordan, Yemen, Sudan, and Mandatory Palestine, which made the Muslim Brothers the most powerful Islamic movement in the world and a key player in the Egyptian political scene. Finding its members largely among students, professionals, and civil servants of the new middle class, the movement amassed substantial funds from followers' donations and was soon effectively running its own "state within a state," including educational institutions, newspapers, factories, hospitals, commercial, financial and insurance enterprises, as well as a private army. In a series of meetings with Banna between 1940 and 1942 to discuss possible collaboration between the Muslim Brothers and the nascent clandestine group of the Free Officers, Anwar Sadat was told of the intention to establish paramilitary "shock battalions". (Banna apparently alluded to the "special section," a secret elite unit that was responsible for most of the society's terrorist attacks during the 1940s.)

The parallel with the Nazi SS was not accidental. Banna was an unabashed admirer of Hitler and Mussolini, who "guided their peoples to unity, order, regeneration, power, and glory." Authoritarian to the core, Banna demanded absolute loyalty from his subordinates and ran the Muslim Brothers in such a heavy-handed manner that a contemporary Egyptian journalist quipped that "If Banna sneezed in Cairo, the Brothers in Aswan would say 'God bless you.'"

Sadat gained an insight into this phenomenon as he listened to Banna praising Mussolini's defiance of the international community through his invasion of Ethiopia and Hitler's use of radio broadcasts to enlighten the German people. In contrast, Banna had nothing but disdain for the Egyptian regime, which used this new invention to corrupt the minds and souls of ordinary Egyptians with songs about love and sex rather than to inculcate them with the virtues of death and martyrdom in the quest for Allah's universal empire. "Death is an art," he famously wrote, "and the most exquisite of arts when practiced by the skillful artist." In Banna's view, the Qur'an commanded its believers to love death as much as others love life. As long as Muslim societies failed to abide by this sacred philosophy they were destined to remain in their current dismal position. "There is no escape from death and it happens only once," he claimed. "Should death come in the path of Allah, it will be a gain in this world and a reward in the other."[5] This reasoning was duly incorporated into the Muslim Brothers' credo: "Allah is our goal; the Qur'an is our constitution; the Prophet is our leader; Struggle is our way; and death in the path of Allah is our highest aspiration."

In the end Banna fell victim to his own cult of violence and death. On February 12, 1949, he was murdered by government agents, apparently in revenge for the assassination of Prime Minister Nuqrashi Pasha a few weeks earlier. Yet the imperial vision and violent ethos he had instilled in the Muslim Brothers was preserved and expanded by his ideological successor, the movement's most influential thinker: Sayyid Qutb.

Like Banna, Qutb was born in 1906 in a small rural locality, graduated from a Cairo teacher-training institution, and worked as a civil servant in the educational field. Unlike Banna, however, he was a born-again Muslim, breaking with his secular life style only in his forties. The metamorphosis took place during Qutb's stay in the United States in 1948–50, when he was sent to explore the possibility of introducing American ideas and methods into the Egyptian educational system. Finding himself isolated from the only world he had hitherto known, and shocked and disgusted by what he regarded as

America's sexual depravity, the lonely and despondent Qutb took increasing solace in Islam. Upon his return to Egypt he began frequenting Muslim Brothers' meetings, and in late 1951 was recruited to the society and almost immediately placed in charge of its propaganda section.[6]

Focusing on Islam's absolutist outlook on world affairs, Qutb viewed human history as a Manichean struggle between the "the party of God [which] stands beneath the banner of God and bears His insignia [and] the party of the Devil [which] embraces every community, group, people, race and individual who do not stand under the banner of God." For a brief period of time, during the age of the Prophet and the four "rightly guided" caliphs (622–61), a true community of believers came into being, having overcome the state of barbaric ignorance (*jahiliya*) prevailing in the Arabian Peninsula prior to Muhammad's advent. Unfortunately, humanity as a whole was not yet prepared for a breakthrough of such cosmic proportions. Islam spread throughout the world with unprecedented rapidity, converting the conquered populations en masse, but successive generations of Muslims lacked the unique training given by the Prophet to the first community of believers, and foreign ideas and sources, from Greek philosophy and ancient Iranian legends to Jewish scriptures and traditions, mixed with the Qur'anic precepts to drag the umma down from the lofty heights it had initially reached. This allowed Satan to recover from the original setback suffered by the advent of Islam, summon his followers, who soon regained the reins of power, and plunge the world into a new and more dangerous state of jahiliya.

Why more dangerous? Because the original jahiliya was confined to those pagans who had not yet embraced Allah's divine message, whereas the new one afflicted Muslim societies as well: "Everything around us is jahiliya— people's beliefs and ideas, habits and traditions, culture, art, and literature, rules and laws, to such an extent that much of what we consider Islamic culture, Islamic sources, Islamic philosophy, and Islamic thought are also constructs of jahiliya!"

Contrary to what is sometimes thought, Qutb's brand of Islamism was not a response to the ascendancy of European imperialism and the growing adoption of Western ideals and practices by Muslim societies. Rather, he traced the "new jahiliya" to the disintegration of the first umma and the creation of the Umayyad and Abbasid empires, where the notion of Allah's universal sovereignty succumbed to the reality of human kingship and hereditary rule in their most decadent and un-Islamic forms. In the following millennium the House of Islam would fluctuate between various levels of attainment, from the low ebbs of the Mongol and crusader invasions to the apogee of Ottoman expansion. Yet it would never manage to rid itself of the new jahiliya, let alone come anywhere near the lofty heights of the first umma.

It is indeed the rejection of Allah's rule on earth and the subordination of man to man that lies at the heart of the new jahiliya: "Not in the simple and primitive manner of the first jahiliya but in the form of claiming that the right to create values, to pass laws and regulations, and to choose one's way of life rests with man, in disregard of what Allah has prescribed." This defiance has resulted in widespread oppression throughout history, both by deviant regimes within the House of Islam and by various systems outside this domain, from communism to capitalism to imperialism: "Such systems—those adopted by mankind in isolation from the guidance of God at any time or place—are inevitably affected by the results of human ignorance, human weakness, and human folly. Hence, in whole or in part they will conflict with human nature, and the soul of mankind will suffer as a result."

In order to break jahiliya's yoke, Islamic societies must undergo a comprehensive conceptual and political transformation spearheaded by a small and dedicated vanguard of true believers who will substitute the umma for the perverted and corrupt regimes that have dominated Muslim societies for over a millennium. This newly resurrected entity will then sustain the struggle until the eventual "conquest of world domination" and the establishment of Allah's sovereignty on earth. "We are the umma of the believers, living within a jahili society," a defiant Qutb told the Egyptian court which was to decide on his execution. "As a community of believers we should see ourselves in a state of war with the state and the society. The territory we dwell in is the House of War."[7]

In sharp contrast to Banna, who shared pan-Arabism's perception of the Qur'an as an Arab book and regarded the Arabs as "Islam's first community and its chosen people," without whom the new religion would have never come into being, Qutb viewed Islam as a universal phenomenon based on an association of believers and rejecting racial, national, linguistic, and regional partisanship. Even the original umma was an Islamic society where an extremely diverse group of peoples—"Arabs, Persians, Syrians, Egyptians, Maghribis, Turks, Chinese, Indians, Romans, Greeks, Indonesians, and Africans"—coexisted in peace and harmony under the banner of Islam. "This great civilization was not 'Arab' even for a single day, but was always 'Islamic,'" Qutb argued. "It was never 'national' but was always 'ideological.'"

Keenly aware of the possible imperialist overtones attending such a "community," let alone a community aimed at transforming Islam into "a worldwide—not just local—order," Qutb went out of his way to disclaim any connection between the two concepts. "There is nothing further from the true understanding of the spirit of Islam than to speak of it as imperial," he argued.

Perhaps the point of formal similarity is that the Islamic world was composed of a number of provinces with widely differing races and cultures ruled from a single center. This is a mark of empire! But it is merely an outward mark. . . . It is more appropriate to say that [Islam] was worldwide in its tendency because of its strong idea of the unity of the world and its goal of gathering all humanity under its banner of equality and brotherhood.[8]

Imperial or not, Qutb knew full well that the creation of the universal umma could not be achieved by peaceful means, just as the original umma had only been created through the relentless military campaigns of the Prophet and the orthodox caliphs. "The establishment of Allah's kingdom on earth, the elimination of the reign of man, the wresting of sovereignty from its usurpers and its restoration to Allah, and the abolition of human laws and implementation of the divine law [shari'a] cannot be only achieved through sermons and preaching," he argued. "Those who have usurped Allah's authority on earth and have enslaved His creatures will not surrender their power merely through preaching. Had this been the case, Allah's messengers would have far more easily achieved the task of establishing His religion across the world. But this runs counter to the history of the prophets and this religion throughout the ages." This is why Allah has established "only one cause for killing—where there is no other recourse—and that is striving for the sake of God (jihad)" and imposed this sacred duty on all Muslims, not as a means to convert individuals or communities to Islam, but as the foremost tool "to establish Allah's sovereignty on earth."[9]

Like Banna, Qutb did not live to see the realization of his vision. On August 29, 1966, after more than a decade in prison, he was executed by the authorities for an alleged "new conspiracy" against the regime. Yet his radical doctrine outlived him and was embraced by a new generation of Islamists, both within and outside Egypt. "Sayyid Qutb's call for loyalty to God's oneness and to acknowledge God's sole authority and sovereignty was the spark that ignited the Islamic revolution against the enemies of Islam at home and abroad," wrote the prominent Egyptian Islamist Ayman al-Zawahiri. "The bloody chapters of this revolution continue to unfold day after day."[10]

Zawahiri knew what he was talking about. With the Muslim Brothers emerging from the decades of Nasserite repression as a regular parliamentary opposition group rather than a revolutionary movement, the violent quest for Allah's empire passed to the society's non-Egyptian branches as well as to new and more militant Egyptian groups. Foremost among these were the Society of Muslims, also known as al-Takfir wa-l-Hijra (Excommunication and Hijra), al-Gamaat al-Islamiya (the Muslim Associations), and Tanzim al-Jihad

(Organization of the Jihad), Zawahiri's own group, which on October 6, 1981, assassinated President Sadat and made an abortive attempt to trigger a nationwide revolt by capturing the southern town of Asyut.

During the 1990s the Egyptian authorities battled against a sustained wave of Islamist terrorism, this time by the Gamaat. This involved attacks on government officials and the country's substantial Coptic minority, the murdering of foreign tourists, as well as an audacious attempt on the life of President Mubarak while on an official visit to Ethiopia in June 1995. The startled president afterward intensified the repressive campaign against the Islamists, arresting thousands of activists, executing some of them, and blocking all avenues of political participation. By the end of the year the movement's capacity for action had been reduced to sporadic hit-and-run attacks from its base in the Nile Valley.

The Islamists were no more successful outside Egypt. Their sustained effort in the late 1970s and early 1980s to topple Syria's ruling Ba'th regime was brutally suppressed, with the town of Hama, the center of Islamist resistance, razed to the ground and tens of thousands of its residents slaughtered. An attempt to overthrow the Algerian regime in the 1990s was similarly defeated after an exceptionally savage war, which claimed over 100,000 lives and saw horrendous atrocities on both sides. Only in Sudan did the Islamists seize power through a coup by sympathetic officers in June 1989. The Muslim Brothers also managed to strike deep roots in the West Bank and the Gaza Strip, occupied by Israel during the Six-Day War of June 1967. The Israelis turned a blind eye to the society's development, despite its outright commitment to Israel's destruction, in the hope that it would act as a counterweight to the far more powerful PLO, equally committed to the Jewish state's demise.

This proved a critical mistake. During the popular uprising of the late 1980s (or the *intifada*), the Palestinian branch of the Muslim Brothers, better known by its Arabic acronym Hamas (Islamic Resistance Movement), earned its stripes by spearheading the struggle against Israel. During the 1990s Hamas increased its power still further as the corrupt and repressive Palestinian Authority that had been established in the territories under the leadership of Yasser Arafat as part of the 1993 Oslo accords failed to deliver the fruits of peace while alienating growing segments of the local population.

Yet far from being an ordinary liberation movement in search of national self-determination, Hamas has subordinated its aim of bringing about the destruction of Israel and the creation of a Palestinian state on its ruins to the wider goal of establishing Allah's universal empire. In doing so, it has followed in the footsteps of its Egyptian parent organization, which viewed its violent opposition to Zionism from the 1930s and 1940s as an integral part of the Manichean struggle for the creation of a worldwide caliphate rather than as a defense of the Palestinian Arabs' national rights. In the words of the senior Hamas leader, Mahmoud al-Zahar: "Islamic and traditional views reject the notion of establishing an independent Palestinian state ... In the past, there was no independent Palestinian state ... [Hence] our main goal is to establish a great Islamic state, be it pan-Arabic or pan-Islamic."[11] "Hamas finds itself at a period of time when Islam has waned away from the reality of life," stated the organization's constitution, echoing Banna's and Qutb's preaching. "The state of truth has disappeared and has been replaced by the state of evil. Nothing has remained in its right place, for when Islam is removed from the scene everything changes."

It was to redress this dismal state of affairs that Hamas was established— not merely to "liberate Palestine from Zionist occupation" but to pursue the far loftier goals of spreading Allah's holy message and defending the weak and oppressed throughout the world: "The Islamic Resistance Movement, while breaking its own path, will ... spare no effort to implement the truth and abolish evil, in speech and in fact, both here and in any other location where it can reach out and exert influence." As the movement's slogan puts it: "Allah is [Hamas's] goal, the Prophet its model, the Qur'an its Constitution, Jihad its path and death for the cause of Allah its most sublime belief."

In other words, the "Question of Palestine" is neither an ordinary territorial dispute between two national movements nor a struggle by an indigenous population against a foreign occupier. It is a holy war by the worldwide Islamic umma to prevent the loss of a part of the House of Islam to the infidels: "When our enemies usurp some Islamic lands, Jihad becomes a duty binding on all Muslims." Like other parts of the world conquered by the forces of Islam, "the land of Palestine has been an Islamic trust (*waqf*) throughout the generations and until the Day of Resurrection, [hence] no one can renounce it or part of it, or abandon it or part of it." This makes the present struggle over Palestine a direct extension of Islam's historic fight against its two foremost medieval enemies—the crusaders and the Mongols:

The Muslims had faced those invasions and planned their removal and defeat, [and] they are able to face the Zionist invasion and defeat it. This will not be difficult for Allah if our intentions are pure and our determination is sincere; if the Muslims draw useful lessons from the experiences of the past, and extricate themselves from the vestiges of the [Western] ideological onslaught; and if they follow the traditions of Islam.[12]

The most ambitious attempt to establish Allah's universal empire, though, came not from the Muslim Brothers and their ideological offshoots but from the Islamic Republic of Iran, created in 1979 by the religious radical Ayatollah Ruhollah Khomeini—"undoubtedly the greatest soldier for Islam in the twentieth century"[13]—on the ruins of the Pahlavi monarchy that had ruled the country since the mid-1920s.

Born on September 24, 1902, into a devout small-town family, Khomeini lost his father when he was five months old and was brought up by his mother. At the age of nineteen he was sent to continue his religious education in the adjacent town of Arak, moving a year later to the city of Qom, a traditional center of learning and pilgrimage, where he quickly established himself as an outstanding scholar and teacher.

Iran at the time was going through dramatic changes and reforms, introduced by the newly installed shah, Reza Pahlavi (1925–41), and aimed at its transformation into a modern and largely secular state. The diminution in the power of the clerics and the repressive means used to enforce these changes gradually drove Khomeini into political activism, and in 1942 he published his first book (titled *The Revelation of Secrets*) in which he derided the shah's Westernizing policies as anti-Islamic. In the following years Khomeini became the foremost religious critic of the regime. When in 1963 Shah Muhammad Reza Pahlavi (1941–79) promulgated the series of far-reaching social, political, and economic reforms that came to be known as the White Revolution, Khomeini embarked on a sustained campaign against the new measures. Matters came to a head in June 1963 when, following a particularly virulent sermon against the shah, Khomeni was arrested and placed in solitary confinement. This triggered widespread riots throughout the country, in which thousands of people were killed in just a few days. In early April 1964 the authorities bowed to intense public pressure and released Khomeini, but not before announcing that he had agreed to refrain from political activity as a condition of his release. The imam, who resumed his anti-regime campaign with renewed vigor, immediately denied the allegation. In November 1964 Khomeini was arrested yet again and sent into exile in Turkey, from where he moved a year later to the holy Shiite town of Najaf, in southern Iraq.

Aside from pandering to public pressure, in agreeing to this move the Iranian regime hoped that Khomeini would be overshadowed by Najaf's prominent religious authorities and reduced to political obscurity. In fact the opposite happened. Khomeini quickly transformed Najaf into a hotbed of anti-Pahlavi activities. All subsequent attempts to suppress the ayatollah's activities backfired, and in January 1978 widespread demonstrations erupted in Qom in what quickly snowballed into a nationwide popular revolt against the regime.

Anxious to stem the mounting tide of public restiveness, the shah pressured the Iraqi authorities to expel Khomeini, and in October 1978 the aged ayatollah arrived in Paris. This proved yet another critical miscalculation. Rather than restricting Khomeini's room for maneuver, the move actually improved his ability to control developments within Iran and catapulted him to international prominence. On January 16, 1979, the shah left Iran, never to return. Two weeks later Khomeini returned from his long exile to a rapturous welcome.[14]

Like Mawdudi and Qutb, Khomeini viewed human history as a millenarian struggle between the forces of Islam and the forces of jahiliya, which include all Muslim states that are not governed in accordance with the Shari'a, and took the early caliphate as a model for a future Islamic government. Yet he did not share Qutb's sweeping dismissal of the Islamic empires; his position on this issue was far more pragmatic. On the one hand, Khomeini had nothing but praise for a number of Islamic empires such as "the great Ottoman State." On the other, he viewed "monarchy and hereditary succession" as an alien import antithetical to Islam's true spirit and pilloried a string of Islamic empires starting with the Umayyad. This is not difficult to understand, given that it was the founder of this empire, Mu'awiya ibn Abi Sufian, who had challenged the authority of the caliph Ali, Shiism's patron imam, and whose son Yazid had been responsible for the killing of Ali's son Hussein, Shiism's foremost martyr.

Like pan-Arab ideologues, Khomeini viewed Western imperialism as the latest manifestation of the millenarian struggle between the House of Islam and the House of War. But while the former invoked past Muslim imperial glories as a justification for the creation of a united pan-Arab empire, Khomeini viewed them as a precedent for the unification of the worldwide Muslim community. In his understanding, after partitioning the umma into artificial separate entities after World War I, the great powers had done their utmost to keep Muslim communities in a permanent state of ignorance and fragmentation. "The imperialists, the oppressive and treacherous rulers, the Jews, Christians, and materialists are all attempting to distort the truth of Islam and lead the Muslims astray," he cautioned:

> We see today that the Jews (may God curse them) have meddled with the text of the Qur'an. . . . We must protest and make the people aware that the Jews and their foreign backers are opposed to the very foundations of Islam and wish to establish Jewish domination throughout the world. Since they are a cunning and resourceful group of people, I fear that—God forbid!— they may one day achieve their goal, and that the apathy shown by some of us may allow a Jew to rule over us one day.[15]

This means that the Middle Eastern states—indeed, the entire contemporary international system—are totally illegitimate, for they perpetuate an unjust order imposed on "oppressed" Muslims by the "oppressive" great powers. Muslims are therefore obliged to "overthrow the oppressive governments installed by the imperialists and bring into existence an Islamic government of justice that will be in the service of the people."[16] An Islamic world order would see the territorial state transcended by the broader entity of the umma.

As the only country where a true Islamic government had been established, ran Khomeini's line of reasoning, Iran had a sacred duty to serve as the core of the umma and as the springboard for worldwide dissemination of Islam's holy message: "The Iranian revolution is not exclusively that of Iran, because Islam does not belong to any particular people. . . . We will export our revolution throughout the world because it is an Islamic revolution. The struggle will continue until the calls 'there is no god but Allah and Muhammad is the messenger of Allah' are echoed all over the world."[17] Khomeini made good his promise of exporting the struggle. In November 1979 and February 1980 widespread riots erupted in the Shiite towns of the oil-rich Saudi province of Hasa, causing many casualties. Similar disturbances occurred in Bahrain, while Kuwait became the target of a sustained terror and subversion campaign. Yet the main thrust of the subversive effort was directed against Iraq, for two main reasons. First, Shiites accounted for some 60 percent of Iraq's total population, and they deeply resented the long-standing discrimination practiced against them by the ruling Sunni minority, about a third their size; the revolutionary regime in Tehran could, and certainly did, entertain hopes that this Shiite community would emulate the Iranian example and rise against its own Sunni "oppressors." As Khomeini put it: "It may be that when the people of Iraq see the progress made by the revolution of Iran, they will begin their own movement."[18]

Second, given Iraq's position as the most powerful Arab state in the Gulf, it was viewed by the revolutionary regime as the main obstacle to Iran's quest for Allah's empire. In the words of the influential member of the Iranian leadership, Hujjatul Islam Sadeq Khalkhali: "We have taken the path of true Islam and our aim in defeating Saddam lies in the fact that we consider Saddam the main obstacle to the advance of Islam in the region."[19]

In June 1979, the revolutionary regime began publicly urging the Iraqi population to rise up and overthrow the secular Ba'th regime, which had governed Iraq since the summer of 1968. A few months later Tehran escalated its campaign by resuming support for the rebellious Iraqi Kurds (which had been suspended in 1975), providing aid to underground Shiite movements in Iraq, and initiating terrorist attacks against prominent Iraqi officials. These reached their peak on April 1, 1980, with a failed attempt on the life of the

Iraqi deputy premier Tariq Aziz while he was making a public speech in Baghdad. Two weeks later, the Iraqi minister of information narrowly escaped a similar attempt. In April alone, at least twenty Iraqi officials were killed in bomb attacks by Shiite underground organizations. When these pressures eventually led to the Iraqi invasion of Iran in September 1980, Khomeini wholeheartedly embraced "the imposed war" as a means of consolidating his regime and furthering its influence throughout the region. The war would continue, he vowed, "until the downfall of the regime governing Baghdad."[20]

Eventually, the exorbitant human toll and economic dislocation of the Iran-Iraq war drove the Iranian leadership to compromise its high principles and Khomeini was finally persuaded to "drink the poison" and authorize the cessation of hostilities. On July 18, 1988, after eight years of bitter fighting, Iran accepted United Nations Security Council Resolution 598 on a ceasefire in the Iran-Iraq war, and shortly afterward embarked on a vigorous campaign to end its international isolation. It mended fences with the Gulf states, re-established diplomatic ties with the major West European powers, and even alluded to a possible dialogue with the United States, the "Great Satan." Yet when a combination of international and regional developments offered new opportunities in the early 1990s, the ayatollahs' imperialist ambitions were quickly reasserted. An expansion of the country's military arsenal was accompanied by sustained efforts to project Iranian influence in the Persian Gulf and the Middle East, as well as in Central Asia and the Transcaucasus.

No less important, Iran renewed and substantially accelerated its nuclear development program. Notwithstanding the war's cost, the Islamic regime has continued to pour substantial sums of money into its nuclear program, and there is a strong consensus among intelligence services and arms-control agencies around the world that Iran is now aggressively seeking nuclear weapons. Iran is known to have been shopping for nuclear know-how and matériel in the West, the successor states to the Soviet Union, especially Russia—from which Iran has acquired two reactors of four hundred megawatts thermal each—and selected Third World countries, such as Brazil, North Korea, and China, which has long been involved in the Iranian program. For their part, the ayatollahs made no secret of their interest in the Bomb, at least until they came under heavy American pressure to bridle their nuclear ambitions following the 9/11 attacks. "It was made very clear during the [Iran–Iraq] war that chemical, bacteriological and radiological weapons are very decisive," stated Ali Akbar Hashemi-Rafsanjani, then speaker of the Iranian parliament and commander-in-chief of Iran's armed forces, shortly after the war. "We should fully equip ourselves both in the offensive and defensive use of chemical, bacteriological, and radiological weapons."[21]

Despite these efforts, Iran's pan-Islamic doctrine has had no greater success than did pan-Arabism in denting the Middle Eastern territorial state system. Not only have most Sunnis rejected it as a distinctly Shiite doctrine, but even Iraq's majority Shiite community found it unconvincing and gave more allegiance to the Iraqi territorial state. Rather than welcoming their self-styled Iranian liberators, they endured the hardships of war in much the same way as other Iraqis, and many of them fought shoulder to shoulder with their compatriots to rebuff the Iranian threat. While the number of Sunni officers in the Iraqi army remained disproportionately high, some Shiite officers were promoted to positions of prestige and responsibility in which they proved their loyalty and patriotism. As for Shiite desertions, these occurred at about the same rate as Sunni desertions and at substantially lower rates than desertions from largely Kurdish units. Isolated terrorist activities notwithstanding, the Shiite community sealed its commitment to the Iraqi state with the blood of its sons; this state of affairs remained unchanged following the 2003 overthrow of Saddam's dictatorship and the attendant rise of the Shiites to political pre-eminence, for the first time since the creation of Iraq in 1921.

This poor record of achievement (Iran's only successful revolutionary export has been the militant Shiite Hizbullah group in Lebanon and the far smaller Islamic Jihad in the Palestinian territories) did not mean that the quest for Allah's empire was over, however. Only now it was personified by an individual, rather than a state, and a Sunni, rather than a Shiite: the Saudi tycoon Osama bin Laden and his al-Qaeda terrorist organization.

Bin Laden's Holy War

The 1981 assassination of Anwar Sadat forced the Islamists to rethink their strategy. The expectation that the "killing of Pharaoh" would trigger a general rising by the Egyptian people against their deviant rulers met with disappointment. The masses remained conspicuously aloof and Sadat's successor, Husni Mubarak, unleashed a repressive anti-Islamist campaign that resulted in the incarceration of thousands of activists and the execution of scores of others. The need for a revised approach was further underscored by the failure of the Iranian revolution to spread its messianic message through a frontal assault on the secular Iraqi Ba'th regime. As successive Iranian human-wave attacks broke against Iraq's formidable line of defense, the Islamists gradually concluded that their offensive against the Arab regimes had to be accompanied by a careful targeting of their international backers: "the Jews and the crusaders." Once these foreign aggressors had withdrawn their support from their local lackeys, these deviant regimes would collapse like a house of cards and the road to the creation of Allah's universal empire would be opened.

"The masters in Washington and Tel Aviv are using the [Arab] regimes to protect their interests and to fight the battle against the Muslims on their behalf," wrote Ayman al-Zawahiri, leader of Tanzim al-Jihad, the group that was behind the Sadat assassination.

If the shrapnel from the battle reaches their homes and bodies, they will trade accusations with their agents about who is responsible for this. In that case, they will face one of two bitter choices: Either personally wage the battle against the Muslims, which means that the battle will turn into [a] clear-cut jihad against infidels, or they reconsider their plans after acknowledging the failure of the brute and violent confrontation against Muslims. Therefore, we must move the battle to the enemy's grounds to burn the hands of those who ignite fire in our countries.

The primary tool for moving the battle to "the enemy's grounds" was terrorism. Its adoption reflected the euphoria attending the defeat of the Soviet occupation of Afghanistan during the 1980s on the one hand, and a keen awareness of Western military and technological superiority on the other. "The mujahid Islamic movement must escalate its methods of strikes and tools of resisting the enemies to keep up with the tremendous increase in the number of its enemies," argued Zawahiri. "The targets as well as the type and method of weapons used must be chosen to have an impact on the structure of the enemy and deter it enough to stop its brutality, arrogance, and disregard for all taboos and customs." In practical terms this meant the infliction of maximum casualties through "martyrdom operations," which were at one and the same time the cheapest and most effective military means at the Muslims' disposal and "the [only] language understood by the West."[1]

In late December 1994 the Algerian Groupe Islamique Armé (GIA), a radical Islamist group engaged in a bitter war against the country's secular regime, hijacked a French airbus at Algiers airport with a view to bringing it down on a major target in Paris. The intended atrocity was averted by the French police, who stormed the airplane while it refueled in Marseille, but in the following year the GIA carried out a sustained bombing campaign in France, "the former colonial power and bitterest enemy of Islam in the West," aimed at forcing the French government to withdraw all support for the Algerian government and thus hasten its collapse. On the other side of the ocean, a car bomb was detonated on February 26, 1993, at New York's World Trade Center in an attempt to bring down this symbol of American prowess. It soon transpired that this first major international terrorist attack on US soil had been carried out by Islamists, inspired by the Egyptian sheikh Omar Abdel Rahman, spiritual guide of Sadat's assassins, who had found refuge in the United States since 1990.[2]

Yet no person has taken the anti-Western jihad to greater lengths than the Saudi multi-millionaire Osama bin Laden. Born in 1957 in Riyadh as the seventeenth son of a small-time builder and contractor who had emigrated from Yemen to Saudi Arabia in the 1930s in search of employment, he was brought up in the Hijaz, where his father expanded his business from its humble beginnings into one of the biggest construction companies in the Middle East. By the time of his death in 1968 in a plane crash, Muhammad bin Laden had become a close confidant of the Saudi royal family and had amassed a fabulous fortune.

Like many of his super-rich Saudi peers, Osama bin Laden led a secular life under the cloak of the country's strict religious piety. Frequenting flashy night-clubs, bars, and casinos in Beirut, then the "Paris of the Middle East," he freely consumed alcohol—something that is strictly forbidden by Saudi Arabia's

Islamic law. His religious transformation apparently occurred during his college days in Jeddah, where he was taught by Muhammad Qutb, Sayyid Qutb's brother, and the militant Palestinian Islamist Abdallah Azzam. Bin Laden was also impressed by the Islamic revolution in Iran in early 1979 and the seizure of the Grand Mosque in Mecca by Muslim zealots later that year. Yet the defining moment in his transformation was undoubtedly the Soviet invasion of Afghanistan in December 1979. Within days of the invasion bin Laden flew to Afghanistan, inspired in his own account by the plight of Muslims in a medieval society besieged by a twentieth-century superpower. "In our religion, there is a special place in the hereafter for those who participate in jihad," he famously quoted the Prophet. "One day in Afghanistan was like one thousand days of praying in an ordinary mosque."[3]

During the 1980s bin Laden established himself at the forefront of the anti-Soviet resistance movement. He participated in many battles and used his family's bulldozers to pave roads and build shelters in the Afghan mountains. He also played a pivotal role in the recruitment and transportation of the twenty thousand-odd Islamists who flocked to the war zone from all over the world (the "Afghan Arabs" as they were commonly known) and bankrolled some of their training camps in Afghanistan. He was also instrumental in channeling funds to the war effort from the Saudi royal family, which viewed the Afghan rebels' cause as a golden opportunity to brandish its religious credentials.

Following the Iraqi occupation of Kuwait in August 1990, bin Laden, who had meanwhile returned home to a hero's welcome, presented the Saudi authorities with a detailed plan for the kingdom's defense against a possible Iraqi invasion. If the "Muslim nation" had successfully evicted the Soviet Union from Afghanistan, he argued passionately, there was no reason why the Saudi army, bolstered by a hard core of seasoned mujahidun, whom he promised to recruit, would not be able to fend off an Iraqi attack. He also proposed the mobilization of the heavy engineering equipment available to large Saudi construction companies to build fortifications along the kingdom's border with Iraq and Kuwait. When the Saudi regime preferred to rely on international support for its survival, however, bin Laden became a vociferous critic of any foreign, particularly American, military presence in Islam's holiest land. As the Saudi royal family decided to retain these forces even after Iraq's eviction from Kuwait, applying ever-growing pressure on the Islamists to desist from their criticism of this move, in April 1991 bin Laden left the country together with his immediate family (his four wives and an unknown number of children), turning up a few months later in Sudan, which since the summer of 1989 had been ruled by an Islamist military junta under the spiritual and political guidance of the prominent cleric Hassan Turabi.[4]

Scion of a dignified religious family, Turabi had received a traditional Islamic education before earning a master's degree from the University of London and a doctorate from the Sorbonne. As the driving force behind the newly established regime, he sought to transform Sudan into the hub of Islamist militancy through the creation of the Popular Islamic and Arab Conference in April 1991, a worldwide coalition of religious zealots, pan-Arab radicals, and assorted terrorist groups aimed at "work[ing] out a global action plan in order to challenge and defy the tyrannical West."[5]

This mindset suited bin Laden perfectly, and he quickly found himself drawn into the tangled web woven by the Sudanese regime. Having known Turabi since the early 1980s, the Saudi émigré was warmly welcomed by the cleric and appointed a member and special adviser of the National Sudanese Islamic Front. Bin Laden reciprocated with a hefty donation to his adoptive party, and in the following weeks began exploring investment possibilities in the country. This developed before long into a mutually beneficial relationship, which enabled bin Laden to construct and equip about two dozen training camps for the thousands of Afghan Arabs arriving in Sudan.[6] The mujahidun then had a second baptism of fire in the Somali civil war, where they participated in the fighting against the UN peacekeeping force that arrived in the country in 1992, including the Mogadishu battle of October 3–4, 1993, which left eighteen US Marines and several hundred Somalis dead.

The hasty retreat of the US-led international forces from Somalia in the face of the domestic turmoil reinforced bin Laden's perception of the United States as a paper tiger that would crumble under the first real terrorist pressure. "The [Islamist] youth ceased seeing America as a superpower," he told ABC television on May 28, 1998.

> After leaving Afghanistan they headed for Somalia and prepared for a long battle, thinking that the Americans were like the Russians, but they were surprised . . . at the low morale of the American soldiers and realized more than before that the American soldiers are paper tigers. After a few blows, they ran in defeat and America forgot about all the hoopla and media propaganda . . . about being the world leader, and the leader of the new world order. After a few blows, they forgot about this title and left, dragging their corpses and their shameful defeat.

By now, bin Laden had become one of the FBI's most wanted fugitives and had had his citizenship stripped by the Saudi authorities. Militants from all over the world flocked to his training camps in Sudan, and the al-Qaeda terrorist organization, which he established in the late 1980s, was implicated in a series of attacks in Europe, Africa, and the Middle East against American and Western targets. It was also implicated in the 1995 attempt on the life of Mubarak during a state visit to Ethiopia, and the 1993 World Trade Center bombing, where the main culprit, Ramzi Ahmad Yusuf, had been closely associated with bin Laden. Al-Qaeda terrorists played an active role in such regional conflicts as Bosnia, Kosovo, Chechnya, and Tajikistan, while the organization financed extremist groups in Egypt and Algeria. Bin Laden is even said to have spent some time in London in 1994, at personal risk of arrest and extradition to Saudi Arabia, at which time he reportedly laid the groundwork for a terrorist network in Western Europe.[7]

In the spring of 1996, bowing to American, Egyptian, and Saudi pressure as well as newly imposed Security Council sanctions, the Sudanese government ordered bin Laden out of the country and he settled in the mountainous Hindu Kush area in Afghanistan, having failed to obtain political asylum in Britain.[8] Yet if there were any hopes that such a move would lead to the curtailment of his terrorist zeal, they were quickly dashed. Not only did an attack on the US military base at Khobar in Saudi Arabia claim nineteen lives within weeks of bin Laden's departure from Sudan, but in August 1996 he released a "Declaration of Jihad Against the Americans Occupying the Land of the Two Holy Places."

Addressed to "Muslim brethren all over the world generally and in the Arab peninsula specifically," the declaration proudly announced the readiness of the Islamist forces to launch a new jihad from the Afghan mountains "where—by the grace of Allah—the largest infidel military force in the world was destroyed." This would start with the liberation of the "Land of the Two Holy Places" from American occupation—the greatest aggression hatched against the world of Islam since the death of the Prophet Muhammad—and would be carried out by the worldwide Muslim community rather than the residents of this specific territory. "Clearly after belief there is no more important duty than pushing the American enemy out of the holy land," the declaration asserted, invoking the Prophet Muhammad's purported deathbed pledge: "If I survive, Allah willing, I'll expel the Jews and the Christians out of the Arabian Peninsula."

Why were the Muslims destined to prevail in their war against the far-richer and better-equipped "Jewish-crusader coalition"? Because they loved death as much as the enemy loved life. "Where was this false courage of yours when the [1983 terrorist] explosion in Beirut took place?" bin Laden ridiculed the US administration's pledge to intensify the fight against terrorism following the Khobar attack. "You were turned into scattered bits and pieces at that time; 241 mainly marine soldiers were killed. And where was this courage of yours when two explosions made you leave Aden in less than twenty hours?" "Our youth believe in paradise after death," bin Laden piled on the scorn:

Those youths are different from your soldiers. Your problem will be how to convince your troops to fight, while our problem will be how to restrain our youths to wait for their turn in fighting and in operations. . . . These youths know that: if one is not to be killed one will die [anyway] and the most honorable death is to be killed in the way of Allah.[9]

Bin Laden's proclamation of jihad was no novelty in and of itself: declaring a holy war against the infidel has been a standard practice of countless imperial rulers and aspirants since the rise of Islam. Nor does bin Laden's perception of jihad as a predominantly military effort to facilitate the creation of the worldwide Islamic umma differ in any way from traditional Islamic thinking, let alone from that of the Muslim Brothers and their Islamist offshoots. But then, bin Laden's historic significance lies not in the novelty of his religious thinking but in his distinct translation of Islam's millenarian imperialist vision into concrete action at the dawn of the twenty-first century. For he is the first Islamist to have not only proclaimed a jihad against the United States but to have actually unleashed such a war—something that even America's sworn enemies, such as Ayatollah Khomeini, refrained from doing.

Bin Laden was deeply influenced by Abdallah Azzam, his university mentor-turned-chief ideologue of the Afghan Arabs, who viewed the anti-Soviet struggle in Afghanistan as a stepping stone to the worldwide restoration of Islam's usurped lands, from Andalusia to the Philippines.[10] But the moving spirit behind the jihad proclamation was apparently Zawahiri, who fled Mubarak's campaign of repression and turned up in Peshawar with scores of his Egyptian followers in the mid-1980s. According to eyewitness accounts, Zawahiri had a commanding influence on bin Laden, establishing himself quickly as his right-hand man and second-in-command. It has even been suggested that it was Zawahiri who convinced bin Laden to form the al-Qaeda organization, so as to sustain the fight for the worldwide spread of Islam after the end of the Afghan war. Zawahiri's growing influence tarnished bin Laden's relations with his spiritual mentor, and in November 1989 Azzam and his two sons were killed by a car bomb in Peshawar while on their way to Friday prayers. The identity of the murderers remains unknown.[11]

In February 1998 bin Laden took his commitment to jihad a step further by creating the International Islamic Front for Jihad Against Jews and Crusaders, an umbrella organization comprising al-Qaeda and four Islamist groups from Egypt, Pakistan, and Bangladesh. The front's founding charter, signed by bin Laden, Zawahiri, and the other three members of the collective leadership, accused the United States of defiling Islam's holiest sites through its military presence in the Arabian Peninsula and attempting to partition the Middle East into tiny entities in order to keep them weak and divided in the face of the

"Jewish-crusader assault." "All these crimes and sins committed by the Americans are a clear declaration of war on Allah, his messenger, and Muslims," the charter declared, laying the ground for issuing the following fatwa:

To kill the Americans and their allies—civilians and military—is an individual duty for every Muslim who can do it in any country in which it is possible to do it, in order to liberate the al-Aqsa Mosque and the holy mosque [Mecca] from their grip, and in order for their armies to move out of all the lands of Islam, defeated and unable to threaten any Muslim. . . . We—with Allah's help—call on every Muslim who believes in Allah and wishes to be rewarded to comply with Allah's order to kill the Americans and plunder their money wherever and whenever they find it. We also call on Muslim ulama, leaders, youths, and soldiers to launch the raid on Satan's US troops and the devil's supporters allying with them, and to displace those who are behind them so that they may learn a lesson.[12]

Within a few months bin Laden delivered on his threat. On August 7, 1998, on the eighth anniversary of the landing of American forces in Saudi Arabia to protect the kingdom from an Iraqi invasion, two simultaneous explosions destroyed the American embassies in Kenya and Tanzania, killing 224 people and injuring over 4,500. The US retaliatory strikes against al-Qaeda targets in Afghanistan and Sudan, its intensified targeting of the organization's international funding, and the announcement of a five-million-dollar bounty on bin Laden's head were to no avail. On October 12, 2000, an attack on the destroyer USS *Cole*, while it was refueling in the Yemeni port of Aden, left seventeen sailors dead. Eleven months later, on September 11, 2001, al-Qaeda terrorists slammed two hijacked airliners into the twin towers of the World Trade Center and one into the Pentagon, killing some three thousand civilians. A fourth plane, apparently on its way to the White House, crashed in Pennsylvania as passengers fought the hijackers.

The 9/11 atrocities afford the starkest demonstration of the global scope of bin Laden's imperialist ambitions. In his 1996 proclamation of jihad he had vowed "to re-establish the greatness of this umma," a pledge he reiterated shortly after 9/11 by quoting from Muhammad's farewell address: "I was ordered to fight the people until they say there is no god but Allah."[13] For his part Zawahiri defined the jihad's objective as nothing short of "the restoration of the caliphate and the dismissal of the invaders from the land of Islam . . . . It is the hope of the Muslim nation to restore its fallen caliphate and regain its lost glory."[14]

In his first-ever televised interview in March 1997, with CNN's Peter Arnett, bin Laden defined the objective of his jihad as "driv[ing] the

Americans away from all Muslim countries", rather than from Saudi Arabia alone. "The cause of the reaction must be sought and the act that has triggered this reaction must be eliminated," he said. "The reaction came as a result of the US aggressive policy toward the entire Muslim world and not just toward the Arabian Peninsula . . . . So, the driving-away jihad against the US does not stop with its withdrawal from the Arabian Peninsula, but rather it must desist from aggressive intervention against Muslims in the whole world."[15]

What is the precise nature of this "aggressive intervention"? Superficially, it is the ongoing US-orchestrated "butchering" of the world's 1.2 billion-strong Muslim community—"in Palestine, in Iraq, in Somalia, in southern Sudan, in Kashmir, in the Philippines, in Bosnia, in Chechnya, and in Assam." But at a deeper level, bin Laden's words echo the standard anti-Western indictment, which attributes Islam's current dismal position to the post-World War I dismemberment of the last Islamic great power, the Ottoman Empire. The 9/11 attacks are therefore a heroic retribution for this historical injustice that targeted "the main enemy who divided the umma into small and little countries and pushed it, for the last few decades, into a state of confusion." "What America is tasting now is only a copy of what we have tasted," bin Laden proudly announced in a videotaped message shortly after the attacks. "Our Islamic nation has been tasting the same for more than eighty years, of humiliation and disgrace, its sons killed and their blood spilled, its sanctities desecrated." Now, for the first time, "the sword fell upon America."

But the story does not end here. Bin Laden's historical reckoning extends well beyond the Ottoman calamity. As he sees it, his jihad against the "Jewish-crusader alliance" is the natural extension of Islam's millenarian struggle for world domination, dating back to the Prophet Muhammad. "We left our country on a jihad in the path of Allah," bin Laden told the al-Jazeera satellite television channel in 1999. "And it is for the sake of Allah, praise and glory be upon Him, that we made this blessed Hijra to facilitate the institutionaliza-tion of the Shari'a."[16] The use of the term "Hijra" to describe al-Qaeda's activities is not accidental. Just as Muhammad was forced to flee his native town of Mecca in order to be able to fight for the worldwide spread of Islam, so bin Laden, a fellow native of the Hijaz, fashions himself as Allah's servant expelled from his homeland by an apostate regime, only to use his exile as a springboard for a holy war in the path of Allah.

In this respect, the "blessed attacks" against the "head of world infidelity" have fully achieved their objectives. They have not only "removed the disgrace that befell our nation" and taught the United States a lesson it will never forget, but have also exposed the incredible fragility of this "modern-day Hubal" (an idol worshiped by pre-Islamic Arabian pagans), thus setting in train a chain of events that, runs the rhetoric, will eventually result in Islam's worldwide triumph. "When people see a strong horse and a weak horse, by nature, they will like the strong horse," bin Laden told a Saudi cleric visiting him in his Afghan hideout shortly after 9/11.

In Holland, at one of the centers, the number of people who accepted Islam during the days that followed the operations was more than the people who accepted Islam in the last eleven years. I heard someone on Islamic radio who owns a school in America say: "We don't have time to keep up with the demands of those who are asking about Islamic books to learn about Islam." This event made people think [about Islam] which benefited Islam greatly.[17]

Bin Laden was keenly aware that, despite these gains, the latest phase in this millenarian struggle for world mastery had only just begun and was bound to be hazardous and prolonged. Yet he had no doubt regarding its ultimate outcome: the triumph of Islam and the consequent destruction of the United States, just as Islam's victory in Afghanistan triggered the disintegration of the Soviet Union. "The Soviet Union entered Afghanistan in the last week of 1979, and with Allah's help their flag was folded a few years later and thrown in the trash, and there was nothing left to call the Soviet Union," bin Laden told ABC correspondent John Miller in May 1998. "We anticipate a black future for America. Instead of remaining the United States, it shall end up separated states [sic] and shall have to carry the bodies of its sons back to America."[18] He reiterated this apocalyptic prediction after 9/11. "God willing, the end of America is close," he prophesied in a videotaped interview shown by al-Jazeera on December 12, 2001. "Its end is not dependent on the survival of this slave to God. Regardless if Osama is killed or survives, the awakening has started, praised be God. This was the fruit of these operations."

Epilogue

When satirical depictions of the prophet Muhammad in a Danish newspaper sparked a worldwide wave of Muslim violence in early 2006, observers naturally focused on the wanton destruction of Western embassies, businesses, and other institutions. Less attention was paid to the words that often accompanied the riots—words with ominous historical echoes. "Hurry up and apologize to our nation, because if you do not, you will regret it", declared Khaled Mash'al, the leader of Hamas, fresh from the Islamist group's sweeping victory in the Palestinian elections:

> This is because our nation is progressing and is victorious. . . . By Allah, you will be defeated. . . . Tomorrow, our nation will sit on the throne of the world. This is not a figment of the imagination but a fact. Tomorrow we will lead the world, Allah willing. Apologize today, before remorse will do you no good.[1]

Such gloating about Islam's prowess and imminent triumph is frequently dismissed by Westerners as delusional, a species of mere self-aggrandizement or propaganda. But the Islamists are perfectly serious, and know what they are doing. As this work shows, their rhetoric has a millennial warrant, both in doctrine and in fact, and taps into a deep imperialist undercurrent that has characterized the political culture of Islam from the beginning. Though tempered and qualified in different places and at different times, the Islamic longing for unfettered suzerainty has never disappeared, and has resurfaced in our own day with a vengeance.

Indeed, unlike other parts of the world, where the demise of empire during the twentieth century has invariably led to the acceptance of the reality of the modern nation-state, the contemporary Middle Eastern state system has been under sustained assault since its formation in the wake of World War I. Aside from Mustafa Kemal (Atatürk), who extricated Turkey from its Islamic imperial legacy and re-established it as a modern nation-state by abolishing the sultanate and caliphate and effecting a separation of state and church, Middle Eastern leaders and Islamist ideologues have remained under the spell of the imperial dream.

Colonel Reza Khan, who in February 1921 seized power in Iran in a military coup and four years later deposed the ruling shah, chose to establish his own royal dynasty rather than transform his country into a republic in an attempt to revive Iran's imperial glory. The Hashemites, who envisaged the substitution of their own empire for that of the Ottomans, acted similarly, as did subsequent generations of pan-Arabists who denounced the new Middle Eastern system as an artificial creation of Western imperialism and urged its replacement by a unified regional state, or rather empire. This created a deep dissonance between the reality of state nationalism and the dream of an empire packaged as a unified "Arab nation." It failed, however, to bring about the creation of such an empire for the simple reason that there is not, and never has been, an Arab nation: its invocation has largely represented a clever ploy to rally popular support behind individual quests for regional mastery.

There had been no sense of "Arabism" among the Arabic-speaking populations of the Middle East prior to the 1920s and 1930s, when Arabs began to be inculcated with the notion that they constituted one nation. They viewed themselves as subjects of the Ottoman sultan-caliph, in his capacity as the religious and temporal head of the worldwide Muslim community, ignored the nationalistic message of the tiny secret Arab societies, and fought to the bitter end for their suzerain during World War I.

Such behavior is not difficult to understand. As the millenarian linchpin of the Middle East's imperial order, Islam would not be easily supplanted by the schizophrenic construct of pan-Arabism, which spoke the new and alien European language of nationalism while pursuing the age-old goal of imperial aggrandizement. For thirteen hundred years Muslims had been conditioned to view themselves as distinct from, and superior to, all other subjects of the House of Islam, and they were not going to give up this privileged status just because they happened to speak the same imperial language (i.e., Arabic) as their non-Muslim neighbors.

There was, of course, a time when Arabism and Islam were fully synonymous, but these days have long since ended. Islam has traveled far from its Arabian origins to become a thriving universal religion boasting a worldwide community of believers of whom Arabs are but a small minority. The last great Muslim empire may have been destroyed and the caliphate left vacant, but the Islamic imperial dream of world domination has remained very much alive in the hearts and minds of many Muslims, as evidenced by the proliferation (in the face of persistent repression by the authorities) of numerous religious groups and organizations throughout the Middle East and the Islamic world. So much so that the avowedly secularist Ba'th Party felt obliged to introduce religious provisions into the Syrian and Iraqi constitutions, notably that the head of state should be a Muslim. For their part the Ba'thist Syrian and Iraqi presidents, Hafiz Assad (1970–2000) and Saddam Hussein (1979–2003), went out of their way to brandish their religious credentials, among other things by inscribing the battle cry of Islam "Allahu Akbar" on the Iraqi flag.

Neither have all Muslims reconciled themselves to the loss of Islam's colonies beyond the Middle East. At a 1980s meeting in Pakistan with representatives of the seven Afghan resistance parties, a group of American officers and diplomats were surprised to see a huge map on which large parts of what was then Soviet Central Asia and China's Xinjiang Province were labeled "Temporarily Occupied Muslim Territory." Chatting with English-speaking mujahidun after the meeting, an American diplomat asked about this labeling and was told, in perfect seriousness: "Yes, Inshallah [God willing], the region will soon be won back for Islam one day."[2]

This yearning for lost imperial dominions has by no means been confined to Asia. To this day many Arabs and Muslims unabashedly pine for the restoration of Spain and consider their 1492 expulsion from the country a grave historical injustice, as if they were Spain's rightful owners and not former colonial occupiers of a remote foreign land, thousands of miles from their ancestral homeland. Edward Said applauded Andalusia's colonialist legacy as "the ideal that should be moving our efforts now," while Osama bin Laden noted "the tragedy of Andalusia" after the 9/11 attacks, and the perpetrators of the March 2004 Madrid bombings, in which hundreds of people were murdered, mentioned revenge for the loss of Spain as one of the atrocity's "root causes."[3]

Even countries that were never ruled by the caliphate have become targets of Muslim imperial ambition. As immigration, conversion, and higher rates of child birth have greatly increased the number of Muslims within Europe (in France one in ten people is a Muslim and a reported fifty thousand Christians convert to Islam every year; in Brussels Muhammad has been the most popular name for male babies for some years; in Britain attendance at mosques is higher than in the Church of England), prophecies of Islam's eventual triumph over the West have become commonplace. Since the late 1980s various Islamist movements in France, notably the Union de Organizations Islamiques des France (UOIF), have begun to view the growing number of French Muslims as a sign that the country has become a part of the House of Islam. This message has been echoed by the creation of an extensive European network of mosques, schools, and Islamic charities by the Muslim Brothers over the past fifty years.

In Germany, which extended a warm welcome to the scores of Islamists fleeing persecution in their home countries, the Muslim Brothers have successfully established themselves, with ample Saudi financing, as the effective voice of the three million-strong Muslim community. Since the early 1990s, in parallel to the European Union's growing integration, the Brothers have invested considerable efforts in integrating their various proxies across the continent via a string of pan-European organizations, such as the Federation of Islamic Organizations in Europe. In September 1996 they launched the Forum of European Muslim Youth and Student Organizations (FEMYSO), with its headquarters in Brussels, the home of the EU's own headquarters, which quickly evolved into the de facto voice of Muslim youth in Europe. It is regularly consulted on issues pertaining to European Muslims and has developed extensive contacts with such key international institutions as the European Parliament, the Council of Europe, and the United Nations, as well as numerous Non-Governmental Organizations (NGOs) at the European level.

In the autumn of 2003, the German public was shocked to learn of the racist and anti-Western messages inculcated in young Muslim children inside Saudi-funded mosques and schools when a journalist infiltrated the King Fahd Academy in Bonn and videotaped classroom teaching. Americans were similarly taken aback by a series of exposés of the supremacist teachings of Islamic schools across the United States, which, among other things, disparaged Christianity and Judaism and alienated children from Western society and culture. In fact, one needs to look no further than the Muslim Brothers' English-language internet homepage, which notes the restoration of the caliphate and the "mastering [of] the world with Islam" as the organization's primary goals.

In Britain, even the more moderate elements of the Muslim community have been candid in setting out their aims. As the late Zaki Badawi, a doyen of interfaith dialogue in the UK, put it, "Islam is a universal religion. It aims to bring its message to all corners of the earth. It hopes that one day the whole of humanity will be one Muslim community".[4]

Dr. Yusuf Qaradawi, a spiritual guide of the Muslim Brothers and one of today's most influential Islamic thinkers, whose views are promulgated to millions of Muslims worldwide through the media and the internet, gave this sweeping vision theological grounding. "The Prophet Muhammad was asked: 'What city will be conquered first, Constantinople or Romiyya?'" he wrote on December 2, 2002, citing a well-known hadith:

He answered: "The city of Hirqil [Emperor Hercalius, that is, Constantinople] will be conquered first" . . . . Romiyya is the city called today Rome, the capital of Italy. The city of Hirqil was conquered by the young 23-year-old Ottoman [sultan] Muhammad bin Morad, known in history as Muhammad the Conqueror, in 1453 [C.E.]. The other city, Romiyya, remains, and we hope and believe [that it too will be conquered]. This means that Islam will return to Europe as a conqueror and victor, after being expelled from it twice—once from the South, from Andalusia, and a second time from the East, when it knocked several times on the door of Athens.

This goal need not necessarily be pursued by the sword; it can be achieved through demographic growth and steady conversion of the local populations by "an army of preachers and teachers who will present Islam in all languages and in all dialects." But should peaceful means prove insufficient, physical force can readily be brought to bear.[5]

This imperialist vision should not be misconstrued for a civilizational struggle between the worlds of Islam and Christendom. World history has rarely, if ever, seen a mighty clash of civilizations. Conflicts and wars among members of the *same* civilization have been far more common, and far more intense, than those between members of rival civilizations. Even in Islam, where Muhammad specifically and categorically forbade fighting among the believers, it took a mere twenty-four years after the Prophet's death for the head of the universal Islamic community, the caliph Uthman, to be murdered by political rivals. This opened the floodgates to incessant infighting within the House of Islam, which has not ceased to date and has exacted far more numerous casualties than conflicts between Muslims and non-Muslims.

Indeed, more often, empires across the civilizational divide have pragmatically cooperated with their counterparts. "East is East and West is West, and never the twain shall meet," Rudyard Kipling, the quintessential champion of nineteenth-century European imperialism, famously rhapsodized. But in fact they have met and mingled continuously, from ancient times. Iran was an early link between civilizations, especially for the exchange of religious ideas. Alexander the Great dreamed of establishing a genuinely cosmopolitan world order, and tried to fuse the cultures of Greece and Iran.

This goal was largely achieved by early Islam, which amalgamated the cultural and scientific riches of these two nations with Arabian traditions to create its own distinct Islamic civilization. Even the millenarian confrontation between the worlds of Islam and Christianity has essentially been a "clash of imperialisms" rather than a "clash of civilizations." This was manifested in the crystallization of a symbiotic relationship between East and West, comprising extensive trade and pragmatic political cooperation. Even during the age of the crusades, the supposed height of civilizational antagonism, all Christian and Muslim rulers freely collaborated across the religious divide, often finding themselves aligned with members of the rival religion against their co-religionists. The legendary Saladin himself spent far more time fighting Muslim rivals than the infidel crusaders; while he was busy eradicating the Latin Kingdom of Jerusalem he was closely aligned with the Byzantine Empire, the foremost representative of Christendom's claim to universalism.

This pattern of pragmatic cooperation reached its peak during the nineteenth century, when the Ottoman Empire relied on Western support for imperial survival. It has also become a regular feature of twentieth- and twenty-first-century Middle Eastern politics. For all their vibrant anti-Western rhetoric, Muslim and Arab rulers have always, in all their wars and intrigues against fellow Arabs and Muslims, sought the support and protection of the "infidel" powers they so vilify, whenever they have deemed it in their interest to do so. Just as the Iranian shahs used the great European powers for personal self-enrichment, so Sharif Hussein fought alongside the British "infidels" against his Muslim suzerain to promote his imperial ambitions, and his great-grandson, King Hussein of Jordan, repeatedly relied on British, American, and Israeli support to prop up his throne.

Just as the Egyptian president Gamal Abdel Nasser, who had built his reputation on standing up to "Western imperialism," introduced large numbers of Soviet troops into Egypt when the War of Attrition he launched against Israel (1969–70) went sour, so Ayatollah Khomeini, the high priest of Islamic imperialism, bought weapons from even the "Great Satan," the United States, in his effort to subvert the Middle Eastern political order and to establish a universal "Empire of Allah." Saddam Hussein used Western support to survive his eight-year war against Iran (1980–88), while Osama bin Laden cooperated with the United States against the Soviet occupation of Afghanistan and sought asylum in Britain following his expulsion from Sudan in the mid-1990s.[6]

Political cooperation, however, has not meant accepting Western doctrines or values, as the events of September 11, 2001, amply demonstrate. Contrary to widespread assumptions, these attacks, and for that matter Arab and Muslim anti-Americanism, have little to do with US international behavior or its Middle Eastern policy. If, today, America is reviled in the Muslim world, it is not because of its specific policies but because, as the preeminent world power, it blocks the final realization of this same age-old dream of regaining the lost glory of the caliphate. As such, it is a natural target for aggression. Osama bin Laden and other Islamists' war is not against America per se, but is rather the most recent manifestation of the millenarian jihad for a universal Islamic empire (or umma).

Nor is this vision confined to a tiny extremist fringe. This we saw in the overwhelming support for the 9/11 attacks throughout the Arab and Islamic worlds, in the admiring evocations of bin Laden's murderous acts during the crisis over the Danish cartoons, and in such recent findings as the poll indicating significant reservoirs of sympathy among Muslims in Britain for the feelings and motives of the suicide bombers who attacked London in July 2005. In the historical imagination of many Muslims and Arabs, bin Laden represents nothing short of the new incarnation of Saladin. In this sense, the House of Islam's war for world mastery is a traditional, indeed venerable, quest that is far from over.

To the contrary, now that this war has itself met with a determined counterattack by the United States and others, and with a Western intervention in the heart of the House of Islam, it has escalated to a new stage of virulence. In many Middle Eastern countries, Islamist movements, and movements appealing to traditionalist Muslims, are now jockeying fiercely for positions of power, both against the Americans and against secular parties. For the Islamists, the stakes are very high indeed, for if the political elites of the Middle East and elsewhere were ever to reconcile themselves to the reality that there is no Arab or Islamic nation, but only modern Muslim states with destinies and domestic responsibilities of their own, the imperialist dream would die.

It is in recognition of this state of affairs that Ayman al-Zawahiri, bin Laden's top deputy, wrote his famous letter to Abu Musab al-Zarqawi, the late head of al-Qaeda in Iraq, in July 2005. If, Zawahiri instructed his lieutenant, al-Qaeda's strategy for Iraq and elsewhere were to succeed, it would have to take into account the growing thirst among many Arabs for democracy and a normal life, and strive not to alienate popular opinion through such polarizing deeds as suicide attacks on fellow Muslims. Only by harnessing popular support, Zawahiri concluded, would it be possible to come to power by means of democracy itself, thereby to establish jihadist rule in Iraq, and then to move onward to conquer still larger and more distant realms and impose the writ of Islam far and wide.[7] Something of the same logic clearly underlies the carefully plotted rise of Hamas in the Palestinian Authority, Hezbollah's participation in the Lebanese government, the (temporarily thwarted) attempt by the Muslim Brotherhood in Egypt to exploit the demand for free elections there, and the accession of Mahmoud Ahmadinejad in Iran.

Whether or not these disparate elements can be forged into a new axis of Islam, especially after Hezbollah's successful war with Israel in the summer of 2006 and the imminent withdrawal of the US-led forces from Iraq, the fact is that the fuel of Islamic imperialism remains as volatile as ever, and is very far from having burned itself out. Only when the political elites of the Middle

East and the Muslim world reconcile themselves to the reality of state nationalism, forswear pan-Arab and pan-Islamic imperialist dreams, and make Islam a matter of private faith rather than a tool of political ambition will the inhabitants of these regions at last be able to look forward to a better future free of would-be Saladins.

Notes

Introduction

1. Bernard Lewis, *From Babel to Dragomans: Interpreting the Middle East* (New York: Oxford University Press, 2004), p. 375. See also Michael Steinberger, "So, Are Civilizations at War?" (interview with Samuel Huntington), *Observer* (London), Oct. 21, 2001; Andrew Sullivan, "This Is a Religious War," *New York Times Magazine*, Oct. 7, 2001; Fiachra Gibbons, "V.S. Naipul Launches Attack on Islam," *Guardian* (London), Oct. 4, 2001.

2. See, for example, Douglas Little, *American Orientalism: The United States and the Middle East since 1945* (Chapel Hill: University of North Carolina Press, 2002); François Brugat, *Face to Face with Political Islam* (London: Tauris, 2003), pp. xxiii–xvii; Abdel Wahab Meddeb, *The Malady of Islam* (New York: Basic Books, 2003), pp. 8–10; As'ad AbuKhalil, *Bin Laden, Islam, and America's New "War on Terrorism"* (New York: Seven Stories Press, 2002), pp. 12–13, 31–44.

3. Karen Armstrong, "Was It Inevitable? Islam through History," in James F. Hoge and Gideon Rose (eds.), *How Did It Happen? Terrorism and the New War* (New York: Public Affairs, 2001), p. 61. See also Johannes J. G. Jansen, *The Dual Nature of Islamic Fundamentalism* (Ithaca: Cornell University Press, 1997), p. 22. For criticism of this approach, see Daniel Pipes, "Jihad and the Professors," *Commentary*, Nov. 2002, pp. 17–21.

4. Bernard Lewis, *What Went Wrong? Western Impact and Muslim Responses* (New York, Oxford University Press, 2001). Written a few years before 9/11 but published in its immediate wake, the book failed to anticipate the attacks, or for that matter any anti-Western terror offensive, yet somehow came to be seen as explaining the general social and cultural background of this momentous event. Lewis amplified this reactive perception of Middle Eastern history in a later article: "Freedom and Justice in the Modern Middle East," *Foreign Affairs*, May–June 2005, pp. 36–51.

   For this standard version see also George Antonius, *The Arab Awakening* (London: Hamish Hamilton, 1938); Arnold Toynbee, "The Present Situation in Palestine," *International Affairs*, Jan. 1931, p. 40; George Kirk, *A Short History of the Middle East: From the Rise of Islam to Modern Times* (New York: Praeger, 1963), chapter 5; Roger Owen, *State, Power, and Politics in the Making of the Modern Middle East* (London: Routledge, 1992), especially Chapters 1 and 4; Bernard Lewis, *The Middle East: 2000 Years of History from the Rise of Christianity to the Present Day* (London: Weidenfeld and Nicolson, 1995), pp. 342–43; Edward W. Said, *Orientalism: Western Conceptions of the Orient* (London: Penguin, 1995).

   For a dissenting view, see Elie Kedourie, *The Chatham House Version and Other Middle Eastern Studies* (London: Weidenfeld and Nicolson, 1970).

5. The term millenarian is used throughout the book in a literal rather than ecumenical or metaphysical sense, namely to designate a tradition, trend, phenomenon, or legacy that is thousands of years old.

6. The literature on empire and imperialism is immense. For some major classical and recent discussions, see Edward Gibbon, *The Decline and Fall of the Roman Empire* (1776–88) (London: Everyman's Library, 1978); David Bromwich (ed.), *On Empire, Liberty, and Reform: Speeches and Letters of Edmund Burke* (New Haven: Yale University Press, 2000); Vladimir Ilich Lenin, *Imperialism, the Highest State of Capitalism* (Chicago: Pluto, 1996); John Atkinson Hobson, *Imperialism: A Study* (London: Unwin Hyman, 1988); Wolfgang J. Mommsen, *Theories of Imperialism* (Chicago: University of Chicago Press, 1982); Richard Koebner, *Empire* (Cambridge: Cambridge University Press, 1961); George Lichtheim, *Imperialism* (New York: Praeger, 1971); Eric Hobsbawm, *The Age of Empire, 1875–1914* (London: Weidenfeld and Nicolson, 1987); Paul Kennedy, *The Rise and Fall of the Great Powers* (New York: Random House, 1987); Michael W. Doyle, *Empires* (Ithaca: Cornell University Press, 1986); Anthony Pagden, *Peoples and Empires* (New York: The Modern Library, 2003).

7. For discussion of the imperial mindset in the pre- and early Islamic era, see Garth Fowden, *Empire to Commonwealth: Consequences of Monotheism in Late Antiquity* (Princeton: Princeton University Press, 1993).

8. Patricia Crone, *Meccan Trade and the Rise of Islam* (Oxford: Blackwell, 1987), p. 246.

9. Ibid. pp. 247, 249, 250. Crone uses the term "primitive" to denote nativist movements that lack political organization: "Either they are members of societies that never had much political organization, as is true of Muhammad's Arabia, or they are drawn from these strata of society that lack this organization, as is true of the villagers who provided the syncretic prophets of Iran. They invariably take a religious form."

10. Muhammad ibn Umar al-Waqidi, *Kitab al-Maghazi* (London: Oxford University Press, 1966), Vol. 3, p. 1113. See also W. Montgomery Watt, *Islam and the Integration of Society* (London: Routledge & Kegan, 1961), pp. 61–67.

11. Crone, *Meccan Trade*, pp. 243–44; Fred McGraw Donner, *The Early Islamic Conquests* (Princeton: Princeton University Press, 1981), Chapter 1; I. M. Lapidus, "The Arab Conquests and the Formation of Islamic Society," in G. H. A. Juynboll (ed.), *Studies on the First Century of Islamic Society* (Carbondale and Edwardsville: Southern Illinois University Press, 1982), pp. 60–61; Philip K. Hitti, *History of the Arabs* (London: MacMillan, 10th edn., 1993), pp. 88–90.

12. W. Montgomery Watt, "Islamic Conceptions of the Holy War," in Thomas Patrick Murphy (ed.), *The Holy War* (Columbus: Ohio State University Press, 1976), pp. 141–43; Hugh Kennedy, *The Prophet and the Age of the Caliphates* (London: Longman, 2nd edn., 2004), p. 21; F. E. Peters (ed.), *The Arabs and Arabia on the Eve of Islam* (Aldershot: Ashgate, 1999), especially chapters 1–3.

13. Hamilton A. R. Gibb, *Studies on the Civilization of Islam* (London: Routledge & Kegan, 1962), pp. 38–39.

14. From the reign of Peter the Great (1672–1725) to the Bolshevik Revolution of 1917, Russia considered itself a European great power and played a key role in Europe's inter-actions with the Ottoman Empire. During the communist era (1917–1991), especially the Cold War years, the Soviet Union was removed from the West by an unbridgeable ideological opposition and hence is not treated here as part of "Western imperialism."

15. Gibb, *Studies*, p. 22.

16. The only partial exceptions to this rule were the Russian and the Austro-Hungarian empires.

17. Hisham Sharabi, *Nationalism and Revolution in the Arab World* (New York: Van Nostrand Reinhold, 1966), p. 7.

18. G. E. von Grunebaum, *Classical Islam: A History 600–1258* (London: Allen & Unwin, 1970), p. 151.

19. *T. E. Lawrence to His Biographers Robert Graves and Liddell Hart* (London: Cassell, 1963), p. 101.

Chapter 1

1. *The Koran*, trans. with an introduction by Arthur J. Arberry (Oxford: Oxford University Press, 1982), sura 96.1–5. While Muslim tradition regards these verses as the Qur'an's first revelation, some believe that sura 74.1–7 was the first.

2. Muhammad ibn Jarir al-Tabari, *Tarikh al-Rusul wa-l-Muluk* (Cairo: Dar al-Ma'arif bi-Misr, 1966), Vol. 2, pp. 298–99; Muhammad ibn Sa'd, *Kitab al-Tabaqat al-Kabir*, English trans. by S. Moinul Haq (Karachi: Pakistan Historical Society, 1967), Vol. 1, pp. 224–26.

3. Patricia Crone, *Meccan Trade and the Rise of Islam* (Oxford: Blackwell, 1987), p. 132.

4. Muhammad ibn Ishaq, *The Life of Muhammad. A Translation of Ibn Ishaq's "Sirat Rasul Allah," with Introduction and Notes by Alfred Guillaume* (Oxford: Oxford University Press, 1955), p. 118; Tabari, *Tarikh*, Vol. 2, pp. 335–37.

5. Hamilton A. R. Gibb, "Pre-Islamic Monotheism in Arabia," and W. Montgomery Watt, "Belief in a 'High God' in Pre-Islamic Mecca," in F. E. Peters (ed.), *The Arabs and Arabia on the Eve of Islam* (Aldershot: Ashgate, 1999), pp. 295–312; F. E. Peters, *Muhammad and the Origins of Islam* (Albany: State University of New York Press, 1994), p. 107; J. Henninger, "Pre-Islamic Bedouin Religion," in Merlin Swartz (ed.), *Studies in Islam* (New York: Oxford University Press, 1981), p. 12; W. Montgomery Watt, *Muhammad's Mecca: History of the Qur'an* (Edinburgh: Edinburgh University Press, 1988), pp. 32–35; Crone, *Meccan Trade*, pp. 189–95; Tor Andrae, *Mohammed: The Man and His Faith* (London: Allen & Unwin, 1956), p. 26.

6. W. Montgomery Watt, *Muhammad at Mecca* (Karachi: Oxford University Press, 1953), pp. 133–36; W. Montgomery Watt, *Muhammad: Prophet and Statesman* (Oxford: Oxford University Press, 1961), Chapter 3. For criticism of Watt's analysis see Crone, *Meccan Trade*, pp. 232–37.

   This is not to say that there was no rejection of the conceptual and ethical tenets of Muhammad's preaching, such as the claim of the bodily resurrection of the dead, a totally alien idea to the Meccans. See, for example, Ignaz Goldziher, *Muslim Studies* (London: George Allen & Unwin, 1967), Vol. 1, pp. 18–44; G. E. von Grunebaum, *Classical Islam: A History 600–1258* (London: Allen & Unwin, 1970), pp. 31–32.

7. Moshe Gil, "The Origin of the Jews of Yathrib," *Jerusalem Studies in Arabic and Islam*, Vol. 4 (1984), pp. 203–24; Gordon Darnell Newby, *A History of the Jews of Arabia: From Ancient Times to Their Eclipse under Islam* (Columbia: University of South Carolina Press, 1988), pp. 17–18, 79–96.

8. Philip K. Hitti, *The Arabs: A Short History* (Chicago: Henry Regnery, 1970), pp. 36–37.

9. Ibn Ishaq, *The Life of Muhammad*, pp. 231–33; Abdel Malik ibn Hisham, *Sirat al-Nabi* (Cairo: Matba'at Hijazi, 1937), pp. 119–23. The Jews were attached to this community as an autonomous group, subject to certain conditions.

10. Muhammad ibn Umar al-Waqidi, *Kitab al-Maghazi* (London: Oxford University Press, 1966), Vol. 1, pp. 13–19; Tabari, *Tarikh*, Vol. 2, pp. 410–15; Ella Landau-Tasserson, "Features of the Pre-Conquest Muslim Army in the Time of Muhammad," in Averil Cameron (ed.), *The Byzantine and Early Islamic Near East. Vol. III—States, Resources, and Armies* (Princeton: Darwin, 1995), pp. 305–07.

11. For the elimination of the Medina Jews see: Ibn Ishaq, *The Life of Muhammad*, p. 464; Waqidi, *Kitab al-Maghazi*, Vol. 1, pp. 176–80, 363–80, Vol. 2, pp. 496–521; Tabari, *Tarikh*, Vol. 2, pp. 479–83, 550–55, 581–94; M. J. Kister, "The Massacre of the Banu Qurayza: A Re-examination of a Tradition," *Jerusalem Studies in Arabic and Islam*, Vol. 8 (1986), pp. 612–96.

12. Ibn Sa'd, *Kitab al-Tabaqat*, pp. 283–87, 292–94; M. J. Kister, *Concepts and Ideas at the Dawn of Islam* (Aldershot: Ashgate, 1997), pp. 92–95.

13. Julius Wellhausen, *The Arab Kingdom and Its Fall* (Calcutta: University of Calcutta, 1927), pp. 18–20; Irfan Shahid, "Pre-Islamic Arabia," in P. M. Holt, Ann K. S. Lambton, and Bernard Lewis (eds.), *The Cambridge History of Islam. Volume I—The Central Islamic Lands* (Cambridge: Cambridge University Press, 1970), p. 24; Patricia Crone and Michael Cook, *Hagarism: The Making of the Islamic World* (Cambridge: Cambridge University Press, 1977), pp. 13–14, 24–26. The process of turning Abraham into the first monotheistic prophet might have already begun prior to Muhammad's move to Medina. See Fazlur Rahman, "Pre-Foundations of the Muslim Community in Mecca," in Peters, *The Arabs*, pp. 197–98.

14. Ibn Ishaq, *The Life of Muhammad*, pp. 504–07; Tabari, *Tarikh*, Vol. 2, pp. 620–22; Waqidi, *Kitab al-Maghazi*, Vol. 2, pp. 571–66. For modern interpretations see Furrukh B. Ali, "Hudaybiya: An Alternative Version," in Uri Rubin (ed.), *The Life of Muhammad* (Aldershot: Ashgate, 1998), pp. 229–44; Michael Lecker, "The Hudaybiya Treaty," *Jerusalem Studies in Arabic and Islam*, Vol. 5 (1984), pp. 1–11.

15. Waqidi, *Kitab al-Maghazi*, Vol. 2, pp. 633–93; Kister, *Concepts and Ideas*, pp. 91–92.

16. Waqidi, *Kitab al-Maghazi*, Vol. 3, pp. 944–45.

17. Von Grunebaum, *Classical Islam*, p. 37; Bernard Lewis, *The Arabs in History* (London: Hutchinson, 4th ed., 1966), p. 39; W. Montgomery Watt, *Muhammad at Medina* (Oxford: Clarendon Press, 1956), p. 143.

18. Sura 7.158. See also Michael Cook, *Muhammad* (Oxford: Oxford University Press, 1983), p. 40; Albert Hourani, *A History of the Arab Peoples* (London: Faber, 1991), p. 22.

19. Watt, *Muhammad: Prophet and Statesman*, p. 37.

20. Maxime Rodinson, *Muhammad* (London: Penguin, 1973), p. 286 (emphasis in the original).

21. Hugh Kennedy, *The Prophet and the Age of the Caliphates* (London: Longman, 2nd edn., 2004), p. 47; Rahman, "Pre-Foundations," p. 192.

22. Kennedy, *The Prophet*, p. 48. See also Fred McGraw Donner, *The Early Islamic Conquests* (Princeton: Princeton University Press, 1981), pp. 56–57.

23. Ibn Ishaq, *The Life of Muhammad*, p. 232.

24. Waqidi, *Kitab al-Maghazi*, Vol. 3, p. 1113.

25. Carole Hillenbrand, *The Crusades: Islamic Perspectives* (Edinburgh: Edinburgh University Press, 1999), p. 92.

26. Sura 9.111. See also suras 2.154, 195, 218; 3.157–58, 169; 4.56–57, 74–77, 94–95; 8.72; 9.14, 36, 68, 72–73, 83–84, 88–89; 19.72–74.

27. Goldziher, *Muslim Studies*, Vol. 1, p. 55.

28. A. L. Tibawi, *Arabic and Islamic Themes* (London: Luzac, 1976), p. 55. This tradition is supported by sura 48.16 ("Say to the Bedouins who were left behind: 'You shall be called against a people possessed of great might to fight them, or they surrender"), construed by some authorities as referring to Byzantium and Iran.

29. Ibn Ishaq, *The Life of Muhammad*, pp. 652–59; Ibn Hisham, *Sirat al-Nabi*, Vol. 4, pp. 279–81. A number of modern scholars doubt whether some, or all, of these letters were actually sent. See, for example, R. B. Serjeant, "Early Arabic Prose," in A. F. L. Beeston et al (eds.), *Arabic Literature to the End of the Umayyad Period* (Cambridge: Cambridge University Press, 1983), pp. 141–42.

30. Waqidi, *Kitab al-Maghazi*, Vol. 3, pp. 1117–27.

31. Watt, *Muhammad at Medina*, p. 117.

Chapter 2

1. Edward Gibbon, *The Decline and Fall of the Roman Empire* (1776–88; London: Everyman's Library, 1978), Vol. 5, pp. 398–99.

2. Philip K. Hitti, *History of the Arabs* (London: Macmillan, 10th edn., 1993), pp. 144–45. See also: Bernard Lewis, *The Arabs in History* (London: Hutchinson, 4th edn., 1966), pp. 55–56; Joseph Hell, *The Arab Civilization* (Cambridge: W. Heffer & Sons, 1926), p. 37; M. A. Shaban, *Islamic History: A New Interpretation. Vol. 1—A.D. 600–750* (Cambridge: Cambridge University Press, 1971), pp. 14, 24–25; Dominique Sourdel, *Medieval Islam* (London: Routledge & Kegan Paul, 1983), pp. 17–18.

3. Fred McGraw Donner, *The Early Islamic Conquests* (Princeton: Princeton University Press, 1981), pp. 221–22, 268–69; Donner, "Centralized Authority and Military Autonomy in the Early Islamic Conquests," in Averil Cameron (ed.), *The Byzantine and Early Islamic Near East. Vol. III—States, Resources, and Armies* (Princeton: Darwin, 1995), pp. 337–60; Hugh Kennedy, *The Prophet and the Age of the Caliphates* (London: Longman, 2nd edn., 2004), p. 58.

4. Theodor Noeldeke, *Sketches from Eastern History* (London: Adam and Charles Black, 1892), p. 73.

5. Abdel Rahman ibn Abdullah ibn Abdel Hakam, *Futuh Misr wa-Akhbaruha* (New Haven: Yale University Press, 1922), p. 65.

6. Abdel Rahman ibn Muhammad ibn Khaldun, *Kitab al-Ibar wa-Diwan al-Mubtada wa-l-Khabar* (Beirut: Dar al-Kitab al-Lubnani, 1961), Vol. 1, p. 278.

7. M. J. Kister, *Concepts and Ideas at the Dawn of Islam* (Aldershot: Ashgate, 1997), p. 284.

8. Ahmad ibn Yahya al-Baladhuri, *Futuh al-Buldan* (Cairo: Dar al-Nashr li-l-Jami'in, 1957), Vol. 2, p. 149.

9. Muhammad Muhi al-Din Abdel Hamid al-Mas'udi, *Muruj al-Dhahb wa-Maadin al-Jawhar* (Beirut: University of Beirut, 1970), Vol. 3, pp. 126–27.

10. Ahmad ibn Yahya al-Baladhuri, *Ansab al-Ashraf* (Beirut: Dar al-Fiqr, 1996), Vol. 10, pp. 361–62.

11. After the conquests the Arabs used the imperial monetary systems of the vanquished peoples. In 696 they minted their own gold coin, the dinar, followed two years later by a silver coin, the dirham. Under the Umayyads the exchange rate was ten dirhams for one dinar, rising during the Abbasid era to twelve dirhams per dinar. E. Ashtor, *A Social and Economic History of the Near East in the Middle Ages* (London: Collins, 1976), pp. 81–84.

12. Muhammad ibn Saad, *al-Tabaqat al-Kubra* (Cairo: Dar al-Tahrir, 1968), Vol. 3, pp. 77, 157–58; Mas'udi, *Muruj*, Vol. 3, pp. 50, 76–77; Ibn Abdel Hakam, *Futuh Misr*, p. 82; Ahmad ibn Abi Ya'qub al-Ya'qubi, *Tarikh al-Ya'qubi* (Beirut: Dar Beirut li-l-Tiba'a wa-l-Nashr, 1960), Vol. 2, p. 154.

13. Ya'qub ibn Ibrahim al-Kufi (Abu Yusuf), *Kitab al-Kharaj* (Cairo: al-Matba'a al-Salafiyya, 2nd edn., 1933), pp. 23–24. See also: Lewis, *The Arabs*, p. 57; Michael G. Morony, "Landholding in Seventh-Century Iraq: Late Sasanian and Early Islamic Patterns," in A. L. Udovitch (ed.), *The Islamic Middle East, 700–1900: Studies in Economic and Social History* (Princeton: Darwin Press, 1981), pp. 135–75.

14. G. E. von Grunebaum, *Classical Islam: A History 600–1258* (London: Allen & Unwin, 1970), p. 57.

15. There are differing views about the origin of the Diwan. According to the prominent ninth-century historian Ahmad ibn Yahya Baladhuri (d. 892), Umar probably borrowed the idea from the "kings of Syria," presumably the Byzantine emperors (*Futuh*, Vol. 3, p. 549). Muhammad ibn Abdus Jashiyari (d. 942) points to Sasanid origin, as does the modern scholar Michael G. Morony. See: Jashiyari, *Kitab al-Wuzara wa-l-Kutab* (Cairo: Mustafa al-Babi, 1938), p. 17; Morony, *Iraq after the Muslim Conquest* (Princeton: Princeton University Press, 1984), p. 56.

16. Baladhuri, *Futuh*, Vol. 1, pp. 33–41, 76–83. A Jewish community nevertheless managed to survive in Yemen until the 1940s.

17. Alfred Freiherr von Kremer, *The Orient Under the Caliphs* (Philadelphia: Porcupine Press, 1978; facsimile reprint of the 1920 English translation, published by the University of Calcutta), p. 118; Hava Lazarus-Yafeh, *Some Religious Aspects of Islam: A Collection of Articles* (Leiden: E. J. Brill, 1981), p. 14; Patricia Crone, *Slaves on Horses: The Evolution of the Islamic Polity* (Cambridge: Cambridge University Press, 1980), p. 30.

18. Baladhuri, *Futuh*, Vol. 1, pp. 216–18; Abu Yusuf, *Kitab al-Kharaj*, pp. 120–21; Wilfred Madelung, *The Succession to Muhammad: A Study of the Early Caliphate* (Cambridge: Cambridge University Press, 1997), p. 74.

19. Abu Yusuf, *Kitab al-Kharaj*, pp. 120–28, 138–49; Bertold Spuler, *The Muslim World: A Historical Survey. Part 1—The Age of the Caliphs* (Leiden: Brill, 1960), pp. 25–27; Hell, *The Arab Civilization*, p. 44. See also C. E. Bosworth, "The Concept of Dhimma in Early Islam," in his *The Arabs, Byzantium, and Iran* (Aldershot: Variorum, 1996), pp. 37–51; Yohanan Friedmann, *Tolerance and Coercion in Islam: Interfaith Relations in the Muslim Tradition* (Cambridge: Cambridge University Press, 2003); Bat Yeor, *The Dhimmis: Jews and Christians under Islam* (Rutherford: Farleigh Dickinson University Press, 1985).

20. Hell, *The Arab Civilization*, pp. 63–64; Morony, *Iraq*, Chapter 8; Samuel S. Haas, "The Contributions of Slaves to and Their Influence upon the Culture of Early Islam" (Princeton: PhD Thesis, 1942); Ira M. Lapidus, "Arab Settlement and Economic Development of Iraq and Iran in the Age of the Umayyad and Early Abbasid Caliphs," in Udovitch (ed.), *The Islamic Middle East*, pp. 177–207.

21. Patricia Crone argues that while pre-Islamic Arabia provided the general context for the *wala* (clientage) it did not provide the institution itself, which derived its crucial features from Roman and provincial law. See Crone, *Roman, Provincial, and Islamic Law: The Origins of the Islamic Patronage* (Cambridge: Cambridge University Press, 1987), esp. pp. 40–88.

22. Daniel C. Dennett, *Conversion and the Poll Tax in Early Islam* (Cambridge: Harvard University Press, 1950); Ignaz Goldziher, *Muslim Studies* (London: George Allen & Unwin, 1967), Vol. 1, pp. 101–36; Julius Wellhausen, *The Arab Kingdom and Its Fall* (Calcutta: University of Calcutta, 1927), pp. 267–311; Crone, *Slaves on Horses*, pp. 49–57; Crone, "Were the Qays and Yemen of the Umayyad Period Political Parties?" *Der Islam*, Vol. 71, No. 1 (1994), p. 24; J. J. Saunders, *A History of Medieval Islam* (London: Routledge & Kegan Paul, 1965), pp. 95–97.

23. Baladhuri, *Futuh*, Vol. 2, pp. 131–49; Wellhausen, *The Arab Kingdom*, pp. 23–24; C. H. Becker, "The Expansion of the Saracens," *The Cambridge Medieval History* (Cambridge: Cambridge University Press, 1st ed., 1911–36), pp. 335–36; Elias Shoufany, *Al-Rida and the Muslim Conquest of Arabia* (Toronto: Toronto University Press, 1973).

24. Muhammad ibn Jarir al-Tabari, *Tarikh al-Rusul wa-l-Muluk* (Cairo: Dar al-Ma'arif bi-Misr, 1966), Vol. 3, pp. 287–301.

25. Wellhausen, *The Arab Kingdom*, pp. 68–70. Muhammad Shaban argued that the Qays-Yemen rivalry was essentially political rather than tribal, but Patricia Crone comprehensively demolished his thesis. See Shaban, *Islamic History*, Vol. 1, pp. 120–21; Crone, "Were the Qays and Yemen of the Umayyad Period Political Parties?"

26. Mas'udi, *Muruj*, Vol. 3, pp. 87–90; Martin Hinds, *Studies in Early Islamic History* (Princeton: Darwin, 1996), pp. 1–55; Hugh Kennedy, "The Financing of the Military in the Early Islamic State," in Cameron, *The Byzantine*, pp. 361–78; von Grunebaum, *Classical Islam*, pp. 56–63.

27. Mas'udi, *Muruj*, Vol. 3, pp. 120–54; Hinds, *Studies*, pp. 56–66.

28. Mas'udi, *Muruj*, Vol. 3, pp. 155–63.

29. Patricia Crone and Martin Hinds, *God's Caliph: Religious Authority in the First Centuries of Islam* (Cambridge: Cambridge University Press, 1990), pp. 4–11; Goldziher, *Muslim Studies*, Vol. 2, pp. 40–41.

30. F. Harb, "Wine Poetry," in Julia Ashtiany et al (eds.), *Abbasid Belles-Lettres* (Cambridge: Cambridge University Press, 1990), p. 224; Von Kremmer, *The Orient*, Chapter 4.

31. Thomas W. Arnold, *The Caliphate* (London: Routledge & Kegan Paul, 2nd edn., 1967), pp. 31–33.

32. Von Kremer, *The Orient*, pp. 163–64.

33. M. J. Kister, "The Battle of the Harra," in Miriam Rosen-Ayalon (ed.), *Studies in Memory of Gaston Wiet* (Jerusalem: Hebrew University, 1977), pp. 30–50.

34. Mas'udi, *Muruj*, Vol. 3, pp. 282–301, 315–19; Ya'qubi, *Ta'rikh*, Vol. 2, pp. 255–68; G. R. Hawting, *The First Dynasty of Islam: The Umayyad Caliphate AD 661–750* (London: Croom Helm, 1986), pp. 46–57.

35. Mas'udi, *Muruj*, Vol. 3, pp. 331–32.

36. Jurji Zaydan, *History of Islamic Civilizations. Part 4: Umayyads and Abbasids*, trans. D. S. Margoliouth (Leiden: Brill, 1907), p. 112.

37. Abd al-Ameer Abd Dixon, *The Umayyad Caliphate 65–86/684–705: A Political Study* (London: Luzac, 1971), Chapter 5.

38. Wellhausen, *The Arab Kingdom*, p. 65. See also W. Montgomery Watt, *Islamic Political Thought* (Edinburgh: Edinburgh University Press, 1968), pp. 54–63; Abd Dixon, *The Umayyad Caliphate*, Chapter 6; Shaban, *Islamic History*, Vol. 1, pp. 95–98, 100–10, 150–52.

39. M. A. Shaban, *The Abbasid Revolution* (Cambridge: Cambridge University Press, 1970), pp. 138–49.

40. Mas'udi, *Muruj*, Vol. 3, pp. 248–59; Ya'qubi, *Ta'rikh*, Vol. 2, pp. 243–47.

41. Tabari, *Ta'rikh*, Vol. 6, pp. 115–16. See also: ibid. pp. 45–114; Ya'qubi, *Ta'rikh*, Vol. 2, p. 307; Mas'udi, *Muruj*, Vol. 3, pp. 272–73. For discussion of the revolt's long-term legacy see S. H. M. Jafri, *Origins and Early Development of Shi'a Islam* (London: Longman, 1979), pp. 235–42; M. G. S. Hodgson, "How Did the Early Shi'a become Sectarian?" *Journal of the American Oriental Society*, Vol. 75 (1955), pp. 4–8.

42. Farouq Omar, *The Abbasid Caliphate* (Baghdad: National Printing and Publishing, 1969), p. 61; Moshe Sharon, *Black Banners from the East: The Establishment of the Abbasid State—Incubation of a Revolt* (Jerusalem: Magnes Press, 1983), pp. 105–07.

43. See, for example, *Akhbar al-Dawla al-Abbasiya wa-fihi Akhbar al-Abbas wa-Waladihi* (Beirut: Dar al-Tali'a li-l-Taba'a wa-l-Nashr, 1971), pp. 173–91.

44. See, for example, Sharon, *Black Banners*, pp. 173–83; Patricia Crone, "On the Meaning of the Abbasid Call to al-Ridda," in C. E. Bosworth et al (eds.), *The Islamic World: From Classical to Modern Times: Essays in Honor of Bernard Lewis* (Princeton: Darwin Press, 1989), pp. 95–111; Saleh Said Agha, *The Revolution Which Toppled the Umayyads: Neither Arab Nor Abbasid* (Leiden: Brill, 2003), pp. xxxiii–xxxvi; Elton Lee Daniel, *Iran's Awakening: A Study of Local Rebellions in the Eastern Provinces of the Islamic Empire, 126–227 A.H. (743–842 A.D.)* (Austin: University of Texas, 1978), Part 1; Daniel *The Political and Social History of Khurasan under Abbasid Rule 747–820* (Minneapolis: Bibliotheca Islamica, 1979), Chapter 1.

45. Wellhausen, *The Arab Kingdom*, pp. 493–98; Sharon, *Black Banners*, pp. 54–71; Shaban, *The Abbasid Revolution*, pp. xv, xvi, 156–57; Moshe Sharon, *Revolt: The Social and Military Aspects of the Abbasid Revolution* (Jerusalem: Hebrew University, 1990).

46. C. E. Bosworth, "Byzantium and the Arabs: War and Peace between Two World Civilizations," in his *The Arabs, Byzantium, and Iran*, p. 64.

47. Khalid Yahya Blankinship, *The End of the Jihad State: the Reign of Hisham ibn Abd al-Malik and the Collapse of the Umayyads* (Albany: State University of New York Press, 1994), pp. 224, 236.

48. Tabari, *Ta'rikh*, Vol. 7, pp. 437–43; Ali ibn Muhammad ibn Athir, *al-Kamil fi-l-Ta'rikh* (Beirut: Dar Sadir, 6th ed., 1995), Vol. 5, pp. 417–21; Wellhausen, *The Fall*, pp. 549–50.

Chapter 3

1. G. E. von Grunebaum, *Classical Islam: A History 600–1258* (London: Allen & Unwin, 1970), pp. 80–81; Albert Hourani, *A History of the Arab Peoples* (London: Faber, 1991), pp. 46–47; Patricia Crone, "The Pay of Client Soldiers in the Umayyad Period," *Der Islam*, Vol. 80, No. 2 (2003), p. 300.

2. S. D. Goitein, *Studies in Islamic History* (Leiden: Brill, 1968), pp. 168–96; Thomas W. Arnold, *The Caliphate* (London: Routledge & Kegan Paul, 2nd edn., 1967), pp. 28–29; Bertold Spuler, *The Muslim World: A Historical Survey. Part 1—The Age of the Caliphs* (Leiden: Brill, 1960), pp. 50–52; Jacob Lassner, *The Shaping of Abbasid Rule* (Princeton: Princeton University Press, 1980), pp. 8–16, 89–102, 177.

3. Muhammad ibn Jarir al-Tabari, *Tarikh al-Rusul wa-l-Muluk* (Cairo: Dar al-Ma'arif bi-Misr, 1966), Vol. 7, pp. 425–28.

4. Patricia Crone and Martin Hinds, *God's Caliph: Religious Authority in the First Centuries of Islam* (Cambridge: Cambridge University Press, 1990), pp. 82, 84–85; Ignaz Goldziher, *Muslim Studies* (London: George Allen & Unwin, 1970), Vol. 2, pp. 60–71; Arnold, *The Caliphate*, pp. 27–28.

5. Goldziher, *Muslim Studies*, Vol. 2, pp. 64, 71–74; Michael Cook, *Commanding Right and Forbidding Wrong in Islamic Thought* (Cambridge: Cambridge University Press, 2000), pp. 65–67, 165–92. See also W. Montgomery Watt, *Islamic Philosophy and Theology* (Edinburgh: Edinburgh University Press, 1962), pp. 58–71.

6. Tabari, *Ta'rikh*, Vol. 7, p. 426; Dominique Sourdel, "The Abbasid Caliphate," in P. M. Holt, Ann K. S. Lambton, and Bernard Lewis (eds.), *The Cambridge History of Islam. Volume I—The Central Islamic Lands* (Cambridge: Cambridge University Press, 1970), Vol. 1, p. 104.

7. E. Ashtor, *A Social and Economic History of the Near East in the Middle Ages* (London: Collins, 1976), p. 71.

8. Hugh Kennedy, *The Early Abbasid Caliphate: A Political History* (London: Croom Helm, 1981), p. 78.

9. M. A. Shaban, *Islamic History: A New Interpretation: Vol. 2—A.D. 750–1055 (A.H. 132–448)* (Cambridge: Cambridge University Press, 1976), pp. 35–36, 90; Ashtor, *A Social and Economic History*, Chapter 2; Simha Sabari, *Mouvements populaires à Bagdad à l'époque abbaside, IXe—XIe siècles* (Paris: Adrien Maisonneuve, 1981), pp. 77–100; Hamilton A. R. Gibb, "An Interpretation of Islamic History," in his *Studies on the Civilization of Islam* (London: Routledge & Kegan Paul, 1962), pp. 19–23; Elizabeth Greene Heilman, *Popular Protest in Medieval Baghdad 295–334 A.H./908–946 A.D.* (Ann Arbor: University Microfilms International, 1989).

10. Ashtor, *A Social and Economic History*, p. 80.

11. Elton Lee Daniel, *The Political and Social History of Khurasan under Abbasid Rule 747–820* (Minneapolis: Bibliotheca Islamica, 1979), Chapter 5.

12. Elton Lee Daniel, *Iran's Awakening: A Study of Local Rebellions in the Eastern Provinces of the Islamic Empire, 126–227 A.H. (743–842 A.D.)* (Austin: University of Texas, 1978), pp. 443–77; Farouq Omar, *al-Abbasiyun al-Awa'il* (Baghdad: n.p., 1982), Vol. 3, pp. 142–57.

13. Tabari, *Ta'rikh*, Vol. 9, pp. 431–37, 470–73, 477–88, 520–26, 534–43, 554–56, 588–99, 602, 622–31; Abdel Rahman ibn Muhammad ibn Khaldun, *Kitab al-Ibar wa-Diwan al-Mubtada wa-l-Khabar* (Beirut: Dar al-Kitab al-Lubnani, 1961), Vol. 1, pp. 142–43; Alexandre Popovic, *The Revolt of African Slaves in Iraq in the 3rd/9th Century* (Princeton: Marcus Weiner, 1999); Theodor Noeldeke, *Sketches from Eastern History*

(London: Adam and Charles Black, 1892), pp. 149–74; Ahmad Olabi, *Thawrat al-Zanj wa-Qaiduha Ali ibn Muhammad* (Beirut: al-Hayat, 1961). Shaban rejects the standard interpretation of the insurrection as a slave revolt, claiming that the Zanj were not slaves but merely "Negroes"; that most rebels were in fact Arabs; and that the freeing of the slaves had never been one of their objectives. In his view, the revolt revolved by and large around the lucrative African trade. See *Islamic History*, Vol. 2, pp. 100–03.

14. Tabari, *Ta'rikh*, Vol. 7, p. 426. There is some confusion regarding the origin of this title. Bernard Lewis claims that the caliph never assumed it: "It was assigned to him by later historians, whose sense of order and propriety required that the first Abbasid, like all his successors should have a regnal title of some sort." Yet Lewis has argued elsewhere that Abul Abbas "was proclaimed as Caliph, with the title Saffah." See "The Regnal Titles of the First Abbasid Caliphs," in *Dr Zahir Husain Presentation Volume* (New Delhi, 1968), p. 15, reproduced in Bernard Lewis, *Studies in Classical and Ottoman Islam* (London: Varium Reprints, 1976), p. 15; *The Arabs in History* (London: Hutchinson, 4th edn., 1966), p. 79.

15. Tabari, *Ta'rikh*, Vol. 7, pp. 450–57; Ibn Khaldun, *Kitab al-Ibar*, Vol. 3, pp. 373–76; Ahmad ibn Abi Ya'qub al-Ya'qubi, *Tarikh al-Ya'qubi* (Beirut: Dar Beirut li-l-Tiba'a wa-l-Nashr, 1960), Vol. 2, pp. 352–57; Ali ibn Muhammad ibn Athir, *al-Kamil fi-l-Ta'rikh* (Beirut: Dar Sadir, 6th ed., 1995), Vol. 6, pp. 21–22.

16. Jurji Zaydan, *History of Islamic Civilizations. Part 4: Umayyads and Abbasids*, trans. D. S. Margoliouth (Leiden: Brill, 1907), pp. 111–12; Farouq Omar, *The Abbasid Caliphate* (Baghdad: National Printing and Publishing, 1969), pp. 260–80; Amikam Elad, "Aspects of the Transition from the Umayyad to the Abbasid Caliphate," *Jerusalem Studies in Arabic and Islam*, Vol. 19 (1995), pp. 92–95.

17. Ya'qubi, *Ta'rikh*, Vol. 2, pp. 352–53; Tabari, *Ta'rikh*, Vol. 7, pp. 429–31; Muhammad Muhi al-Din Abdel Hamid al-Mas'udi, *Muruj al-Dhahb wa-Maadin al-Jawhar* (Beirut: University of Beirut, 1970), Vol. 3, pp. 268–70; Goitein, *Studies*, pp. 169–70; Amikam Elad, "The Siege of Wasit (132/749)," in Moshe Sharon (ed.), *Studies in Islamic History and Civilization in Honor of Professor David Ayalon* (Jerusalem: Cana, 1986), pp. 59–64.

18. Tabari, *Ta'rikh*, Vol. 7, pp. 468–69, 479–94; Ibn Athir, *al-Kamil*, Vol. 5, pp. 468–81; Ibn Khaldun, *Kitab al-Ibar*, Vol. 3, pp. 385–90; Ya'qubi, *Ta'rikh*, Vol. 2, pp. 366–69; Mas'udi, *Muruj*, Vol. 3, pp. 302–06.

19. Goitein, *Studies*, p. 182.

20. For the fall of the Barmakids see Muhammad ibn Abdus Jashiyari, *Kitab al-Wuzara wa-l-Kutab* (Cairo: Mustafa al-Babi, 1938), p. 234; Omar, *al-Abbasiyun al-Awa'il*, Vol. 3, pp. 21–27; Abdel Aziz Duri, *al-Asr al-Abbasi al-Awal* (Baghdad: Matba'at al-Tafayud al-Ahliya, 1945), pp. 156–76; Dominique Sourdel, *Le Vizirat abbaside de 749 à 936* (Paris: Damas, 1959), pp. 169–81.

21. Hugh Kennedy, *The Prophet and the Age of the Caliphates* (London: Longman, 2d ed., 2004), p. 124; Daniel, *Iran's Awakening*, p. 68.

22. Julius Wellhausen, *The Arab Kingdom and Its Fall* (Calcutta: University of Calcutta, 1927), pp. 499–500; W. Montgomery Watt, "Shiism under the Umayyads," *Journal of the Royal Asiatic Society*, 1960, pp. 170–72.

23. *Akhbar al-Dawla al-Abbasiya wa-fihi Akhbar al-Abbas wa-Waladihi* (Beirut: Dar al-Tali'a li-l-Taba'a wa-l-Nashr, 1971), p. 130.

24. R. Rubinacci, "Political Poetry," in Julia Ashtiany et al (eds.), *Abbasid Belles-Lettres* (Cambridge: Cambridge University Press, 1990), p. 194.

25. Tabari, *Ta'rikh*, Vol. 7, pp. 556–609, 649–66; Ibn Athir, *al-Kamil*, Vol. 5, pp. 529–42, 560–65; Yaqubi, *Ta'rikh*, Vol. 2, pp. 454–56; Noeldeke, *Sketches*, pp. 122–25; Reynold A. Nicholson, *A Literary History of the Arabs* (1907; Cambridge: Cambridge University Press, 1953), p. 258.

26. For general studies of the Fatimids see Heinz Hal, *The Empire of the Mahdi: The Rise of the Fatimids* (Leiden: Brill, 1996); Yaacov Lev, *State and Society in Fatimid Egypt*

(Leiden: Brill, 1991); Paul E. Walker, *Exploring an Islamic Empire: Fatimid History and Its Sources* (London: Tauris, 2002); Sadik A. Asaad, *The Reign of al-Hakim bi Amr Allah: A Political Study* (Beirut: Arab Institute for Research and Publication, 1974).

27. Shaban, *The Abbasid Revolution*, pp. 163–68.
28. Lassner, *The Shaping*, pp. 129–36.
29. David Ayalon, "Preliminary Remarks on the Mamluk Military Institution in Islam," in V. J. Perry and M. E. Yapp (eds.), *War, Technology, and Society in the Middle East* (London: Oxford University Press, 1975), p. 49.
30. Ibid., pp. 54–56. See also Ayalon, "The Military Reforms of Caliph al-Mu'tasim: Their Background and Consequences" (unpublished paper, Jerusalem, 1963); Ayalon, "Aspects of the Mamluk Phenomenon," *Der Islam*, Part 1 (1976), pp. 196–225; Part 2 (1977), pp. 1–32; Daniel Pipes, *Slave Soldiers and Islam: The Genesis of a Military System* (New Haven and London: Yale University Press, 1981); Patricia Crone, *Slaves on Horses: The Evolution of the Islamic Polity* (Cambridge: Cambridge University Press, 1980), Chapter 10; Matthew S. Gordon, *The Breaking of a Thousand Swords: A History of the Turkish Military of Samarra 200–275 A.H./815–889 C.E.* (Albany: State University of New York, 2001), pp. 6–9; C. E. Bosworth, "Recruitment, Muster, and Review in Medieval Islamic Armies," in Perry and Yapp, *War, Technology, and Society*, pp. 59–77.
     Shaban disputes the description of this force as based on slave-soldiers. See *Islamic History*, Vol. 2, pp. 65–67.
31. Kennedy, *The Prophet*, pp. 201–02.
32. Edward Gibbon, *The Decline and Fall of the Roman Empire* (1776–88; London: Everyman's Library, 1978), Vol. 5, pp. 373–74; Reinhart Dozy, *Spanish Islam* (London: Chatto & Windus, 1913), pp. 230–41; Derek W. Lomax, *The Reconquest of Spain* (London: Longman, 1978), pp. 10–16; Abdulwahid Dhanun Taha, *The Muslim Conquest and Settlement of North Africa and Spain* (London: Routledge, 1988), pp. 99–101.
33. Hugh Kennedy, *Muslim Spain and Portugal* (London: Longman, 1996), p. 15.
34. C. R. Haines, *Christianity and Islam in Spain* (London: Kegan Paul, 1889); Stanley Lane-Poole, *The Moors in Spain* (London: Fisher Unwin, 1888).
35. E. Levi-Provençal *Histoire de l'Espagne musulmane* (Paris: Maisonneuve, 1950), Vols. 1 and 2; Roger Collins, *The Arab Conquest of Spain 710–797* (Oxford: Blackwell, 1989).
36. Abu Ali Ahmed ibn Muhammad (Ibn Miskawayh), *Tajarib al-Umam* (Leiden: Brill, 1909), Vol. 1, pp. 162–63.
37. Richard Frye, *The Golden Age of Persia: The Arabs in the East* (London: Weidenfeld and Nicolson, 1975), Chapter 10; Von Grunebaum, *Classical Islam*, pp. 141–58; Kennedy, *The Prophet*, pp. 210–47; Arnold, *The Caliphate*, pp. 70–98; C. E. Bosworth, *The Islamic Dynasties* (Edinburgh: Edinburgh University Press, 1980), pp. 83–119.

Chapter 4

1. Muhammad ibn Umar al-Waqidi, *Kitab al-Maghazi* (London: Oxford University Press, 1966), Vol. 3, p. 1113.
2. Abdel Rahman ibn Muhammad ibn Khaldun, *Kitab al-Ibar wa-Diwan al-Mubtada wa-l-Khabar* (Beirut: Dar al-Kitab al-Lubnani, 1961), Vol. 1, p. 408. For modern-day discussion of the doctrine of jihad see: Majid Khadduri, *War and Peace in the Law of Islam* (Baltimore: John's Hopkins University Press, 1955); Rudolph Peters, *Jihad in Classical and Modern Islam* (Princeton: Marcus Weiner, 1996); Bernard Lewis, "Politics and War," in Joseph Schacht and C. E. Bosworth (eds.), *The Legacy of Islam* (Oxford: Clarendon Press, 1974), pp. 156–209; Andrew G. Bostom, *The Legacy of Jihad: Islamic Holy War and The Fate of Non-Muslims* (New York: Prometheus Books, 2005).

3. W. Montgomery Watt, *Islam and the Integration of Society* (London: Routledge & Kegan Paul, 1961), p. 89.

4. Gaston Wiet, "L'Empire néo-byzantin des Omeyyades et l'empire néo-sasanide des Abbasides," *Journal of World History*, Vol. 1 (1953–54), pp. 63–71.

5. Hamilton A. R. Gibb, *Studies on the Civilization of Islam* (London: Routledge & Kegan Paul, 1962), pp. 51–57; Oleg Graber, "Islamic Art and Byzantium," *Dumbarton Oaks Papers*, 18 (1964), p. 88.

6. Gustave E. von Grunebaum, *Medieval Islam* (Chicago: University of Chicago Press, 2nd edn., 1962), p. 294; S. D. Goitein, *Studies in Islamic History* (Leiden: Brill, 1968), pp. 54–70; C. E. Bosworth, "The Persian Impact on Arabic Literature," in A. F. L. Beeston et al (eds.), *Arabic Literature to the End of the Umayyad Period* (Cambridge: Cambridge University Press, 1983), pp. 483–501; Richard Frye, *The Golden Age of Persia: The Arabs in the East* (London: Weidenfeld and Nicolson, 1975), pp. 150–85; L. E. Goodman, "The Greek Impact on Arabic Literature," in Beeston, *Arabic Literature*, p. 481; Goodman, "The Translation of Greek Materials into Arabic," in M. J. L. Young et al (eds.), *Religion, Learning, and Science in the Abbasid Period* (Cambridge: Cambridge University Press, 1990), pp. 477–97; De Lacy O'Leary, *How Greek Science Passed to the Arabs* (London: Routledge & Kegan Paul, 1964).

7. W. Montgomery Watt, *The Influence of Islam on Medieval Europe* (Edinburgh: Edinburgh University Press, 1972), p. 11.

8. Thus, for example, while foreign nationals were subjected to a 10 percent custom on the value of their merchandise and Dhimmis had to pay a 5 percent tax, Muslim merchants were liable to only a 2.5 percent tax. Goitein, *Studies*, p. 232.

9. Daniel C. Dennett, "Pirenne and Muhammad," *Speculum*, Vol. 23, No. 2 (April 1948), p. 168.

10. J. H. Krammers, "Geography and Commerce," in Thomas Arnold and Alfred Guillaume (eds.), *The Legacy of Islam* (Oxford: Oxford University Press, 1931), pp. 100–10; Archibald R. Lewis, *Naval Power and Trade in the Mediterranean A.D. 500–1100* (Princeton: Princeton University Press, 1951), pp. 174–75; E. Ashtor, *A Social and Economic History of the Near East in the Middle Ages* (London: Collins, 1976), pp. 100–06; C. E. Bosworth, "The City of Tarsus and the Arab-Byzantine Frontiers in Early and Middle Abbasid Times," in his *The Arabs, Byzantium, and Iran* (Aldershot: Variorum, 1996), p. XIV.

11. Henri Pirenne, *Mohammed and Charlemagne* (London: Allen & Unwin, 1939); Pirenne, *Economic and Social History of Medieval Europe* (London: Kegan Paul, Trench, Trubner & Co., 1936). For discussion of the thesis see: Dennett, "Pirenne and Muhammad"; Robert S. Lopez, "Mohammed and Charlemagne: A Revision," *Speculum*, Vol. 18, No. 1 (Jan. 1943), pp. 14–38; Eliyahu Ashtor, "Quelques observations d'un orientaliste sur la thèse de Pirenne," *Journal of the Economic and Social History of the Orient*, Vol. 22 (1970), pp. 166–94; A. S. Ehrenkreutz, "Another Orientalist's Remarks Concerning the Pirenne Thesis," *Journal of the Economic and Social History of the Orient*, Vol. 25 (1973), pp. 94–104; Richard Hodges and David Whitehouse, *Mohammed, Charlemagne, and the Origins of Europe* (London: Duckworth, 1983).

12. Watt, *The Influence of Islam*, p. 19; Claude Cahen, "Commercial Relations between the Near East and Western Europe from the Seventh to the Tenth Centuries," in Khalil I. Semaan (ed.), *Islam and the Medieval West* (Albany: State University of New York Press, 1980), p. 5; Ashtor, *A Social and Economic History*, pp. 100–06.

13. Wilhelm von Heyd, *Histoire du commerce du Levant au moyen-âge* (Leipzig: Harrassowitz, 1923), Vol. 1, pp. 98–108, 125–28; Robert S. Lopez, *The Commercial Revolution of the Middle Ages 950–1350* (Cambridge: Cambridge University Press, 1976), pp. 60–70; S. D. Goitein, *A Mediterranean Society: The Jewish Communities of the Arab World as Portrayed in the Documents of the Cairo Geniza. Volume 1—Economic Foundations* (Berkeley: University of California Press, 1967), p. 317; Pirenne,

Mohammed, pp. 178–80; Moshe Gil, "The Radhanite Merchants and the Land of Radhan," *Journal of the Economic and Social History of the Orient,* Vol. 17 (1974), pp. 299–328; Armand O. Citarella, "Patterns in Medieval Trade: the Commerce of Amalfi before the Crusades," *Journal of Economic History,* Vol. 28, No. 4 (Dec. 1968), pp. 531–55; Robert S. Lopez and Irving W. Raymond, *Medieval Trade in the Mediterranean World: Illustrative Documents Translated with Introductions and Notes* (New York: Norton, 1967).

14. Hilmar C. Krueger, "The Italian Cities and the Arabs before 1095," in Kenneth M. Setton (editor-in-chief), *A History of the Crusades. Volume I: The First Hundred Years* (Philadelphia: University of Pennsylvania Press, 1955), pp. 40–53; Armand O. Citarella, "The Relations of Amalfi with the Arab World before the Crusades," *Speculum,* Vol. 42, No. 2 (Apr. 1967), pp. 299–312; Fred E. Engreen, "Pope John the Eighth and the Arabs," *Speculum,* Vol. 20, No. 3 (July 1945), pp. 318–30.

15. See, for example, *The Chronicle of Theophanes Confessor: Byzantine and Near Eastern History A.D. 284–813,* trans. with an introduction and commentary by Cyril Mango and Roger Scott (Oxford: Clarendon Press, 1997), pp. 484–85, 503, 506–07.

16. See, for example, E. Levi-Provençal, "Un échange d'ambassades entre Cordoue et Byzance au IX siècle," *Byzantion,* Vol. 12 (1937), pp. 1–124.

17. F. W. Buckler, *Harunu'l-Rashid and Charles the Great* (Cambridge: Medieval Academy of America, 1931); Einar Joranson, "The Alleged Frankish Protectorate in Palestine," *American Historical Review,* Vol. 32, No. 2 (Jan. 1927), pp. 241–61; Aziz S. Atiya, *Crusade, Commerce, and Culture* (Bloomington: Indiana University Press, 1962), pp. 34–40.

18. Fulcher of Chartres, *A History of the Expedition to Jerusalem 1095–1127,* ed. with an introduction by Harold S. Fink (Knoxville: University of Tennessee Press, 1969), p. 71.

19. Edward Peters (ed.), *The First Crusade: The Chronicle of Fulcher of Charters and Other Source Materials* (Philadelphia: University of Pennsylvania Press, 1971), pp. 3, 9.

20. The classic study on these states remains Joshua Prawer's *The Latin Kingdom of Jerusalem: European Colonialism in the Middle Ages* (London: Weidenfeld and Nicolson, 1972).

21. Steven Runciman, "Byzantium and the Crusades," in Thomas Madden (ed.), *The Crusades: The Essential Readings* (Oxford: Blackwell, 2002), p. 220. See also Runciman, *The History of the Crusades: Volume 2—The Kingdom of Jerusalem and the Frankish East 1100–1187* (Cambridge: Cambridge University Press, 1952), pp. 32–55, 121–26; A. C. Krey, "Urban's Crusade—Success or Failure," *American Historical Review,* Vol. 53, No. 2 (Jan. 1948), pp. 235–50; Ralph B. Yewdale, *Bohemond I, Prince of Antioch* (New York: AMS Press, 1980); Robert Lawrence Nicholson, *Tancred* (Chicago: Chicago University Press, 1940); Thomas S. Asbridge, *The Creation of the Principality of Antioch 1098–1130* (Woodbridge: Boydell Press, 2000).

22. Claude Cahen, "The Turkish Invasion: The Selchukids," in Setton, *A History,* Vol. 1, pp. 135–76.

23. Ali ibn Muhammad ibn Athir, *al-Kamil fi-l-Ta'rikh* (Beirut: Dar Sadir, 6th ed., 1995), Vol. 10, p. 285; Bertold Spuler, *The Muslim World: A Historical Survey. Part 1—The Age of the Caliphs* (Leiden: Brill, 1960), p. 89; Cahen, "The Turkish Invasion," p. 166.

24. Ibn Athir, *al-Kamil,* Vol. 10, p. 284; Abdel Rahman ibn al-Jawzi, *al-Muntazam fi T'arikh al-Muluk wa-l-Umam* (Beirut: Dar al-Kutub al-Ilmiyya, 1992), Vol. 17, pp. 43, 47–48; Muhammad al-Azimi, *Ta'rikh Halab* (Damascus: n.p., 1984), p. 360.

25. Carole Hillenbrand, *The Crusades: Islamic Perspectives* (Edinburgh: Edinburgh University Press, 1999), pp. 104–10; Emmanuel Sivan, *L'Islam et la croisade: idéologie et propagande dans les réactions musulmanes aux croisades* (Paris: Librairie d'Amérique et d'Orient, 1968), pp. 25–28.

26. The situation was in fact more complex. Following Duqaq's death his brother Baktash claimed to be his rightful heir and established himself in the Hauran, south of

Damascus, from where he sided with the Franks in opposition to Tughtigin's then pro-Egyptian policy. W. B. Stevenson, *The Crusaders in the East* (Cambridge: Cambridge University Press, 1907), p. 48.

27. Ibn Athir, *al-Kamil*, Vol. 10, pp. 496–97; H. A. R. Gibb, *The Damascus Chronicle of the Crusades. Extracted and Translated from the Chronicle of Ibn al-Qalanisi* (London: Luzac, 1932), pp. 140–42.

28. Ibn Athir, *al-Kamil*, Vol. 10, pp. 459–66; Nicholson, *Tancred*, pp. 170–79; Runciman, *The History of the Crusades*, Vol. 2, p. 45.

29. Ibn Athir, *al-Kamil*, Vol. 10, pp. 483–87; *The Damascus Chronicle*, pp. 112–13; Azimi, *Ta'rikh Halab*, p. 365.

30. *The Damascus Chronicle*, pp. 76–78, 91–93, 106, 114–19, 148–53, 159–61, 172–73.

31. *The Travels of Ibn Jubayr*, trans. by R. J. C. Broadhurst (London: Jonathan Cape, 1952), p. 301.

32. Fulcher of Chartres, *A History*, pp. 271–72.

33. Joshua Prawer, *Crusader Institutions* (Oxford: Clarendon Press, 1980), pp. 201–14; Jonathan Riley-Smith, "The Survival in Latin Palestine of Muslim Administration," in P. M. Holt (ed.), *The Eastern Mediterranean Lands in the Period of the Crusades* (Westminster: Aris & Phillips, 1977), pp. 9–22; Benjamin Z. Kedar, "The Subjected Muslims of the Frankish Levant," in James M. Powell (ed.), *Muslims under Latin Rule, 1100–1300* (Princeton: Princeton University Press, 1990), pp. 143–74.

34. *The Damascus Chronicle*, p. 167. See also Umar ibn Adim, *Zubdat al-Halab min Ta'rikh Halab* (Damascus: al-Mash'had al-Faransi bi-Dimashq li-l-Dirasat al-Arabiya, 1951), Vol. 2, pp. 131, 133, 134, 137, 141.

35. *The Travels of Ibn Jubayr*, pp. 315–17, 321–22.

36. P. M. Holt, *The Age of the Crusades: the Near East from the Eleventh Century to 1517* (London: Longman, 1986), p. 38; Michael A. Kohler, *Allianzen und Verträge zwischen fränkischen und islamischen Herrschern im Vorderen Orient: eine Studie über das zwischenstaatliche Zusammenleben vom 12. bis ins 13. Jahrhundert* (Berlin: Walter de Gruyter, 1991), p. 316; Andrew S. Ehrenkreutz, *Saladin* (Albany: State University of New York, 1972), pp. 234–38; Malcolm Cameron Lyons and D. E. P. Jackson, *Saladin: The Politics of Holy War* (Cambridge: Cambridge University Press, 1990), p. 240.

37. See, for example, Sivan, *L'Islam*, pp. 44–49.

38. Hans Eberhard Mayer, *The Crusades* (London: Oxford University Press, 1972), p. 91.

39. Nikita Elisséeff, "The Reaction of the Syrian Muslims after the Foundation of the First Latin Kingdom of Jerusalem," in Madden, *The Crusades*, pp. 229–31; H. A. R. Gibb, "The Career of Nur-ad-Din," in Setton, *A History*, Vol. 1, pp. 513–27.

40. The best example of such pragmatism was perhaps the 1159 alliance with Emperor Manual Comnenus, who for his part viewed Nur al-Din as a useful counterweight to Latin expansion in Syria and to the Seljuk pressure in Anatolia. For general accounts of Nur al-Din's career see Nikita Elisséeff, *Nur ad-Din: un grand prince musulman de Syrie au temps des croisades* (Damascus: Institut Français de Damas, 1967); Hassan Habashi, *Nur al-Din wa-l-Salibiyun* (Cairo: Dar al-Fikr al-Arabi, 1948).

41. Actually, mention of the Abbasid caliph had already been made in the Friday sermon of September 10, two days prior to Adid's death, albeit not on a written order from Saladin. Ibn Athir, *al-Kamil*, Vol. 11, pp. 368–71; Baha al-Din ibn Shaddad, *Min Kitab al-Nawadir al-Sultaniya wa-l-mahasan al-Yusufya: Sirat Salah al-Din al-Ayyubi* (Damascus: Manshurat Wizarat al-Thaqafa wa-l-Irshad al-Qawmi, 1979), p. 53.

42. Ehrenkreutz, *Saladin*, pp. 98–99.

43. Ibn Athir, *al-Kamil*, Vol. 11, pp. 352–53, 371–73, 392–94, 396–98, 402; *A History of the Ayyubid Sultans of Egypt*, trans. from the Arabic of al-Maqrizi, with an introduction and notes by R. J. C. Broadhurst (Boston: Twayne Publishers, 1980), pp. 35–46.

44. Ehrenkreutz, *Saladin*, p. 117.

45. Lyons and Jackson, *Saladin*, p. 245.

46. H. A. R. Gibb, "The Rise of Saladin, 1169–1189," in Setton, *The History*, Vol. 1, p. 569. Gibb takes his cue from Stanley Lane-Poole's classic, *Saladin and the Fall of the Kingdom of Jerusalem* (New York: Putnam, 1898). For the original works of Saladin's "official" biographer see Imad al-Din al-Isfahani, *al-Fath al-Qussi fi-l-fath al-Qudsi* (Cairo: al-Dar al-Qawmiya lil-Tiba'a wa-l-Nashr, 1965); Baha al-Din ibn Shaddad, *al-Nawadir al-Sultaniya*.

47. Maqrizi, *A History*, p. 75.

48. David Abulafia, "Trade and Crusade, 1050–1250," in Michael Goodich, et al (eds.), *Cross-Cultural Convergences in the Crusader Period* (New York: Peter Lang, 1999), pp. 1–20; Andrew S. Ehrenkreutz, "The Crisis of Dinar in the Egypt of Saladin," *Journal of the American Oriental Society*, Vol. 76, No. 3 (July–Sept. 1956), pp. 180–83; David Jacoby, "The Supply of War Materials to Egypt in the Crusader Period," *Jerusalem Studies in Arabic and Islam*, Vol. 25 (2001), pp. 102–29; Charles M. Brand, "The Byzantines and Saladin, 1185–1192: Opponents of the Third Crusade," *Speculum*, Vol. 37, No. 2 (April 1962), pp. 167–70.

49. Ibn Shaddad, *al-Nawadir al-Sultaniya*, pp. 78–79, 82–85.

50. Maqrizi, *A History*, pp. 81–82; Ibn Athir, *al-Kamil*, Vol. 11, pp. 478–79, 502, 529–30, 538.

51. Maqrizi, *A History*, pp. 85–86.

52. Ibid. p. 97; Ibn Athir, *al-Kamil*, Vol. 11, pp. 553–57.

53. Ibn Athir, *al-Kamil*, Vol. 12, pp. 95–96.

54. Lyons and Jackson, *Saladin*, pp. 193–94.

55. Ibn Shaddad, *al-Nawadir al-Sultaniya*, pp. 24–25.

Chapter 5

1. For general surveys of the Ayyubis see: *A History of the Ayyubid Sultans of Egypt*, trans. from the Arabic of al-Maqrizi, with an introduction and notes by R. J. C. Broadhurst (Boston: Twayne Publishers, 1980); Stephen R. Humphreys, *From Saladin to the Mongols: the Ayyubis of Damascus 1193–1260* (Albany: State University of New York, 1977).

2. On the Mamluks see: David Ayalon, *The Mamluk Military Society* (London: Variorum, 1979); Robert Irwin, *The Middle East in the Middle Ages: The Early Mamluk Sultanate 1250–1382* (London: Croom Helm, 1986).

3. Ala-ad-Din Ata-Malik Juvaini, *Genghis Khan: The History of the World Conqueror*, trans. by J. A. Boyle (Manchester: Manchester University Press, 1997), pp. 96–97, 105.

4. For general surveys of Mongol imperialism see: *The Secret History of the Mongols: A Mongolian Epic Chronicle of the Thirteenth Century*, trans. and annotated by Igor de Rachewiltz (Leiden: Brill, 2004); J. J. Saunders, *The History of the Mongol Conquests* (London: Routledge & Kegan Paul, 1971); David O. Morgan, *The Mongols* (Oxford: Basil Blackwell, 1986); Thomas Allsen, *Mongol Imperialism* (Berkeley: University of California Press, 1987).

5. The famous story about this historic episode, which has Mu'tasim locked up in a tower and left to starve amid his gold and silver dishes, is apparently an unfounded extrapolation of Hulagu's conversation with the caliph. See J. A. Boyle, "The Death of the Last Abbasid Caliph," *Journal of Semitic Studies*, Vol. 6, No. 2 (autumn 1961), pp. 145–61.

6. Reuven Amitai-Preiss, *Mongols and Mamluks: The Mamluk-Ilkhanid War, 1260–1281* (Cambridge: Cambridge University Press, 1995); Amitai-Preiss, "Mongol Imperial Ideology and the Ilkhanid War against the Mamluks," in Reuven Amitai-Preiss and David O. Morgan (eds.), *The Mongol Empire and Its Legacy* (Leiden: Brill, 1999), pp. 57–72.

7. J. A. Boyle, "Dynastic and Political History of the Il-Khans," in J. A. Boyle et al (eds.), *The Cambridge History of Iran* (Cambridge: Cambridge University Press, 1968),

pp. 378–80; Charles Melville, "*Padshah-i Islam*: The Conversion of Sultan Mahmud Ghazan Khan," in Melville (ed.), *Persian and Islamic Studies: In Honor of P. W. Avery* (Cambridge: Center for Middle Eastern Studies, 1990), pp. 159–77.

8. Halil Inalcik, *The Ottoman Empire: The Classical Age 1300–1600* (London: Weidenfeld and Nicolson, 1973), pp. 5–8.

9. Halil Inalcik, "The Rise of the Ottoman Empire," in M. A. Cook (ed.), *A History of the Ottoman Empire to 1730* (Cambridge: Cambridge University Press, 1976), pp. 17, 31–40; G. Amakis, "Gregory Palamas among the Turks," *Speculum*, Vol. 26, p. 110.

10. Bernard Lewis, *The Muslim Discovery of Europe* (London: Weidenfeld and Nicolson, 1982), p. 32. The literature on the rise of the Ottoman Empire is immense. See, for example, Herbert Adams Gibbons, *The Foundation of the Ottoman Empire: A History of the Osmanlis up to the Death of Bayezid I, 1300–1403* (Oxford: Clarendon Press, 1916); Paul Wittek, *The Rise of the Ottoman Empire* (1938; London: Royal Asiatic Society of Great Britain and Ireland, rep. 1963); M. Fuad Koprulu, *The Origins of the Ottoman Empire* (Albany: State University of New York, 1992); Colin Imber, *The Ottoman Empire 1300–1481* (Istanbul: Isis Press, 1990); Stanford Shaw, *History of the Ottoman Empire and Modern Turkey. Vol. 1, Empire of the Gazis: The Rise and Decline of the Ottoman Empire, 1280–1808* (Cambridge: Cambridge University Press, 1977).

11. In fairness to Murad, it should be noted that it was Mehmed II who institutionalized the practice whereby upon his accession a sultan murdered his brothers together with his brothers' male offspring as a means of preventing wars of succession. See Norman Itzkowitz, *Ottoman Empire and Islamic Tradition* (Chicago: University of Chicago Press, 1972), p. 31.

12. See, for example, Albert Howe Lybyer, *The Government of the Ottoman Empire in the Time of Suleiman the Great* (Cambridge: Harvard University Press, 1913), pp. 91–97; Alexander Pallis, *In the Days of the Janissaries: Old Turkish Life as Depicted in the "Travel-Book" of Evliya Chelebi* (London: Hutchinson, 1951); Avigdor Levy, "Military Reform and the Problem of Centralization in the Ottoman Empire in the Eighteenth Century," *Middle Eastern Studies*, Vol. 18 (1982), pp. 227–49.

13. For the English text of the treaty, see J. C. Hurewitz (ed.), *The Middle East and North Africa in World Politics* (New Haven: Yale University Press, 2nd edn., 1975), Vol. 2, pp. 92–101.

14. Emile Laloy, *Les Plans de Cathérine II pour la conquête de Constantinople* (Paris: Rahir, 1913); Nicolae Iorga, *Geschichte des Osmanischen Reiches: nach den Quellen dargestellt* (Gotha: Friedrich Andreas Perthes, 1913), Vol. 5, pp. 71–99.

15. For accounts of the 1860 massacres see France, Ministère des Affaires Etrangères, *Documents diplomatiques* (Paris, 1861), Vol. 1, pp. 193–233; François Lenormant, *Histoire des massacres de Syrie en 1860* (Paris: Hachette, 1861); Baptistin Poujoulat, *La vérité sur la Syrie et l'expédition française* (Paris: Gaume Frères et Duprey, 1861); H. H. Jessup, *Fifty-Three Years in Syria* (New York: Fleming H. Revell, 1910), Vol. 1, pp. 157–214; Hussein Ghadhan Abu Shaqra (ed.), *al-Harakat fi-l-Lubnan ila Ahd al-Mutassarrifiya* (Beirut: Matba'at al-Ittihad, n.d.), pp. 99–136; Leila Tarazi Fawaz, *Occasion for War: Civil Conflict in Lebanon and Damascus in 1860* (London: Tauris, 1995).

16. Skene to Bulwer, July 9, 1860, FO 78/1603 (London: Public Record Office; unless otherwise indicated, all British archival source material cited in this book is taken from the PRO).

17. British Foreign Office, "Affairs of Turkey. Crimean War 1854–55. Part 5. Eastern Papers. Communications Respecting Turkey, Made to Her Majesty's Government by the Emperor of Russia with the Answers Returned to Them January to April 1853," Presented to the Houses of Parliament by Command of Her Majesty, 1854.

18. Elie Kedourie, *England and the Middle East: The Destruction of the Ottoman Empire 1914–1921* (London: Bowes & Bowes, 1956), p. 15; Barbara Tuchman, *The Guns of*

August (New York: Dell, 1962), p. 161; Arnold J. Toynbee and Kenneth P. Kirkwood, *Turkey* (London: Ernest Benn, 1926), p. 6. For general surveys of the Eastern Question see J. A. R. Marriott, *The Eastern Question: An Historical Study in European Diplomacy* (Oxford: Clarendon Press, 2nd rev. edn., 1918); M. S. Anderson, *The Eastern Question 1774–1923* (London: Macmillan, 1966); A. L. Macfie, *The Eastern Question 1774–1923* (Essex: Longman, 1989); Edouard Driault, *Question d'Orient depuis ses origines jusqu'à nos jours* (Paris: Felix Alcan, 4th edn., 1909); Albert Sorel, *La Question d'Orient au XVIIIe siècle* (Paris: E. Plon, 1878); Max Choublier, *La Question d'Orient depuis le Traité de Berlin* (Paris: Rousseau, 2nd edn.,1899); Malcolm MacColl, *The Eastern Question: Its Facts and Fallacies* (London: Longmans, Green & Co., 1877).

19. L. Carl Brown, *International Politics and the Middle East* (London: Tauris, 1984), p. 5.

20. For the text of the agreements see Hurewitz, *The Middle East,* Vol. 1, pp. 271–75.

21. The discussion in this section draws on Efraim Karsh and Inari Karsh, *Empires of the Sand: The Struggle for Mastery in the Middle East 1789–1923* (Cambridge: Harvard University Press, 1999), Chapter 5.

22. For discussion of this episode see below pp. 107–08.

23. See, for example, Albert Hourani, *A History of the Arab Peoples* (London: Faber, 1991), p. 283; Ronald Robinson and John Gallagher, with Alice Denny, *Africa and the Victorians: The Official Mind of Imperialism* (London: Macmillan, 2nd edn., 1981), p. 159.

24. Dufferin to Granville, June 24, 1882, FO 78/3397, No. 168; Granville to Dufferin, June 25, 1882, FO 78/3395, No. 302; Dudley W. R. Bahlman (ed.), *The Diary of Sir Edward Walter Hamilton, 1880–1885* (Oxford: Clarendon Press, 1972), Vol. 1, pp. 208, 212, 297.

25. Gladstone to Granville, July 13, 1882, PRO 30–29/126; *Hamilton Diary,* p. 306.

26. Granville's dispatch to Dufferin, CAB 37/9, p. 15; A. J. P. Taylor, *The Struggle for Mastery in Europe, 1848–1918* (New York: Oxford University Press, 1971), p. 90.

27. Grey to Erskine, Aug. 20, 1914, FO 371/2138/42268; Grey to Beaumont, Aug. 7, 1914, "Correspondence Respecting Events Leading to the Rupture of Relations with Turkey, Presented to Both Houses of Parliament by Command of His Majesty, Nov. 1914, Cmd. 7628," No. 5, p. 2 (hereafter—Cmd. 7628); Churchill to Enver, Aug. 15, 1914, Martin Gilbert, *Winston S. Churchill* (London: Heinemann, 1972), Companion Vol. 3, Part 1, p. 38.

28. Grey to Beaumont, Aug. 16, 1914, Cmd 7628, No. 17, p. 5; Grey to Mallet, Aug. 18, 1914, ibid., No. 21, p. 7; Mallet to Grey, Aug. 21, 1914, ibid., No. 27, p. 9; Sazonov to Giers, Aug. 23, 1914, in *Ministère des Affaires Étrangères: recueil de documents diplomatiques, négociations ayant précédé la guerre avec la Turquie 19 juillet (1 août)–19 octobre (1 novembre) 1914* (Pétrograd, 1915), No. 34.

29. Intercepted ciphered telegrams from Enver Pasha, July 10, 15, 26, 27, 1914. Sent by the political resident in the Persian Gulf (Major S. G. Knox) to the foreign secretary to the government of India in the foreign and political dept., Simla, on Sept. 26 and Oct. 1, 1914, FO 371/2144/64214.

30. For the making of the Ottoman-German alliance see: Wangenheim to Foreign Office, July 21, 22, 1914, Karl Kautsky (ed.), *Die Deutschen Dokumente zum Kriegsausbruch* (Charlottenburg: Deutsche Verlagsgesellschaft für Politics und Geschichte m.b.h., 1919), Vol. 1, No. 99, p. 123 and No. 117, pp. 134–36; the Kaiser's comments on Wangenheim's report of July 23, 1914, ibid., No. 149, pp. 162–63; Jagow to Wangenheim, July 24, 1914, ibid., Vol. 1, No. 144, p. 158; Count Wedel (Minister in the Imperial Suite) to Foreign Office, July 24, 1914, ibid., No. 141, p. 158; Wangenheim to Foreign Office, July 28, 1914, ibid., Vol. 2, no. 285, p. 7; Wangenheim to Foreign Office, 30 July 1914, ibid., No. 411; Admiral Alfred P. Tirpitz, *My Memoirs* (London: Hurst & Blacket, 1919), Vol. 2, pp. 80–83.

31. Sazonov to Benckendorff, Nov. 1, 1914, FO 371/2145/66389; Grey to Mallet, Oct. 30, 1914, Cmd. 7628, No. 179, p. 72; Gilbert, *Churchill,* Vol. 3, p. 216.

32. Arnold J. Toynbee, *Turkey: A Past and a Future* (New York: George H. Dorn, 1917), pp. 28–29.

Chapter 6

1. For this received wisdom see: Elie Kedourie, *Politics in the Middle East* (Oxford: Oxford University Press, 1992), p. 93; Malcolm Yapp, *The Making of the Modern Middle East 1792–1923* (London: Longman, 1987), p. 266; Feroz Ahmad, "The Late Ottoman Empire," in Marian Kent (ed.), *The Great Powers and the End of the Ottoman Empire* (London: Cass, 1996), pp. 15–16; David Fromkin, *A Peace to End All Peace: The Fall of the Ottoman Empire and the Creation of the Modern Middle East* (New York: Avon, 1989), pp. 48–50; Y. T. Kurat, "How Turkey Drifted into World War I," in K. Bourne and D. C. Watt (eds.), *Studies in International Diplomacy* (London: Longman, 1967), p. 297; Ahmed Emin, *Turkey in the World War* (New Haven: Yale University Press, 1930); Feroz Ahmad, *The Young Turks: The Committee of Union and Progress in Turkish Politics, 1908–1914* (Oxford: Clarendon Press, 1969); Frank G. Weber, *Eagles on the Crescent: Germany, Austria, and the Diplomacy of the Turkish Alliance 1914–1918* (Ithaca: Cornell University Press, 1970).

2. Robert D. Kaplan, "At the Gates of Brussels," *Atlantic Monthly*, Dec. 2004 (internet edn.).

3. Edward Said, "My Right of Return," interview with *Ha'aretz Magazine*, Aug. 18, 2000; Moustafa Bayoumi and Andrew Rubin (eds.), *The Edward Said Reader* (London: Granta Books, 2001), p. 430.

4. See (Russia's) Foreign Secretary Nesselrode's instructions to the ambassador in Constantinople, Feb. 23/March 7, 1821, in Ministerstvo inostrannykh del SSSR, *Vneshniaia politika Rossii XIX i nachala XX veka: dokumenty rossiiskogo ministerstva inostrannykh del* (Moscow: Nauka, 1980), Ser. 2, Vol. 7, pp. 36–38; Russian Circular No. 8, March 18/30, 1821, in Barbara Jelavich, *Russia and Greece during the Regency of King Othon 1832–1835: Russian Documents on the First Years of Greek Independence* (Tessalonika: Institute of Balkan Studies, 1962), Appendix I, pp. 123–24. For the Greek national awakening see, for example, Richard Clogg, *The Movement for Greek Independence, 1770–1821* (London: Macmillan, 1976); Douglas Dakin, *The Greek Struggle for Independence, 1821–1833* (London: B. T. Batsford, 1973).

5. PRO, Proclamation addressed to the Janissary Aghas on May 8, 1821, FO 78/98.

6. Stratford to Castlereagh, May 1, 1821, encl. in FO 78/98; Stratford to Londonderry, June 12, 1821, FO 78/99/46; Russian despatch, June 22/July 4, 1821, in Jelavich, *Russia and Greece*, Appendix. II, pp. 124–28.

7. For the text of the London Protocol see Thomas Erskine Holland (ed.), *The European Concert in the Eastern Question: A Collection of Treaties and Other Public Acts* (Oxford: Clarendon Press, 1885), Text I.

8. Holmes to Elliot, Sept. 28, 1875, encl. in No. 32, in Great Britain, Foreign Office, "Turkey, No. 2 (1876), Bosnia and Herzegovina. Correspondence Respecting Affairs in the Bosnia and Herzegovina"; hereafter "Turkey, No. 2 (1876)."

9. For Ottoman attempts to crush the uprising see Safvet Pasha to Musurus Pasha, Aug. 9, 1875, doc. 10; Safvet Pasha to Musurus Pasha, Aug. 22, 1875, doc. 15; proclamation by Server Pasha in Holmes to Derby, encl. 2 in No. 28; promulgation of reforms by Sultan Abdul Hamid on Oct. 3, 1875, encl. in No. 29; Holmes to Elliot, Sept. 28, 1875, encl. in No. 32; Reshid Pasha to Musurus Pasha, No. 54; Règlement respecting the functions of the executive council, No. 61, all in Turkey, No. 2 (1876).

10. The discussion of the Armenian genocide draws on Efraim Karsh and Inari Karsh, *Empires of the Sand: The Struggle for Mastery in the Middle East 1789–1923* (Cambridge: Harvard University Press, 1999), Chapter 10.

11. For population figures see, for example, Mallet to Grey, Oct. 7, 1914, FO 371/2137/56940; "Turkey: Annual Report, 1913. By the Embassy," FO 371/2137/79138, p. 25.

12. See Fontana to Lowther, March 25, 1913, FO 371/1773/16941; Lowther to Grey, April 5, 10, 1913, FO 371/1773/16736; Admiralty to FO, April 15, 1913, FO 371/1775/17825.

13. Ironside to Foreign Office, March 3, 1915, and War Office to the Foreign Office, March 4, 1915, FO 371/2484/25073 and 25167; Foreign Office to Ironside, March 9, 1915, FO 371/2484/28172 and 22083.

14. The polemical literature on this issue is immense. See, for example, Talaat Pasha, "Posthumous Memoirs of Talaat Pasha," *New York Times Current History*, Vol. 15, No. 2 (Nov. 1921); *Vérité sur le mouvement révolutionnaire arménien et les mesures gouvernementales* (Constantinople, n.p., 1916); *Aspirations et agissements révolutionnaires des comités arméniens avant et après la proclamation de la constitution ottomane* (Constantinople, n.p., 1917); Ahmed Rustem Bey, *The World War and the Turco-Armenian Question* (Berne: Staempfli & Co., 1915); Kamuran Gürün, *The Armenian File: The Myth of Innocence Exposed* (London: K. Rustem & Weidenfeld and Nicolson, 1985).
    Some Western scholars have accepted the Turkish apologia at face value. See, for example, Stanford J. Shaw and Ezel Kural Shaw, *History of the Ottoman Empire and Modern Turkey: Vol. II: Reform, Revolution, and Republic: The Rise of Modern Turkey, 1808–1975* (Cambridge: Cambridge University Press, 1977), p. 315; Bernard Lewis, interview with *Le Monde*, Nov. 16, 1993. Interestingly enough, in the first and second editions of his book *The Emergence of Modern Turkey* (Oxford: Oxford University Press, 1961 and 1968), Lewis described these tragic events as "the terrible holocaust of 1915, when a million and half Armenians perished," p. 356.
    For the opposite approach see, for example, Haigazn Kazarian, "The Turkish Genocide," *Armenian Review*, Vol. 30 (spring 1977); Richard G. Hovannisian (ed.), *The Armenian Genocide in Perspective* (New Brunswick: Transaction Books, 1987); Hovannisian (ed.), *The Armenian Genocide: History, Politics, Ethics* (London: Macmillan, 1992); The Permanent Peoples' Tribunal, *A Crime of Silence: The Armenian Genocide* (London: Zed Books, 1985); Navasard Derymenjian, "An Important Turkish Document on the 'Exterminate Armenians' Plan," *Armenian Review*, Vol. 14 (1961), pp. 53–55; William Yale, *The Near East: A Modern History* (Ann Arbor: University of Michigan Press, 1958), pp. 230–31.

15. Viscount Bryce, *The Treatment of Armenians in the Ottoman Empire: Documents Presented to Viscount Grey of Fallodon, Secretary of State for Foreign Affairs. Laid Before the Houses of Parliament as an Official Paper and Now Published by Permission* (London: Hodder and Stoughton, 1916), pp. 645–49.

16. Ibid., pp. 641–42; Johannes Lepsius, *Der Todesgang des armenischen Volkes* (Potsdam: Missionshandlung und Verlag, 1930), pp. 301–04.

17. Bryce, *The Treatment of Armenians*, pp. 649–51; "Annex F: Statistical Estimate Included in the Fifth Bulletin of the American Committee for Armenian and Syrian Relief, Dated New York, 24th May 1916," ibid., pp. YY2; Johannes Lepsius, *Deutschland und Armenien, 1914–1918* (Potsdam: Tempelverlag, 1919), pp. lxv, 256; Lepsius, *Der Todesgang*, pp. 301–04; Aaron Aaronsohn, "Pro Armenia," Nov. 16, 1916, p. 13, Aaronsohn Archives (Zichron Yaacov, Israel), File 2C/13; Aaronsohn, "On the Armenian Massacres: Memorandum Presented to the War Office, London, November 1916," Aaronsohn Archives, File 2C/14.

Chapter 7

1. Roger Savory, *Iran under the Safavids* (Cambridge: Cambridge University Press, 1980); Rula Jurdi Abisaab, *Converting Persia: Religion and Power in the Safavid Empire*

(London: Tauris, 2004); Laurence Lockhart, *The Fall of the Safavi Dynasty and the Afghan Occupation of Persia* (Cambridge: Cambridge University Press, 1958).

2. Hamid Algar, *Religion and State in Iran 1785–1906: The Role of Ulama in the Qajar Period* (Berkeley: University of California Press, 1969); Said Amir Arjomand, *The Turban for the Crown: The Islamic Revolution in Iran* (New York: Oxford University Press, 1988), pp. 12–15.

3. Ahmad Tajbakhsh, *Siyasathayi Ist'mari-i Rusiyah-i Tizari, Inglistan va Faransah dar Iran: Nimah-i Avval-i Qarn-i Nuzdahum* (Tehran: Iqbal, 1983); A. V. *Fadeev, Rossia i Kavkaz, Pervoi Ttreti XIX v.* (Moscow: Akademi Nauk U.S.S.R., 1960); Muriel Atkin, *Russia and Iran 1780–1828* (Minneapolis: University of Minnesota Press, 1980), Chapters 2–4.

4. See, for example, Abbas Mirza to His Majesty the King, as translated in the enclosure of Ouseley to Wellesley, June 1, 1812, FO 60/6, No.15 (p. 168).

5. See Marquis Wellesley to the Secret Committee of the Honourable the Court of Directors, "Persian Embassy and Treaty, and advantages thus secured. Why an European ambassador, in state, was required," Sept. 28, 1801, in Sidney J. Owen (ed.), *A Selection from the Despatches, Treaties and Other Papers of the Marquess Wellesley, during his Government of India* (Oxford: Clarendon Press, 1877), pp. 607–08.

6. For the text of the treaty, see J. C. Hurewitz (ed.), *The Middle East and North Africa in World Politics* (New Haven: Yale University Press, 2nd ed., 1975), Vol. 1, pp. 68–70.

7. See, for example, Warren to Hawkesbury, Feb. 17, 1804, FO 65/54.

8. Bonaparte, Empereur des Français à Feth Ali, Schah des Persans, 16 février et 30 mars, 1805, in *Correspondance de Napoleon I, publiée par ordre de l'empereur Napoleon III* (Paris: Henri Plon, 1858–70), Vol. 10, pp. 184–86, 342–44, 362–63; Napoléon au Schah de Perse, 20 avril et 5 mai 1807, ibid., Vol. 15, pp. 73–76, 148–49, 237–38. For the text of the treaty see Hurewitz, *The Middle East*, Vol. 1, pp. 184–85.

9. For the text of the agreements see: C. U. Aitchison (ed.), *A Collection of Treaties, Engagements, and Sanads Relating to India and Neighboring Countries* (Calcutta: Government of India, 1933), Vol. 12, pp. 45–46, 48–53; Hurewitz, *The Middle East*, Vol. 1, pp. 199–201.

10. Ouseley to Castlereagh, Jan. 16, 1813, FO 60/8; Fath Ali Shah to His Majesty the King, May 1812, FO 60/6, p. 170.

11. For the official text of the treaties see FO 60/553; Hurewitz, *The Middle East*, Vol. 1, pp. 197–99.

12. The Marquis of Salisbury to Sir Henry Drummond Wolff, No. 14, Feb. 29, 1888, FO 60/491. For the text of the proposed treaty see "Draft Convention between Her Majesty and the Shah of Persia, most secret," undated, FO 65/1097.

13. Salisbury to Wolff, Feb. 29, 1888, FO 60/491; Treaty series 14B. Persia, FO 93/75/14B, Oct. 24, 1888.

14. See "Correspondence respecting the Reuter and Falkenhagen Concessions 1872–75," FO 539/10.

15. Peter Avery, *Modern Iran* (London: Benn, 1965), p. 100. See also *Asnad-i Siyasi-yi Dawran-i Qajariyya*, compiled and ed. by Ibrahim Safa'i (Tehran: Sharq Press, 1967–68); Shaul Bakhash, *Iran: Monarchy, Bureaucracy, and Reform under the Qajars: 1858–1896* (London: Ithaca, 1978); Firuz Kazemzadeh, *Russia and Britain in Persia 1864–1914: A Study in Imperialism* (New Haven: Yale University Press, 1968); George N. Curzon, *Persia and the Persian Question* (London: Longman, 1892).

16. For the text of the tobacco concession see Wolff to Salisbury, April 3, 1890, FO 539/60, No. 3 (104). See also FO 60/553; Acting Consul-General Robert Paton to Kennedy, Aug. 19, 1891, FO 60/553, No. 202.

17. For the Régie crisis and its aftermath see Nikki R. Keddie, *Religion and Rebellion in Iran: The Tobacco Protest of 1891–1892* (London: Cass, 1966); Jean-Baptiste Feuvrier,

Trois ans à la cour de Perse (Paris: Imprimerie Nationale, 1906); Edward G. Browne, *The Persian Revolution of 1905–1909* (Cambridge: Cambridge University Press, 1910).

18. T. H. Sanderson to R. W. Grosvenor, March 11, 1892, FO 60/555.

19. Lascelles to Rosebery, Jan. 26, 1894, FO 65/1484, No. 22 and Feb. 11, 1894, FO 65/1484, No. 42; Greene to the Earl of Kimberley, March 13, 1894, FO 65/1485, No. 67; Lascelles to Rosebery, Jan. 20, 1894, FO 65/1484, No. 18.

20. A. Hardinge to Lansdowne, Dec. 30, 1902, FO 60/600, No. 183.

21. The Bahai faith was established by Mirza Ali Muhammad (1819–50), a merchant from the Iranian city of Shiraz who claimed to be the Hidden Imam, whose return had been anticipated by Twelver Shiites since the ninth century, and a new manifestation of God. He was summarily executed, but his ideas were developed to a full fledged religion by one of his disciples, Mirza Hussein Ali (1817–92), who styled himself Baha'ullah ("Glory of God")—the messenger foretold by Ali Muhammad.

22. E. Eldred to Hardinge, enclosure in Hardinge to Landsowne, FO 60/666, No. 102.

23. Hardinge to Lansdowne, April 27, 1903, FO 60/665, No. 64.

24. Nikki R. Keddie, "The Assassination of Amin as Sultan (Atabak-i Azam) 31 August 1907," in C. E. Bosworth (ed.), *Iran and Islam* (Edinburgh: Edinburgh University Press, 1971), pp. 315–30; Gad Gilbar, "The Big Merchants (*tujjar*) and the Constitutional Movement of 1906," *Asian and African Studies*, Vol. 11 (1977), pp. 275–303; V. A. Martin, "The Anti-Constitutional Arguments of Shaikh Fazlallah Nuri," *Middle Eastern Studies*, Vol. 22, No. 2 (April 1986), pp. 181–91; Ahmed Kasravi, *Tarikh-e Mashruteh-e Iran* (Tehran: Ahmed Kabir, 1984); Fereidun Adamiyat, *Ideolozhi-ye Nehzat-e Mashrute'h Iran* (Tehran: Payam, 1976); Djafar Shafiei-Nasab, *Les Mouvements révolutionnaires et la constitution de 1906 en Iran* (Berlin: Klaus Schwarz, 1991); Ervand Abrahamian, "The Causes of the Constitutional Revolution in Iran," *International Journal of Middle East Studies*, Vol. 10 (August 1979), pp. 318–414; Edward G. Browne, *The Persian Revolution of 1905–1909* (Cambridge: Cambridge University Press, 1910); Ann K. S. Lambton, "Secret Societies and the Persian Revolution of 1905–06," in Albert Hourani (ed.), *Middle Eastern Affairs*, No. 1, St. Antony's Papers, No. 4 (1959), pp. 43–61; Lambton, "Persian Political Societies 1906–1911," in Albert Hourani (ed.), *Middle Eastern Affairs*, No. 3, St. Antony's Papers, No. 16 (1963), pp. 41–98.

25. Said Amir Arjomand, "The Ulama's Traditionalist Opposition to Parliamentarianism: 1907–1909," *Middle Eastern Studies*, Vol. 17, No. 2 (April 1981), pp. 174–90; Spring-Rice to Grey, June 13, 1907, FO 416/33/22389; Eugène de Schelking, *Recollections of a Russian Diplomat* (New York: Macmillan, 1918), p. 240.

26. Spring-Rice to Grey, June 13, 1907, FO 416/33/22389.

27. Viscount Grey of Fallodon, *Twenty-Five Years, 1892–1916* (New York: Frederick Stokes, 1925), Vol. 1, pp. 243–44, 246.

28. Hurewitz, *The Middle East*, Vol. 1, pp. 538–40.

29. Grey, *Twenty-Five Years*, Vol. 1, p. 254.

Chapter 8

1. "Report of the Committee on Asiatic Turkey," June 30, 1915, CAB 27/1, pp. 4, 29.

2. "Correspondence between Sir Henry McMahon, His Majesty's High Commissioner at Cairo, and the Sherif of Mecca July 1915–March 1916, presented by the Secretary of State for Foreign Affairs to Parliament by Command of His Majesty," Cmd. 5957, London, 1939, p. 3 (hereafter "Hussein-McMahon Correspondence").

3. "Intelligence Report," Dec. 28, 1916, FO 686/6, p. 176; *Arab Bulletin*, June 23, 1916, p. 47 and Feb. 6, 1917, pp. 57–58, FO 882/25; McMahon to Grey, Oct. 20, 1915, FO 371/2486/154423.

4. Eliezer Tauber, *The Emergence of the Arab Movements* (London: Frank Cass, 1993), Chapter 28.

5. T. E. Lawrence, "Syria: the Raw Material" (written early in 1915 but not circulated), *Arab Bulletin*, No. 44, March 12, 1917, FO/882/26.

6. David Hogarth, "Mission to King Hussein," *Arab Bulletin*, Jan. 27, 1918, pp. 22–23.

7. Lawrence, July 30, 1917, FO 686/8; Mark Sykes, "Notes on Conversations with the Emirs Abdullah and Faisal," May 1, 1917, FO 882/16, p. 233.

8. Hussein-McMahon Correspondence, p. 10; Munib Madi and Suleiman Musa, *Ta'rikh al-Urdunn fi-l-Qarn al-Ishrin* (Amman: Maktabat al-Muhtasab, 1959), pp. 132–36.

9. McMahon's letter of Dec. 14, 1915, in Hussein-McMahon Correspondence, p. 12. See also his letter from Jan. 25, 1916: "We are greatly pleased to hear of the action you are taking to win all the Arabs over to our joint cause, and to dissuade them from giving any assistance to our enemies." Ibid., p. 14.

10. This claim has been almost universally accepted by Arab and Western historians. See, for example, George Antonius, *The Arab Awakening* (London: Hamish Hamilton, 1938); Arnold Toynbee, "The Present Situation in Palestine," *International Affairs*, Jan. 1931, p. 40; Amin Said, *al-Thawra al-Arabiya al-Kubra* (Cairo: Isa al-Babi al-Halabi, 1951); Suleiman Musa, *al-Haraka al-Arabiya: Sirat al-Marhala al-Ula li-l-Nahda al-Arabiya al-Haditha, 1908–1924* (Beirut: Dar al-Nahar, 1970); Abu Khaldun Sati al-Husri, *Yawm Maisalun: Safha min Tarikh al-Arab al-Hadith* (Beirut: Dar al-Ittihad, 1964); Zeine N. Zeine, *The Emergence of Arab Nationalism with a Background Study of Arab-Turkish Relations in the Near East* (Beirut: Khayat's, 2nd. rev. edn., 1966); Zaki Hazem Nuseibeh, *The Ideas of Arab Nationalism* (Ithaca: Cornell University Press, 1956).

   For criticism of this approach see Elie Kedourie, *England and the Middle East: The Destruction of the Ottoman Empire 1914–1921* (London: Bowes & Bowes, 1956); Efraim Karsh and Inari Karsh, *Empires of the Sand: The Struggle for Mastery in the Middle East 1789–1923* (Cambridge: Harvard University Press, 1999).

11. Abu Khaldun Sati al-Husri, *al-Uruba Awalan* (Beirut: Dar al-Ilm li-l-Malain, 1955), pp. 11–13; Walid Khalidi, "Thinking the Unthinkable: A Sovereign Palestinian State," *Foreign Affairs*, July 1978, pp. 695–96; Hisham Sharabi, *Nationalism and Revolution in the Arab World* (New York: Van Nostrand Reinhold, 1966), pp. 3–4.

12. General Nuri al-Said, *Arab Independence and Unity: A Note on the Arab Cause with Particular Reference to Palestine, and Suggestions for a Permanent Settlement to Which Are Attached Texts of All the Relevant Documents* (Baghdad: Government Press, 1943), p. 8.

13. *Baghdad Radio*, Aug. 8, 1990; *Iraqi News Agency*, Aug. 28, 1990.

14. Abu Khaldun [Sati] al-Husri, review of Anthony Nutting's *Nasser*, *Journal of Palestine Studies*, winter 1972, p. 135.

15. Yusuf Haikal, *Filastin Qabla wa-Ba'd* (Beirut: Dar al-Ilm li-l-Malain, 1971), pp. 20–41; Sylvia G. Haim (ed.), *Arab Nationalism: An Anthology* (Berkeley: University of California Press, 1964), p. 36.

16. Abdel Rahman Kawakibi, *Umm al-Qura* (Aleppo: al-Matba'a al-Asriya, 1959), pp. 29–30.

17. Husri, *al-Uruba Awalan*, p. 12; Husri, *Ara wa-Ahadith fi-l-Qawmiya al-Arabiya* (Cairo: Maktabat, al-Khanji, 1951), p. 107.

18. Haim, *Arab Nationalism*, pp. 57, 64; Edward W. Said, *Peace and Its Discontents* (New York: Vintage, 1996), p. 79.

19. Quoted in Walter Laqueur, *Nasser's Egypt* (London: Weidenfeld and Nicolson, 1956), p. 23.

20. *President Gamal Abdel Nasser on Colonialism* (Cairo: Ministry of Information, 1963), p. 37.

21. Aharon Cohen, *Israel and the Arab World* (London: W. H. Allen, 1970), p. 381.

22. According to contemporary British and German sources. See, for example, E. C. Blech (Jerusalem) to Sir Nicholas O'Conor, Nov. 16, 1907, FO 371/356/40321. The Arabic-

speaking population of Palestine at the time was estimated at between 600,000 and 700,000. Arthur Ruppin, the head of the Zionist Palestine Office, estimated the Jewish population at the outbreak of the war at the lower figure of 85,000. See Ruppin, *The Jews in the Modern World* (London: Macmillan, 1934), pp. 55, 389. Yet, in his address to the Eleventh Zionist Congress in September 1913, Ruppin subscribed to the 100,000 figure.

23. Colonel Richard Meinertzhagen, *Middle East Diary, 1917–1956* (London: Crescent Press, 1959), p. 7; "Report on the Existing Political Condition in Palestine and Contiguous Areas", by the Political Officer in Charge of the Zionist Commission, Aug. 27, 1918, FO 371/3395/147225, p. 5 (231).

24. Hussein's letter of Nov. 5, 1915, Hussein-McMahon Correspondence, p. 8; McMahon's letter of Dec. 14, 1915, ibid., pp. 11–12; CO 732/3, fol. 366. For elaborate discussion of this dispute, see Karsh and Karsh, *Empires of the Sand*, Chapter 15.

25. "Secretary's Notes of a Conversation Held in M. Pichon's Room at the Quai d'Orsay, Paris, on Thursday, 6 February 1919, at 3 p.m." *Foreign Relations of the United States–Peace Conference*, Vol. 3, pp. 889, 890, 892 (hereafter FRUS).

26. Walter Laqueur (ed.), *The Israel-Arab Reader* (Harmondsworth: Penguin, 1970), p. 37.

27. Said, *Arab Independence and Unity*, p. 11.

28. Golda Meir's verbal report to the Provisional State Council on May 12, 1948, Israel State Archives, *Provisional State Council: Protocols, 18 April–13 May 1948* (Jerusalem, 1978), p. 40.

29. Haza al-Majali, *Mudhakkirati* (Amman: n.p., 1960), pp. 63–64.

30. Hearing before the Anglo-American Committee of Inquiry, Washington, D.C., State Department, Jan. 11, 1946, Central Zionist Archive (Jerusalem), V/9960/g, pp. 5–6.

31. *New York Times*, Aug. 25, 1947 and Jan. 19, 1948; *Damascus Radio*, March 8, 1974.

32. "Fortnightly Intelligence Newsletter No. 57, issued by HQ British Troops in Palestine for the period 6 Dec–18 Dec 1947," WO 275/64, p. 2.

33. John Laffin, *The PLO Connections* (London: Corgi Books, 1983), p. 127.

34. Hagana Archives (HA), 105/257.

35. HA 105/114, p. 24; HA 105/215, pp. 19, 25, 51, 101; HA 105/143, p. 174; HA 105/257; American Consulate (Port Said) to Department of State, April 29, 1948, RG 84, 800—Refugees.

36. Sir J. Troutbeck, "Summary of general impressions gathered during week-end visit to the Gaza district," June 16, 1949, FO 371/75342/E7816, p. 123.

37. David Hogarth, "Mission to King Hussein."

38. Gerard Lowther (Istanbul) to Grey (London), July 28, 1910, FO 371/1007, doc. 433; Elie Kedourie, *Arabic Political Memoirs and Other Studies* (London: Frank Cass, 1974), pp. 107–09; Sami Dahhan, *Abdel Rahman Kawakibi 1854–1902* (Cairo: n.p., 1955); Ahmad Shafiq, *Mudhakarati fi Nisf Qarn* (Cairo: Matbaat al-Misr, 1936), Vol. 2, Part 2, pp. 269–70.

39. Kawakibi, *Umm al-Qura*, pp. 212–14.

40. "Secretary's Notes of a Conversation Held in M. Pichon's Room"; "Memorandum by the Emir Feisal, Jan. 1, 1919," FO 608/80.

41. Zeine N. Zeine, *The Struggle for Arab Independence* (Beirut: Khayat's, 1960), p. 50.

Chapter 9

1. Negib Azury, *Le Réveil de la Nation Arabe dans l'Asie Turque* (Paris: Libraire Plon, 1905), p. 246; Daniel Pipes, *In the Path of God: Islam and Political Power* (New York: Basic Books, 1983), p. 59.

2. Sylvia G. Haim (ed.), *Arab Nationalism: An Anthology* (Berkeley: University of California Press, 1964), pp. 46–47.

3. Yehoshua Porath, *In Search of Arab Unity 1930–1945* (London: Cass, 1986), p. 158.

4. For the background to the 1952 putsch see Ahmad Hamrush, *Thawrat 23 Yulyu* (Cairo: al-Hai'a al-Misriya al-Amma li-l-Kitab, 1992), Vol. 1, pp. 127–74.

5. *Qala al-Rais: Majmuat Khutub wa-Ahadith al-Rais Gamal Abdel Nasser* (Cairo: Dar al-Hilal, 1958), pp. 130–31.

6. Mohamed H. Heikal, *Cutting the Lion's Tail: Suez through Egyptian Eyes* (London: Corgi, 1986), p. 44; Joachim Joesten, *Nasser: The Rise to Power* (London: Oldhams Press, 1960), p. 115.

7. Miles Copeland, *The Games of Nations* (London: Weidenfeld and Nicolson, 1970), pp. 163–64 (emphasis in the original).

8. Ibid., pp. 56–57; Nejla Abu Izzedin, *Nasser of the Arabs: An Arab Assessment* (London: Third World Centre, 1981), p. 327; Jean Lacouture, *Nasser: A Biography* (New York: Knopf, 1973), pp. 190, 386.

9. Yeroham Cohen, *Leor Hayom Uvamahshah* (Tel Aviv: Amikam, 1969), pp. 212–13.

10. Gamal Abdel Nasser, *Egypt's Liberation: The Philosophy of the Revolution* (Washington, D.C.: Public Affairs Press, 1955), p. 24.

11. Copeland, *The Games of Nations,* p. 56.

12. Gamal Abdel Nasser, *Filastin* (Cairo: Maslahat al-Isti'lamat, 1964), p. 11.

13. "President Gamal Abdel Nasser's Speech at the Inaugural Session of the Second Afro-Asian Economic Conference Held at the Chamber of Commerce Headquarters in Cairo, Apr. 30, 1960," *President Gamal Abdel Nasser on Colonialism* (Cairo: Information Department Press, 1964), p. 36.

14. Bernard Lewis, *Semites and Anti-Semites* (London: Weidenfeld and Nicolson, 1986), pp. 208–09.

15. Peter Mansfield, *Nasser's Egypt* (Baltimore: Penguin, 1965), p. 54.

16. Lacouture, *Nasser,* pp. 183–84.

17. Keith Wheelock, *Nasser's Egypt: A Critical Analysis* (New York: Praeger, 1960), pp. 251–52; Robert St. John, *The Boss: The Story of Gamal Abdel Nasser* (New York: McGraw Hill, 1960), p. 275.

18. Nasser, *The Philosophy,* pp. 106, 108–09.

19. Taha Riyad (ed.), *Mahadir Mubahathat al-Wahda* (Cairo: al-Ahram, 1963), p. 244.

20. Hans E. Tutsch, *Facets of Arab Nationalism* (Detroit: Wayne University Press, 1965), p. 59.

21. BBC, *Survey of World Broadcasts* (hereafter SWB), June 4 and July 21, 1954.

22. P. J. Vatikiotis, *Nasser and His Generation* (London: Croom Helm, 1978), pp. 54, 60, 73.

23. Joesten, *Nasser,* p. 179; St. John, *The Boss,* p. 285.

24. Nasser, *The Philosophy,* pp. 86–87.

25. *Look Magazine,* June 14, 1957.

26. *New York Times,* April 4, 1955. See also Ahmad Abul Fath, *L'Affaire Nasser* (Paris: Plon, 1962), pp. 239–40.

27. Wheelock, *Nasser's Egypt,* pp. 220, 266–68.

28. Patrick Seale, *The Struggle for Syria* (1965; London: Tauris, 1986), p. 225.

29. *Middle East News Agency* (Cairo; hereafter MENA), Aug. 6, 1955.

30. Tom Little, *Modern Egypt* (London: Ernest Benn, 1967), pp. 192–93; St. John, *The Boss,* p. 276; James Jankowski, *Nasser's Egypt: Arab Nationalism and the United Arab Republic* (Boulder: Lynne Reinner, 2002), pp. 120–21.

31. *Akhar Sa'a,* March 12, 1958, as quoted in Wheelock, *Nasser's New Egypt,* p. 262.

32. Jankowski, *Nasser's Egypt,* p. 169.

33. *Majmu'at Khutub wa-Tasrihat wa-Bayanat al-Rais Gamal Abdel Nasser* (Cairo: Ministry of National Guidance, n.d.), Vol. 3, p. 550.

34. *President Gamal Abdel Nasser's Pre-Election Speeches in Asiut, Minia, Shebin el Kom, Mansura* (Cairo: Information Ministry, 1965), pp. 28–29, 68.

35. Anwar Sadat, *In Search of Identity: An Autobiography* (New York: Harper & Row, 1978), pp. 171-72; *al-Ahram*, May 23, 1967.

36. Muhammad Fawzi, *Harb al-Thalath Sanawat, 1967-1970* (Cairo: Dar al-Mustaqbal al-Arabi, 1980), pp. 71-72.

37. Abdel Muhsin Kamel Murtagi, *al-Fariq Murtagi Yarwi al-Haqa'iq: Qaid Jabhat Sinai fi Harb 1967* (Cairo: Dar al-Watan al-Arabi, 1976), p. 64; Indar Jit Rikhye, *The Sinai Blunder* (London: Cass, 1980), pp. 11-12.

38. On three occasions the Soviet ambassador to Israel was invited by the Israeli authorities to visit the border area, but declined to go. Sydney D. Bailey, *Four Arab-Israeli Wars and the Peace Process* (London: Macmillan, 1990), p. 190.

39. Sadat, *In Search of Identity*, p. 172. Heikal, who also participated in the meeting, essentially confirmed Sadat's description, though he argued that Nasser estimated the risk of war after the closure of the straits at 50 percent. Another participant corroborating Sadat's account of the meeting was Zakaria Muhieddin, second vice-president in 1967. See: Muhammad Hassanein Heikal, *1967: al-Infijar* (Cairo: al-Ahram, 1990), pp. 514-19; Richard B. Parker, "The June War: Some Mysteries Explored," *Middle East Journal*, Vol. 46, No. 2 (spring 1992), p. 192.

40. Nasser's speech on the anniversary of the Egyptian revolution, July 23, 1967, in Walter Laqueur (ed.), *The Israel-Arab Reader* (Harmondsworth: Penguin, 1970), p. 248.

41. *New York Times*, May 27 and 30, 1967.

42. Ibid. May 27, 1967; Abdel Latif Baghdadi, *Mudhakirat* (Cairo: al-Maktab al-Misri al-Hadith, 1977), Vol. 2, p. 271; *al-Usbu* (Cairo), Jan. 24, 1976.

43. Nasser's speech to Arab trade unionists, May 26, 1967, in Laqueur, *The Israel-Arab Reader*, pp. 215-18.

44. Samir A. Mutawi, *Jordan in the 1967 War* (Cambridge: Cambridge University Press, 1987), pp. 11-12; Moshe Dayan, *Story of My Life* (London: Sphere Books, 1978), p. 314.

45. Rikhye, *The Sinai Blunder*, p. 21; *Baghdad Radio*, June 1, 1967.

46. Richard Parker, *The Politics of Miscalculation in the Middle East* (Bloomington: Indiana University Press, 1993), pp. 97-98.

47. See, for example, Nasser's speech of July 23, 1967; Robert Stephens, *Nasser: A Political Biography* (London: Allen Lane, 1971), p. 489.

48. Israel Defense Forces, Southern Command, "The Four-Day War, 1967" (an internal IDF document, June 1967; Hebrew). The existence of operational plans to occupy Israeli territory was also confirmed by Egyptian military sources. See, for example, Muhammad Abdel Ghani al-Gamasy, *Mudhakirat al-Gamasy: Harb October 1973* (Paris: al-Manshurat al-Sharqiya, 1990), pp. 70-71, 73-74.

49. William B. Quandt, "Lyndon Johnson and the June 1967 War: What Color was the Light?" *Middle East Journal*, Vol. 46, No. 2 (spring 1992), p. 221, fn. 68.

50. Hussein of Jordan, *My "War" with Israel* (London: Peter Owen, 1969), p. 55; Mutawi, *Jordan*, p.110; Sadat, *In Search of Identity*, p. 174; Heikal, *1967*, pp. 1062-63.

51. Mahmoud Riad, *The Struggle for Peace in the Middle East* (London: Quartet Books, 1981), p. 23.

52. Laqueur, *The Israel-Arab Reader*, p. 226.

Chapter 10

1. The foremost proponent of this theory was Muhammad Hassanein Heikal, but it gained wide currency in Egypt and the Arab world and had its share of dedicated supporters among Western observers of the Middle East. See, for example, Heikal, *Nasser: The Cairo Documents* (London: New English Library, 1972), Chapter 7; Heikal, *Sphinx and Commissar: The Rise and Fall of Soviet Influence in the Middle East* (London: Collins, 1978), Chapter 10; Heikal, *1967: al-Infijar* (Cairo: Ahram, 1990), pp. 317-30,

371–80, 419–25, 490–500. See also, Anwar Sadat, *In Search of Identity: An Autobiography* (New York: Harper & Row, 1978), pp. 282–83; Mahmoud Riad, *The Struggle for Peace in the Middle East* (London: Quartet Books, 1981), p. 26; Muhammad Abdel Ghani al-Gamasy, *Mudhakirat al-Gamasy: Harb October 1973* (Paris: al-Manshurat al-Sharqiya, 1990), Chapters 1–2; Ahmad Hamrush, *Qisat Thawrat 23 Yuliu. Vol. 5: Kharif Abdel Nasser* (Beirut: al-Mu'asasa al-Arabiya li-l-Dirasat wa-l-Nashr, 1978), pp. 145–71; Anthony Nutting, *Nasser* (New York: E. P. Dutton, 1972), Chapters 19–20; Ibrahim Abu-Lughod (ed.), *The Arab-Israeli Confrontation of June 1967: An Arab Perspective* (Evanston: Northwestern University Press, 1970).

2. See, for example, Sadiq Jalal Azm, *al-Naqd al-Dhati Ba'da al-Hazima* (Beirut: Dar al-Tali'a, 1968); Kamal Faramawi, *Yawmiyat Sajin fi-l-Sijn al-Harbi* (Cairo: Dar al-Thaqafa, 1976); Abdallah Laroui, *The Crisis of the Arab Intellectual* (Berkeley: University of California Press, 1976).

3. Samir A. Mutawi, *Jordan in the 1967 War* (Cambridge: Cambridge University Press, 1987), Chapters 8–9; Hussein of Jordan, *My "War" with Israel* (London: Peter Owen, 1969), pp. 106–07.

4. Sadat, *In Search of Identity* pp. 179–80.

5. Riad, *The Struggle*, p. 48.

6. For Soviet acceptance of the need for Israel's retention of some of the territories occupied during the 1967 war see, for example, *Pravda*, Feb. 18, June 6, 21, Aug. 19, 1968; *Izvestiya*, Feb. 2, 1968.

7. P. J. Vatikiotis, *Nasser and His Generation* (London: Croom Helm, 1978), p. 245.

8. Abdel Magid Farid, *Nasser: The Final Years* (Reading: Ithaca Press, 1994), p. 202. Farid served as secretary-general of the Egyptian presidency for eleven years until 1970.

9. See, for example, Saad el-Shazly, *The Crossing of Suez: The October War, 1973* (London: Third World Centre, 1980), p. 64; Muhammad Hassanein Heikal, *The Road to Ramadan* (London: Fontana, 1976), pp. 121–30; Yitzhak Rabin, *The Rabin Memoirs* (London: Weidenfeld and Nicolson, 1979), p. 149; Henry Kissinger, *Years of Upheaval* (Boston: Little, Brown, 1982), p. 201.

10. *New York Times*, Dec. 28, 1970.

11. Arab Republic of Egypt, *White Paper on the Peace Initiatives Undertaken by President Anwar Sadat [1971–77]* (Cairo: Ministry of Foreign Affairs, n.d.), pp. 5–16; "UN Document S/10070/Add. 2," March 5, 1971; Rabin, *The Rabin Memoirs*, p. 157.

12. *New York Times*, Dec. 28, 1970; Heikal, *The Road to Ramadan*, p. 206.

13. Hani A. Faris and As'ad Abdul Rahman, "Arab Unity," in Nasser H. Aruri (ed.), *Middle East Crucible: Studies on the Arab-Israeli War of October 1973* (Wilmette: Medina University Press International, 1975), p. 98.

14. For the Egyptian war objectives see Gamasy, *Mudhakirat*, pp. 372–95, and his interview with the Lebanese *al-Hayat*, Oct. 9, 1991. See also the interview by General (ret.) Hassan Abu Sa'ada (commander of the Egyptian Second Army during the war) with *al-Hayat*, Oct. 8, 1992. For the Syrian objectives see Muhammad Zuhair Diab and Amid Khuly, *al-Mun'ataf al-Kabir* (Damascus: Tishrin, 1979), pp. 18–19, 28–35.

15. Kissinger, *Years of Upheaval*, p. 506.

16. Shazly, *The Crossing*, pp. 74–75; Anwar Sadat, *Those I Have Known* (London: Cape, 1985), pp. 68–69.

17. For the text of the 1975 agreement, and its secret annexes see Edward Sheehan, *The Arabs, Israelis, and Kissinger* (New York: Readers' Digest, 1976), pp. 245–57.

18. Muhammad Ibrahim Kamel, *The Camp David Accords: A Testimony* (London: KPI, 1986), p. 365.

19. Jalal al-Din al-Hamamsi, *Hiwar Wara'a al-Aswar* (Cairo: al-Maktab al-Misri al-Hadith, 1976), p. 85; Sami Jawhar, *al-Samitun Yatakalamun: Abdel Nasser wa-Madhbahat al-Ikhwan* (Cairo: al-Maktab al-Misri al-Hadith, 1976).

20. Tawfiq al-Hakim, *The Return of Consciousness* (London: Macmillan, 1985), pp. 24–25, 34, 37, 43, 44, 50.

21. Kamel, *The Camp David Accords*, pp. 44, 367.

22. Saddam's interview with *al-Siyasa* (Kuwait), May 24, 1982; Shahram Chubin and Charles Tripp, *Iran and Iraq at War* (London: Tauris, 1988), p. 147.

23. *International Herald Tribune*, Nov. 27, Dec. 5, 1984; *Hadashot* (Tel Aviv), Nov. 13, 15, 1987; *Davar* (Tel Aviv), Nov. 12, 1987.

24. E. Lauterpacht, C. J. Greenwood, M. Weller, and D. Bethlehem (eds.), *The Kuwait Crisis: Basic Documents* (Cambridge: Grotius Publications, 1991), p. 281.

25. Pierre Salinger and Eric Laurent, *Secret Dossier: The Hidden Agenda behind the Gulf War* (London: Penguin, 1991), p. 160.

26. Ibid., p. 156; Tlas's interview with *Ukaz* (Saudi Arabia), Feb. 24, 1991.

27. *New York Times*, March 16, 1991; "A New Beginning," *US News & World Report*, Sept. 13, 1993, p. 30.

28. Arafat's interview with *al-Anwar* (Beirut), Aug. 2, 1968.

29. Ibid.

30. *Al-Arabi* (Cairo), June 24, 2001.

31. "Political Program for the Present Stage Drawn up by the 12th PNC, Cairo, June 9, 1974," *Journal of Palestine Studies*, summer 1974, pp. 224–25.

32. *Palestinian Authority Television*, Oct. 2, 2000. For discussion of the origin of the latest Palestinian-Israeli war see Efraim Karsh, *Arafat's War: The Man and His Battle for Israel Conquest* (New York: Grove, 2003).

33. Kamel, *The Camp David Accords*, p. 321.

34. Ephraim Dowek, *Israeli-Egyptian Relations 1980–2000* (London: Cass, 2001), pp. 120–21.

35. Damascus Radio, Dec. 13, 1981.

Chapter 11

1. Edward Said, "The Morning After," *London Review of Books*, Oct. 21, 1993, p. 3.

2. For further discussion of this issue see Efraim Karsh and Inari Karsh, "Myth in the Desert, or Not the Great Arab Revolt," *Middle Eastern Studies*, April 1997, pp. 267–312.

3. Albert Hourani, *The Emergence of the Modern Middle East* (London: Macmillan, 1981), pp. 209–10.

4. For the text of the Sykes-Picot agreement, as well as a memorandum by its two authors accompanying the draft agreement, see CAB 42/11/9. See also E. L. Woodward and R. Butler (eds.), *Documents on British Foreign Policy 1919–1939*, 1st Ser. (London: HMSO, 1960), Vol. 4, pp. 241–51 (hereafter "DBFP").

5. For further discussion of this issue see Elie Kedourie, *In the Anglo-Arab Labyrinth: The McMahon-Husayn Correspondence and Its Interpretations 1914–1939* (Cambridge: Cambridge University Press, 1976); Efraim Karsh and Inari Karsh, *Empires of the Sand: The Struggle for Mastery in the Middle East 1789–1923* (Cambridge: Harvard University Press, 1999), esp. Chapter 15.

6. Other factors that undermined the agreement were Russia's departure from the war after the 1917 Bolshevik Revolution and its repudiation of the wartime secret agreements, as well as Anglo-French-Italian rivalries and American dithering regarding the desired shape of the postwar arrangements.

7. *A Speech Delivered by Ghazi Mustapha Kemal: President of the Turkish Republic, October 1927* (Leipzig: K. F. Kohler, 1929), pp. 16–19.

8. David Fromkin, *A Peace to End All Peace: The Fall of the Ottoman Empire and the Creation of the Modern Middle East* (New York: Avon, 1990), p. 17.

9. CO 732/3, fols. 409–12; "Sherifian Policy in Mesopotamia & Trans-Jordania," CO 732/3/10127, fols. 418–22; Churchill to Lloyd George, received at the Colonial Office at 8.30 p.m., March 14, 1921, CO 732/4/17976, fol. 167. For discussion of the episode see Karsh and Karsh, *Empires of the Sand*, Chapter 20.

10. "Sherifian Policy in Mesopotamia & Trans-Jordania," Feb. 25, 1921, CO 732/3, fols. 420–21.

11. "First Conversation on Trans-Jordania, Held at Government House, Jerusalem, March 28, 1921," FO 371/6343, fols. 99–101.

12. "Second Conversation on Trans-Jordania," "Third Conversation on Trans-Jordania" ibid., fols. 101–02.

13. "Letter from Mr. Churchill to Sir Herbert Samuel, at Sea," April 2, 1921, ibid. fols. 102–03.

14. Edward Said, *The Pen and the Sword: Conversations with David Barsamian* (Edinburgh: AK Press, 1994), p. 136.

15. For discussion of the US-Israel influence relationship see Efraim Karsh, "Cold War, Post-Cold War: Does It Make a Difference for the Middle East?" *Review of International Studies*, Vol. 23, No. 3 (July 1997), pp. 271–91.

16. See, for example, *Pravda*, Feb. 18, 1968, June 6 and 21, 1968, Aug. 19, 1968; *Izvestiya*, Feb. 2, 1968; "Soviet Government Statement on the Middle East," *Tass*, April 28, 1976; "Soviet Proposal Concerning a Middle Eastern settlement," *Tass*, Oct. 1, 1976.

17. See, for example, Damascus Radio, Feb. 22, Mar. 8, 1971; Assad's interview with the Bulgarian Communist Party organ *Robotnichenko Delo*, Feb. 2, 1971, and with *al-Anwar* (Beirut), Aug. 10, 1972.

18. Mahmoud Riad, *The Struggle for Peace in the Middle East* (London: Quartet Books, 1981), p. 102; Muhammad Hassanein Heikal, *Sphinx and Commissar: The Rise and Fall of Soviet Influence in the Middle East* (London: Collins, 1978), Chapter 11; Heikal, *The Road to Ramadan* (London: Fontana, 1976), pp. 79–83; Jean Lacouture, *Nasser: A Biography* (New York: Knopf, 1973), pp. 330–31.

19. Richard Nixon, *RN: The Memoirs of Richard Nixon* (New York: Simon & Schuster, 1990), pp. 884–85; Henry Kissinger, *Years of Upheaval* (Boston: Little, Brown, 1982), pp. 279–97, 463; *Pravda*, Sept. 26, 1973; Hanoch Bartov, *Dado* (Tel Aviv: Maarachot, 1978), Vol. 1, p. 314.

20. Efraim Karsh, *Soviet Policy towards Syria: The Asad Years* (London: Routledge, 1991), Chapter 1.

21. See, for example, *Pravda*, July 21, 1988; *Izvestiya*, Sept. 8, 1989; *Literaturnaya Gazeta*, May 31, 1989; *Tass*, Sept. 5, 1988. See also interview with Vladimir Poliakov (head of the Near East Department in the Soviet Foreign Office), in *Le Quotidien de Paris*, Oct. 13, 1988, and in *Izvestiya*, Sept. 8, 1989.

22. *Tass*, June 19, 1985, Oct. 28, 1988, Nov. 1, 1988; *Pravda*, June 20, 1985; *Krasnaya Zvezda*, Nov. 1, 3, 1988; Moscow Radio, Apr. 24, 1987; *al-Anba* (Kuwait), interview with Konstantin Geyvendov (*Izvestiya*'s Middle Eastern commentator), Sept. 12, 1987.

23. Secret Memorandum, Executive Office of the President: from Henry A. Kissinger to the Secretary of State and Secretary of Defense, "Follow-Up on the President's Talk with the Shah of Iran," June 15, 1972.

24. John D. Stempel, *Inside the Iranian Revolution* (Bloomington: University of Indiana Press, 1981), pp. 72–74; James A. Bill, *The Eagle and the Lion: The Tragedy of American-Iranian Relations* (New Haven: Yale University Press, 1988), pp. 202–09.

25. William Shawcross, *The Shah's Last Ride: The Story of the Exile, Misadventures and Death of the Emperor* (London: Chatto & Windus, 1989), Chapter 2; "Iran's Birthday Party," *Newsweek*, Oct. 25, 1971, pp. 16–17.

26. *Guardian*, Oct. 9, 1971; *AFP*, June 24, 1974; *DPA*, June 10, 1976; Amin Saikal, *The Rise and Fall of the Shah* (Princeton: Princeton University Press, 1980), pp. 146–47.

27. Bill, *The Eagle*, p. 173.

28. Henry Kissinger, *White House Years* (Boston: Little, Brown, 1979), p. 224.

29. House Select Committee on Intelligence Report (The Pike Report) on American Involvement in the Kurdish Insurrection, as reprinted in *Village Voice* (New York), Jan. 26, 1976. The main findings of the report also formed the basis for two articles by William Safire: "Mr. Ford's Secret Sell-Out," *New York Times*, Feb. 5, 1976; "Son of Secret Sell-Out," *New York Times*, Feb. 12, 1976.

30. There were, of course, occasional warnings of the risks attending the shah's ambitious development programs. Some of these even questioned the prudence of predicating American national interests on the fortunes of one person, however powerful. Yet even these manifested expressions of self-doubt would normally conclude on a positive note, emphasizing the remoteness of the identified threats and the effective control exercised by the shah. See, for example, "Religious Circles," US Embassy, Iran, May 15, 1972; "The Conduct of Relations with Iran," secret report by the Department of State, Office of the Inspector General, Oct. 1974; "Iran: An Overview of the Shah's Economy," confidential memorandum, CIA, Oct. 16, 1974; "Iran's Modernizing Monarchy: A Political Assessment," secret aerogram from Richard Helms to United States Department of State, July 8, 1976.

31. "The Future of Iran," Department of State, Bureau of Intelligence and Research, drafted by Franklin P. Huddle, Jan. 28, 1977.

32. See, for example, "Iran in the 1980s," secret report, CIA, Oct. 5, 1977; William H. Sullivan, *Mission to Iran* (New York: Norton, 1981), p. 155.

33. "Your appearance before the House International Relations Committee, Thursday, 18 July, 10 a.m., on the Sale of AWACS to Iran," memorandum to Cyrus Vance from Alfred Roy Atherton, July 27, 1977.

34. "Iran in the 1980s," Secret Report, CIA, Aug. 1977; "Iran in the 1980s," secret report, CIA, Oct. 5, 1977.

35. Cyrus Vance, *Hard Choices: Critical Years in America's Foreign Policy* (New York: Simon & Schuster, 1983), pp. 325, 329; "Pessimism about Iranian Stability," confidential memorandum by Theodore H. Moran, consultant to Policy Planning Staff, to Department of State, Oct. 4, 1978; "Iran: Political Assessment," secret briefing, Department of State, drafted by Henry Precht, Oct. 18, 1978; "The Policies of Ayatollah Khomeini," intelligence memorandum, CIA, Nov. 20, 1978; "Iran Update on Moharram," secret alert memorandum, CIA, Dec. 5, 1978.

36. Zbigniew Brzezinski, *Power and Principle: Memoirs of the National Security Adviser 1977–1981* (London: Weidenfeld and Nicolson, 1983), pp. 371–82; Bill, *The Eagle*, pp. 249–57.

37. The analysis in this section draws on Lawrence Freedman and Efraim Karsh, *The Gulf Conflict 1990–1991: Diplomacy and War in the New World Order* (Princeton: Princeton University Press, 1993).

Chapter 12

1. Elie Kedourie, *The Chatham House Version and Other Middle Eastern Studies* (Hanover: University Press of New England, new ed., n.d.), pp. 177–207.

2. Abul Ala Mawdudi, *Political Theory of Islam* (Lahore: Islamic Publications, 1961), pp. 26, 30; Mawdudi, *al-Jihad fi Sabil Allah* (Beirut: Dar al-Fikr, 1960), p. 35 (emphasis in the original).

3. For Banna's biography see: *Hassan al-Banna: Shaheed* (Karachi: International Islamic Publishers, 1981); Richard P. Mitchell, *The Society of the Muslim Brothers* (New York: Oxford University Press, 1993); Robert St. John, *The Boss: The Story of Gamal Abdel Nasser* (New York: McGraw Hill, 1960), pp. 41–42.

4. Hassan Banna, "al-Ikhwan al-Muslimun Tahta Rayat al-Qur'an," in *Min Rasail al-Ikhwan al-Muslimin* (Cairo: Dar al-Kitab al-Arabi fi Misr, n.d.), p. 13.

5. St. John, *The Boss*, pp. 41–42; Mitchell, *The Society*, pp. 297, 328; Anthony Shadid, *Legacy of the Prophet: Despots, Democrats, and the New Politics of Islam* (Boulder: Westview, 2001), pp. 54–55; Henry Munson, *Islam and Revolution in the Middle East* (New Haven: Yale University Press, 1988), pp. 76–77; Olivier Roy, *The Failure of Political Islam* (Cambridge: Harvard University Press, 1994), pp. 110–11; Anwar Sadat, *Asrar al-Thawra al-Misriya* (Cairo: Dar al-Hilal, 1957), pp. 44–53, 60–67, 90–92; Hassan Banna, *al-Salam fi-l-Islam* (Jeddah: al-Dar al-Suudiya li-l-Nashr, 1971), p. 12; Banna, "Fan al-Mawt," in *Majmuat Maqalat Hassan al-Banna* (Damascus, n.d.)., p. 62; Banna, "Risalat al-Jihad," in *Min Rasail*, pp. 2, 32.

6. Gilles Kepel, *Muslim Extremism in Egypt: The Prophet and Pharaoh* (Berkeley: University of California Press, 1985), pp. 39–41; Charles Tripp, "Sayyid Qutb: The Political Vision," in Ali Rahnema (ed.), *Pioneers of Islamic Revival* (London: Zed Books, 1994), p. 159.

7. Sayyid Qutb, *The Religion of Islam* (Palo Alto: Al-Manar Press, 1967), pp. 34, 65–67, 77, 87; Qutb, *Maalim fi-l-Tariq* (Ramallah: Dar al-Kutub al-Thaqafiya, 1987), pp. 8, 13–19, 149–50; Qutb, *Islam and Universal Peace* (Plainfield: American Trust Publications, 1977), pp. 72–73; Emmanuel Sivan, *Radical Islam: Medieval Theology and Modern Politics* (New Haven and London: Yale University Press, 1985), pp. 85–86.

8. Hassan Banna, *Da'watuna fi Tawr Jadid* (Khartum: Dar al-Ibada wa-l-Nashr al-Islamiya, 1979), pp. 12–14; Sayyid Qutb, *Social Justice in Islam* (Leiden: Brill, 1996), pp. 106–08, 289; Qutb, *Maalim*, pp. 52–53.

9. Sayyid Qutb, *Maalim*, pp. 60–61; Qutb, *The Religion of Islam*, pp. 87, 89; Qutb, *Islam and Universal Peace*, p. 72.

10. Ayman al-Zawahiri, *Knights under the Prophet's Banner*, serialized by *al-Sharq al-Awsat* (London) and translated by FBIS-NES-2002–0108, Dec. 2, 2001, p. 16.

11. "Exclusive Interview with Hamas Leader," *The Media Line*, Sept. 22, 2005 (http://www.themedialine.org/news/news_detail.asp?NewsID=11354); Walid Mahmoud Abdelnasser, *The Islamic Movement in Egypt: Perceptions of International Relations 1967–81* (London: Kegan Paul, 1994), p. 39.

12. Hamas Constitution, Articles 8–11, 15, 35.

13. Johannes Jansen, *The Dual Nature of Islamic Fundamentalism* (London: Hurst, 1997), p. 69.

14. Ayatollah Ruhollah Khomeini, *Islam and Revolution: Writings and Declarations*, trans. and ed. Hamid Algar (London: KPI, 1985), pp. 13–23.

15. Ibid. pp. 31, 49, 127.

16. Ibid. pp. 31, 48–49; James P. Piscatori, *Islam in a World of Nation-States* (Cambridge: Cambridge University Press, 1986), p. 113.

17. Farhad Rajaee, *Islamic Values and World View: Khomeini on Man, the State and International Politics* (Lanham: Universities of America Press, 1983), pp. 82–83.

18. Khomeini, *Islam and Revolution*, pp. 327–28.

19. Tehran Radio, July 24, 1982.

20. British Broadcasting Corporation (BBC), *Summary of World Broadcasts* (SWB), April 4, 1983.

21. Cited in Leonard Spector, "Nuclear Proliferation in the Middle East: The Next Chapter Begins," in Efraim Karsh et al (eds.), *Non-Conventional Weapons Proliferation in the Middle East: Tackling the Spread of Nuclear, Chemical, and Biological Capabilities* (Oxford: Clarendon Press, 1993), p. 143. For further details of Iran's nuclear program see Frank Barnaby, "Capping Israel's Nuclear Volcano," in the same volume; Geoffrey Kemp, *Forever Enemies? American Policy and the Islamic Republic of Iran* (Washington, D.C.: Carnegie Endowment, 1994); Shahram Chubin, *Iran's National Security Policy: Capabilities, Intentions, and Impact* (Washington, D.C.: Carnegie Endowment, 1994).

Chapter 13

1. Ayman al-Zawahiri, *Knights under the Prophet's Banner*, serialized by *al-Sharq al-Awsat* (London) and translated by FBIS-NES-2002–0108, Dec. 2, 2001, pp. 78, 79.

2. Gilles Kepel, *Jihad: The Trail of Political Islam* (Cambridge: Harvard University Press, 2002), pp. 266–67, 282–83, 300–02. It has also been suggested, though without credible evidence, that Saddam Hussein initiated the attack in revenge for his defeat in the 1991 Gulf war.

3. Yossef Bodansky, *Bin Laden: The Man Who Declared War on America* (New York: Forum, 1999), pp. 3–7; Kamel Isam et al, *Bin Laden: Rajul fi Muwajahat al-Alam* (Cairo: Matabi al-Ahrar, 2001), pp. 11–12; Kepel, *Jihad*, p. 314; Scott Macleod and Dean Fisher, "The Paladin of Jihad," *Time*, Vol. 147, Issue 19 (June 5, 1996; internet edition).

4. Bodansky, *Bin Laden*, pp. 28–31; Peter Bergen and Frank Smith, "Holy Warrior," *New Republic*, Aug. 31, 1998 (internet edition).

5. Bodansky, *Bin Laden*, p. 36.

6. For bin Laden's Sudan period, see Khaled Khalil Asaad, *Muqatil min Mekka* (London: al-A'lam li-l-Nashr, 2000), pp. 77–93; *al-Quds al-Arabi* (London), Nov. 24, 2001.

7. Bodansky, *Bin Laden*, pp. 101–02; Judith Miller, *God Has Ninety-Nine Names* (New York: Simon & Schuster, 1996), p. 118.

8. Youssef M. Ibrahim, "Saudis Strip Citizenship from Backer of Militants," *New York Times*, April 10, 1994; Chris Hedges, "Sudan Linked to Rebellion in Algeria," *New York Times*, Dec. 24, 1994; "Sudan Asserts a Militant Financier Has Left," *New York Times*, June 5, 1996; Jeff Gerth and Judtih Miller, "Funds for Terrorists Traced to Persian Gulf Businessman," *New York Times*, Aug. 14, 1996; Craig Pyes, Judith Miller, and Stephen Engelberg, "One Man and a Global Web of Violence," *New York Times*, Jan. 14, 2001; Daniel McGrory, "The Day when Osama bin Laden Applied for Asylum—In Britain," *The Times* (London), Sept. 29, 2005.

9. "Declaration of Jihad against the Americans Occupying the Land of the Two Holy Places: A Message from Usama bin Muhammad bin Laden to his Muslim Brethren All Over the World Generally and in the Arab Peninsula Specifically," Part 1, p. 2; Part 2, pp. 5, 7–8, www.terrorismfiles.org/individuals/declaration_of_jihad1.html.

10. Abdallah Azzam, *al-Difa an Aradi al-Muslimin Ahamm Furud al-A'yan* (Amman: Maktabat al-Risala al-Haditha, 1987), pp. 23–24, 33–34; Azzam, *Jihad Sha'b Muslim* (Israel [?]: n.p., 1992), pp. 63–64.

11. Pyes, Miller and Engelberg, "One Man and a Global Web of Violence."

12. For the English translation of the declaration see www.fas.org/irp/world/para/docs/980233–fatwa.htm.

13. "Transcript of Usama bin Laden Video Tape," mid-Nov. 2001, www.fas.org/irp/world/para/ubl_video.htm.

14. Zawahiri, *Knights*, pp. 72, 80.

15. The full text of the interview can be found at www.anusha.com/osamaint.htm.

16. Jamal Abdel Latif Ismail, *Bin Laden wa-l-Jajeera . . . wa-Ana*, (Qatar: Dar al-Hurriya, 2000), p. 119.

17. "Declaration of Jihad," Part 2, p. 4; "Bin Laden's Recorded Statement, December 27, 2001," al-Jazeera Television; *www.fas.org/irp/world/para/ubl-video.htm*; "Transcript of Osama bin Laden's Video Tape."

18. *http://www.pbs.org/wgbh/pages/frontline/shows/binladen/who/miller.html*; http://www.pbs.org/wgbh/pages/frontline/shows/binladen/who/interview.html#video.

Epilogue

1. The Middle East Media Research Institute (MEMRI), Special Dispatch Series—No. 1087, Feb. 7, 2006 (memri.org).
2. Anonymous, *Through Enemies' Eyes: Osama bin Laden, Radical Islam, and the Future of America* (Washington, D.C.: Brassey's, 2002), p. 21.
3. Edward Said, "A Desolation, and They Called it Peace," *Al-Ahram Weekly Online*, June 25–July 1, 1998; slate.msn.com/id/1008411.
4. Gilles Kepel, *Jihad: The Trail of Political Islam* (Cambridge: Harvard University Press, 2002), p. 306; Michel Gurfinkiel, "Islam in France: The French Way of Life Is in Danger," *Middle East Quarterly*, Vol. 4, No. 1 (March 1997; internet edition); Lorenzo Vidino, "The Muslim Brotherhood's Conquest of Europe," *Middle East Quarterly*, Vol. 12, No. 1 (Winter 2005; internet edition); *Observer* (London), Nov. 4, 2001; Anthony Browne, "The Triumph of the East," *Spectator* (London), July 24, 2004; *New York Daily News*, March 30, 2003; Latimes.com, Feb. 7, 2002; Washingtonpost.com, Oct. 16, 2001; *Chicago Tribune*, "A Rare Look at Secretive Brotherhood in America," Sept. 19, 2004. For the spread of Islamism to the United States see Daniel Pipes, *Militant Islam Reaches America* (New York: W. W. Norton, 2003).
5. MEMRI, "Special Dispatch Series, No. 447," Dec. 6, 2002.
6. *The Times* (London), Sept. 29, 2005.
7. For an English translation of the letter see *The Weekly Standard*, Oct. 12, 2005, www.weeklystandard.com/Content/Public/Articles/000/000/006/203gpuul.asp.

Index

Abbas, Mahmoud, 199
Abbas Shah, 120
Abbas Hilmi, khedive, 147, 212
Abbasid Empire, 10
　　creation of, 40–42, 215
　　foreign influences, 43–44
　　religious pretences, 44–46
　　claim to the caliphate, 52–53
　　economic apogee, 47
　　intellectual and scientific
　　　awakening, 47
　　corruption, 47–48
　　internecine strife, 5, 6, 48–49,
　　　57–59
　　state violence, 49–52
　　economic and political relations
　　　with Europe, 68–73
　　and the crusades, 76–87
　　decline and fall, 54–65, 90, 93, 119
Abdallah, King, 132, 133, 134, 135, 142,
　　143–45, 147, 149, 155, 196–98, 212
Abdel Malik, Caliph, 36, 39, 41
Abdel Rahman I, Caliph, 61
Abdel Rahman III, Caliph, 62
Abdel Rahman, Omar, 226
Abdul Hamid II, Sultan, 103–105, 113,
　　114
Abdul Mejid, Sultan, 100–101, 105
Abu Bakr, Caliph, 6, 11, 13, 25, 29, 30,
　　33, 35
Abu Lahab, 10, 12
Abu Muslim, 42, 50–51, 52
Abu Nidal, 180–81
Abu Sufian ibn Harb, 18
Abu Talib, 10, 12, 52

Abul Abbas, Caliph, 42, 44, 45, 49–50,
　　51, 55, 58
Abul Huda Sayyadi, 104
Achaemenid Empire, 44, 119, 203
Acre, 78, 86, 100
Adid, Caliph, 83
Adrianople, 92, 117
Aegean Sea, 92, 113
Afghanistan, 40, 48, 63, 120, 121, 122,
　　123, 124, 131, 226, 227, 228, 229, 230,
　　233, 235
Aflaq, Michel, 138, 158
Africa, 49, 69, 137, 154, 155–56, 228
Agha Muhammad, Khan, 121, 122
Aghlabid dynasty, 62, 70
Ahmad Khan, 122
Ain Jalut, Battle of (1260), 90
Alawites, 174
Aleppo, 78, 79, 81, 82, 90, 100, 104, 118,
　　134, 193
Alexander the Great, 119, 238
Alexander I, 122
Alexandria, 26, 100, 104, 142, 189
Algeria, 62, 100, 102, 209, 218, 226, 229
Ali ibn Abi Talib, Caliph, 6, 10, 11, 18,
　　25, 29, 32–33, 36, 38, 39–40, 52–53,
　　54, 71, 120, 134, 220
Amalfi, 69, 70, 71
Amer, Abdel Hakim, 160–61, 172, 178
Amin, Caliph, 57, 58, 62
Anatolia, 73, 74, 77, 90, 91, 92, 96, 99,
　　100, 114, 116, 117, 192
Andalusia, 60, 230, 236
　　see also Spain
Ankara, 117, 193

Ansar, 13, 35
Antioch, 74, 77, 79, 80
Al-Aqsa mosque, 83, 186
"Al-Aqsa Intifada", 186
Arab Higher Committee, 144, 146
Arab imperial dream, 132–48, 155, 223
    decline of, 172–80, 212
    resurgence, 182–90
Arab-Israeli conflict, 140, 143, 149–90, 198–202
Arab League, 140, 152, 158, 171, 174, 178, 182, 185, 208
Arab nationalism 7–9, 133, 135, 137, 234
    see also Pan-Arabism
Arab world 7, 8
Arabian Peninsula, 6, 10, 15, 24, 198, 228, 229
    on the eve of Islam 2, 4, 5, 11–12, 21
    and the Fertile Crescent, 25
    under Muhammad's domination, 7, 16–18, 21 30–31
    cleansed of Jews and Christians, 15, 27–28
    loses imperial mastery, 32–33
    scene of inter-Muslim strife, 37, 48, 54, 55, 95
    in World War I, 132–33
Arafat, Yasser
    expelled from Lebanon, 180–81
    supports Iraq's occupation of Kuwait, 183–85
    signs the Oslo accords, 185–86, 218
    advocates Israel's destruction, 185–87
    war of terror, 185–87, 199
    rejects peace with Israel, 198–99
Aref, Abdel Rahman, 167
Armenia, 80, 120, 134, 193
    Islamic colonization, 48, 57
    Ottoman repression, 109, 113–14
    World War I genocide, 115–18
Assad, Hafiz, 144–45, 174, 175, 182, 189, 201–202, 235
Assassins, 76, 78, 90
Assyria, 2, 115, 137
Assyrians, 134

Austro-Hungary, 106
    see also Habsburg Empire
Ayyam al-Arab, 4
Ayyarun, 48
Ayyubi dynasty, 55, 88–89, 149
Azzam, Abdallah, 227, 230
Azzam, Abdel Rahman, 140, 152
Azerbaijan, 48, 57, 62, 87, 120, 128
Aziz, Tariq, 208, 210, 222–23
Azuri, Najib, 135

Babak, 48–49, 62–63
Babylon, 2, 14, 115, 203
Badr, Battle of (624), 14, 177
Baghdad, 2, 27, 44, 46, 48, 49, 52, 55, 57, 58, 59, 61, 62, 64, 65, 71, 72, 76, 77, 78, 79, 90, 94, 120, 136, 179, 195, 210, 223
    pact (1955), 155, 157, 158
Bahais, 128
Bahrain, 37, 222
Baldwin I, King, 78
Balfour Declaration (1917), 139, 142, 143
Balkans, 62, 92, 93, 94, 96, 102, 105, 112, 113, 114
Banna, Hassan, 213–14, 216
Banu Hanifa tribe, 30
Barak, Ehud, 187, 189
Barmakids, 51–52
Basra, 27, 32, 36, 38, 49, 53, 136, 158, 195
Ba'th Party, 138, 147, 158, 160, 163, 174, 179, 222, 225, 235
Baybars I, Sultan, 88–89, 90
Bayezid I, Sultan, 92, 93, 94, 105
Begin, Menachem, 178, 188, 198
Beirut, 100, 134, 140, 179, 226, 229
Berbers, 28
    resisting Islamic colonization, 4, 37, 61–62
    invading Spain, 59–61
Berlin Congress (1878), 113, 114
Bin Laden, Osama
    imperialist vision, 1, 224, 230–33, 239
    personal background, 226–28
    embarks on a jihad, 228–33
    envisages US destruction, 232–33
    mourns Islam's loss of Spain, 235
    seeks asylum in Britain, 239

Black Sea, 89, 94, 96, 101, 102, 107, 113, 116
Black September (1970), 172
Bosnia–Herzegovina, 97, 111–12, 113, 229, 232
Brezhnev, Leonid, 200
Britain, 156, 236
  imperialism, 27, 185
  and the Ottoman Empire, 100–102, 112, 123
  occupies Egypt, 100–105
  and World War I, 106–08, 115, 132–35, 137–38, 141–43, 192–93, 238
  and Iran, 122–31
  post-World War II policies, 151, 152, 155, 157, 159, 203, 204
  and Kuwait crisis, 208
Bukhara, 63, 89
Bulgaria, 89, 92, 112, 113
Bush, George, 207, 210
Bush, George W., 199
Buyid dynasty, 60, 64, 119
Byzantium, 18, 19, 96, 139
  on the eve of Islam 2, 4, 27
  imperial vision, 6, 67
  encounters with Islam 21, 25, 76
  influence on Islamic civilization, 28–29, 67–68
  trade relations with Islamic empires, 69–70
  political relations with Islamic empires, 71
  and the Holy Roman Empire, 72
  and the Seljuks, 73, 74, 91
  and the crusades, 74, 76, 79, 80, 82
  fall, 76, 93
  and Saladin, 85, 87
  and the Ottomans, 91–92, 237

Cairo, 27, 74, 81, 94, 142, 158, 159, 160, 162, 168, 172, 173, 178, 181, 213, 214
  conference (1921), 195–97
Camp David Accords (1978), 178–79, 188
Canaanites, 137
Capitulations, 95
Carlowitz, Treaty of (1699), 96
Carolingian dynasty, 71–73
Carter, Jimmy, 198, 205, 206

Caspian Sea, 54, 59, 63, 64, 124
Catherine the Great, 96, 122
Caucasus, 41, 89, 90, 121, 124, 223
Central Asia, 23, 40, 41, 48, 76, 89, 91, 94, 119, 120, 122, 223, 235
Chamoun, Camille, 156
Charlemagne, 72–73
Chechnya, 229, 232
China, 23, 41, 89, 90, 223, 235
Christians and Christianity, 21–22, 68, 88
  encounter with Islam 1, 15, 18, 23, 238
  early development 6
  imperialist vision 6, 7
  influence on Islam, 11, 15
  under Muslim rule, 22, 27–29, 94, 97, 101, 109–10, 113–14, 128, 139
  vilified, 225, 230, 236
Churchill, Winston, 106, 195–98
Clash of Civilizations, 1, 67, 73, 237, 238
Clinton, Bill, 191, 199
Cold War, 186–87, 203, 211, 212
Comnenuns, Alexius, Emperor, 73, 74, 79
Constantinople, 2, 21, 41, 60, 73, 74, 87, 91, 92, 93, 134
Constitution of Medina (622), 13, 18–20
Copts, 28, 218
Crimea, 93, 96
Crimean War (1854–56), 102, 124
Crusades, 69, 70, 73–87, 215
  Christian-Muslim cooperation, 77–78, 238
  Muslim-Christian peaceful coexistence, 80–81, 88
  modern-day evocation, 138–40, 185, 189–94, 219, 229, 230
Ctesiphon, 2, 44
Cyprus, 159
Cyrus the Great, 203
Czechoslovakia, 159

Damascus, 35, 36, 38, 39, 40, 43, 45, 60, 67, 76, 77, 78, 79, 80, 82, 83, 84, 90, 97, 100, 134, 137, 143, 158, 160, 163, 164, 173, 180, 181, 196, 198, 201

Danube, 93, 95, 101, 102, 111
Djemal Pasha, 107
Dhimmis, 27–28, 37
Dome of the Rock, 45, 67
Dufferin, Lord, 103, 104

East India Company, 122
Eastern Question, 97–108
Edessa, 74, 78, 79, 82
Egypt
    ancient empires, 2
    Muslim occupation and
        colonization, 7, 23, 25, 26, 27,
        32, 36
    on the eve of Islam, 11
    under the Abbasids, 48, 55, 59, 62
    under the Fatimids, 69, 70, 83
    and the crusades, 76, 77
    under the Ayyubis, 88
    under the Mamluks, 88–89, 90, 94
    under the Ottomans, 93, 95
    Napoleonic invasion, 99, 122
    under Muhammad Ali, 99–100,
        111
    British occupation, 102–106
    Arabism, 133, 135, 149
    in World War I, 141, 192, 193
    denies Palestinian statehood, 145,
        151
    and Arab-Israeli conflict, 146,
        149–79, 184, 187–88, 199–200
    abortive union with Syria, 147,
        158–61
    and Iraq, 154, 155, 179, 207, 208
    under Nasser, 149–72
    under Sadat, 172–79
    under Mubarak, 188–89
    institutionalized anti-Semitism,
        188–89
    and the great powers, 198
    Islamism, 213–19, 229, 230–31
Enver Pasha, 106, 107, 116
Ethiopia, 4, 12, 18, 19, 22, 214, 218, 229
Euphrates, 23, 27, 32, 90, 117, 152
Europe
    imperialism 2, 4, 6, 7, 8
    invaded by Islam, 2, 23, 60–62, 92
    economic decline, 47
    economic relations with Islamic
        empires, 68–70, 88–89
    political relations with Islamic
        empires, 70–74
    during the crusades, 73–74, 88–89
    and the Ottoman Empire, 92–108,
        109, 111, 136
    and the Kuwait crisis, 207, 210
    and Islamist terrorism, 226, 228
    targeted by Islamists, 236–37

Fahd, King, 180, 236
Fahmi, Ismail, 202
Faisal, king of Saudi Arabia, 172,
    174–75
Faisal I, king of Iraq, 132, 133, 135, 136,
    138, 142–43, 147–48, 195–96, 197,
    198, 212
Farouq, King, 149, 150, 212
Fars, 37, 53, 63, 64
Fath Ali, Shah, 122, 123
Fatima, 10, 38, 40, 52, 53
Fatimids, 10, 38, 54–55, 62, 64, 69, 70,
    74, 76, 77, 78, 80, 83, 84, 149
Fawzi, Muhammad, 164
Fertile Crescent, 7, 21, 22, 24, 32, 47, 54,
    76, 135, 136, 154
Finland, 69
France, 72, 154, 156, 185
    Muslim invasions, 23, 41, 59–60,
        71
    revolution, 96, 206
    occupies Algeria and Tunisia, 100,
        102
    defends Ottoman Empire, 102, 103
    and Iran, 122–23, 126, 129
    and World War I, 106–07, 192–93
    and Egypt, 157
    and Syria, 134, 143, 195, 196, 197
    and Israel, 170
    and Iran, 204, 205
    and Kuwait crisis, 210
    and Islamism, 226, 236
Frantz Ferdinand, Archduke, 107
Fulcher of Charters, 80
Fustat, 27, 32

Galilee, 76, 81, 90, 145, 181
Gallipoli, 92
Gaza Strip, 145, 146, 168, 173, 178, 184,
    185, 186, 187, 199, 218
Geneva Conference (1973), 201

Genghis Khan, 89–90
Georgia, 87, 121–22, 123, 124
Germany, 106, 107, 108, 129, 192, 236
Ghassanids, 27
Ghazw, see razzia
Gibbon, Edward, 23
Gibraltar, 23, 60
Gladstone, William Ewart, 103, 105, 125
Golan Heights, 78, 81, 85, 170, 174, 189
Golden Horde, 89, 90, 91, 93
Gorbachev, Mikhail, 181, 201
Granville, Lord, 103, 105, 106
Great Arab Revolt, 132–33, 141, 145, 195, 196, 213
Great Game, 119, 122, 130–31
Greater Syria, 7, 143, 144, 152, 155
Greece, 93, 113, 134
    imperial past, 24, 60
    influence on Islamic civilization, 67–68, 215, 238
    under the Ottomans, 96, 237
    war of independence, 110–11
Gregory VII, Pope, 73
Grey, Edward, 102, 106, 107, 108, 130–31
Gulf of Aqaba, 22, 164–65, 166
Gulf war (1991), 183–84
Gulistan, Treaty of (1813), 124

Habsburg Empire, 96, 112
    see also Austro-Hungary
Hadi, Caliph, 57, 58
Haifa, 141, 167, 172
Hakim, Tawfiq, 177–78
Hama, 218
Hamas, 184–85, 187, 218–19
Harun al-Rashid, Caliph, 45, 46, 51–52, 54, 57, 58, 62, 72
Hashemi-Rafsanjani, Ali Akbar, 223
Hashemites, 12, 132–35, 137, 139, 142, 147, 149, 154, 160, 192–93, 195, 196, 197, 198, 234
Hashemiyya, 40, 50, 53
Hassan, Imam, 10, 33
Hebron, 145
Heikal, Muhammad Hassanein, 150, 155, 166, 168
Heraclius, Emperor, 74
Herat, 124, 125
Herzl, Theodor, 141

Hijaz, 2, 10, 53, 83, 93, 148, 196, 226, 232
Hijra, 4, 13–14, 35, 232
Hisham, Caliph, 39, 41, 42, 50, 60
Hitler, Adolf, 214
Hitti, Philip, 13, 144
Hittin, Battle of (1187), 86
Hittites, 137
Hizbullah, 224
Holy Roman Empire, 72
House of Islam, 7, 66–68, 76, 83, 84, 93, 138, 215, 216, 219, 221, 236
House of War, 66, 76, 90, 138, 221
Hudaibiya, Treaty of (628), 16–17
Hulagu, 90–91, 255 n. 5
Hungary, 89, 93
Hurmoz, 120
Husri, Sati, 136, 138, 149
Hussein, Imam, 10, 38, 221
Hussein, King, 156, 160, 161, 166–67, 168, 171, 172, 174, 239
Hussein, Saddam, 147, 179–81, 182–84, 187, 207–08, 235, 239
Hussein, Sharif, 132–34, 135, 147, 148, 157, 192–93, 212, 234, 238
Husseini, Faisal, 186
Husseini, Jamal, 146

Ibn Abdel Wahhab, Muhammad, 95–96
Ibn Abi Ubaid, Mukhtar, 38, 39, 40
Ibn Aghlab, Ibrahim, 62, 70
Ibn al-As, Amr, 26
Ibn Athir, Ali, 77, 87
Ibn Awam, Zuabir, 25
Ibn Habib, Masalma, 30
Ibn Hanafiyya, Muhammad, 39–40, 52, 54
Ibn Haritha, Zaid, 11, 21
Ibn Jubayr, 79, 81
Ibn Khaldun, Abdel Rahman, 25, 49, 66
Ibn Laith, Ya'qub, 63
Ibn Nusair, Musa, 59–60
Ibn Qalanisi, 80
Ibn Ubaidallah, Talha, 26
Ibn Yusuf, Hajjaj, 36–37
Ibn Zaid, Tareq, 59–60
Ibn Ziyar, Mardavij, 62–63
Ibn Zuabir, Abdallah, 35–37, 39, 71
Ibrahim, Caliph, 39
Ibrahim Pasha, 99–100, 111, 153

Idrisids, 54, 62, 70

Ifriqiya, 58, 70

India, 7, 23, 41, 47, 94, 122, 123, 126, 131, 147

Indian Ocean, 203

Iran
ancient empires, 2, 119
and the rise of Islam, 2, 4, 18, 21
Muslim occupation and colonization, 6, 7, 23, 24, 40, 140
influence on the Islamic world, 28, 47, 67–68, 215, 238
during the Abbasid era, 44, 48, 51–52, 57, 58, 59, 62–65, 76, 77, 119–20
Mongol invasion, 90–91, 120
under the Safavids, 94, 120–121
and the Great Game, 119, 122–23
and the Ottoman Empire, 120
under the Qajars, 121–31
tobacco riots, 126–27
partitioned, 130–31
joins Baghdad Pact, 155
under the Pahlavis, 161, 202–205
Islamic republic, 179, 198, 220–23
and Iraq, 179, 183, 199, 205, 222–24, 225
and the United States, 202–205
nuclear ambitions, 205, 223

Iran–Iraq war (1980–88), 179, 183, 199, 206, 207, 224, 225, 238

Iraq, 21, 46, 78, 135–38, 147, 151, 220, 235
Muslim occupation and colonization, 23, 24, 25, 32, 33, 37, 41
anti-Umayyad resistance, 37–38, 41, 42
imperial metropolis, 43–44, 46, 47, 134
internecine strife, 49, 59, 62
rivalry with Syria, 76, 147
ravaged by Mongols, 89, 90
under the Ottomans, 93, 148
creation of modern state, 195–96, 198
and Egypt, 154, 155, 160, 179
and Kuwait, 136, 147, 158, 182–84, 199, 206–11, 227

and Arab-Israeli conflict, 167, 170, 174
and Israel, 179, 183–84
and Iran, 179, 183, 199, 205, 222–24, 225
under Saddam Hussein, 179–80, 182–83, 238

Isfahan, 64

Islamic Jihad, 187, 224

Islamism, 212–31

Ismail Pasha, 156

Ismail Shah, 120, 121

Ismailiya, 54–55

Israel
destruction advocated, 109, 139, 150, 159, 162, 166–69, 171–72, 185–88, 199, 201
established, 144
attacked by Arabs, 145–46
and Egypt, 150–52, 157, 161–69, 173–79, 188, 200–201
designs on its territory, 151
Six-Day War, 163–69, 170–72
invades Lebanon, 180–81
and the end of the Cold War, 181
and Kuwait crisis, 183–84, 208
and Oslo process, 185–87, 191
and Hamas, 218–19
helps Arab states, 238

Istanbul, 93, 95, 96, 100, 101, 102, 103, 106, 114, 117

Italy, 69, 72, 85, 89
Muslim invasions, 61, 70–71
occupies Libya, 102
arms Iran, 204

Jaffa, 141, 142, 172

Jahiliya, 215–17, 221

Janissaries, 94

Jarring, Gunnar, 173

Jerusalem, 15, 45, 72, 73–74, 76, 77, 80, 82–83, 84, 86, 87, 88, 101, 141, 143, 145, 182, 187, 199

Jesus Christ, 7, 18

Jews and Judaism, 18, 68
influence on Islam, 14–15, 215
establish Medina, 13
relations with Muhammad, 14–17
under Muslim rule, 17, 27–29, 109, 128, 134

bridge between Islam and Europe,
  69
and the crusades, 74, 80
expelled from Spain, 140
historical attachment to Palestine,
  140–41
vilified, 188–89, 221, 225, 229, 231,
  236
Jihad 2, 5, 20, 22, 23, 24, 25, 33, 65–66,
  77, 82, 83, 86, 87, 89, 91, 92, 101, 166,
  213–32, 236–38
Johnson, Lyndon, 168, 204
Jordan
  denies Palestinian statehood, 145
  and Egypt, 158, 160, 161
  and Arab-Israeli conflict, 163,
    166–67, 170–71, 172, 174
  and the Palestinians, 172
  peace with Israel, 187
  Islamism, 213
Jordan River, 163, 170, 186
Judea and Samaria, 145

Kamel, Muhammad Ibraihm, 175
Karak, 83, 85, 86
Karbala, 39
Kawakibi, Abdel Rahman, 135, 137,
  147–48
Kazakhstan, 40
Kemal, Mustafa (Atatürk), 193–95, 234
Khadija, 10–11
Khaibar, 17
Khaled, King, 180
Khalkhali, Sadeq, 222
Khallal, Abu Salama, 50, 55
Kharijites, 32–33, 37–38, 42, 49, 50, 62
Kharg Island, 224
Khartoum Summit (1967), 171
Khomeini, Ayatollah
  imperialist vision 1, 221–23, 230,
    238–39
  seizes power, 206
  personal background, 220–21
  anti-Semitism, 221
Khuarasan, 40–42, 44, 48, 52, 53, 55, 57,
  58, 62, 63, 70, 89
Khuzistan, 38, 49, 64
Kissinger, Henry, 174, 202
Klibi, Chadly, 208
Kosovo, 92, 229

Kuchuk Kainardji, Treaty of (1774), 96
Kufa, 27, 32, 33, 37, 38–39, 42, 49, 50, 52
Kurds, 109, 114, 121, 134, 139, 193, 205,
  224
Kutahia, 99
  Peace of, 100
Kuwait, 136, 158, 172, 182–84, 193, 199,
  206–11, 222, 227

Latin Kingdom of Jerusalem, 74, 78,
  81–82, 84, 85–88, 89, 90
Lausanne, Treaty of (1923), 188
Lawrence of Arabia 8, 133, 134, 195, 196
Lebanon, 151
  and the crusades, 77, 78, 83, 143
  massacres of Christians, 97
  and Arab-Israeli conflict, 146, 163,
    182, 183
  victim of Nasser's imperial dream,
    159
  Israeli invasion, 180–81
  Syrian invasion, 199
Levant, 22, 55, 62, 69, 70, 74, 76, 77, 80,
  85, 88, 93, 95, 100, 118, 122
Libya, 102, 173, 180, 182
Lloyd George, David, 196
Louis I, 72, 73

Macedonia, 113
Madrid
  conference (1991), 184, 191
  bombings (2004), 235–36
Maghreb, 38, 41, 54, 58, 62, 69
  see also North Africa
Mahdi, Caliph, 44, 45, 55, 57, 58
Mahfuz, Naguib, 166
Mahmud II, Sultan, 105, 110, 111
Mamluks, 57–58, 62, 88–89, 94, 95, 140,
  149
Ma'mun, Caliph, 45, 46, 49, 52, 57, 58,
  62, 63, 72, 73
Mansur, Caliph, 44, 45, 46, 50, 51, 53,
  55, 57, 58, 71
Manzikert, Battle of (1071), 73, 74, 91
Maronites, 97
Martel, Charles, 23, 60, 71
Marwan I, Caliph, 36, 39
Marwan II, Caliph, 42, 39
Mawali, 29, 37, 42, 44, 50, 57
Mawdudi, Abul Ala, 212–13

McMahon, Arthur Henry, 132, 134, 142, 192–93

Mecca, 5, 10, 11, 12, 13, 14, 15, 16, 17, 18, 36, 37, 50, 52, 54, 55, 85, 93, 96, 131, 146, 192, 196, 227, 232

Medina, 4, 13–22, 26, 32, 35–36, 45, 48, 50, 54, 55, 67, 93
    see also Yathrib

Mediterranean, 69, 78, 88, 96, 135, 145, 186

Mehmed II, Sultan, 94, 105, 237

Mehmed III, Sultan, 94, 105

Meir, Golda, 144

Merv, 42, 57

Mesopotamia, 109
    see also Iraq

Millet, 109–10, 111

Mitterand, François, 210

Mongols
    origins, 89
    imperial self-image, 24, 89
    destroy the Abbasid Empire, 65, 90, 94, 215, 219
    assimilated into Islam, 90–91

Montenegro, 112, 113

Morocco, 54, 61–62, 70, 179

Mosul, 78, 79, 82, 87, 195

Mu'awiya ibn Abi Sufian, Caliph, 6, 18, 33, 35, 38, 39, 41, 67, 71, 221

Mu'awiya II, Caliph, 39

Mubarak, Husni, 180, 181, 187–88, 207, 218, 225, 229, 230

Mughal Empire, 94

Muhajirun, 13, 14, 36

Muhammad, Prophet, 10, 29, 32, 38, 39, 40, 44, 45, 52, 53, 54, 68, 135, 138, 177, 214, 215, 219
    imperialist vision and legacy, 1, 4, 5, 18–26, 35, 43, 65, 213, 229, 231
    flees Mecca, 4, 12–13, 22, 36
    introduces the concept of jihad, 5, 20–22, 25
    death, 6, 18, 21, 22, 23, 26, 237
    temporal and religious leader 6, 7, 13–17, 19–21, 26, 30, 48
    early activities, 10–12
    creates the first umma, 13, 19–20
    and the Medina Jews, 14–17, 27

Muhammad Ali, 99–100, 111, 136, 149, 153, 156, 212

Muhammad Reza, Shah, 161, 202–205, 220–21

Muhammad "The Pure Soul," 10, 53

Muqtadir, Caliph, 58, 59

Murad I, Sultan, 92, 94, 105

Murad III, Sultan, 94, 105

Murad V, Sultan, 105, 113

Muslim Brothers, 154, 176–77, 213–19, 230, 236–37

Mussolini, Benito, 214

Mustakaff, Caliph, 58, 59

Mu'tamid, Caliph, 47, 58

Mu'tasim, Caliph, 46, 49, 58, 65, 90, 255 n. 5

Mutawakil, Caliph, 46, 58, 59

Muttaqi, Caliph, 58, 59, 60–61

Muzaffar al-Din, Shah, 128–30

Nadir Shah, 120–21, 122

Nadir tribe, 13, 14

Naguib, Muhammad, 150, 154

Najd, 2, 148

Naples, 70, 71

Napoleon I, 96, 99, 105, 122, 123

Nasser, Caliph, 58, 65, 86

Nasser al-Din, Shah, 124–28

Nasser, Gamal Abdel, 136, 238
    uses crusades analogy, 139–40, 166
    denial of Palestinian statehood, 145, 151
    union with Syria, 147, 159–61
    personal background, 149–50
    endorses Arab imperial dream, 150, 153–58
    and Israel, 150, 152, 157, 162–72, 200
    dismissive of Arabs and Arabism, 151
    admiration for Zionism, 151–52
    domestic repression and corruption, 157, 159, 176–78
    Yemen blunder, 161–62
    triggers 1967 war, 163–69
    partial disillusionment, 170–72
    legacy discredited, 176–78

Nationalism 8, 9, 106, 109–10, 111

Negev, 151, 163, 168

Netanyahu, Benjamin, 187

Nicholas I, Tsar, 98, 100, 101, 102
Nile, 23, 152, 218, 239
9/11, 1–2, 207, 223, 231, 233, 242 n. 4
Nixon, Richard, 200, 102, 204
Nuqrashi Pasha, 214
North Africa, 4, 23, 59, 60, 69, 70, 71, 87, 93, 95, 135
    see also Maghreb
Norway, 69
Nur al-Din, Mahmoud, 81, 82–84

October War (1973), 165, 173–74, 176–77, 199, 200–01
Oil embargo (1973–74), 174, 202, 205
Orhan, Sultan, 92, 105
Oslo process (1993–2000), 185–87, 191, 218
Osman Bey, 91–92, 105
Ottoman Empire, 5, 6, 8, 105, 119, 136, 141, 147, 149, 154, 158, 185, 212, 232, 234
    destruction of 6, 7, 8, 26, 108, 109, 132–34, 139, 193, 195, 196
    rise of, 91–92
    imperialist vision, 92, 93
    expansion, 92–94, 215
    decline, 94–97
    collaborates with European powers, 96–108, 191–92, 239
    failed reforms, 97
    and World War I, 99, 106–09, 141–43, 192, 193
    begs Britain to take Egypt, 103–105
    perceived legacy, 109–10
    loses European colonies, 110–12
    represses minorities, 110–18
    and the Armenian genocide, 115–18
    and Iran, 120

Pahlavi dynasty, 161, 202–205, 220–21, 234
Pakistan, 7, 154, 155, 213, 232
Palestine, 140, 143, 238
    and early Islam, 22
    under the Umayyads, 45
    under the Abbasids, 50, 55
    under the crusaders, 74, 76–81, 140
    under League of Nations mandate, 140, 197

Jewish historical attachment, 140–41
Jewish national revival, 141–43
allegedly a "twice promised land," 142
partition, 144
1948 war, 144, 145–46, 149, 151, 152, 154–55, 162, 168, 170
and pan-Arab maneuvering, 162–69, 182–84, 187–88
reject peace with Israel, 198–99
Islamism, 208, 218–19
Palestine Liberation Organization (PLO), 163, 166, 179–81, 184–88, 198–99, 201–02, 218
Palestinians
    mistreated by Arab states, 144–45, 151, 166, 171, 174, 180–81, 182–83, 184
    animosity toward Arab states, 145–46, 172
    refugees, 145–46
    and Oslo process, 185–87, 191
Pan-Arabism 7, 8, 9, 135–41, 147–48, 149, 150–63, 170–73, 176–79, 224
Pan-Islamism 7, 9, 137–38
Paris Peace Conference (1919), 143, 148
Paul I, Tsar, 122
Persian Gulf, 27, 150, 179, 203, 207, 223
Peter the Great, 96
Pippin the Short, King, 71
Poitiers, Battle of (732), 23, 60, 71
Portugal, 120
Protocols of the Elders of Zion, 152, 189

Qaddafi, Mu'ammar, 180, 182
Qadisiyya, Battle of (637), 24
Qaeda, 219, 228–31, 239–41
Qahir, Caliph, 46, 58, 59
Qainuqa tribe, 13, 14
Qajar Empire, 121–31, 191
Qaradawi, Yusuf, 237–38
Qassem, Abdel Karim, 160
Qauqji, Fawzi, 144
Qays tribe, 30, 36, 41, 42, 62
Quraish tribe, 18, 32, 36
Quraiza tribe, 13, 14, 15
Qur'an 10–12, 14, 15, 18, 20, 27, 33, 44, 46, 68, 214, 215, 216, 220, 221
Qutb, Sayid, 214–17, 221, 227

Rabin, Yitzhak, 185, 186, 189
Radi, Caliph, 58, 59
Razzia, 5
Red Sea, 14, 85
Reuter, Baron Paul Julius von, 125, 126
Reynald of Châtillon, 85–86
Reza Shah, 220, 234
Riad, Mahmoud, 168
Richard the Lion-Heart, 86
Ridda, 30, 36
Rikhye, Indar Jit, 167
Rogers, William, 173
Roman Empire, 2, 13, 24, 29, 45, 61, 67, 72, 140
Romania, 95, 111, 115
Rome, 70, 71, 72, 237
Rumelia, 93
Russia, 69, 89, 93, 96, 100, 101, 102, 106–08, 112, 113, 114, 115, 116, 119, 120, 121, 122, 123, 124, 125, 126, 128, 129, 130, 131, 152, 189, 192, 206, 223

Sadat, Anwar, 46
    career, 154, 172
    and 1967 war, 165
    and Nasser, 171, 172, 173, 176–78
    drops the imperial dream, 173–79
    makes peace with Israel, 173, 175, 178, 188, 191
    launches October war, 173–74, 199–201
    and Islamists, 176–77, 213–14
    assassinated, 180, 188, 218, 225, 226
    breaks with the Soviet Union, 200–01
    courts the United States, 202
Safavid Empire, 94, 120–21
Saffarid dynasty, 64
Said, Edward, 109, 138, 191, 199, 235
Said, Nuri, 135, 155, 157, 160
Saladin
    imperialist vision, 1, 84, 87, 88
    gains control of Egypt and destroys the Fatimid dynasty, 55, 84
    fights Muslim rulers, 82, 84, 89, 238

    peaceful coexistence with the crusaders, 82, 84–85, 87
    personal background, 83, 139
    conquers Jerusalem, 83, 84, 86
    alliance with Byzantium, 85
    defeats the crusaders, 86–87
    modern-day aspirants, 166, 182, 187, 189–90, 239, 240, 241
Salisbury, Lord, 124–25
Samanid dynasty, 63
Salonika, 92, 112
Samarra, 49, 58
San Stefano, Treaty of (1878), 113
San'a, 26
Sarajevo, 105, 112
Sarraj, Hamid, 160
Sasanid Empire, 2, 4, 23, 24, 41, 64, 119, 120
Saud, King, 156
Saudi Arabia, 144, 151, 154, 155, 156, 158, 175, 180, 208, 222, 226–27, 228, 229, 237
Sazonov, Sergei, 102, 106
Selim I, Sultan, 93, 105
Selim II, Sultan, 94, 105
Selim III, Sultan, 99, 105
Seljuks, 64–65, 73, 74, 76, 77, 78, 79, 82, 91, 119–20, 140
Serbia, 92, 93, 112, 113
Sèvres, Treaty of (1920), 193
Shari'a, 45, 176, 217
Shazly, Saad al-Din, 174
Shiites, 10, 94
    anti-Umayyad resistance, 37–38, 41, 42
    origins, 38–39
    challenge the Abbasids, 48, 52–55, 75
    factions, 54–55
    dominate the Abbasid Empire, 63
    in Iran, 120, 121, 220–23
    in Iraq, 222–24
Shuqeiri, Ahmad, 166
Sicily, 62, 70, 71, 72
Sidon, 100
Siffin, Battle of (657), 33
Sinai Peninsula, 157, 164, 165, 167
Six-Day War (1967)
    origin, 163–69, 199
    consequences, 170–82, 218

Somalia, 228, 232
Soviet Union, 159, 164, 172, 174, 176,
    181, 193, 198–202, 203, 204, 223, 226,
    227, 230, 233, 235, 238
    see also Russia
Spain
    Muslim occupation and
        colonization, 2, 23, 41, 59, 70,
        71, 72, 92, 140
    resisting Muslim colonization,
        60–62, 88–89
    Muslim hopes of re-colonization,
        234–38
Spinoza, Baruch, 188
Sudan, 48, 171, 193, 213, 218, 227–29,
    232
Suez Canal, 150, 154, 157, 170, 173, 175,
    178, 203
Suez War (1956), 157, 161, 164, 177
Suleiman, Caliph, 39
Suleiman the Magnificent, Sultan, 93,
    94, 105
Sunnis, 48, 65, 76, 82, 94, 120, 121, 223,
    224
Sweden, 69
Sykes–Picot Agreement (1916), 192–93
Syria: 7, 14, 21, 22, 23, 151, 235
    on the eve of Islam, 4, 11, 12, 14
    Muslim occupation and
        colonization, 6, 7, 23, 26–28
    as imperial center, 33–34, 36, 37,
        41, 42, 57
    under the Abbasids, 50, 55, 64
    and the crusades, 74, 76–83
    under the Ayyubis, 88
    Mongol invasion, 90
    under the Ottomans, 99–100, 116,
        117, 118
    in World War I, 133, 143, 148
    and Arab-Israeli conflict, 138, 142,
        144, 145, 163–65, 170, 174, 175,
        199–202
    under Faisal's rule, 143, 198
    and Egypt, 147, 154, 155, 158–61,
        171, 172, 173, 174, 175, 180,
        181–82, 183, 184
    Islamism, 213, 218

Tabriz, 120, 131
Taherid dynasty, 63

Taif, 12, 36
Tajikistan, 40, 229
Talaat Pasha, 107
Tamerlane, 91, 93, 94, 121
Tancred, Prince, 78, 79
Tehran, 121, 127, 129, 179, 222
Tel Aviv, 141, 166, 167, 225
Thawri, Sufian, 45
Third Reich, 7
Third World, 4, 152, 207
Tiberias, 86
Tikrit, 83, 182
Tilsit, Treaty (1807), 123
Tlas, Mustafa, 184
Transjordan, 22, 40, 83, 84, 143, 144,
    145, 147, 154, 155, 196–98
Transoxania, 63
Tripoli, 74, 82, 100, 180
Tughtigin, 78, 79
Tunisia, 62, 178
Turabi, Hassan, 227–28
Turkey, 87, 155, 193, 195, 220, 234
Turkmanchai (1828), 124
Turks: 41, 55, 57, 58, 59, 63, 64–65, 73,
    76, 77, 79, 80, 91, 92, 93, 109, 112,
    118, 119, 134, 139

Uhud, Battle of (625), 14, 16
Ulama, 121, 126–27, 128, 129, 130
Umar ibn al-Khattab, Caliph, 25, 26–29,
    31, 36, 73, 187
Umar II, Caliph, 29, 39, 41, 50, 60
Umayyad Empire 5, 6, 18, 32, 33–42, 43,
    44, 45, 46, 49, 50, 51, 55, 57, 59–62,
    67, 71, 72, 134, 215, 221
Umma 5, 6, 7, 9, 13, 14, 17, 19–21,
    26–28, 31–32, 33, 35, 38, 43, 212–13,
    215–17, 221–22, 234–41
United Arab Republic, 159–61
United Nations, 146, 201, 229
    Partition Resolution, 144, 181
    pulls out of Egyptian border,
        164–65, 166, 167
    mediation of Arab-Israeli peace,
        173
    and Kuwait crisis, 210–11
    and Iran–Iraq war, 223
    Resolution 242, 171–72, 175, 181,
        199, 200
    Resolution 338, 175, 199

United States, 1, 151, 155, 156, 157, 159,
224
   and Arab-Israeli conflict, 167,
      168, 169, 170, 174, 181, 183–84,
      188, 191, 198, 199, 235, 240,
      241
   and Iran, 202–206, 223
   and the Kuwait crisis, 206–11
   and bin-Laden, 228–33, 239–40
Urabi, Ahmad, 103, 105
Urban II, Pope, 73–74, 80
Uthman ibn Affan, Caliph, 6, 25–26, 29,
   31–33, 35, 36, 45, 237
Uzbekistan, 40

Vatican, 50, 73
Venice, 69
Vienna, 93, 96

Wahhabiya, 95–96
Walid I, Caliph, 39
Walid II, Caliph, 39, 42, 55
Waqidi, Muhammad ibn Umar, 21
War of Attrition (1969–70), 176, 199,
   200, 238
Wasit, 50, 53
Wathiq, Caliph, 46, 58, 59
Weizmann, Chaim, 143
West
   imperialism 2, 6
   nationalism 8

   influence on Islamic civilization,
      68
West Bank, 145, 146, 178, 184, 185, 186,
   187, 199, 218
Wilson, Arnold, 195–96
World War I, 7, 8, 26, 99, 106–08, 109,
   114–18, 132, 133, 135, 136, 139, 145,
   155, 221, 234
World War II, 198

Yathrib, 12, 13, 14
   see Medina
Yazid I, Caliph, 35, 36, 39, 221
Yazid II, Caliph, 39
Yazid III, Caliph, 39, 42, 55
Yemen 2, 4, 8, 11, 26, 31, 36, 38, 41, 42,
   54, 62, 84, 109, 140, 148, 151, 161–62,
   172, 177, 213, 226, 229, 231
Young, Hubert, 195, 196

Zaghlul, Saad, 144
Zahar, Mahmoud, 219
Zaidiya, 54
Zaman Shah, 122, 123
Zangi, Imad al-Din, 81–82, 83, 84, 87
Zanj, 37, 49
Zawahiri, Ayman, 217–18, 225–26, 230,
   231, 240
Zionism, 118, 139, 140–41, 143, 151–52,
   173, 183, 187–88, 218, 219–20
Zuraiq, Qustantin, 138